Diamonds
& Demons

Diamonds & Demons

DAVID BERNSTEIN

The Joseph Gutnick story

Lothian
BOOKS

Thomas C. Lothian Pty Ltd
11 Munro Street, Port Melbourne, Victoria 3207

National Library of Australia
Cataloguing-in-Publication data:

Bernstein, David H., 1944—.
    Diamonds & demons: the Joseph Gutnick story.
    Bibliography
    Includes index.

    ISBN 0 7344 0094 2.

    1. Gutnick, Joe. 2. Businesspeople – Australia – Biography.
    3. Football team owners – Australia – Biography. 4. Rabbis –
    Australia – Biography. 5. Mines and mining – Australia.
    6. Jews – Australia – Social life and customs – Biography.
    7. Judaism – Australia – Customs and practices.
    I. Title.

338.092

Design by David Constable
Index by Russell Brooks
Typeset by J&M Typesetting
Printed by Griffin Press Pty Limited

CONTENTS

LIST OF MAPS

ACKNOWLEDGEMENTS

I would like to record my debt to Joseph Gutnick for the time he gave me and for the openness and candor he displayed in a series of interviews I conducted with him between August and December 1999. Those interviews, which took place in Melbourne and 'on location' in Western Australia, form the backbone of this book.

My thanks go to Joseph's wife, Stera, and his father, Rabbi Chaim Gutnick, for their kind cooperation — as well as to Joseph's secretary, Moira Stewart, for her invaluable help in fitting me into her boss's hectic schedule. I would like to thank the Gutnick family, too, for giving me access to the photographs that accompany this text.

It would be appropriate also to acknowledge my enormous debt to the dozens of business and sports reporters — too many to mention here — who have chronicled and commented on the various facets of the Gutnick story over the past decade. I have relied heavily on their efforts, as the attribution notes at the back of this book will testify. Likewise, the notes will show, I am deeply indebted to the authors of several extremely useful background texts — most particularly David Landau (*Piety & Power: The World of Jewish Fundamentalism*); Edward Hoffman (*Despite All Odds: The Story of Lubavitch*); and Simon Jacobson (*Towards a Meaningful Life: The Wisdom of the Rebbe*).

Thanks, too, to *Age* business writer Rod Myer and former *Age* sports writer Ashley Browne, who kindly agreed to read my manuscript and draw my attention to any gross gaffes I might have made in their respective areas of expertise. I, of course, bear full responsibility for the finished product.

Finally, a very special thank you to my family — Marion, Yaniv and Noa — for having had to put up with my obsessive-compulsive 'Gutnicking' over the past year. I know I will have tried their patience, as well as that of the various friends and acquaintances unfortunate enough to have crossed my path during that period.

Yossel and Me

'HOW'D YOU LIKE to do a book on Joe Gutnick?'

I thought my agent must be joking. Gutnick hated me. Just a few months earlier — in December 1998 — he had told *Age* journalist Peter Ellingsen that he wanted to buy the *Australian Jewish News*, which I was editing at the time, and fire me. He didn't like my 'lefty' views on Israel, and felt the paper was unbalanced. In the event, I saved him the trouble — and the money. A long-running feud I had with the management of the *News* over editorial independence and related matters came to a head in April 1999, and I quit. I was out of a job. And Joseph had his Bernstein-less *Jewish News*, without even having to put his hand in his pocket. It was one of the few bright spots in a year that saw Bibi Netanyahu lose the election in Israel, the price of gold plummet dramatically, and the Demons languish near the bottom of the ladder after an inspiring season the previous year.

So me do a book on him? You must be kidding! But, with more time than I wanted on my hands, I agreed to think it over. And the more I thought about it, the more the idea intrigued me.

Yes, Yossel — as he is almost invariably known in the Jewish community — and I had had several confrontations over the years. We stood at polar extremes on the Israel/Arab issue.

I was a lefty who had lived in Israel for over twenty-five years before arriving in Australia at the beginning of 1989 and was a strong supporter of the Rabin/Peres land-for-peace line; he was the Rebbe's Special Emissary for the Integrity of the Land of Israel, charged with doing all in his power to thwart that line. He loathed what I was writing on Israel, both in the *Jewish News* and in the general press. And he was particularly incensed by an article I wrote for the *Age* to coincide with Israel's fiftieth anniversary — in which I tried to imagine how I would be looking back on the previous century had I been born a Palestinian. It was my attempt, as an Israeli, to listen to what Henry Reynolds would have called 'the whispering in my heart'. Yossel was also angered by a piece I wrote — provocatively titled, but not by me, 'Alas! The Butcher of Beirut is Back' — about one of his favourite right-wing Israeli politicians, Ariel Sharon.

Then came the open clash we had in the opinion pages of the *Age* a few months later, in August 1998, over the J B Were affair. I had written an article questioning the editorial judgement the paper had displayed in running, on its front page, what seemed like something of a 'beat-up' concerning a few mildly offensive comments made about Gutnick in private conversation by two senior Were brokers. This made a huge mountain out of a very small molehill, I wrote — the sort of precious over-reaction to perceived racial insults that, I felt, was giving multi-culturalism a bad name. Yossel did not like that at all, seeing it, quite mistakenly, as a criticism of himself rather than of the *Age*. And he wrote a counter-article a day or two later, questioning my journalistic competence and integrity for failing to obtain the full transcript of the comments made about him before rushing to judgement. It was an understandable reaction — especially when one saw the transcript, large chunks of which the *Age* eventually published. It contained some pretty nasty stuff. I published an apology a couple of days later.

Ironically, I wrote the J B Were article some two years after I had come to view Joseph Gutnick not just as the most colourful and inter-esting personality the Jewish community had produced in the ten years I had been in Australia but as a major Australian multicultural icon. This had happened in the space of a few remarkable weeks in August/September 1996 — when Yossel burst out of Melbourne's St Kilda *shtetl*,[1] put on a red-and-blue yarmulka (skullcap), and set about challenging the dry economic rationalism that was pushing the Melbourne and Hawthorn football clubs towards a deeply unpopular merger. My first response to this bearded little Orthodox Jewish rabbi-cum-goldminer emerging as the most unlikely of saviours of Victoria's supremely blue-blooded, establishment football club was, like that of most onlookers in both the Jewish and the broader Australian community, one of incredulity and mirth. It was bizarre — all a bit of a joke. And it prompted me to write a snide column in the *Australian Jewish News*, replete with all the smart-arsed chortling that charac-terised much of the initial reaction to Yossel's latest *meshugas* (folly). I called it 'Yossel Gutnick performs a footy mitzvah':

> One can only speculate on what has motivated Rabbi Gutnick. Did the late Lubavitcher Rebbe come to him in a dream, anointing him his Special

Emissary for the Integrity of Victorian Football? (It has been pointed out that last Saturday was *Tet b'Elul*, the same date on the Jewish calendar that the Rebbe told him to look for diamonds in the Kimberleys.) Or perhaps he just doesn't like mergers — not kosher,[2] a bit like mixing milk and meat, or Likud and Labour in an Israeli National Unity Government?

Yossel Gutnick himself has a much more mundane explanation. Like any other dinky-di Aussie, he told Doug Aiton on Melbourne's Radio 3LO, footy is well and truly in his blood. Not only was he a useful player himself, for Yeshivah College in Hotham Street ('Is that a big footy school?' an innocent Aiton asked), but he has been a mad-keen Demons supporter for years!

There is absolutely no reason to doubt any of this, and there is a certain pleasure in the thought of a frustrated Yossel spending all those Sabbaths in synagogue when he really would far rather have been down at the G. But why Melbourne, one would have to ask — arguably the WASPiest club in the League. St Kilda, yes — if only for reasons of geographic logic. And perhaps even Carlton, which is almost Jewish. But Melbourne? Whatever the case, if those Demons members determined to save their club from the impending merger with Hawthorn were praying for a Messiah, it would seem that they have got the next best thing . . .

I returned to the subject less than a month later, in another column in the *Jewish News*. This time, most — if not all — of the snideness had disappeared. And what I wrote was a much more serious, reasoned reflection on what I had come to recognise, in the space of less than a month, was a highly significant sociological development that said as much about Australia as it did about Joseph Gutnick:

Whatever his initial motivation, Yossel Gutnick's foray into the world of Aussie Rules Football has provided a remarkable new insight into the mysterious workings of Australian multiculturalism. No one could say that Yossel looks or feels exactly at home in the football world. He has appeared several times on Channel Nine's hugely popular *The Footy Show*, on each occasion looking decidedly out of place alongside Don Scott, Ian Ridley, Sammy Newman and all the other denizens of the blokey, foul-mouthed, locker-room world of Aussie Rules. But — and this emerged equally clearly — he was greeted with a kind of puzzled, quizzical acceptance, with little hint of hostility or animosity. There was no ugly, malicious innuendo, as there might so easily have been, of 'Jewish big money' taking over football . . .

Plainly, a society that can accept with equanimity a pair of Governors-General with names like Sir Isaac Isaacs and Sir Zelman Cowen has little difficulty in coming to terms with Joseph Gutnick, president of the Melbourne Football Club — an encouraging affirmation of Australia's traditional, and enduring, tolerance towards Jews. On the other side of the equation, if Yossel Gutnick has been accepted by the footy world, he has also shown that he has something very real to offer football — beyond the three million dollars he has pledged, and beyond even the business acumen and contacts he can undoubtedly bring to the Melbourne Football Club. He has demonstrated, instinctively, an uncanny grasp of football culture beyond *The Footy Show* and the locker room. A profound, visceral understanding of the passions that drive football and make nonsense of the sterile economic rationalism that has infested Ross Oakley, Graeme Samuel and their blinkered mates at the AFL.

Where does an Ultra-Orthodox Jew,[3] who has supposedly spent a culturally secluded life in the East St Kilda ghetto, come by such understanding? As a Jew, he clearly knows all about survival, against overwhelming odds. He also knows all about the importance of tradition, and resisting all attempts to compromise or weaken that tradition. But it is, I believe, as a Lubavitcher rabbi that he has come instinctively to understand that the kind of passion and yearning for simple, transcendental gratification that fires many footy fans is not very different (psychologically, at least) from that which has drawn tens of thousands of young Jews to his Chabad movement, making it the most phenomenally successful and vibrant Jewish religious cult in the world today. If 'Demon Joe' can harness that passion and bring even an iota of that success to the Melbourne Football Club — watch out the Dees!

So, when the question was popped some time in June 1999, I had long been intrigued by Yossel — not only as the subject of a great yarn, but as an important sociological phenomenon. Yes, this was a story I wanted to tell. And one I felt I could tell, despite our open, quite irreconcilable political differences, both fairly and well. The problem, I warned my prospective publisher, was — how would Joseph respond to the idea of me, of all people, writing a book about him? Would he co-operate? I felt there was more than enough material on the public record to write a good book without his co-operation, but that it would be a much better book *with* it. Also, I didn't much like the idea of writing a book behind Yossel's back, feeding suspicions on his part and expectations in the Jewish community that this was 'payback time' — that I was out to 'Get Shorty'. So, I bit the bullet and called him. The conversation went something like this:

'Mr Gutnick? David Bernstein here.'

'David Bernstein? The David Bernstein from the *Jewish News*?'

Gulp. 'Yes, that's the one.'

Silence.

'I've been invited by my publisher to write a book about you.'

Silence.

'Why should you want to write a book about me? And why should I co-operate? You know I'm against you?'

'Yes, Mr — er — do you mind if I call you Joseph?'

'Joseph's fine.'

'I think you have a great story, and I'd like to tell it. And I think I can do it, fairly and, I hope, entertainingly — with or without your co-operation.'

'You'll go ahead, even without my co-operation?'

'Yes.'

'So it would be in my interests to co-operate?'

'Probably. It would certainly make for a better book.'

And so on, for about half an hour. Finally:

'Let me think about it. I need to talk to a few people. My wife. My father. Meanwhile, put what you propose in writing.'

This I did. And two weeks later, I had an appointment to see him at his office in South Melbourne.

◊ ◊ ◊

Joseph conducts his mining empire from a square, squat building at 210 Kings Way, about five minutes from Melbourne's CBD. Buff-coloured, with huge green-tinted, ornate-paned windows, it looks like something out of *Arabian Nights*. It wouldn't be out of place, one imagines, in Brunei. Or in one of the oil-rich Gulf emirates. There's a prestige car dealership on the ground floor. It sells sheikhly-looking Rolls-Royces and Bentleys.

As you enter the lobby, you are greeted by a couple of polite, athletic footy player types in neat suits. You tell them you have an appointment with Joseph. (He's 'Joseph' to everyone around here. You discover that when you call and ask to make an appointment with 'Mr Gutnick'.) They sign you in, escort you to the lift, and take you up to the fourth floor.

You step out into a large, hushed anteroom. A golden-hued mining scene dominates one wood-panelled wall. There are pictures of mines, looking like cratered moonscapes, on the others. Mining and business magazines are stacked neatly on a couple of side tables next to two dark plush couches. You take a seat. Today's papers are on the large perspex table in front of you, and you browse through one as you wait for your appointment.

'Joseph won't be long.'

The willowy, fair-haired receptionist smiles sweetly behind her desk. She has the kind of gentile beauty that gives Jewish mothers sleepless nights. Another attractive young woman, in a beautifully tailored pants suit, comes into the room to put a pile of files on her desk.

A couple of young men drift through. They have full beards and black yarmulkas. One of them stops to chat with the receptionist. He tells an amusing story. She smiles again.

'Joseph will see you now.'

You are led into the inner sanctum. A heavy door swings open silently. A huge colour portrait of the Rebbe greets you. He seems like a very nice man. You turn to the right where, at the other end of an enormous office, Joseph rises from his seat to greet you. He is a small man — smaller than you had expected — and the office makes him look even smaller. He has a friendly smile and an easy manner.

He returns to his seat, on the other side of a long curved desk mounted with several computer screens, and motions you to sit down. Joseph can see the Rebbe, in the distance, from where he is seated. Just a reminder, out of the corner of his eye, of why he is in this place, at this time, doing whatever it is he is doing. You, his guest, are spared the Rebbe's relentless gaze, unless you make the effort to twist your neck to the right.

Behind Joseph is a wall full of photographs and other memorabilia. A collage of his current interests and obsessions.

There are pictures of his wife Stera, his eleven children, and his three grandchildren. There will be many more grandchildren, God willing. Joseph, as he constantly reminds you, is still a young man. Barely forty-seven.

There are also pictures of Joseph with Bibi Netanyahu — the man he is credited with having helped get across the line in the 1996 Israeli election. Netanyahu has fallen on hard times since. And pictures of Joseph, wearing a hard hat, touring his mines. They, too, are not doing as well as they used to, with gold prices at a twenty-year low.

Joseph seems to read your mind: 'No, it hasn't been a good year for me.'

There is also, prominently displayed on the long shelf behind the desk, the *tsedakah* (charity) box.

But the wall is dominated by a large photo of the current Demons football team and other Demons memorabilia. There are various photos of himself, wearing his familiar red-and-blue yarmulka, posing with players and senior club officials. And one of him, wearing a Demons jumper, with a famous footy mate — Carlton president John Elliott.

You are surprised by how big a part the Demons appear to play in Joseph's life.

Your interview begins . . .

An hour and a bit later Joseph still hasn't made up his mind. He is clearly intrigued with the idea, and would love to see a book about himself. You also sense that having me, of all people, write it appeals to his sense of mischief:

'You know they'll think I'm crazy?'

'Probably,' I agree, enjoying the shared irony, '– but it won't be the first time.'

He wants to talk it over further with his wife Stera, and perhaps his father Chaim. Can I come back the following day? He'll try to arrange for Stera to be there as well.

A much more private person than Joseph, Stera is clearly uneasy about public exposure — and, I suspect, about me in particular doing the exposing. I try to reassure her: she and Joseph can see the manuscript before publication. Not for their approval or veto, but to make sure that it is factually accurate and that there is no inadvertent misrepresentation. I explain to Joseph that there will inevitably be stuff in the book that he may not like, but as long as it is fair, accurate and not libellous it will remain in. After about half an hour, Joseph has made up his mind.

'OK, I'm on . . . '

The Gutnick Odyssey

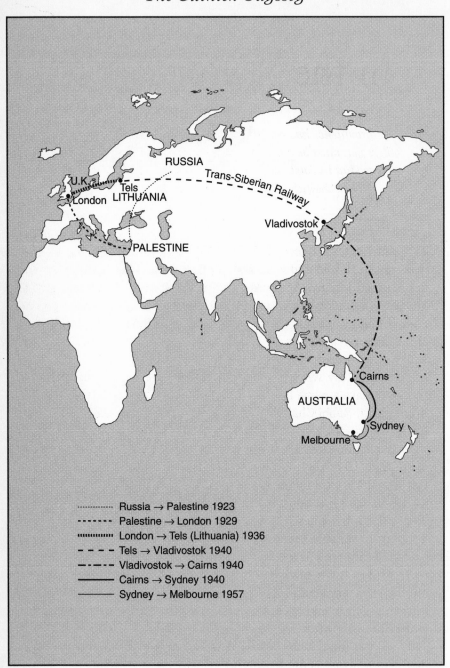

```
············  Russia → Palestine 1923
- - - - - -   Palestine → London 1929
·············  London → Tels (Lithuania) 1936
– – – –       Tels → Vladivostok 1940
–·–·–·–       Vladivostok → Cairns 1940
————          Cairns → Sydney 1940
————          Sydney → Melbourne 1957
```

In the Beginning . . .

*'As providence has led you to this country that is a sign that
there you must be, and I do not advise you to come to America
but to stay in Australia.'*

The Lubavitcher Rebbe, in a telegram to Chaim Gutnick, 1941

THE BIRTH REGISTRY records in Sydney will show that a son, Jeremy,
was born to Harold and Rose Gutnick on 8 June 1952. But Jeremy was
never called Jeremy. At home, the Gutnicks' second son was always
Yossel — the Yiddish diminutive for his Hebrew name Yosef, or Joseph.
And, formally, until he changed his name by deed poll to Joseph Isaac
some fifteen years later, he was known not as Jeremy but, for some
unexplained reason, as Geoffrey.

'I think in my wife's mind it might have been a safeguard that he
shouldn't have a name in school where the kids would laugh at him or
think it odd,' Rabbi Chaim Gutnick explained, a little defensively, in an
interview forty-seven years later.[1] 'He should go to school and they
would call him Yossel? She wanted him to have a nice Australian
name, like Geoffrey, or George ... I don't know why she chose
Geoffrey. It's a nice name. A nice intellectual name.'

It was quite common at that time for Jews in Australia[2] to
Anglicise their names in this way. Australian society in general was
not very hospitable to foreigners, and Jews in particular took great
pains not to stand out too much, fearing, among other things, that this
could lead to anti-semitism.[3] The older, pre-World War II Jewish community was especially sensitive, and when Jewish refugees from
Europe began to arrive in Australia just before the war, and in much
larger numbers after the war, they were seen — with their thick
Yiddish[4] accents, loud voices, and sometimes gross, ostentatious
manners — as an acute threat and embarrassment. In May 1939, for
instance, on the very eve of the Holocaust that was to wipe out most

of Europe's Jews, the *Australian Jewish News* published the following 'advice' to the new arrivals:

> Modulate your voices. Do not make yourself conspicuous anywhere by walking with a group of persons, all of who are loudly speaking a foreign language. Remember that the welfare of the old-established Jewish communities in Australia, as well as of every migrant depends on your personal behaviour. Jews are judged by individuals. You, personally, have a very great responsibility.[5]

This was a form of cultural cringe that would have gone completely against the grain for someone like Chaim Gutnick. He had a very robust, independent-minded sense of both his Jewish and his Australian identity. His wife, Rose, on the other hand, had a background that made her much more vulnerable to the pressures Jews were under to keep a 'low profile'. She had come to Australia before the war, as a small child. Her parents were typical Polish Jews: relatively simple, uneducated people from a small Polish *shtetl*, who had escaped from Europe to build new lives in a new country. Her grandfather was a ritual slaughterer,[6] and her father a jeweller. Although observant religious Jews at home, they accepted the prevailing wisdom that they should not make themselves conspicuous. Thus, they readily changed their family name from Sochaczeska to Chester, and their daughter Rushka called herself Rose at the prestigious Sydney Girls' High School which she attended.

'I'm sure they would have been influenced in that way,' Chaim reflects. 'They came before the war, and I'm sure they must have felt the difference of being a foreigner, of being Jewish, of being religious . . . It could be that my wife chose the name Geoffrey for that reason.' There was a certain irony in this for Chaim, too, had found himself 'christened' — albeit reluctantly — with a more acceptable 'Aussie' name shortly after arriving in Australia more than a decade before. Hence the 'Harold' on 'Jeremy''s birth certificate. But more about that later . . .

◊ ◊ ◊

Schneur Chaim Gutnick had arrived in Australia on his own in 1940, after a long and rather unusual odyssey. It had begun nineteen years earlier, in 1921, in the small town of Zolotmonosh in the Ukraine, where he was born into a prominent rabbinical family. His father, Reb Mordechai Ze'ev Gutnick,[7] was a brilliant young rabbi belonging to the Lubavitcher sect.

Also known as 'Chabad' — from the Hebrew acronym for *chochmah* (wisdom), *binah* (understanding) and *da'at* (knowledge) — the Lubavitcher movement was an early branch of Hasidism, the joyous, mystic form of populist Judaism that emerged in the first half of the eighteenth century as a reaction to the dry, elitist, text-based Judaism of the time.

The founder of the Hasidic movement was a charismatic miracle-worker called Israel ben Eliezer, better known as the Baal Shem Tov (Master of the Good Name), who would travel from town to town in Russia curing the sick and those in despair. Using simple language that ordinary uneducated folk could readily understand, the Baal Shem Tov took classic Jewish mystical themes about the nature of human existence and its relationship with the divine, and cast them in the form of appealing stories. His central tenet was that every individual had a specific God-given mission to accomplish on earth, whether it was to sweep the streets, heal the sick or raise children. (Or, he might have added, to look for gold and diamonds.) 'No two individuals have the same abilities,' the Baal Shem Tov declared. 'Each man should work in the service of God according to his own talents. If one man tries to imitate another, he merely loses the opportunity to do good through his own merit.'[8]

The Hasidic movement spread like wildfire throughout Eastern Europe as disciples of the Baal Shem Tov set up courts of their own in Galicia, Poland, Russia, the Ukraine, the Austro–Hungarian Empire — and even Lithuania, home of the great Talmudic academies against which Hasidism had rebelled. These disciples, who became known as Rebbes (derived from the word *rabbi*, or teacher), were held in total awe by their followers, or *Hasidim* (literally, 'pious men'). The Rebbe was considered to be a *Tsadik* (a perfectly righteous man); not only did his followers believe in the 'extraordinary power of his individual spiritual contemplation of and encounter with God', but they saw him as 'a mystical intermediary to God'.[9] He was viewed as a perfect role model and spiritual guide:

> If he stressed long earlocks and beard, in strict adherence to the biblical injunction not to cut off the 'hair on the sides of your head or the edges of your beard' (Leviticus 19:27), or wore a sash around his waist during prayer to separate the higher and lower parts of his body; if he took to wearing knickers or a fur hat, his hasidim would do this too, in the belief that this would perfect their spiritual repair and make them better Jews . . . [10]

Moreover, the Rebbe was the absolute authority and the final arbiter of all aspects of the Hasid's life:

> ... nothing was considered beneath their purview. Through both group and individual involvement, followers sought out their Rebbe for advice on livelihood, family matters and health problems. They saw the Rebbe as an intercessor in the heavenly courts, an expounder of mysteries through both study and meditation, and a wise figure who could guide them through the straits of everyday existence ... [11]

One of these early Hasidic Rebbes was Rabbi Schneur Zalman of Liady (1745–1812). A brilliant scholar, Rabbi Schneur Zalman, or the Alter Rebbe (the Old Rabbi) as he is known to his followers, had been a disciple of the Baal Shem Tov's direct heir, Rabbi Dov Baer of Meztrich (known as the *Maggid*, or preacher). Some time in the late eighteenth century, he set up court in the small White Russian town of Lubavitch — hence the name of the movement he founded — and wrote what has come to be its definitive text, a mystical treatise known as the *Tanya*. He taught meditative practices designed to help individuals to attain closer communion with God, an endeavour that was viewed as heretical by the powerful non-Hasidic rabbinical establishment in White Russia. So vicious, in fact, was the rabbis' opposition to Hasidism in White Russia that most Hasidic groups left for other, more hospitable regions. The Czar was no friendlier, and the Alter Rebbe was twice imprisoned on charges of subversion. But he and his followers displayed a remarkable tenacity and held firm in Lubavitch against all odds. Leadership was passed on by succession[12] and a century after the first Rebbe's death in 1812 disciples still came to study at the prevailing Lubavitcher Rebbe's feet in the small White Russian town. Among them was Chaim Gutnick's father Reb Mordechai Ze'ev.

Reb Mordechai was a favourite of Rabbi Sholom Dov Baer, the fifth Lubavitcher Rebbe, and was very close to his successor, Rabbi Yosef Yitzhak Schneersohn, who became the Sixth Lubavitcher Rebbe in 1920. It was Rabbi Yosef Yitzhak who sent Reb Mordechai as his emissary to the Jews of Tiplis (Tiblisi) in the Caucasus, some time in 1921. This was a dangerous calling at that time, as the new Soviet regime proved to be no friendlier than the Czars had been, and had begun to crack down on all forms of religious expression. 'Down with the priests, down with the rabbis!' is the first Russian phrase Chaim remembers learning. He had picked it up in the streets while out with his mother, when he was barely two years old. And it was not long before Reb Mordechai came to the attention of the Soviet secret police and was arrested. His young wife, Chaya, the daughter of a wealthy Russian landowner who had lost all his property in the 1917 Revolution, managed to secure his release. It was clear, however, that they had no future in Russia. And like millions of despairing Jews before them, they began to plan their emigration.

Over two million Jews had left Russia since 1881 — the year Czar Alexander II was assassinated, precipitating an unprecedented wave of pogroms in which thousands of Jews were murdered. The vast bulk of them had headed for the United States — the 'Goldeneh Medineh', or 'Golden Country' as it was known. Smaller numbers settled in France, England, Germany, Argentina, Canada and South Africa. A trickle even found its way to Australia. By 1921, the United States had begun to close the door on mass immigration, and other countries soon followed suit. So when Reb Mordechai and his young family decided to make their move, in 1923, their options would have been severely restricted.

There was one country open to large-scale Jewish migration. Palestine had been conquered from the Ottoman Turks by Britain six years earlier, in 1917. And following intense lobbying by Jewish activists, the British Government pledged to help create a 'national home' for the Jewish people in their ancient homeland. For many Jews, this was a dream come true. The destruction of the Temple by the Romans in the first century had ended Jewish national sovereignty in the Land of Israel, and in the ensuing centuries most of the Jewish population had been slaughtered, had assimilated, or had drifted off to other places. By the beginning of the seventh century, only a tiny handful of Jews remained, living in small, impoverished communities under a succession of foreign rulers. The Jews had become predominantly a Diaspora people, living in a web of interconnected communities scattered around the world. This did not mean that Jews had abandoned their claim to the Land of Israel as their God-given birthright, or had lost any of their religious or emotional attachment to the land. But for the almost two millennia during which they remained in the Diaspora, most Jews viewed both their exile and their eventual redemption as part of a divine plan. Each year at Passover, the festival of liberation and redemption, they would pray 'Next year, in Jerusalem', and hope that one day, in God's good time, the Messiah would come and the exiles would be ingathered. Until such time, it was incumbent on Jews, whatever the hardship, to keep faith with God, to obey his commandments, and in this way to hasten the coming of the Messiah.

With the growing secularisation of European society over the past two centuries, accompanied by the emancipation of the Jews and their integration into general society, religious belief and the fatalistic acceptance of God's will began to lose their hold on many Jews. And when the growth of secular nationalist movements in various parts of Europe during the course of the nineteenth century gave rise to an upsurge in xenophobia and anti-semitism, these Jews began to seek a secular, nationalistic response to their predicament. Zionism — the Jewish nationalist movement which envisaged the establishment of a sovereign Jewish state in the ancient Land of Israel — emerged as an increasingly potent ideology. It was an ideology that drew on several of the central religious motifs of traditional Judaism, particularly the notion of the Land of Israel as the God-given birthright of the Jews. But Zionism was fundamentally secular, sometimes even virulently anti-religious, in its general mindset. The goal of Zionists was to find a political solution to what they saw as a burning political problem. They had neither the time, nor the inclination, to pray for the coming of the Messiah.

The British occupation of Palestine in 1917 gave the Zionists their chance. Jews began to flood into the Land of Israel to participate in the great Zionist enterprise of building a homeland where Jews could once again be masters of their own destiny. Many of them were genuinely committed Zionists, secular Jews who aimed to create a new Jew in an old–new land, shucking off the centuries of what they saw to be the debilitating fatalism that had characterised Jewish life in the Diaspora. But many others were simply frightened Jews seeking to escape the growing horrors of Jewish life in Eastern Europe. They did not necessarily share the Zionist dream, but were happy to find a haven in Palestine. And if things didn't work out in Palestine, there was always the possibility of moving later to America or elsewhere. Perhaps even to Australia.

Some time in 1923 — just before the Soviet authorities put a stop to all Jewish emigration from Russia — Reb Mordechai Ze'ev Gutnick, his wife Chaya, and their two small sons, Chaim and Sholem, received the Rebbe's blessing and boarded a ship for Palestine. Reb Mordechai would not, of course, have been a Zionist, and he would have had little in common with the secular Zionists who were building their new secular society in Palestine — although, unusually for a Lubavitcher at this time, there is evidence that he may not have been entirely unsympathetic to them. His alleged 'Zionist tendencies' once even earned him a ticking-off from Rabbi Yosef Yitzhak Schneersohn, the Sixth Lubavitcher Rebbe, who, like most religious Jews, was vehemently opposed to Zionism as a blasphemous attempt by Godless opportunists to short-circuit God's own Messianic plan. Reb Mordechai, however, had already shown an independent streak not usual among Lubavitchers at this time. He had studied such 'profane' subjects as Law, Mathematics and Philosophy — something he had in common with the man who was to become the Seventh Lubavitcher Rebbe, Rabbi Menachem Mendel Schneerson. But it does not appear that either his alleged pro-Zionist leanings or his interest in the profane in any way alienated him from the Rebbe, with whom he had an especially close rapport (not unlike the rapport that his son, Chaim, and grandson, Joseph — both of whom would also display strong 'Zionist leanings' — later came to enjoy with his successor).

The Gutnicks settled in Hebron, a holy city in what is now the West Bank, where the biblical patriarchs are buried. Reb Mordechai had a job as a secretary in the Tel Aviv Rabbinate, and the family divided its time between Hebron and Tel Aviv, where Chaim attended the Tachkemoni School. His father felt frustrated in his job at the Rabbinate, however; and when the opportunity arose in 1927 to head the Lubavitcher community in London, he jumped at it.[13] Chaya, his wife, was not keen to uproot her family for a second time in less than four years, and chose to remain behind while Reb Mordechai established himself in London. It was a courageous move for a woman with two young children.

Palestine at this time was a more hospitable place for religious Jews than Russia had been. But it was no bed of roses. There was a large indigenous Arab population, who bitterly resented the sudden influx of Jews from Europe. Their hostility was apparent from the outset. It erupted into widespread insurrection in 1929, in the course of which the Arabs in Hebron went on a rampage and slaughtered almost seventy of the town's Jews. Fortuitously, Chaya was in Tel Aviv with the two boys at the time of the outrage. But shaken by what had happened in Hebron, she decided the time had come to join her husband in England.

The family lived a secluded life for their first few years in London. Reb Mordechai wouldn't even let his children attend school, and had tutors in to teach them secular subjects. But when he died quite suddenly in 1932, aged just thirty-five, Chaya could no longer afford this arrangement.

Chaim was sent to the Jewish Free School, an English government school for Jewish students, where he learned English and acquired a life-long love for the game of cricket. On finishing school at fourteen, he followed in the family tradition and started his rabbinical studies at the local Etz Chayim *yeshivah* (religious seminary). He was a bright student, and his mother wanted him to go on to study at one of the major seminaries in Europe. He was too young to go to the main Lubavitcher yeshivah in Warsaw — where the Rebbe had relocated by this time, the situation in the Soviet Union having finally become intolerable — but was offered a place at the famous Tels Yeshivah in Lithuania, one of the finest Jewish rabbinical seminaries in pre-war Europe. Tels was a strange choice for a young Lubavitcher, being a non-Hasidic institution, and the Rebbe's permission was needed before he was allowed to go. 'The Rebbe's reply was that at that yeshivah they learn *Musar* — ethics — so he agreed,' Chaim recalls. He left London for Lithuania in 1936, when he was barely fifteen years old. It was to be a dozen years before he saw his mother again.

Tels was an unusual institution. Although deeply conservative and rigorously Orthodox, in the strict *Litvak* tradition, it would not tolerate any form of extremism or fanaticism, and placed little importance on the outward signs of piety. Chaim was chastised by the head of the yeshivah once for trying to grow a beard. He was told in no uncertain terms to devote more attention to the content of Jewish piety and less to its superficial symbolism. It was a useful lesson, and one that came to characterise Chaim's approach to religion. It was also at Tels that he acquired two of the characteristics that were to mark him for the rest of his life: he learned to 'fit in' with people from a religious and social background very different from his own, and he learned the importance of moderation, of the middle way.

In 1940, the Russians annexed Lithuania. Among the first things they did was to close down the yeshivah and expel all foreign nationals. Fortunately, Chaim was given his *smichah* (rabbinical certification) just before Tels was closed. That would not normally have happened so early, as he was barely nineteen and still had much to learn. But it was wartime and nobody knew what the future held, so all the students received their certification before they left. The young rabbinical student was fortunate to have acquired British citizenship while living in England. This meant he could be evacuated, along with 340 other British subjects in Lithuania, to Vladivostok in the Soviet Far East, where they were picked up by a British ship and brought to Australia.

The Gutnick saga Down Under was about to begin.

◊ ◊ ◊

The evacuees landed in Cairns, in northern Queensland, where they were welcomed by the British High Commissioner before being dispersed around Australia. Chaim and seven other yeshivah students were billeted in Brisbane. Although grateful to have a refuge, the students did not want to remain in Australia. Almost immediately they had encountered the hostility of the established Jewish community to Jewish 'reffos', especially religious Jews who, it was feared, would stand out and draw attention to the community. Rabbi Jacob Danglow — doyen of Australia's religious establishment and a man Chaim describes as having been 'more English than the King' — made his antipathy plain. Soon after arriving in Australia, two of the students were delegated to go to Melbourne, even then the largest Jewish centre in Australia, to look into the possibility of starting a yeshivah there. They were politely received, and were treated to a community dinner. Danglow was the reluctant host. The fact that the guests were British subjects may have been a mitigating factor, but he was incensed when the two students refused to touch the meat they were served, suspecting that it might not be kosher. 'We're going to have trouble from these fellows,' he growled. 'We'd better persuade them not to stay in the country.' The two returned to Brisbane and reported: 'This is not the place for us here. They said if we establish a yeshivah it will increase anti-semitism. Australia's not used to it. They would prefer us to go somewhere else.' Chaim recalls he was even offered money to find another place to go.

To leave Australia, the students would need a letter from a yeshivah or some other religious institution abroad saying they were accepted as students. Chaim wrote to his spiritual leader, the Lubavitcher Rebbe — who had recently escaped from Nazi-occupied Warsaw and established himself in New York — asking to come to America. The Rebbe replied:

> As providence has led you to this country that is a sign that there you must be, and I do not advise you to come to America but to stay in Australia. The war's going to finish one day and there'll be thousands of Jews who will look for a new country in which to settle after Europe. Australia will be one of them. Someone should be there to establish Jewishness and to bring back to them the God whom they thought had forsaken them.

And so Chaim stayed.

◊ ◊ ◊

Then began a remarkable chapter in Chaim's life, one that was to mould the strong sense of pride and self-assurance he had in his dual identity as proud Jew and proud Australian. In 1942, he volunteered to join the Australian Army.

'Your name?' the red-faced sergeant at the recruiting office in Sydney barked.

'Schneur Chaim Gutnick,' Chaim replied, giving his full name.

'What? You can't have a name like that in the army. We'll lose the [bleep]ing war! From now on we're calling you Harold James Gutnick.'

So Harold James it was, or 'Harry' to his new army mates. In fact, Chaim notes a little sheepishly, that was the formal name he used for the next sixteen years, until he moved to Melbourne to become Rabbi Chaim Gutnick of Elwood Synagogue in 1957. And it remains his name to this day on his driver's licence — as well as in the telephone directory, which lists him as 'Rabbi H J Gutnick'.

The military authorities may not have thought much of the fighting qualities of this strange new arrival from Lithuania. They posted him to the Medical Corps to become a medic, but they had underestimated their man. Chaim told them he wanted to fight. He had come from Europe and knew what was happening there. He wanted to be in a fighting unit. His persistence paid off, and he was eventually transferred, as he proudly recalls, 'to the Second First Machine Gun Battalion of the 9th Divvy'.

It was a gutsy move for a young, deeply observant Jew, recently arrived in Australia straight from one of Eastern Europe's most rigorous, conservative seminaries. The contrast in lifestyles could not have been starker. Chaim did meet a few fellow Jews in the army, although no one from anything like his own deeply Orthodox background. By and large, he was on his own. But he had no trouble mixing, and remembers encountering no animosity or prejudice because of his Jewishness. 'It never arose.'

Chaim had grown up in England, and spoke good English, which would have helped enormously. But food was a problem. There was no possibility of maintaining the kind of strict kosher eating regime he would normally observe, but he did his best:

> I remember that Sunday was a 'Pork Day' in the army. They used to serve a pork dinner. And when I used to come into the mess, the boys used to call out: 'Hey Cooky — bring out the cheese, the rabbi's here!' Things like that. But it was very difficult . . . I pacified myself that I was in the army, that we were at war, and that it was a holy war in my eyes, to defeat the Germans. So I justified everything I was doing.

Observing the Sabbath was another difficulty. The army did its best to accommodate him, although this was not always possible. 'They used to give me mess duty on *Shabbat* (the Sabbath),' Chaim recalls.

'But when we went on bivouac, on manoeuvres, I had to go.' It was a question of *pikuach nefesh*, the Jewish law venerating the sanctity of life. It was wartime, and he was being trained to fight. 'I had to learn how to fight, or else I'd be shot when I got to the front.'

In the event, Chaim did not get to the front. He was on a ship due to leave for Malaya some time in 1943 when he was ordered to disembark and undergo an officers' training course in Sydney. Meanwhile, his mother, in far off England, had heard he was in the army. She was horrified. It was not what she had in mind for her budding young rabbi. He should at least be an army chaplain. She contacted the Chief Rabbi in London, who in turn got in touch with Rabbi Danglow. Chaim was ordered to present himself at a Sydney hotel for an interview with the man they called 'Anglo Danglow'.

It was, Chaim recalls, the most peculiar interview he had had in his life:

> I thought that when Rabbi Danglow came to interview me he wanted to test my scholastic ability. The custom was, when you came to visit a rabbi, the student would begin by telling him about some topic he is learning, and you'd have a discussion. So I started talking, and for about twenty minutes I talked and he never said a word. 'Uh-oh,' I thought, 'that's the end of me! I'm probably not making any sense.' In the end Rabbi Danglow said: 'Young man, I haven't delved in these matters for forty years. I couldn't follow very closely what you were saying.' So I asked: 'Then what was the purpose of the interview?' He replied: 'I want to see if you're officer material.' And how did he propose to do that? 'I want you to walk up and down the room.' So I walked up and down the room for him, in my khaki shorts. He shook his head, and said: 'I can't see you being a captain!' A chaplain had to be a captain. So that was the end of that.

Not long after, in 1944, Chaim was discharged. He had completed his officer's training at Randwick, but before he was commissioned he underwent a medical test and it was found he had several deficiencies: 'One arm was shorter than the other, one leg was shorter than the other. In the family we suffer from extra bones in the body. At any rate, I was discharged as being medically unfit.' He wasn't especially sorry. 'To tell you the truth, I was fed up. I hadn't seen any action. I wasn't sent overseas. I kept being sent from one barracks to the other. I was glad to get out.' He has never forgotten his debt to the army, though: 'The army fashioned me in such a way that I could mix comfortably with non-Jews . . . I felt very Australian since I joined the army.'

Once out of the army, Chaim set about establishing himself in

Sydney. He boarded with a religious family, the Wises, and earned his keep by giving religious instruction to Jewish high-school students, and private lessons to Jewish children evacuated from England along with their mothers while their fathers were away fighting in the war. He was also involved, as 'honorary rabbi', with the Mizrachi Synagogue in Bondi, established to cater to the city's growing population of Jews from Eastern Europe. He could have sought a permanent rabbinical position, but life was going well for him, and he was prepared to see out the war in this fashion, before asking the Rebbe if he would reconsider and permit him to join his mother in England. 'I kept thinking that I'd go back to England one day, to my mother.'

Then he met Rose Chester. Chaim was about twenty-three at the time, a strikingly handsome, highly eligible young man with, he concedes, quite an eye for the ladies. And they, it seems, had quite an eye for him: 'I had a few incidents that made me decide it was time to get married,' Chaim recalls. 'I was too vulnerable. A nice looking young man with all these grass widows who were here from England and so forth. So I wrote to the Rebbe. I asked should I wait till I went back to England to my mother, or should I look for a bride. His reply was I should get married, and he told me what kind of a girl I should choose.'

One of the schools Chaim taught at was Sydney Girls' High. 'I used to have girls in the higher classes, sixteen, seventeen, that I used to teach. I noticed that all the girls used to put lipstick on to make themselves look attractive, because the handsome young rabbi was coming. One girl stood out by the fact that she did not. She didn't try to impress me. She didn't want to make herself conspicuous, but she was conspicuous by her non-conspicuousness.' Also, Chaim remembers wistfully, she wore braids. 'Lithuanian Jewish girls used to wear these long braids . . . '

Rose, for her part, was equally smitten: 'He was a junior Jewish Studies teacher in school when I was a senior doing my Leaving,' she related in a 1991 *Australian Jewish News* interview. 'Even the Christian girls used to sneak out of their religious instruction lessons to hear him . . . He was so handsome. He asked to marry me. I said yes but I wanted to get my Matric first.' Chaim agreed to the delay, and received the Rebbe's blessing. They were married in 1945.

Chaim then went into his new father-in-law's jewellery business. He worked there in the mornings, selling watches, gold and diamonds. In the afternoons, he continued with his private lessons and rabbinical work. Meanwhile, he and Rose started a family of their own. Their firstborn was a girl, Pnina, who was later to achieve considerable notoriety as an audacious searcher for diamonds in the Australian desert (see Chapter 9). She was followed by another daughter, Chana ('Annette'), now married to a prominent New York rabbi, Rabbi Sholom Ber Hecht, and the mother of fourteen children. Then came the first son, Mottel ('Martin'), today a well-known rabbi in Melbourne, followed by Yossel ('Geoffrey'). Two further sons were born after the family moved to Melbourne in 1957: Moshe, who also went on to become a prominent rabbi, in Sydney; and Avraham, who later became the first and only Jewish community police chaplain in New South Wales.

The fact that his first two children were girls was 'quite providential', Chaim observes, 'because there wasn't a *mohel* (ritual circumciser)[14] in Sydney satisfactory for my standards.' He also wouldn't touch meat for the first eight years 'because I was never sure it was kosher enough'. Then a Rabbi Bernard came to serve the Hungarian community in Sydney, and he met with Chaim's approval both as a *mohel* and as a *shochet* (ritual slaughterer). 'That was when I started eating meat — and had my first boy, Mottel.'

The Gutnicks lived a strictly Orthodox[15] lifestyle in Sydney. The children went to the Jewish school, Moriah College, which Chaim had been instrumental in establishing. English was the language of the home, both between Chaim and Rose, and with the children. They spoke Yiddish — the Hebrew–German patois of East European Jewry — with Rose's parents, and with the other Eastern European Jews who used to visit the house regularly on Sabbaths and Jewish holidays, and all the children picked it up.

This was very much the lifestyle the Gutnick children experienced in their paternal grandparents' home, too. Once Chaim had married and started a family, the Lubavitcher Rebbe instructed his mother, Chaya, and her second husband, Rabbi Osher Abramson, to move from London to Sydney. This they did in 1947. It was the first time Chaim had seen his mother since leaving for Tels in 1935, as a boy of barely fifteen.

For all the richness of their Jewish home life, Chaim was determined not to let himself, or his family, sink into a ghetto-style existence. 'There was no ghetto feeling in my home, ever,' Chaim insists. 'I would probably have restricted what my children watched on TV, but I would not have banned the TV from my home. I used to take them to the pictures, to see films . . . I would be ninety per cent open to the outside world.' His children had non-Jewish friends, and his two daughters went to a non-Jewish high school — Elwood High — after the family moved to Melbourne in 1957.

Chaim saw no contradiction between being a fully observant, religious Jew and participating fully in Australian life. He might be said to have been an early pioneer of what is now called Australian multi-culturalism:

> I always felt very comfortable as an Australian, and I never regarded myself as belonging to an 'ethnic entity'. I have always regarded myself as being an Australian, and my religion as being Jewish. As far as I can remember, I was always comfortable with non-Jews. I can't remember not being able to mix freely, even though most of my company was Jewish most of the time ... I was never ashamed of wearing a *kipah* [skullcap], I was never afraid of refusing to eat out. That was my religion and it was accepted as such.

Chaim was also a keen sports fan, going back to his school days in London. 'I was always a great cricket fan,' he says. 'And if you asked me what won the Melbourne Cup, I'd be able to tell you. I have always liked to have a bit of a punt.' Being involved in sport is important, Chaim believes, not only for the intrinsic pleasure it brings, but also because it enables people with little else in common to build bridges:

> If you meet a non-Jewish person you can talk to him about football. You can talk to him about the Melbourne Cup or something like that. You have a common language with him. But if he lives in football, and you live in some other thing, you've got no conversation with him. I can't talk to him about *Gemarah* [part of the Talmud, or codification of Jewish Oral Law] or things like that.

What anti-semitism Chaim might have encountered during his time in Australia, he appears to have taken with a grain of salt — and a healthy self-deprecating sense of humour. He relates how someone had once called him a 'fat Jew', dismissing the slur as a piece of unsolicited 'dietary advice'.[16]

Chaim insists that his ability to live easily and comfortably in both worlds was not merely the result of his personal history or philosophy, but lay at the core of his belief as a Lubavitcher Jew: 'The Rebbe under-lined on a number of occasions that the object of a Jewish person is not to enclose himself in a ghetto, but to go out into society. Into the world. Into the Jewish world and into the non-Jewish world.' There was, Chaim explains, a profound socio-theological reason for this:

> It was the Jews' mission in the world to promote a love and respect for God among all mankind. And how do I make God beloved? By living a lifestyle

that brings respect to His name. If I am a Jewish person and I walk around non-Jews and they say, 'Oh, he's a fine fellow' that reflects on my God. If I behave in an indecent way, that reflects detrimentally on my God. So it's entirely wrong from a Lubavitcher point of view to isolate yourself both from the Jewish community and from the non-Jewish environment. We have to go out there, and live our lifestyle, and they should see what a beautiful lifestyle it is . . . I don't have to go on the rooftop and shout about it. But I don't have to be embarrassed by my religion. I think my religion is a very beautiful one, taken all around, and compares more than favourably with all the others, and there's nothing to be ashamed of . . . Whether we perform it correctly or not is a different question. But that is our obligation. This was impressed on my family all the time.

It was a potent message for all of Chaim's children — none more so than the young Yossel, who was singled out very early on in life by his mother, Rose, as someone who was going to succeed in the outside world.

◊ ◊ ◊

In 1956 Chaim was approached by the Elwood Synagogue in Melbourne to be their rabbi. This was a large congregation, made up mostly of Eastern European Holocaust survivors who had arrived in the bayside suburb since the war. These were Jews who did not fit comfortably in to Melbourne's existing congregations in the area — especially the nearby St Kilda Synagogue, which remained a bastion of Melbourne's old 'Anglo–Jewish' establishment. Its long-time rabbi was Chaim's old nemesis, Rabbi Danglow, who epitomised the antipathy many of Melbourne's English-speaking, thoroughly 'Australianised' Jews still felt towards the Yiddish-speaking newcomers. Danglow had little patience with the newcomers' insistence on hanging on to their old ways, and advised them to 'shake the dust off their feet and leave, if they don't like it here'. Needless to say, the newcomers did not take kindly to this advice, and returned Danglow's contempt — with interest. It was they who dubbed him 'Anglo Danglow' and made fun of the fact that he had changed his name from the original 'Danglowitz'. By dropping the give-away 'witz', they joked, 'he had lost his wits!'[17] For most of them, the horrific experience of the Holocaust had only served to reinforce their determination not to dilute or diminish their Jewish distinctiveness for the sake of blending into Australian society. To do so, many believed, would be 'to give Hitler a posthumous victory'. If they were to participate in Australian society,

Australian society would have to accept them for what they were — openly proud Jews. They would not become 'trembling Israelites'.

Much of this mutual antipathy had all but disappeared by the mid-1950s, but there remained (and perhaps still remains) a residue of tension between members of the old established community and the post-war Jewish refugees, which Chaim was uniquely qualified to defuse.

While he may have been a little reluctant to uproot his family from Sydney, Chaim had two compelling reasons to accept the Elwood Synagogue's offer. The Rebbe in New York had been exerting relentless pressure on him to become a full-time rabbi. 'He was the one who was pushing me all the time to become a rabbi. He said I had unique talents, and it would be a pity to waste them.' The Rebbe had earlier wanted Chaim to accept a pulpit in Adelaide, where the small Jewish community was desperately in need of a rabbi. But, Chaim explains, under the Adelaide Synagogue's constitution, the rabbi had to wear a cap and gown — 'You know, like what the priests wear.' So Chaim sent the Rebbe a telegram explaining this, and the Rebbe replied: 'Yes, it seems to me this is forbidden according to the Torah.' There was no such requirement at Elwood.

But the clincher was probably the make-up of the Elwood congregation. The previous Rebbe, when he had instructed Chaim to remain in Australia after he arrived in 1940, had stressed that thousands of Holocaust survivors were likely to be arriving there after the war and that 'someone should be there to establish Jewishness and to bring back to them the God whom they thought had forsaken them.' Chaim could not now refuse this mission. Besides, he himself was obsessed with the Holocaust. He had lost some distant members of his family in the 1941 Babi Yar Massacre,[18] and had been shocked to his soul by the immense catastrophe that had engulfed the Jewish people in Europe. 'I don't know what it was. I became obsessed by it. I used to be angry with myself that I had escaped and hadn't shared ... I begrudged myself ...,' the usually articulate Chaim tries to explain, struggling for the words. 'I remember I was always, since the end of the war ... I used to read snippets during the war, and I used to think it was propaganda. But then after the revelation of what happened ... I remember, on my free days in Sydney, I used to go to the port to welcome these refugees. I felt I wanted to serve them in some way ...'

Chaim came to Elwood over the High Holy Days in 1956, on a trial basis. The community liked what they saw, and he was offered a permanent contract. Chaim was concerned, however, about the amount of time that had elapsed since he had abruptly completed his rabbinical studies in Lithuania. 'I didn't want to become a rabbi until I had renewed my knowledge. I was frightened that even though I got my *smichah* when I left Tels, that was now null and void because of the years in between.' So he studied with Rabbi Hertz in Sydney, who renewed his accreditation. And in 1957, he and his family moved to Melbourne.

All of Melbourne's rabbis were invited to his induction ceremony, with the sole exception of 'Anglo Danglow'. This was his congregation's decision: 'They rejected Rabbi Danglow, my people, because he wore the round collar, and they couldn't stand it.' But Danglow came to see Chaim privately after the induction, and the two rabbis soon became staunch friends. 'He had mellowed, and he regretted that that time he had seen me in Sydney he didn't make me a chaplain,' Chaim relates. 'Every Tuesday afternoon we used to meet and have tea. I used to go to his place, or he used to come to mine. And he eventually handed over to me all his positions — the army chaplaincy, chaplain of prisons, chaplain of hospitals, all his honorary titles.' And, irony of ironies, when Rabbi Danglow retired a couple of years later, 'they approached me to become the Rabbi of St Kilda'. Chaim considered the offer, but eventually turned it down. 'I felt my mission was with the survivors at Elwood.'

Chaim felt an enormous empathy for the members of his new congregation, and saw a great challenge, after the horror they had been through in Europe, in not only helping them rebuild their lives in their new country but also restoring their faith in God. 'I wanted to bring them back their God,' he says. And he shared the immense reverence his congregants felt for the newly established State of Israel. For him, like them, the Holocaust and Israel were bound up with each other as the two pivotal events of recent Jewish history. That the Jewish people could rise like a phoenix from the depths of despair, from the ashes of the Holocaust, and create a brave new future for themselves in Israel was something, he believed, 'that is beyond human understanding'.

Chaim had a presence and a demeanour that not only impressed established Australianised Jews like Rabbi Danglow (eventually) and his congregants at St Kilda, but won him a large following among Australia's non-Jewish population as well. A fine orator, he was a regular guest on the religious television program *Epilogue*. This was well watched and Chaim was a star turn, receiving hundreds of letters from viewers after each appearance. This earned him great respect in the Jewish community, which, in a survey carried out in the early 1960s, rated him as one of the 'most important Jews in Melbourne'.[19] Chaim was also a very active Freemason. 'I wasn't prone to work together with the priests, with the churches, as Danglow had. But I wanted an avenue to get through to the non-Jewish population, and I did that through Freemasonry. I had some doubts about the philosophy of Freemasonry, but it was for me an avenue that covered my conscience that I had access to the non-Jewish world through them. And I rose quite high in the Freemasons.'

◊ ◊ ◊

Yossel was just five years old when the family moved to Melbourne. He has few memories of his early years in Sydney, his strongest recollections being of his paternal grandparents, the Abramsons, and their home at 40 Ocean Street, Bondi. Even after moving to Melbourne, he would go back to visit them several times a year. 'I had a very close relationship with my grandparents,' he recalls. Other childhood memories: 'I remember when my brother Mottel was bitten by a redback spider and taken to hospital . . . I remember playing Monopoly . . . I remember going to Bondi Beach . . . I remember Moriah College and the Mizrachi synagogue . . . and I remember the family home, at 365 Old South Head Road; just before we left, my brother Mottel and I wrote a message that we had lived there, and buried it in a bottle in the ground — I'd like to go back some day and see if that bottle is still there . . . '

Once settled in Melbourne, Yossel, or 'Geoffrey' as he was still known at school, attended the Jewish school next door to his father's synagogue, also called Moriah College. One of his schoolmates of that period — Robert 'Red' Bingham, who had attended Moriah as a child and later went on to achieve fame as the anarchist who slugged the future Treasurer, Peter Costello, at Monash University in the 1970s — remembers him as a somewhat lonely, withdrawn child. 'We used to call him Gutnick the Sputnik,' he recalls — the first of the many colourful nicknames Joseph was to acquire over the years. He is also remembered as the 'Marbles King', in recognition of his early talent for accumulating what in a schoolyard context would have been considered great 'wealth'. This was a trait his mother, Rose, had noticed very early. 'From the time I was six or seven, my mother used to say to her friends: "Yossel will be very successful and very wealthy",' Joseph recalls. 'She said it all the time. It was a mother's intuition.'

Joseph himself had mixed feelings about his time at Moriah. He had great respect for the principal of the school, Reverend Wreschner. 'He had a very unusual philosophy,' Joseph recalls. 'He used to treat us as little adults, and always referred to us as "people".' But although religious in orientation, the school was not strictly Orthodox. It was co-ed, for a start — something Joseph says he would not tolerate for his own children. 'Maybe that's the cause of some of my problems today, my liberalism, because I went to a school like Moriah,' he laments. He also appeared to resent that his brothers all went directly to the strictly religious Lubavitcher school, Yeshivah College, while he had to attend Moriah until the end of Grade 5. This was because the school was attached to his father's synagogue and, as the rabbi, Chaim was under some obligation to send at least one of his children there. 'I was the scapegoat,' Joseph recalls a little ruefully.

In general, it would seem, Joseph regretted, at least in retrospect, the lack of overt Lubavitcher identification and rigorous Lubavitcher lifestyle that characterised his and his family's life at this time: beards for men, head coverings and modest clothing for women — all the outward signs that marked off Lubavitcher Jews from the general Jewish community. The family was, of course, strictly religious, and was always aware and proud of its Lubavitcher affiliation (as we have seen, Chaim had remained in regular correspondence with the Lubavitcher Rebbe). But this tended to be in the background, Joseph recalls, and was not an all-encompassing factor of everyday life. 'We were a Lubavitcher family, but my father was a modern, Orthodox rabbi in the Elwood Synagogue. He didn't have a beard . . . It wasn't a typical Lubavitcher family.'

The Lubavitcher community was, in fact, very small — barely more than a handful of families — when Chaim arrived in Melbourne in 1957. It had its origins in the country town of Shepparton, about 150 kilometres north of Melbourne, where five Lubavitcher families had been sent from Paris by the Rebbe in 1949 to join Moishe Feiglin, whose family had been orchardists there since the late 1920s. They started a yeshivah there, attracting a few students from both Melbourne and Sydney. But it wasn't long before they, like most Jewish migrants who had started out in rural Victoria, were drawn to Melbourne. By 1954, they had established themselves in East St Kilda, in the heart of Jewish Melbourne.

They struggled at first, and Chaim, who was in regular contact with them, even wrote to the Rebbe suggesting they might be better off moving to Sydney and earning their living in a factory he would set up for them. 'But the Rebbe replied that he didn't approve,' Chaim recalls. 'They weren't sent here to work in factories. They were sent to spread Jewishness, and should remain in Melbourne.' The community eventually took root, and established a yeshivah and primary school in Hotham Street, St Kilda. In 1958, the Rebbe sent a special emissary, Rabbi Yitzchok Dovid Groner, to lead the nascent community.

Chaim got on well with Rabbi Groner from the start, and took an active interest in the Lubavitcher community. But his first commitment was to his own congregation in Elwood, and he wore his outward Lubavitcher identity lightly — clearly more lightly than Joseph would have liked. Chaim, however, points out that many of the outward signs of Jewish religiosity so important to Joseph and other Lubavitchers today — the emphasis on beards, skullcaps, strict separation of the sexes — were not so important when he was growing up in London before World War II. 'Even for Lubavitcher Jews', genuine Jewish learning and Jewish observance were what really mattered. Joseph, on the other hand, believes that the 'temptations' of late-twentieth-century materialism make it much more necessary for Jews to be strict about these outward symbols than might have been the case in the past. Especially in an open, multicultural society like Australia, where it is very easy for Jews to assimilate and lose their identity.

In Grade 6, Joseph finally joined his brother Mottel at Yeshivah College, which by this time had grown quite considerably, as had the Lubavitcher community. The college, which took great pride in providing a sound secular education combined with rigorous, Orthodox Jewish learning in the Lubavitcher tradition, was headed by Rabbi Groner, a massive Falstaffian figure with a huge bushy beard and piercing black eyes. He came from a leading Lubavitcher family in the United States, and ran the Yeshivah College with a passion that rubbed off on his students — not least, it would seem, the young Joseph Gutnick, who remembers him as 'a fantastic teacher'. Joseph excelled at both his religious and his secular studies, and became increasingly involved with and committed to the Lubavitcher movement.

As his Lubavitcher identity deepened — spurred on by his growing friendship with Rabbi Groner's son, Yossi, and an enthusiastic group of Lubavitcher rabbinical students who had come over from the United States — Joseph grew more and more uncomfortable with the name Geoffrey, which he still used formally. His Hebrew name, 'Yosef Yitzhak', had a powerful resonance in the Lubavitcher world, being that of the Sixth Lubavitcher Rebbe. So, when he was about fifteen, he decided to get rid of the Geoffrey once and for all, and changed his name by deed poll to Joseph Isaac — the English equivalent of Yosef Yitzhak.

Joseph was also deeply relieved at about this time that his father had decided to finally grow a beard. He was more or less forced to do so when his daughter, Pnina, married into a prominent Lubavitcher family. All the men would have beards, and it would not be becoming for her father — a rabbi, with a proud Lubavitcher pedigree, to boot — to be the only clean-shaven adult male at the wedding. But for Joseph, who had always looked up to Chaim as a role model, the fact that his father now sported a beard like all other Lubavitcher fathers removed another anomaly which, like the name Geoffrey, had become increasingly irksome. Chaim, who was always a little vain about his looks, used to trim his beard, though. And the young Joseph lived in constant fear that he 'would wake up one day and find he had shaved it off!' He needn't have worried. For at about this time, too, in the mid-1960s, Chaim Gutnick began to develop a strong personal relationship with the Lubavitcher Rebbe — something which, Joseph believes, inevitably 'strengthened his Lubavitcher commitment, outwardly and internally'. It also strengthened the bond between father and son, especially in later years, when Joseph developed his own very special relationship with the Rebbe.

One area of tension still remained. Chaim, despite his Lubavitcher background, was a deeply committed Zionist and had always been a strong supporter of Israel. He was, for several years, president of the Jewish National Fund (JNF)[20] in Victoria, which raised money for the Jewish state, and was an eloquent spokesman for the Zionist cause both from his pulpit and in the general community. This was not well received by many in the local Lubavitcher community, which was still ambivalent about the 'Godless' Jewish state that the secular Zionists were creating in the Holy Land. But here Joseph was firmly on his father's side, and was proudly and defiantly pro-Zionist and pro-Israel well before this became generally accepted by most Lubavitchers.

'I used to become very uptight and tense about it, and defensive of my father being president of the JNF', Joseph recalls, pointing out that while 'certain hard-core Lubavitcher circles' in Melbourne were very critical of his father, Chaim had sought and received the Rebbe's permission before taking on the position. This tension continued until after the 1967 Six Day War, when the mood in the Lubavitcher movement changed radically, and it became perhaps the most enthusiastically pro-Israel of all Ultra-Orthodox Jewish sects. In Melbourne, the new tone was set by the movement's leader, Rabbi Groner, who from that time on was a regular guest speaker for the United Israel Appeal — along with the JNF, the main Zionist fundraising organisation in Australia.

At school, Joseph was deeply absorbed in his Jewish studies, especially after the group of senior rabbinical students came out from

New York in 1967. Their enthusiasm, commitment and learning were an eye-opener for the young student, and profoundly influenced him. One in particular, Leibl Kaplan, became a very close friend. He was a brilliant student who went on to become one of the leaders of the Lubavitcher movement in Israel — and, later, the recipient of a great deal of Joseph's philanthropy, which, in turn, signalled the start of Joseph's direct philanthropic and, eventually, high-profile political involvement in the Jewish state. At one stage, Joseph even seriously considered following the rabbinical students' example and devoting himself entirely to his rabbinical studies, dropping out of school and going straight on to yeshivah. But his mother, who had placed a very high premium on her own secular education, had other ideas.

Joseph was very close to his mother, especially as a child, and it was Rose rather than Chaim who had the greater influence over him. Even when it came to his Jewish studies, Joseph does not recall his father showing much interest. 'He was very busy. As long as things were going well, he was prepared to leave things to the school.' His main influence was as a role model, Joseph explains. 'He used to lead by example.' His mother, on the other hand, 'was much more involved in my education, school, and day-to-day activities than my father was'. And, with her 'mother's intuition' about the great future that lay in store for her little Yossel, she encouraged him to excel in his secular studies as well. Joseph was, in fact, very good at secular subjects, especially commercial studies. Had he gone on to university, Joseph says, he probably would have studied economics and accounting (although if he were to go to university now — something he does not rule out at some point in the future — he says he would probably study geology).

Tertiary study was, however, not a serious option at the time. His father was not opposed to university education in principle. But, he once explained: 'If you have a limited span of time, you use that time for the best purposes that you can. The main aim of Jewry is not to send sputniks up to heaven, but to bring heaven down here. The Gutnicks will help bring the sputniks down from heaven.'[21] His mother felt strongly, however, that Joseph's vocation lay in the world of business, and encouraged him to pursue that direction. And Chaim, while he was quite prepared to leave it to Joseph's teachers at school to provide him with his Jewish education, guided his son's first steps into the stock market. 'My father was involved in shares,' Joseph recalls. And it was more than just the odd flutter. 'He was a trader. I learnt about the share market from him.'

Joseph became quite adept at stock trading himself, long before he left school. He remembers the first shares he bought — in a stock called Sunhill. He was about sixteen at the time. 'I used to follow the market a lot. We'd hear tips, and read about it. I was always attracted to the resource sector. There was an opportunity to make money.' Especially at the time of the phenomenal Poseidon nickel boom in 1970, when students would be on the phone to their brokers during lunch breaks. 'Everyone got onto Poseidon. Every kid was involved,' Joseph recalls. 'My father, us kids, everyone was talking about Poseidon . . . I did my own little thing. I always had a feel for it and saw an opportunity on the stock market to make money.' And make money he did — enough to finance his trip to New York, via Israel, after he finished school. 'And a few bucks besides . . . '

At Yeshivah College, Joseph developed his first and, it turned out, abiding interest in Australian Rules football, as both a fan and a player in the school playground. 'As a kid I was a small rover,' he recalled in a 1996 interview.[22] 'But I used to pick up a lot of kicks and score goals.' (He saved many more goals, though, as goalkeeper for the Hakoah soccer club, soccer being the more popular code among his peers at that time.) He also became a passionate Demons supporter, noting that, when he arrived in Melbourne as a small boy in 1957, Melbourne was the best team in town. And, like most small boys, he wanted to support a winner. His strict religious beliefs prevented him from watching many live games as they were almost invariably played on Saturdays — and Joseph refused to desecrate the Sabbath. But he remained an avid follower.

Joseph's football interests — and, he claims, his stock market interests as well — had to be put on hold for a few years after he completed his schooling in 1970. Despite his obvious taste, and talent, for making money, he did not go directly into business. Nor was he encouraged to do so. Instead, after a year at the Yeshivah Gedolah post-high school seminary in Melbourne, he went on to pursue his rabbinical studies in New York — at the feet of the man who was to become his guiding influence for the rest of his life: Rabbi Menachem Mendel Schneerson, the Seventh Lubavitcher Rebbe.

The Sage of New York

'Anyone who fails to understand the influence of the Rebbe on Gutnick fails to understand Gutnick.'
Christopher Webb, the *Age*, 17 July 1997

RABBI MENACHEM MENDEL Schneerson is widely regarded as one of the most remarkable religious figures of the twentieth century. Born in 1902, in the small Ukrainian town of Nikolayev, he was a brilliant religious scholar and a favourite of the Sixth Lubavitcher Rebbe, Rabbi Yosef Yitzhak Schneersohn. He fled the increasingly oppressive Soviet Union in 1928, settling first in Warsaw, where he married the Rebbe's daughter, Chaya Mushka, before moving to Germany. There he studied Mathematics and Science at the University of Berlin but, with the rise of Hitler in 1933, he left Berlin for Paris, continuing his studies at the Sorbonne. When the Nazis occupied Paris in 1941, Rabbi Menachem Mendel and his wife were forced to flee once again, this time leaving Europe for the safety of the United States. They arrived in New York on 23 June 1941.

The Lubavitcher movement was just beginning to establish itself in New York, where the Sixth Rebbe had fled in 1940 from Warsaw with a handful of his disciples. He had realised that Lubavitch in Europe was doomed, along with the rest of European Jewry. Supported by his American followers, the Rebbe and his disciples acquired a property at 770 Eastern Parkway in Crown Heights, then a comfortable, middle-class section of Brooklyn. And from there, with a small team of dedicated young rabbis — including Rabbi Menachem Mendel, who headed the movement's educational arm, its social service organisation and its publishing house — they began to spread the Lubavitcher message, first across the United States and then out to the rest of the Jewish world.

Rabbi Menachem Mendel became the Seventh Lubavitcher Rebbe in January 1951 — a year after the death of his father-in-law. He was reluctant at first to assume the mantle, doubting that he was up to the task. But it was unanimously agreed that he was the one man who had the lineage, spiritual depth, character and intellect required to lead the movement. And lead it he did, for the next forty-four years. By the time he died, on 12 June 1994, Lubavitch had become by far the most dynamic and successful movement of popular Jewish religious revival to have emerged from the Holocaust — with over 200,000 members and more than 1400 centres (known as Chabad Houses) serving the spiritual needs of Jewish communities in thirty-five countries on six continents. It had transformed itself, in less than fifty years, 'from an Eastern European Chassidic dynasty to an outward-looking group helping to influence the entire Jewish world'.[1]

The Rebbe touched and influenced people far beyond the confines of his own Lubavitcher sect — beyond, even, the confines of Judaism. So much so that, after he died, he was awarded the United States' highest civilian honour, the Congressional Gold Medal, for his 'outstanding and lasting contributions toward improvements in world education, morality, and acts of charity'.[2] All who came into direct contact with him were awed by his magnetism, and the aura of what could only be described as 'holiness' that appeared to surround him. Nobel laureate Elie Wiesel, speaking at a dinner in honour of the Rebbe in 1992, described his first meeting with the sage thirty years before: 'It lasted a very long time and I came back again and again. I recall every question and answer. Time in his presence began running at a different pace. In his presence you feel examined and begin wondering about a quest that should be yours. He sends out an emanation of mystical quality that touches even people who have never heard of him.'[3]

If this was the effect the Rebbe could have on a man like Wiesel, who was not a Lubavitcher, it was magnified many times over where his own followers were concerned. They regarded him as living on a plane quite different from that inhabited by ordinary men. The thousands who attended his famous *farbrengens* — the remarkable 'teachins' he gave several times a month in the central Lubavitcher synagogue — would hang on his every word, as though it were the word of God Himself. They would listen in awe, swaying on their feet, their faces quiet in peace and inspiration as the Rebbe spoke from a raised platform at the front of the great room. They would punctuate his intense discourse, which would often go on for four hours or more, with singing and toasts of *l'chaim* (the traditional Jewish toast, from the Hebrew for 'to life'). And when he was finished, his followers would break out into ecstatic song as the Rebbe briskly departed the synagogue

with his entourage, waving his arms in rhythm. Each and every word
he had uttered would have been committed to memory by a team of
'oral scribes'. Later, tens of thousands of Lubavitchers around the
world would pore over the published text of the discourse, reading,
analysing, dissecting and pondering all that the Rebbe had said.[4]

Even the briefest encounter with the Rebbe was something a
Lubavitcher Jew would remember and cherish for the rest of his or her
life. Small tokens, like the dollar bills he gave to his followers each
Sunday for charity, or the drop of vodka he would pour his followers
on the Sabbath, became, for many, treasured possessions. The vodka,
for instance, would be 'carefully decanted into other bottles of vodka,
and those into others, so that no Lubavitch house was ever without its
precious stock of "the Rebbe's vodka".'[5] It is unlikely that the Rebbe
himself either approved or encouraged this. From his point of view,
giving out the dollar bills and the vodka were symbolic acts of kindness, of doing good to other people. But those receiving these gifts often
appeared to attach to them a magical dimension that derived from the
sheer awe in which the Rebbe was held.

The Rebbe wielded incredible authority over all his followers.
Many, even quite sophisticated people, would not contemplate the
most mundane personal matter — such as moving house or changing
a job — without first consulting him. The Rebbe, for his part, would
invariably respond, and the recipient of his advice would unhesitat-
ingly act on it. This was part of a long tradition in Hasidic Judaism —
something called, in Hebrew, 'emunat chachamim,' or 'faith in wise
men'. But in the case of the Seventh Lubavitcher Rebbe, this faith
appears to have gone rather further and deeper. For example, in
January 1991 as the United Nations deadline on Iraq approached and
there was a real threat that Israel could be drawn into a devastating
war, the Rebbe declared that Israel was 'the safest place on earth'. His
followers, many of whom held foreign passports and could quite easily
have left, stayed put. Not only that, Lubavitchers planning to visit
Israel went ahead with their visits at a time when governments around
the world were warning their nationals to stay away. 'The Rebbe said
everything would be all right,' one of them explained on landing at the
semi-deserted Tel Aviv Airport. 'The Rebbe says that the Torah says
that God looks after the Holy Land . . .' It is doubtful that their faith in
the Rebbe's word would have wavered even as they huddled in sealed
rooms, gas masks over their faces, as Iraqi Scud missiles began to fall.
And who is to say their faith was not vindicated? There was not one
casualty as a direct result of the Scud attacks, even though dozens were

fired on the Jewish state. Israeli journalist David Landau, who cites the above example in his book *Piety & Power*, goes on to note that this 'blind obeisance to rabbis' is one of the most difficult aspects of Lubavitch and Ultra-Orthodox Judaism in general for the outsider to accept or to understand. For the Ultra-Orthodox themselves, however, nothing could be simpler or more self-evident. To them, 'religious reverence is a seamless web'. God Himself, the Bible, the Talmud, the rabbinical writings, the rabbis themselves — all are 'intertwined in an unbroken thread that extends from Abraham and Moses to the *gedolim* (great rabbis) of the present day, and on into the future'.[6]

Eventually, most Lubavitchers came seriously to believe that the Rebbe might be the Messiah — and even after his death there were still some who refused to believe he was not the Messiah, and awaited his resurrection (see Chapter 6). But even those who did not take their reverence for their Rebbe to such extremes clearly felt that he was a 'holy man' — that he had some kind of special relationship with God, some special insight into the workings of God's universe. For all that, the Rebbe was a remarkably warm, accessible man of great humility. One of his close associates in the Lubavitcher movement, Rabbi Simon Jacobson, has described his 'personal spirit' as being 'a combination of gentleness and strength, of simplicity and profundity, of sheer accessibility and remarkable intellect'.[7]

◊ ◊ ◊

This, then, was the man who, for the next four years, was to guide and mould the thoughts of the young rabbinical student from Australia when he arrived at Lubavitch headquarters, in Crown Heights, New York.

Joseph had never met the Rebbe before, though his father, Chaim, had enjoyed a close personal relationship with the sage. This had begun in 1964, when Chaim went overseas for the first time since arriving in Australia some twenty-four years earlier. He was accompanying his elder daughter, Pnina, to a women's religious seminary in England, and decided to take the opportunity to go to New York and meet the Rebbe, with whom he had been in regular correspondence for many years. 'I was one of the first in the world to write to him accepting him as my Rebbe way back in 1950,' Chaim recalls. 'He was reluctant to accept the position and I wrote to him urging him to do so, saying that I accepted his authority.' So to meet him personally was a big event. 'Somehow or other we took to each other straight away,' Chaim relates, and from that time on, he made the trip to New York nearly every year to see him.

The Rebbe, who was inundated with requests from followers around the world for a personal audience when they were in New York, could usually spare little more than a few minutes. But he always appeared to have time for Chaim. Once, Chaim recalls, he 'walked in at eleven-fifteen one night, and didn't come out until seven the next morning.' That they shared a special friendship transcending the usual Rebbe–disciple relationship was obvious to anyone who saw them together, and this emerges clearly even from the brief encounters captured on video when Chaim attended his 'dollars' — as Lubavitchers used to call the Rebbe's Sunday morning dollar-giving ritual. While the Rebbe would deal quite formally, and even perfunctorily, with the hundreds of people who filed past him, hearing their requests and giving his blessing, his whole body seemed to smile when he saw Chaim. The mutual enjoyment they appeared to get from each other's company was palpable, tempering the sometimes overwhelming awe in which the Rebbe's disciples — including Joseph — held him, and giving it a more human dimension without in any way diminishing the ultimate respect Chaim accorded him.

Despite the special relationship Chaim had with the Rebbe, Joseph appears to have enjoyed no special privileges or special access during the time he spent in New York. The Rebbe would have been aware of him as Chaim's son — 'I always used to give him the names of my children and ask for his blessing,' Chaim recalls. One of these blessings, Joseph remembers, was, in fact, highly unusual. 'He should grow up to be a High Priest,' the Rebbe had said. This had greatly puzzled Joseph at the time, and he wrote to the Rebbe asking for an interpretation. None was forthcoming. But twenty-five years later, Joseph relates, at one of his meetings with the Rebbe, the Rebbe asked him: 'So, are you getting ready to be a High Priest?' Joseph was flabbergasted. Here was his reply after all those years. The Rebbe went on to explain that every Jew had the potential to reach the top, to be a High Priest in the Temple — and, as far as Joseph was concerned, this meant that he would be very successful. Joseph notes, in passing, that the High Priests at the Temple in Jerusalem were known to be very wealthy — 'besides the corrupt ones at the time of the Second Temple'.

The future High Priest, however, did not have much personal contact with the Rebbe when he first arrived in New York. 'The Rebbe couldn't accommodate everyone,' Chaim explains. 'Even if Yossel had a private audience, on his birthday perhaps, he would have gone in for one or two minutes, got a blessing, and out he went. There was no *protektsia* (special pull).' Joseph confirms this, noting that the first time he met the Rebbe face to face had been at one of the brief birthday audiences he gave to all his students. 'And I was just another student.'

Joseph recalls that there were, perhaps, two occasions during the four years he spent at Crown Heights on which the Rebbe did display overt personal affection for him. The first was quite soon after he arrived in New York. The young student was unhappy during his early months at Crown Heights. He had looked forward to meeting up and studying with a pen-pal he had written to for years before coming to America, the brother of his sister Chana's husband. But the two didn't hit it off. Joseph was lonely, did not like the lifestyle in Crown Heights, and was homesick. He wanted to return to Melbourne, and told his father this when he next visited New York.

The Rebbe, however, insisted that he stick it out, telling him that while he might think his heart was telling him he wanted to go back to Australia, deep in his heart he knew he should stay and study in America. '*Le'olam yilmod adam bamakom shelibo chofetz*,' the Rebbe recited: 'A person should always learn in the place where his heart craves.' This, Joseph explains, was a subtle variation of the original saying: '*Le'olam yilmod adam bamakom shelibo rotzeh*' ('A person should always learn in the place where his heart desires') — the interpretation being that the word *rotzeh*/desires indicates an outward, or superficial, drive, while the word *chofetz*/craves indicates something much more profound. And so Joseph stayed.

The second occasion was about eighteen months later, when Joseph was accidentally hit in the eye by an orange someone had thrown at a Friday night dinner. His glasses had shattered, and some glass had lodged in his left eye. He was rushed to hospital, where he was told he might have lost the sight of the eye — 'but not to worry, the Israeli general Moshe Dayan managed fine with one eye!' Before he would let the doctors remove the glass, Joseph insisted on getting the Rebbe's permission. Two of his friends went around to the Rebbe's house at about two o'clock on a Saturday morning, and the Rebbe said they must do whatever the doctors saw fit. In the event, the glass had just missed the retina, and, although he received twenty-six stitches in the eye, Joseph did not lose his sight. But the Rebbe maintained a close interest in the case, and some nine months later chided Joseph for not keeping him personally informed of his progress.

Another incident from his time in New York that remained indelibly etched on Joseph's mind was the Rebbe's reaction to the 1973 Yom Kippur War in Israel. 'It was weird,' he recalls. Normally the Rebbe was always very serious. But on the eve of Yom Kippur, the Day of Atonement, the most mournful day in the Jewish year, the Rebbe suddenly said everyone should be joyful and start dancing. 'On Yom Kippur eve, we were dancing in the synagogue!' This was the Rebbe's way, Joseph explained, of 'annulling negativity through positivity, through joyfulness'. But the next day, Yom Kippur, Egypt and Syria attacked Israel on two fronts, and came perilously close to overrunning the surprised Israelis before they were able to regroup and take the fight to the enemy. The Rebbe broke down and cried. Every Jewish soldier who died in that war was a 'saint', he said, free from sin, who would go straight to heaven. 'It was very moving,' Joseph recalls. 'We saw how precious every Israeli soldier was to him.'

While Joseph was undoubtedly a solid and competent student, and graduated at the end of his four years as a qualified rabbi, he did not stand out as an '*ilui*', or prodigy of Torah study. 'I didn't have the *zitzfleish* (backside) for that,' he concedes. Or the background. For while he had received a reasonably intensive Jewish education before arriving in New York, and had been taught by one or two good teachers at Yeshivah College in Melbourne, the standard at the time was nothing like it is today — and fell well short of what most of his American peers had enjoyed.

'So what chance did I have?' Joseph asks. Besides, as the Baal Shem Tov had said 200 years before: 'Each man should work in the service of God according to his own talents.' And Joseph's talents, and life's work in the service of God, clearly lay in other directions — something his mother had divined years before, when she predicted that the small boy clinging to her dress would one day be 'very successful and very wealthy'. This had disappointed some of his fellow students in New York, who tried to persuade him that the highest possible calling for a Lubavitcher Jew was to become one of the Rebbe's emissaries, and to spread the word across the world. 'But it had always been my ambition to become the Rebbe's *gvir* (wealthy benefactor),' Joseph explains:

> There are lots of people who make successful rabbis, and I wouldn't be able to accomplish as much as I knew I would in business . . . Perhaps my mother had indoctrinated me . . . I just knew, from as far back as I can remember, that I wanted to be a successful businessman and help Lubavitch. Lubavitch was struggling, and didn't have a lot of financial support. So if I had a flair for business, which I thought I had, then this was the way I could help the movement. That was the only justification for me going into business . . . There are many of the Rebbe's emissaries around the world, but not many who can leave their mark by giving financial support.

Joseph concedes that his time in New York 'was not the happiest in my life', but it was profoundly rewarding and played a crucial role in his religious, intellectual and moral development. He regularly attended the Rebbe's *farbrengens*, and, like everyone else who attended them, came away with understanding and insight that would help guide him for the rest of his life. 'They were very precious, those times.' Even in those more worldly areas where Joseph's talents were destined to take him, a cursory glance through some of what the Rebbe had to say about such matters as work, ambition, determination, wealth and philanthropy would suggest how these might have helped shape and form, in one way or another, the astonishingly successful businessman–philanthropist he was to become.[8]

Take, for instance, the following passage:

> Each of us is born with tremendous resources and inestimable abilities; part of being productive is discovering these strengths. When we fully apply ourselves, we will accomplish far beyond our expectations. As the sages say: ' If someone should tell you, "I have toiled but I have not found," do not believe him; if he says, "I have not toiled but I have found," do not believe him; but if he says, "I have toiled and I have found," believe him.'[9] ... We must be persistent: if one method doesn't succeed try another ... We must fully use all the resources available to us, and remember that accountability is crucial for success.

Then there is what the Rebbe had to say about wealth:

> Some people feel that they and they alone are responsible for their success, that their intelligence and abilities brought it about. This is the challenge of wealth, and a serious challenge it is: to not be deceived by your own ego. 'You must remember that it is G-d[10] who gives you the power to become prosperous' [Deuteronomy 8:18]. Without this recognition money becomes the ultimate symbol of the selfish ego, our contemporary 'golden idol'.

That was not to say that wealth and success were not the result of one's own efforts, the Rebbe continued, and 'you must do everything possible to ensure success, not just sit back and wait for money to come your way.' But, he cautioned, 'you must acknowledge that it is G-d's blessing, and not your effort alone that creates wealth.'

Moreover, the Rebbe would warn, money, on its own, could be a curse:

> Because it is the epitome of materialism, money — and wealth — are mercurial by nature. Money can therefore cause endless anxiety, for no matter

how much you have, you are never sure whether you have enough or whether you will somehow lose it all. [But] when you put money in perspective and recognise why it was given to you, it becomes a blessing instead of a curse. And by using your wealth for charitable and philanthropic purposes, which are for posterity, instead of spending it on the desire of the moment, your money becomes eternal.

Giving to charity, or *tsedakah*, is a central tenet of all forms of Judaism — and one which the Rebbe stressed tirelessly as a deeply spiritual, even mystical, act:

Charity is one of the simplest yet most profound ways to help refine the material world and unite with your fellow man and with G-d — and therefore to fulfil our cosmic mission ... Charity enables us to spiritualize the material, and to actualize our practical intentions.

But, cannily recognising the 'what's in it for me' tendency of human nature, the Rebbe would point out that giving to charity was not only a deeply spiritual, mystical act — it was also 'good business':

One may argue that, from a pure business perspective, charity simply reduces one's financial resources. But when we recognize that G-d's blessing is the ultimate source of wealth, charity becomes the wisest investment there is. If someone is having financial difficulty in his business, he should increase the amount of his charitable contributions in order to increase G-d's blessing for wealth. As the sages say, 'Tithe, so that you may prosper.' Charity opens up new channels of wealth from above. Indeed, before determining how much to bless a person in the future, G-d often watches to see how he gave of his previous wealth.

It does not take a great deal to imagine how the ideas contained in these snippets might have affected a man who was destined to become one of Australia's most energetic, successful and wealthy mining magnates — as well as one of the Jewish world's most generous philanthropists.

But there was one other subject on which the Rebbe's views were to be, if anything, even more obviously decisive — and certainly more controversial — in shaping Joseph's public persona in the years ahead: Israel.

The Rebbe had a complex — and to the outsider, puzzling and contradictory — attitude to Israel. He had never set foot in the Jewish state, was vehemently opposed in principle to the very name it had taken for itself, and had little use for the modern, secular society that was taking shape in the Holy Land. The term 'State of Israel' for the secular state the Zionists had created in part of the Biblical Land of Israel[11] was, to the Rebbe, an illegitimate debasement or distortion of the name God Himself gave to the land he had pledged to the Jews as their eternal birthright. And he rejected, on principle, the notion that the Jewish right to the Land of Israel could rest on anything other than the Bible.

'The fact that 70 or 80 years ago Jews went to the Land of Israel, purchased land and lived there,' the Rebbe said, in an obvious dig at the early Zionist settlers, 'is not the source of our right to the Land.'[12] There were many other nations who had purchased land and lived there, he pointed out, and what was to stop any of them making a similar claim? Likewise, prior possession in and of itself was no basis for such a claim. On those grounds, he argued, the United States would have to be given back to the native Americans (or, he might well have added, Australia returned to the Aborigines) — plainly an absurd position, he said. He was even more dismissive of the claim that the Land of Israel belonged to the Jews because it had been 'pledged' to them by Britain in 1917, or that the United Nations had voted to give them a state in part of the land thirty years later. The United Nations had 'no authority to give away what did not belong to it,' he pointed out — besides, 'what will we do if the nations of the world change their mind and decide to reverse their decision?'

For the Rebbe the sole legitimate basis to the claim that the Land of Israel belonged to the Jews was 'God's promise in the Torah'. Anyone attempting to ignore or marginalise this fundamental, divine premise and, turning their backs on their past, to base their claim to ownership on one or another secular premise, would be 'undercutting the whole basis on which our ownership of the Land of Israel rests'.

The Rebbe not only rejected the secular theoretical underpinnings of the Jewish state the Zionists were creating in the Land of Israel, he also did not share their ultimate article of faith — that all Jews should live in Israel. On the contrary. He felt that, before the coming of the Messiah, this would be imprudent and even dangerous. The 'very lack of concentration of the remnants of our nation was a source of our salvation throughout centuries of persecution and pogroms,' he said soon after becoming Rebbe in 1951. 'Our history in exile is an unbroken chain of the emergence and disappearance of such centers in country after country.'[13]

For all his antipathy to secular Zionism, and to the secular society the Zionists were creating in the Land of Israel, the Rebbe was always deeply concerned about the fate of the Jews living there — as he was about the physical safety and spiritual well-being of Jews everywhere. Of particular concern were the hundreds of thousands of displaced Jews from the Arab countries of the Middle East and North Africa, who had flooded into Israel after 1948 and were being vigorously encouraged by the Israeli establishment of the time to cast aside the 'primitive' cultural baggage they had brought with them and to become modern, westernised Israelis. Much of this 'primitive' baggage included deeply held religious customs and traditions nurtured over many centuries of rich Jewish life in the Muslim world. The Rebbe was determined to reach out to these Jews, and 'save' them from being forcefully assimilated into a Godless, secular Israel. He was highly successful in this, through his emissaries and followers operating out of Kfar Chabad — the village they had established in 1948 — and many Oriental Jewish families remain closely connected to and deeply influenced by Lubavitch (or Chabad as it is better known in Israel) to this day.

In 1956, after an Arab terrorist attack on the synagogue at Kfar Chabad had left five students and their teacher dead, the Rebbe's focus began to shift from concern not only for the spiritual well-being of the Jews living in the Land of Israel but for their physical safety as well. And in 1967, as Arab armies in neighbouring Egypt, Jordan, and Syria began to mobilise for what their propagandists proclaimed — and many Jews in Israel and around the world feared — would be a final assault on the Jewish state, the spectre of another Holocaust loomed and the Rebbe responded by launching an extraordinary worldwide 'Spiritual Campaign'. He insisted that this had played a decisive role in Israel's 'miraculous' victory in the Six Day War, when Israeli forces launched a dramatic pre-emptive strike and drove the Syrians out of the Golan Heights, the Egyptians out of the Sinai Desert, and the Jordanians out of the West Bank. 'When a Jew in Moscow read the Psalms, and another Jew in Buffalo put on *tefillin* [phylacteries] on that day,' he proclaimed, 'it helped the Jews to defeat their enemies in the Land of Israel.'

The Rebbe was deeply disappointed, and angered, that the Israeli leadership, and Israelis generally, had not recognised the hand of God in their miraculous victory. And he was even more angered by Israel's readiness to give back the land it had captured — including the holy Biblical patrimony in Judea and Samaria — in return for peace with the Arabs. The Rebbe saw this as a slap in the face for God, a wanton spurning of the gift God had given His people. Moreover, the Rebbe insisted: 'The Land of Israel in its entirety was given by God to the eternal people for eternity, and no one has the authority to give back a single inch — especially as this involves a grave security risk and endangers life.' On this point, the Rebbe was unequivocal. *Pikuach nefesh* — the sanctity of life — was paramount, more important even than the sanctity of the Land of Israel itself.[14]

Meanwhile, the Rebbe said, it was essential to settle in every part of the Land of Israel — as 'irrefutable proof of God's promise "To your seed have I given this land".' As for the fact that those territories were inhabited by some two million Palestinian Arabs when they were captured in 1967, the Rebbe had a clear, hard-edged response: 'The entire Land of Israel belongs to the Almighty Blessed Be He, and it was His will to give it to them and His will to take it from them and give it to us . . .'

It was while he was still studying in New York that Joseph's mother, Rose, decided that it was time to find him a wife. She already had her eye on someone: Stera, the young daughter of Mendel (Max) and Assia New. Mendel, a wealthy textile merchant, came from another Hasidic sect, the Gerer; while Assia's family — the Kluwgants — was one of the five original Lubavitcher families the Rebbe had sent to Shepparton after the war. Stera was, from Rose's point of view, an ideal catch. Attractive, intelligent, from a good — and well-off — home with strong Hasidic connections. A perfect match for the immensely wealthy, successful businessman she had always known Joseph was destined to become. Moreover, Stera, it turned out, had long had her eye on Joseph. When she was just eight or nine years old, she had started to practise writing her name 'S Gutnick' — because, even then, Joseph relates, 'she thought I was the only boy she wanted to marry.' ('Perhaps I just couldn't think of anybody else at the time!' Stera retorts, when reminded about the incident; 'Destined to be . . .' replies Joseph.) Joseph, for his part, had seen Stera 'once or twice' and knew the New family. But the two had never actually met. There was little or no mixing of the sexes in the Lubavitcher community, and certainly no romantic dalliances, until the time came to find a partner. And that time, Rose believed, after talking to Stera's uncle, Rabbi Sholom Mendel Kluwgant, had now come.

Rose flew to New York some time in 1973, accompanied by her husband Chaim, determined to arrange the match. Chaim was less certain about it all. In the first place, he felt that Joseph, at just twenty-one, was too young to get married. Also, Joseph says, Chaim would have preferred his son to follow the example of his two sisters, Pnina and Chana, and his brother, Mottel, and marry someone from a rabbinical family. Mendel New, although from solid Hasidic stock — 'was just a businessman'. Chaim even had a couple of what he considered to be more suitable candidates in mind. He and Rose met with the Rebbe to discuss the matter — and, Joseph relates, 'the Rebbe sided with my mother.' The Rebbe also chided Chaim for casting aspersions on Stera's lineage, pointing out that her maternal grandfather, Rabbi Isser Kluwgant, happened to be a cousin of his. 'And what's wrong with my *yichus* [pedigree]?' he asked. A few months later, the Rebbe sent his young student to Australia — with an instruction that he should get acquainted with Stera. This he did, and a couple of weeks later they became engaged.

Joseph went back to New York to complete his rabbinical studies. When he returned to Melbourne a qualified rabbi in 1974, he and Stera got married. The young couple spent a further year in New York, where Joseph continued his post-rabbinical studies. Then it was back to Australia, this time for good. Rabbi Groner — Joseph's old principal at Yeshivah College and the Rebbe's emissary in Melbourne — offered the young rabbi an opportunity to teach at his old school, Yeshivah College, as well as to become involved with Ohel Chana, the girls' seminary he was setting up. Joseph accepted. It soon emerged that the wage he was offered was barely adequate. Joseph was also not happy with his situation at Ohel Chana, which was slow to get off the ground, and after about a year he sought the Rebbe's permission to leave the seminary and go and work for his father-in-law, who needed help with his rapidly expanding business.

'It wasn't a strong endorsement from the Rebbe,' Joseph concedes. 'It wasn't a straight "yes".' The Rebbe had said he should sound out leaders of the local Lubavitch community before making the move. This he did, and the consensus was that it would be best for all concerned if he went into Mendel New's textile business. Stera was the only one not entirely happy with the move. 'My wife wanted me not to go into business,' Joseph relates. 'I was an above-average rabbinical student, a qualified rabbi. I could easily have gone on to be a rabbi or open a Chabad House somewhere. Stera would have been prepared to do it.' But that was not to be, and, some time in 1976, Joseph went to work for Max New Australia in Flinders Lane, heart of the Melbourne Jewish *shmatte* (textile) trade.

For the next ten years, Joseph was completely immersed in establishing himself and his rapidly growing family, and had little direct contact with the Rebbe. He remained strongly committed to the Lubavitch movement, however, and never forgot his long-term ambition to become 'the Rebbe's *gvir*'. First, though, he had to make his fortune . . .

The Young Tyro

'From the time I was six or seven, my mother used to say: "Yossel will be very successful and very wealthy." It was a mother's intuition.'

Joseph Gutnick, September 1999

IT WAS AN inauspicious start for the Rebbe's *gvir*. 'For the first few months I used to cut fabric, and sweep the cuttings from the floor,' Joseph recalls of his initiation into his father-in-law's textile business. 'I learnt the hard way.' He was paid reasonably well, though — better than he had been by Rabbi Groner — and his prospects, once he had learned the ropes, were good.

Like any economically savvy young man just starting out, Joseph set up a family trust for Stera and himself — Edensor Nominees Pty Ltd. The name had been registered as a shelf company with the Arnold Bloch Leibler law firm, and Joseph liked it because it contained the word 'Eden'. In future years this was to evolve into the multi-million-dollar private investment vehicle that stood at the apex of Joseph's mining empire. For now he used it to buy a few small investment properties, with some help from his father-in-law Mendel New.

Then, in 1979, after almost a decade in the doldrums, the stock market burst back into life and gold prices started to soar. Up to this point, Joseph had been totally involved in Max New Australia. He was virtually running the business by this time, and oversaw its move to larger premises in Collingwood. But now, after a break of almost ten years, Joseph revived his schoolboy's interest in stocks. Using Edensor as an investment vehicle, he bought a few shares, borrowed some money and bought more. 'I went to my bank manager and borrowed $20,000,' he recalls. 'And then $50,000, $100,000, $200,000.' He began 'taking up strategic positions in the resources sector', and set about building up a portfolio of mining stocks.

Joseph's first major coup was a small company called Centaur Mining & Exploration Ltd, which he went into in 1980 with a close friend at the time, Harry Cooper. Incorporated in Victoria in 1969, Centaur had been engaged, with little success, in mineral exploration — in Western Australia (nickel at Mount Clifford), Victoria (gold/antimony at Bell Top Hill) and New South Wales (tin at Ardlethan). By 1974 it had abandoned exploration, returning to the field in 1979, when it acquired several tenements with nickel and cobalt potential in Western Australia, near Kalgoorlie. This coincided with Joseph's renewed interest in mining stocks, and he and Cooper — 'who was also my lawyer and liked a bit of a punt' — acquired small stakes in the company. In 1980, they managed to get themselves elected onto the board. 'Basically, we bluffed ourselves on,' Joseph confesses, before going on to explain:

> There was this fellow, Don Smith, who was on the board but didn't have many shares. So I bought a couple of per cent, and Harry and myself got ourselves nominated onto the board and pushed him out. Then I made an alliance with two other fellows, Jeff Banks and a fellow called Duncan Purcell, a Scotsman. They had another company, Consolidated Exploration Ltd [Cons Ex], and the two companies acquired cross-shareholdings in each other: Centaur owned 19 per cent of Cons Ex and Cons Ex owned 19 per cent of Centaur.

By 1982 Joseph was chairman of Centaur and also had himself appointed to the board of Consolidated Exploration, which proceeded to report good gold prospects at its Lady Bountiful site north of Kalgoorlie. Concurrently, Centaur took out tenements just to the east of Lady Bountiful, at a site named Lady Bountiful Extended — a move that was to become a hallmark of Joseph's exploration strategy in the years ahead, when he would consistently buy up land around promising strikes.

Harry Cooper, Joseph's sidekick in the Centaur venture, was his closest business associate in those early years. A couple of years older than Joseph, Cooper was a well-known lawyer, and a solicitor for several prominent businessmen in the Jewish community — among them future Coles Myer boss Solomon Lew. He wasn't from a Lubavitcher family (he had been educated at Melbourne's mainstream Jewish day school, Mount Scopus College) but, Joseph relates, he later 'grew a beard and became a great follower and disciple of Rabbi Groner'. This, in turn, led to a deep involvement with the Yeshivah Centre and the Lubavitch community in general. Joseph was to use Cooper both as a lawyer and as an executive director of several of his companies, in some of which Cooper had a substantial personal stake.[1]

One of Joseph and Harry Cooper's lesser known early ventures was a highly speculative — and singularly unsuccessful — search for oil in Israel. Finding oil has long been a dream of the Israelis, living as they do on the edge of one of the world's great petroleum regions. For Joseph, with his strong Zionist sentiments, looking for oil in the Land of Israel would have been an obvious interest. Especially as Centaur was already engaged in oil exploration in the United States, where it had acquired control of an oil and gas exploration company (Oceanic Oil and Gas, which it renamed Centaur Oil and Gas Corporation). So he embarked on the project with some enthusiasm. Like so many other oil explorations in Israel (before and since), though, nothing came of it, and Joseph soon lost interest.[2]

In 1982 another of Joseph's early business associates, car dealer and neighbour Henry Herzog,[3] persuaded him to invest in a company he was involved with, called Kingsway Group Ltd. This had been incorporated in New South Wales as N B Finance Development Corporation Ltd, back in 1958. It changed its name to Kingsway Group in 1964, and developed a sporadic interest in property and minerals. Those interests were revitalised and refocussed after Joseph was appointed chairman of the company in 1982. It became involved in the Torrington Topaz Project in north-eastern New South Wales, and a joint venture gold mining project with Coopers Resources at Mount Pleasant in Western Australia. Renamed Australia Wide Industries Ltd in 1986, it was to evolve into one of the eight core companies in Joseph's future mining empire.

◊ ◊ ◊

Joseph was now devoting more time to the stock market and his mining interests, and less to his father-in-law's business. He had set himself up in an office at Max New, with a terminal linking him directly to the Stock Exchange. He also had his own secretary, dealing exclusively with his shares. 'I'd only spend a couple of hours a day on the business,' he recalls — the rest of the time being spent on the market.

During this period, the early 1980s, Joseph became closely involved with Sydney insurance tycoon and stock market guru Larry Adler. This was the first of several remarkable 'odd couple' relationships Joseph was to strike up at strategic points in his career over the years. He greatly admired Adler, who had come out from Hungary after the war as a penniless refugee, and had gone on to build one of Australia's largest insurance companies, FAI. 'Rags to riches,' Joseph observes admiringly. Adler didn't much like religious Jews.[4] 'He had had a bad experience with Orthodox Jews as a child', Joseph explains in his defence: 'He sort of stereotyped all Orthodox Jews as being similar to the teacher he had when he was a young guy in Hungary, who used to strap the daylights out of him. And he also associated all Orthodox Jews as being dirty, not washing ... He didn't look favourably at the Shylock image ...' But, despite his antipathy towards Orthodox Jews, Adler did take a shine to Joseph, whom he first met through Joseph's brother-in-law, Rabbi Pinchos Feldman. 'He always used to say how he liked myself and my father,' Joseph recalls, 'because we used to dress properly, that he could have a discussion with us on all different types of topics. We were approachable ...'

Adler's son Rodney remembers Joseph at that time as a quietly spoken man with a passion for gold shares. 'He came to us to borrow a small amount of money to buy gold shares,' he recalled in a 1990 interview.[5] 'We found we could do business with him, and the relationship just grew from there.' Larry Adler came, in fact, to be the single most important business influence on Joseph in his early years, teaching him much of what he knew about stocks and trading:

> I looked up to him as a mentor, in the stock market ... He had a special talent and flair in creating situations. He was a born trader and market player ... So I developed this relationship with him ... I met him once, and he lent me some money ... And then I bought some other shares, then he bought some Cons Ex shares and made money on it. And when I used to raise money, Larry used to underwrite it. I did lots of deals with Larry, buying backwards, forwards. And we became really close ... I used to meet him every couple of weeks, talk to him for hours. We used to talk about Judaism, and I even got him, at one stage, a letter from the Rebbe ...

It was Adler who got Joseph involved in financial services, and they went into a number of ventures together. One of these was First Investors Security, which ran a series of very speculative and, for a while, very lucrative investment funds — ABC Fund Managers. Three of the funds, which Joseph managed directly, were rated in the top ten in a 1987 performance survey, and produced outstanding returns for the thousands of small investors who subscribed to them. They had names such as 'Aggressive Growth' and 'Trading Fund', and were generally sold on the basis that they would be aggressive, high-risk traders. And they invested heavily in Joseph's companies, providing a useful stream of investment capital.

By 1985, through a series of corporate manoeuvres, Joseph and

Adler controlled, with combined holdings of up to forty per cent, at least five small listed companies: Western Ventures, Kingsway Group, Mincorp Petroleum, Consolidated Exploration and First Investors Security. 'The two cannot be regarded as associates,' it was remarked at the time, 'but it seems they share a common investment strategy.'[6] Adler also encouraged Joseph to invest in FAI, lending him the money to buy almost ten per cent of the shares in the company. Adler's longer-term goal, it later emerged, was to bring Joseph onto the board of FAI, to take charge of its resources division.

◊ ◊ ◊

Joseph, by this time, was beginning to attract the interest of the business press, which didn't know quite what to make of the share-trading, paper-shuffling, gold-mining, wheeling-and-dealing, bearded little rabbi. In what was to be a familiar pattern in the years ahead, he was treated as something of a curiosity, eliciting a mixture of amusement, bemusement and good-natured banter.

An early example was Hamish Fraser's 'City Beat' column in the *Australian* on 24 July 1985. Fraser was intrigued by the fact that 'the mysterious on-market buyer of a 12.2 per cent stake in First Investors was a certain Rabbi Gutnick'. He contacted Joseph at his office at Max New, and was assured that, despite the entry in the Melbourne telephone directory, and despite the fact that he had once studied to be a rabbi, Joseph was a bona fide businessman, not some cleric dabbling in shares on the side. 'He cursed Telecom for according him the unwarranted honorific,' Fraser wrote, and revealed that he had 'dabbled in shares since childhood and had made his first million'. His strategy was to look where other people were investing — and Larry Adler was one of the people he watched. 'At the rate he is going,' Fraser concluded, 'one day others will be watching him.' Hamish Fraser may not have realised just how prophetic those last words were.

In 1986 Joseph moved out of Mendel New's business in Collingwood, and set himself up in his own offices on St Kilda Road. 'My father-in-law wasn't happy,' Joseph recalls, 'but he saw that there was a bigger world out there for me than the textile business.' He started off with a staff of just three, but quickly built this up until by the next year he had a team of some thirty-five people working for him. He was strongly supported by Henry Herzog, Harry Cooper and another close friend and fellow Lubavitcher, Emmanuel Althaus.[7] 'One of the first ten people I employed was Emmanuel,' Joseph recalls. 'When I first started he was someone I trusted. I needed someone loyal and trusted in the company when I first started off.' Perhaps most significantly of all, from the perspective of his future success, he engaged the services of a young geologist who had recently fallen on hard times, Eduard Eshuys — the man whose name, for the next thirteen years, was to be inextricably linked with Joseph's in one of the most daring and phenomenally successful exploration teams the Australian gold industry had seen.

Up to this point, Joseph had used consulting geologists to advise him on the prospects of the mining companies he wanted to invest in or acquire. But the time had come to hire someone on a permanent basis. In October 1986 he advertised for a geologist, and Eshuys applied. 'Ed was in a company that didn't do well,' Joseph recalls. 'A coal company in Tasmania. He almost lost his pants, I think . . . So he was looking for a position. He was a businessman–geologist, which was right up my alley.' Joseph was more interested in buying gold shares than exploring at this stage — 'my main priority was to make money, and gold shares were the prize' — and, although Eshuys did do some quite serious exploration, Joseph took him on primarily to advise him about what shares to buy.

What happened over the next twelve months had even the most seasoned market analysts rubbing their eyes. The catalyst was Centaur's sale, in October 1986, of its cross-holding in Consolidated Exploration for some $18 million — enabling the company to establish a significant strategic investment portfolio. 'That was where I got my first chunk of money,' Joseph recalls. 'It was my first big deal. I took control of the Centaur board, and then I started getting involved with other companies.' Cashed up and looking for bargains, and with Eshuys at his shoulder to advise him, Joseph immediately made takeover offers for two mining companies which, like Centaur and Kingsway (Australia Wide), were to become an integral part of his future mining empire: Mount Kersey Mining and Great Central Mines.

Mount Kersey Mining Ltd had been formed in November 1985 to acquire and evaluate tenements in the Wadgingarra Mining Centre northeast of Yalgoo in Western Australia for gold and other minerals. It was listed on the Stock Exchange the following July, and Centaur acquired a twenty per cent stake in the company in November. In February 1987 Joseph became chairman of the company, and exploration began in the Yalgoo region under the direction of Eshuys, who had, by this time, been appointed Joseph's general manager of exploration.

Great Central Mines Ltd had also been formed in Western Australia, in February 1985, to acquire a portfolio of gold prospects in the state's

Yilgarn Craton region. It was listed on the Stock Exchange the following August, at about which time it entered into an option agreement to acquire ninety-five per cent in an exploration licence 170 kilometres north-east of Meekatharra. The exploration site meant little to anyone then, but within five years it was to emerge as one of Western Australia's biggest and most exciting new gold provinces in decades: Plutonic.

Joseph, like everyone else at the time, would have had no inkling as to what the future held in store at Plutonic. But he was very interested in Great Central's Great Lady Prospect near Mount Pleasant — in the same Black Flag area just north of Kalgoorlie where Consolidated Exploration's Lady Bountiful and Centaur's even more promising Lady Bountiful Extended were exploring. 'I had the philosophy, even before Ed Eshuys, that if there was a discovery I'd take all the land around it,' Joseph explains. This was a shrewd, and quite transparent strategy: let others spend their money doing the exploring, and then move quickly to buy up and start drilling out the surrounding area. Conversely, wary that others might do the same to him, Joseph was always very careful to tie up as much land as possible around his exploration sites well before he had made a discovery. Great Central fitted in perfectly with Joseph's strategy, and in January 1987 Centaur confirmed that it had acquired 19.9 per cent of the company's issued capital. In May, Joseph was appointed chairman, and soon afterwards Eshuys began drilling out the Great Lady Prospect.

As might have been expected, Joseph's raids on promising mining companies in Western Australia did not always go down well with the local stakeholders, who resented 'carpet-baggers' from out East muscling in on their territory and making off with cheap assets. Joseph was made aware of this when he moved on Great Central Mines in 1987, by Perth millionaire and fellow director Phil Crabb. 'The prospect of cashed-up Eastern State millionaires walking away with prime assets cheap is not very appealing to Crabb, noted for his fighting qualities,' the *Sydney Morning Herald* reported in 1987.[8] Crabb attempted to mount a boardroom coup against Joseph the following year — but this failed when Joseph turned the tables on the feisty Western Australian by mustering fifty per cent of the board and ousting Crabb instead.[9] It could be a tough game, and Joseph knew how to fight in the clinches, when he had to.

Meanwhile, Joseph continued buying up companies, and accumulating chairmanships. In June 1986, Australia Wide Industries gained control of Phoenix Oil and Gas Ltd along with associated companies

Coopers Resources NL, Charter Mining NL and Mistral Mines NL —
Joseph becoming chairman of all four companies, which had exploration interests in several oil and gas projects around Australia as well
as a number of gold prospects in the Yilgarn. Earlier, in April,
Australia Wide also gained control of Great Fingall Mining Company.
As Larry Adler's son Rodney observed in May 1987, when FAI
Insurance took a 19.7 per cent stake in Australia Wide Industries, the
company had become 'the holding company of the Gutnick group, and
was the appropriate vehicle for FAI's investment in Mr Gutnick's
activities'.[10]

The buying spree continued, at an accelerated pace, throughout
1987. Edensor Nominees, Joseph's private holding company, acquired
a controlling interest in Johnson's Well Mining NL — the fifth of
Joseph's 'core' companies — when it was floated in January that year,
and Joseph was appointed chairman in February. Ground held by
Johnson's Well complemented Mount Kersey's in the Yalgoo area. In
March, Centaur made a takeover bid for yet another company that was
to play a key role in Joseph's future exploration: Astro Mining NL.
Astro had been formed in Western Australia in 1983 to explore for
gold mainly in the Mount Pleasant area near Kalgoorlie — hence
Joseph's interest after it was listed on the Stock Exchange in August
1986. The company also had a number of other gold prospects,
including a joint venture near Meekatharra and a speculative project
in New Zealand. Joseph was appointed chairman in May, and the
process of augmenting his prospective gold holdings in Mount Pleasant
continued apace; through Great Central and Astro, Centaur acquired
yet another piece of prospective ground, the Northern Lady Project,
near Lady Bountiful Extended.

In what was probably Joseph's most daring market foray up to this
point, Australia Wide Industries floated an audacious new 'cashbox'
company, Australian Gold Resources Ltd, on the Stock Exchange in
August 1987, raising some $75 million. Australian Gold Resources had
already acquired a controlling interest in another company, Helm
Resources Ltd — which, renamed Quantum Resources Ltd, was also
to become a permanent fixture in Joseph's mining stable — and two
associated mining companies, Mt Carrington Mines Ltd and Ando
Minerals Ltd. Joseph became chairman of all three companies, which
held gold prospects in north-east New South Wales and western
Victoria.

Joseph's modus operandi was, by now, unmistakable: acquire a
stake in a company, seize control of the board, and use the company as

a vehicle to invest in other companies through a series of cross-shareholdings. That is what he had done with Centaur in 1980, and he replicated it, with phenomenal success, in 1986/87, targeting mainly small mining companies in Western Australia. He repeated the process time and again, building up a pyramid of intricately interconnected companies, all with cross-shareholdings in each other. Centaur, for instance, eventually had as many as twelve Gutnick-related companies — seven of them public — on its register.

'A lot of others were doing that as well,' Joseph explains. 'It was a trend at the time. Not to drive up prices, but to get an interest. This way, instead of concentrating in one entity, you get a number of them, and with cross-holdings. And this way you have control of the companies without spending your own money, through cross-shareholdings. That's how the system was in those days.'

Joseph Gutnick had built his empire with incredible speed, earning nicknames such as 'Golden Joe' and 'Midas of St Kilda Road'. One broker at the time said he had not yet analysed Joseph's holdings because 'he sort of went by like an express train'.[11] And business writer Trevor Sykes, writing the following year, described the Gutnick empire before the October 1987 stock market crash as 'a dynamic beast which changes like the chameleon before your eyes', with Joseph trading 'in and out of big positions with such chutzpah that his forays dazzled the market'.[12] Market analysts, brokers, and journalists alike found it difficult to know quite what to make of him. But they were intrigued. And in March 1987, almost a decade before Sam Newman was to do his 'Fiddler on the Roof' number on *The Footy Show*, the cover of *Australian Business* featured a huge caricature of Joseph dancing to his fiddle, under the heading: 'How Gutnick Makes his Gold Shares Dance'. The extensive story inside, by Shirley Skeel, was titled 'Gutnick's Midas Touch'.[13]

By 1987 most of Joseph's acquisitions were, as we have seen, junior gold exploration and mining companies with ground in the Black Flag belt just north of Kalgoorlie in Western Australia. Whether it was the Gutnick name or whether, as Joseph claimed, the market was only waking up to the potential of the area the companies were exploring, all of their share prices had leapt dramatically. In the six months up to April 1987, for instance, Centaur exploded from $1 to an astonishing $5.50, Astro from 30 cents to $1.35, and Great Central from 20 cents to $3.80.

To raise the funds necessary to buy into these companies and to finance their exploration programs, Joseph had exploited the bull market of the time with great audacity and adroitness. He formed a cashbox company called Security and Equity Investments which raised $20 million at the end of 1986; and another company, Security and Equity Resources, did the same in January 1987. Emboldened by these successes, Joseph formed Australian Gold Resources, which, as we saw, raised a massive $75 million at its float in August 1987. Then Centaur raised a further $72 million in a 3-to-1 premium issue the following month. These four companies between them raised an astonishing $200 million in less than a year. All this, it was noted, 'on little more than the strength of Gutnick's name',[14] which by this time was on every speculative investor's lips. Golden Joe was the darling of the bourse, and the investment community came up with various terms of endearment for him: Little Joe, Joey G, Sputnik, the Midas of St Kilda Road. 'Whatever the moniker, he was the resources sector sweetheart . . . You'd have been forgiven for believing that Gutnick was going to mine nuggets as big as bullocks' hearts.'[15]

A large proportion of those investing in Joseph's companies at this time were perceived to be fellow Jews. Shirley Skeel, for instance, suggested in April 1987 that Joseph would buy into a company — 'with probably a good chunk of the Melbourne Jewish community in tow' — and 'steamshovel' the target company's price to dramatic highs.[16] And *Australian Business* made a similar point a few months later, when it wrote that 'once hit with the buying of two or three of Gutnick's vehicles (eg, Centaur and First Investors Resources), and again with his backline of Jewish followers and Gutnick groupies',[17] the prices in such companies would soar. Harry Cooper, of course, was heavily invested in Joseph's companies — as was Joseph's father-in-law, Mendel New, who owed much of his later fortune, when he became one of Australia's richest men, to his very substantial holdings in his son-in-law's companies.[18] And there were many others, including a company called Lof Investments Pty Ltd — owned 50 per cent by Michael Lansky and 25 per cent by Izzy and Henry Herzog — which had a 10 per cent holding in Quantum and, Trevor Sykes pointed out, usually worked 'in sympathy with Gutnick'.[19]

Joseph has conceded that there probably was always a considerable number of wealthy Jewish investors in his companies, both in Australia and later in the United States (mainly New York), but claims that the significance of this has sometimes been exaggerated:

I used to have a mixture of Jewish investors. There were people from the community who invested before '87. It was the in thing to be in the market, in shares. Because I was a Lubavitcher — this may have been more after 1988, when the Rebbe was more involved in the situation — there are a lot of overseas people who became involved . . . But all the money I raised over the years wasn't based on the Jewish community. Even before 1987. Take the money I raised for Centaur and Australian Gold Resources. That came from the institutions. $75 million didn't come from the Melbourne Jewish community. The bulk came from Australian and overseas investment funds.

It was not only other people's money that Joseph was risking, however, Jewish or otherwise. In addition to the tens of millions he was raising through his cashbox companies and his ABC investment funds, he had millions of dollars of his own money at stake. For instance, his family company, Edensor Nominees, had paid $15 million to take up the Centaur issue in September 1987, and subscribed the same amount to the AGR float a month earlier. That made a total of $30 million that Joseph had invested — just weeks before the stock market crash.

By the middle of 1987 Joseph was an extremely wealthy man. At least on paper. He had made it onto *Business Review Weekly*'s 'Rich 200' list, with an estimated net worth of $65 million. 'More than $100 million in paper profits from share market trading has rocketed Joseph Isaac Gutnick from a rag-trader to Australia's most successful gold-share trader,' *Business Review Weekly* wrote. 'In just one year, the 34-year-old father of five has become the chairman of 18 companies and a substantial shareholder in several others.'[20] The rival *Australian Business* was equally impressed, if a touch more acerbic: 'Gutnick has too many deals to his name to count. But his best has to be the one he made with himself — to play high-risk stakes in return for a swipe at the title of top Australian gold producer. As a speculator in gold explorers he has a long way to go, but the mini-empire he has built in 12 short months is astounding . . .'[21]

The Rebbe's *gvir* had arrived — and Joseph had not forgotten his ambition to use his wealth to further the Lubavitch cause. He had given sums of money to the movement over the years — including $50,000 for the Yeshivah Gedolah (post-secondary men's seminary) in Melbourne — but was now in a position to do something much more substantial. His father, Chaim, recalls how Joseph's first really major contribution to Lubavitch — some US$300,000 — came about.

Some time in the mid-1980s, it emerges, the Rebbe had commissioned a Torah scroll to be written. Jews around the world were to contribute a dollar for each of the almost 400,000 letters making up the scroll, comprising the first five books of the Bible. In theory, this should have been a lucrative fundraiser for the Lubavitcher movement. But the Rebbe had underestimated the costs involved — and he was left with a US$300,000 shortfall. 'I'm looking for someone to give me a loan,' he told Chaim during one of his periodic visits to New York. Chaim recalls that, to his shame, it did not occur to him at the time that Joseph would be able to come up with the money. But when he got back to Australia, he told his son: 'Listen, it's a terrible thing. The Rebbe said to me he needs $300,000 and I didn't volunteer to get it. I want you write to him, with me, a note that we will supply him with the money.' Joseph immediately agreed — but, Chaim remembers, he checked with the Rebbe first: 'The $300,000 — was it Australian or American dollars?' he asked — and the Rebbe replied: 'American!' That, says Chaim, 'was the first major contribution he gave, and that's when it started.'

Clearly impressed with Joseph's generosity, the Rebbe began to take a close interest in Joseph's business activities. But he wanted assurances that his young *gvir* was not losing focus, and that he was not neglecting his religious studies. He even asked for a list of what Joseph was studying — and, after perusing this, told him he'd have to improve his act. Joseph agreed. (He has been diligent in keeping up with his studies ever since, despite the huge demands that his business activities make on his time. 'That's very important for me, to study and learn,' Joseph explains. 'The Rebbe demanded of me as part of my success in business I have to be happy, think positively and study as much as I can.')

Joseph clearly valued, and would undoubtedly have been flattered by, the Rebbe's keen interest. But it was not long before this led to a remarkable and bizarre test of faith for Joseph — what came to be a watershed event in his life. In May 1987, Larry Adler, who already had a 19.99 per cent stake in Centaur, put in a $208 million takeover bid for the company — which was coming up with some very promising gold findings in the Lady Bountiful area north of Kalgoorlie. One of the main reasons for the bid, according to Joseph, was that Adler had wanted to buy him out of Centaur and bring him onto the FAI board to look after its resources sector. It was an enticing offer. The money

The Lubavitch Connection. The Sixth Lubavitcher Rebbe, Rabbi Yosef Yitzhak Schneersohn (left), after whom Joseph was named, with his son-in-law Rabbi Menachem Mendel Schneerson (the future Rebbe, who was to guide and inspire Joseph to such a remarkable degree), in a village near Vienna in 1934.

Chaim and Rose Gutnick, Joseph's parents, on their wedding day in 1945. Chaim was smitten by Rose when he taught her religion at Sydney High — because she wore no lipstick and had braids.

Captain Chaim Gutnick, Royal Australian Army Chaplain. Chaim was proud of his Army service, both as a war-time soldier 'in the Second First Machine Gun Battalion of the 9th Divvy' and later, as a chaplain.

Geoffrey (Joseph), aged about four, in Sydney. 'Yossel used to be a very soft, sweet boy,' Chaim recalls.

At Moriah College, Elwood, after the Gutnicks moved to Melbourne in 1958. The school was attached to his father's synagogue, and, as the rabbi, Chaim was under some obligation to send at least one of his children there. 'I was the scapegoat,' Joseph recalls a little ruefully.

Rites of Passage. Joseph at his bar mitzvah in 1965, flanked by his parents Chaim and Rose, his grandmother Chaya and her second husband Rabbi Osher Abramson — both had a considerable influence on the young Joseph — and his two brothers Moshe (in front of Chaim) and Mordechai.

he would receive for his own 35 per cent stake in Centaur would have enabled him to retire a substantial part of the massive $100 million debt he owed Adler, much of it money the tycoon had lent him to build up his 10 per cent stake in FAI. He might even have used some of the money to increase his stake in the insurance giant. ('It was a $2 billion company,' Joseph points out — 'who knows where it was headed?') All in all, it was very tempting. And Joseph was very tempted. But the Lubavitcher Rebbe, in far-off New York, vetoed it. He told Joseph that he was not, under any circumstances, to sell out to Adler.

This was an extremely tough call for Joseph. For it pitted the judgement of the Rebbe, a sage he revered but who had no direct experience of the financial world, against that of Larry Adler, a man whom Joseph all but worshipped as an absolute master of that world. Joseph was being forced to choose between two gurus. While some people might have attempted to separate the two realms — defer to the Rebbe in matters spiritual, and to Larry Adler in matters financial — that was not an option open to someone like Joseph. If he accepted the Rebbe as his Rebbe, his word was final and absolute — in all areas. He explains:

> If I wouldn't have had a Rebbe, and wouldn't have asked him questions, and I wouldn't have based and directed my life on his instructions I could decide myself what I wanted to do. But my wife and myself decided we would direct our lives according to his instructions. I am a disciple of his, and I follow his instructions.

Joseph had no choice. The deal was off.

Both sides put a 'rational' spin on the failed bid, and no mention was made, at the time, of the Rebbe's intervention. The Centaur board, which went along with Joseph's Rebbe-induced decision not to sell, reaffirmed — not without reservation — its confidence in the company. It noted that the ultimate profitability of Centaur would depend largely on the results of future exploration and the performance of the gold price on commodity markets — neither of which could be forecast with certainty. However, 'by extrapolation of the favourable results achieved from exploration activities conducted in the Lady Bountiful district', the directors were confident of the presence of commercial mineralisation which would, in turn, 'result in the development and mining of the gold resource in the medium to long-term future'. Rodney Adler, who was investments manager of his father's Cumberland Credit Corporation which was making the bid, also put on a brave face, explaining that the deal had fallen through because Centaur had been 'revalued' and was 'just out of the reach of Cumberland'.[22]

Joseph refuses to speculate on why the Rebbe was so adamantly opposed to the deal with Larry Adler. 'The Rebbe told me to remain independent' is all he will say — and, like a good Lubavitcher, he complied. But it marked the end of an era for Joseph, the parting of the ways with Adler, his business guru, in deference to the will of the Rebbe, who in the years ahead was to play an increasingly crucial role in Joseph's business life.[23]

◊ ◊ ◊

Joseph was riding the crest of a wave in 1987, and there seemed to be no limit to what he might achieve. But there was already an uneasiness in investment circles about the fact that he owned far more paper than he did assets, and there was a strong suspicion that his main purpose was to 'mine the market' rather than the ground. Joseph strongly disputed this. 'My aim is my profit will come from gold production, not share trading,' he insisted. 'I've got a basic belief that is two-pronged: I want to build up a large financial services group and a large gold group.' He did not convince the sceptics. The astounding success that saw him take over gold explorers which then shot up five or ten times in value, naturally enough, sparked intense speculation. 'A lot is on paper and he has not shown that much to contribute towards exploration,' one broker was quoted as saying, expressing a widely held view at the time. Another broker described Joseph's cash flow as 'dicey'. Yet another asked 'where he would stand if his wheelbarrow full of paper profits was to lose a wheel'.[24] Larry Adler, too, told him that he had 'too many companies' and was vulnerable.

While this unease was understandable — especially in view of what was to take place barely six months later — it would be wrong to conclude that Joseph was only a 'paper shuffler' and had no genuine interest in exploration — even if this was, by his own admission in later years, secondary to the market. He had budgeted a not inconsiderable $12 million for exploration in 1987, while Centaur, Astro and Great Central all held extensive ground around Consolidated Exploration's Lady Bountiful Mine north of Kalgoorlie. Ed Eshuys had, in fact, drilled the area like the proverbial Swiss cheese — reminiscent of the techniques he was to display with such spectacular success in the years ahead, at Plutonic, Bronzewing and Jundee. Exploration activity continued at other sites as well, including in western Queensland (where Australian Gold Resources was active), western Victoria (Ando), New South Wales (Mount Carrington), and the Yalgoo area in Western Australia (Mount Kersey and Johnson's Well).

Ultimately, Joseph was, even then, a self-confessed gold junkie. 'I've studied markets since I was a kid,' he told the *Financial Review* in March 1987 — 'and I'm a super bull when it comes to gold . . . There is no substitute for gold, and Australian gold shares are cheaper than the rest. There is no gold tax here, there are supply problems overseas, our production is increasing and so is the dollar price we are getting for it.' He also said, with some prescience: 'I like gold because the world is in a hell of a mess. I see a financial crisis hitting the world in six months' or six years' time, and the haven will be gold.'[25]

Joseph was right about the crisis — if, that is, one takes the lower end of his predicted time frame. Just seven months later the world was, indeed, 'in a hell of a mess'. But so too was Joseph's business empire.

Crash

*'Come October 20 1987 and Gutnick disappeared from public
view like a pantomime demon going through a trapdoor in a
puff of smoke . . .'*

Trevor Sykes, *Australian Business*, 10 August 1988

ANYONE STUMBLING ACROSS a diagrammatic representation of Joseph's
mining and business empire towards the end of 1987 could have been
forgiven for immediately picking up the phone and calling ASIO, the
Australian Security and Intelligence Organisation. The convoluted
mess of intricately interconnected boxes and arrows looked for all the
world like the state-of-the-art circuitry for Australia's first homegrown
Sputnik. Sadly, it was nothing like as sophisticated . . . more like a
house of cards. And, on 'Black Tuesday', 20 October 1987, as the stock
market lost one quarter of its value in the first hour of trading, the
whole precarious edifice came crashing down.

'I was in my office and watching the screen, flabbergasted, as FAI,
the glamour stock in which we had a 10 per cent stake, fell from $10 to
$3.50 in a second,' Joseph recalled in a survey conducted by the
Financial Review to mark the tenth anniversary of the crash.[1] 'I
thought the whole world was caving in like an earthquake.'

Unfortunately, the crash came at the short end of Joseph's prediction: 'The crash happened three or four months too early for me,' he
reflected ruefully about a year later. And when he later reaffirmed 'I
was always expecting a crash and my philosophy was that when the
time came, gold stocks would be the big runners',[2] he was not the only
one. One prominent expert, Capita's investment chief, Nigel Weaver,
predicted, in the days after the crash, that foreign investors would be
looking for somewhere to park their money — adding that Australia,
which had 'some of the best quality gold-stocks in the world', would be
an attractive option. He noted that with the Australian dollar weak

and markets crashing, gold was bound to look good as an alternative and Australian gold shares looked about the best medium-term proposition. He cautioned, however, that 'in a panic all stocks tend to go down together, regardless of prospects and fundamentals.'[3] Also, unfortunately for Joseph, most of his companies were still junior explorers, and he had yet to bring a commercially significant gold mine on stream. The Australian gold stocks that did attract interest were the heavyweights and producers, while the emerging producers and explorers, like most of Joseph's companies, were to become nearly unsaleable.

Joseph, like many others, was probably surprised, not only at the timing of the crash, but at its severity. 'Nobody picked the savagery of this,' observed one experienced market watcher, Nestor Hinzack, research chief at Ord Minnett.[4] 'The chartists will be able to justify it only in hindsight. We'll have to find a whole new set of benchmarks.'

Some analysts felt that because the bull market was shattered in such an unprecedented way, the resulting bear market would also be a different creature from anything previously seen — and some of the more optimistic operators anticipated that there would be good opportunities to snap up some bargains. Tricontinental's Ian Johns, for instance, pointed out that the Australian market remained very liquid. 'There is a lot of cash in the marketplace. Everyone has some to spare.' He noted that many big private investors had lately been drawing money out of the share market to invest in property, and speculated that it was quite possible they might return as shares fell to lower levels, perhaps raising money on their now wholly-owned properties.'[5] But not all investors had the luxury of being that complacent. Small investors, and anyone who had gone into debt to buy shares, were dealt a savage blow.

It was not long before Joseph was to learn of the impact that the 'earthquake' had had on his own business empire. By December, investors had all but abandoned his companies, whose value plummeted across the board. Thanks to the extraordinary degree of cross-shareholding in Joseph's companies, in the bull-market conditions before the crash they tended to haul each other ever higher. However, now the reverse occurred: they were dragging each other down. Thus, for example, his Centaur Mining — whose shares plunged to just $0.60, compared with over $6 before the crash (wiping out some $40 million of the $72 million it had raised just two months earlier) — had a 19.5 per cent stake in Mount Kersey, which plummeted from $3.30 to just 30 cents a share; a 67 per cent stake in Astro Mining, down to $1.95, from a year high of $3.95; and 15 per cent of Tern Minerals, down to $0.60 compared with a year high of $4.

Joseph's financial services companies fared no better. Worst hit was his Security & Equity Resources 'cashbox'. Launched in January 1987, it raised $20 million on an empty prospectus. By December it had lost $19.5 million, 'thus joining the small but spectacular list of Australian companies that have managed to wipe out shareholders' funds in their first year of existence.'[6] His other cashbox companies also recorded huge losses. The most ambitious of these, Australian Gold Resources, which was floated in July 1987 and raised $75 million in shares, lost $14.2 million; Security and Equity Investments, $13.3 million; First Investors Resources, $8 million; and First Investors Security, $9.9 million. In all, these five companies lost a total of some $65 million.

Joseph's ABC funds were another disaster. These were heavily invested in speculative stocks — including many of his own companies — which were reduced to rubble, leaving hundreds of small investors badly bruised. 'Jo [sic] Gutnick, at least, still has his mansion in East St Kilda, with its fleet of cars parked out the front on a Sunday morning,' the *Sydney Morning Herald*'s Ben Hills commented bitterly a couple of years later. 'Many of the people who trusted him were left with nothing but paper . . .'[7]

Joseph had, of course, taken his fair share of lumps along with other shareholders. He had always been prepared to put up his own money, had lost a fortune in the crash (on paper, as much as $135 million), and as Damon Frith pointed out in a 1993 article in the *Australian*, 'even his detractors don't question the sincerity of his belief in his companies and their prospects'.[8]

Yet, some thirteen years after the crash, one still hears of a residual resentment in Melbourne's Jewish community on the part of people who claim they were 'burned by going with Yossel in '87'. Such comments pain Joseph:

Of course I've heard people say that. And I've had, from time to time, some nasty letters from people . . . On a personal level it hurts. It hurts deeply, and I can't do anything about it . . . That's the business I'm in. I'm in the stock market. In the mining game. And in resources, you must rely on the capital of others. It's big risk money. You're talking about hundreds and hundreds of millions of dollars, which a normal person doesn't have and wouldn't risk in projects like that . . . I'd prefer that only institutions invested in my stock. But I can't help it if little old ladies buy . . . Some little old ladies could have made a fortune if they'd bought Great Central, and other little old ladies can lose. I hope that at the end of the day life works out that everyone will be winners. But life's cruel, it's not so simple.

And ultimately the onus is on the investor:

> The stock market is not for the faint-hearted. But go talk to people. You can't change human nature. Can you convince people not to go to Crown Casino? They enjoy it . . . But you have to be brave when you go into the stock market, especially at the speculative end . . . You buy at highs and sell at lows, you lose your pants . . . But if anyone had bought Great Central before '87, they would have made an absolute fortune if they'd hung on. The same with Johnson's Well, and the same with Australia Wide . . . Some of my stocks did go badly. SER and others didn't do well . . . All the advice I can give to anyone: You buy in gloom and sell in boom . . .

As for himself, Joseph concedes he has had to develop 'a very thick skin' — something that has saddened his father: 'Yossel used to be a very soft, sweet boy,' Chaim recalls, 'when he was younger. But I think going through the crash and all that he has become hardened a bit.' Joseph, however, believes he has had no choice:

> Sometimes if you start feeling too bad about it you won't be able to continue . . . I wouldn't survive. So many people try to throw arrows and spears at me, for whatever reason. Whether it's jealousy, whether it's envy, whether it's hurt — because people are legitimately hurt. They throw spears and arrows, and I've got to be able to survive in this financial jungle. And it is a jungle . . . You have to make tough decisions. You have to sack people. That's hard. That means you have to be ruthless, and you can't have pity . . . If I would show compassion to one and not to another, there would be trouble . . . It really hurts. But you've just got to do it . . .

The same, he says, applies to people who may have invested money in his companies and lost. Some people have confronted him, demanding compensation, wanting their money back. Some quite hard cases. But he can't show compassion, however much he might wish to. 'If I give to one, I'd have to give to thousands. Everyone who lost money in me I'd have to go compensate them — there'd be no end.'

Which raises an ethical question. Joseph, after all, claims he was only in business because he had received the Rebbe's blessing — and because he wanted to do good. But people were getting hurt as a result. For that reason, Joseph concedes, 'the Rebbe didn't like stock markets. Innocent people could get hurt . .' Yet, Joseph claims, he actively encouraged his own involvement:

The Rebbe was very positive about my shares when they went up, and very upset when they went down. He always used to ask, why aren't my shares going up? I can show you his handwritten notes, asking why didn't I show him the comparison from last week. Why did the prices go down? . . . And I never got a word from the Rebbe, in thousands of written responses, against being involved in the stock market . . . Would I prefer to be in a business where innocent people wouldn't get hurt? Yes I would . . . It's unfortunate that it's my lot in life that I'm a stock-market player.

Joseph is confident, moreover, that he has done nothing wrong or illegal in the conduct of his business activities, either before the 1987 crash or subsequently. 'What,' Ben Hills asked him about two years after the crash, when his companies were still being investigated by the then National Companies and Securities Commission, 'if the . . . Commission should find that you have done something wrong along the way?' Joseph's reply: 'What if you should rob a bank? You didn't, did you? So you have nothing to worry about. Neither have I done anything wrong . . .'[9] And that was, in fact, what the Commission found. Asked a similar question — 'have you done anything illegal or wrong?' — ten years and umpteen fruitless Australian Stock Exchange and Securities Commission inquiries later, Joseph replies with the same laconic self-assurance: 'I've got parking fines.'

◊ ◊ ◊

While he may have been down, Joseph was far from out. And, unlike many of his fellow 'paper shufflers', he did manage to survive the crash.[10] 'I was very worried in 1987 that I was going to go under,' he admits. His empire was in ruins and he was massively in debt, to the tune of some $220 million. Almost half of this was owed to Larry Adler, for the close to 18.5 million shares he held in FAI — a debt he could easily have repaid before the crash, had he taken up Adler's offer for Centaur. And Adler, who had himself taken a serious knock in the crash, was playing hardball. 'He was sure I'd survive,' Joseph recalls, 'despite the fact that he was putting enormous pressure on me . . . At the time of the crash I owed Larry $100 million. Big money . . . Larry was my biggest problem. But he always said I would survive.'

In March 1988 Joseph sold most of his shares in FAI to George Soros in New York for almost $90 million. He made a $10 million profit on his investment. 'Before the crash I was making a $150 million profit on my FAI shares,' he recalls ruefully. 'I wanted to sell them. Larry was reluctant to let me sell them. In the end I still made money.

I sold at $4.50. My average must have been about $3.50. But the shares had been as high as $10. I would have made another $100 million if I'd sold before the crash. . . . Larry was a tough player . . .'

It was, however, not Larry Adler but the Lubavitcher Rebbe in New York to whom Joseph turned at this time of crisis: 'It was a test of my faith' . . .

> It was the Rebbe who told me not to sell out to Larry. And now the crash had come. Everything had fallen. Where was I to end up? What was going to happen to me? Things were getting worse and worse. I was using up all my money. And you weren't able to raise money. How was I going to survive? . . . Larry was still on top of the world, and there I was almost on the verge of bankruptcy. So it was a major test. And maybe that was a challenge to the Rebbe as well. From the point of view that he had given me advice not to accept Larry's bid, then the crash came and here Joseph was in trouble. So did the Rebbe feel any responsibility for the advice he had given me?

When push came to shove, though, Joseph's total and utter reason-defying faith in the Rebbe was never really in question. If anything, it grew stronger in adversity. Joseph tells the story of two Hasidic Jews debating the merits of their respective Rebbes:

> So one Hasid said to the other: 'My Rebbe promised me if I do this and this, I'd become wealthy, I'd be successful, I'd give lots of charity. And it all happened. He was a great Rebbe.' The other Hasid said: 'My Rebbe told me to do this and this, and as yet it hasn't happened. But I still have great faith in him and I still follow him. So he's much greater than your Rebbe.'

So 'the Rebbe would still be my Rebbe,' Joseph concludes. 'I'd still follow him, even if — God forbid — these things [his predictions] didn't come true. Because I know he's a wise and righteous person.'

By now, Joseph was in regular correspondence with the Rebbe, writing to him every Friday and getting a reply, unfailingly, twenty-four hours later (the time difference between Melbourne and New York facilitated this, enabling Joseph to fax his weekly report, which usually ran to several pages, before the Sabbath started in Melbourne, and the Rebbe to make his reply before the Sabbath started in New York). His father, Chaim, claims that this is quite unique in the annals of the Lubavitcher movement:

> I don't know of any other person since the establishment of Lubavitch who had such a two-way dialogue — notes back and forth — that the Rebbe had with Joseph. It was apparently so important to him that he answered

immediately — whereas others might wait for months or not get answers at all. He used to get answers from the Rebbe straight away . . .'

Joseph has kept all that correspondence, carefully transcribed and bound in twenty-four volumes, with the words *Ma'anot Kodesh* (Sacred Replies) embossed on their spines. The volumes include not only Joseph's personal correspondence with the Rebbe, but that between the Rebbe and other members of his family pertaining to him when he was a child. Thus, the first letter in the collection dates back to 1955, and is from the Rebbe to Joseph's grandfather, Rabbi Abramson in Sydney, blessing Joseph on the occasion of his third birthday (an important milestone, when Lubavitchers and other strictly Orthodox Jews traditionally give their sons their first haircut). The correspondence is almost exclusively in Hebrew, even though the Rebbe knew English quite well and used Yiddish in speech, and covers a gamut of subjects, from personal blessings and advice, through the most detailed business correspondence pertaining to Joseph's business activities, to an equally detailed correspondence relating to Joseph's political involvement on the Rebbe's behalf in Israel.

Joseph also has all the original letters, notes, comments and marginalia — literally hundreds of them, all in the Rebbe's own handwriting — which he keeps carefully preserved in a special folder. The Rebbe's replies were almost invariably transcribed by the Rebbe's secretaries and then faxed or sent to the recipients, the originals remaining in the archives in Crown Heights. Joseph, however, had persuaded the secretaries to let him have the originals after the Rebbe's death in 1994, and they are his most prized possession. 'My answers here are unique,' Joseph says proudly. 'In his older age, between 1987 and 1992, the Rebbe wouldn't usually answer . . . That I should have a collection of that many [replies] . . . No one in Chabad would have had such a constant, weekly answer. The effort he put in there. It's just a very special privilege. In the latter years of his life . . .'

One of these early business exchanges with the Rebbe related to the state of Joseph's shares in the aftermath of the crash. The Rebbe had given a public speech about Wall Street soon after the crash, in the course of which he said that what had occurred had been a '*yeridah letsorech aliyah*' — a descent in order to rise. He sent Joseph a newspaper clipping, showing Wall Street was going up and asked: 'Wall Street's going up — why aren't your shares going up?' Joseph replied that 'those were solid shares with solid earnings, and my shares were speculative shares'. The Rebbe didn't like that, Joseph recalls:

He was quite annoyed with that answer . . . He told Rabbi Klein (his secretary) that when he said '*yeridah letsorech aliyah*' on Wall Street, he meant me. The whole world works on that system. You have to go down, and then up. That's why the soul comes down to the body, and the soul is elevated. If you live a moral and correct and positive life in this world then it's worth the soul coming down because it reaches a higher level . . .

So, among other things, Joseph made certain that he continued giving to charity. This was the one way, he explains, in which man could 'test' God:

> I gave, in '87, even if it was much harder . . . It's one *mitzvah* [good deed] with which you're able to test God. You give charity; you're allowed to test him. If you give 10 per cent, then he'll give back 90 per cent. God asked one of the prophets: 'Test me. Give charity and I'll open up the treasures from the heaven.' Whether it's treasures in the ground, or the harvest, or business — whatever it is . . .

But giving to charity alone, the Rebbe made clear, was not going to release Joseph from his predicament. He had to remain positive, keep focussed, and work his way out of the crisis. 'I wasn't in a spiritual crisis,' he insists; 'I was in a monetary crisis.' And, as the Rebbe pointed out, 'they were only paper losses I had suffered'.

◊ ◊ ◊

Joseph conceded that 'up to the crash, I was a paper shuffler. Paper was the king as far as I was concerned.'[11] However, he said, on another occasion: 'I have learnt from my mistakes. I have learnt that it is important to have real assets and core cash-flow and not to be reliant on share trading . . . At the time paper was king and since the crash it is cash-flow that is king.' He was quick to point out, all the same, that without share trading he would not have built these assets in the first place: 'I started from nowhere and I built it up from paper.'[12]

The challenge now was to come through the storm and build up those 'real assets and core cash-flow'.

The Comeback Kid

'The fortunes of man are like a turning wheel. He who sits atop
the wheel and laughs is a fool, for should the wheel turn, he
may find himself lower than those at whom he was laughing.
And he who lies beneath the wheel and bewails his fate is
also a fool. Indeed, the very fact that he is now at the wheel's
lowest point means that on its very next movement, his
fortunes will improve.'

Jewish parable, often retold by the Lubavitcher Rebbe

JOSEPH'S FIRST, AND most urgent, priority after Black Tuesday was to reduce his huge debt, which stood at a massive $220 million just before the crash. And he moved quickly to do so. Fortunately, the debt-to-equity ratios of his companies were relatively low, and he was well cashed up, as a result of the money he had raised on the market in the months before the crash. He was also able to raise large sums by getting rid of his controlling interest in First Investors Security as well as his huge stake in FAI — thus selling out of financial services. And by August 1988, his debt was down to a still large but much more manageable $50 million.

He also set about assessing and restructuring what remained of his mining empire. He got rid of some of his more peripheral assets, such as the Phoenix Oil and Gas Company he had acquired in 1987. But Henry Herzog, his fellow director, announced just two months after the crash, in December 1987, that there would be 'no frantic sell-off of interests', noting that one of the smart things the group had done had been to raise plenty of cash so that the group as a whole was not over-geared. (Australia Wide, for instance, had shareholders' funds of $37.6 million and liabilities of $26.4 million; while Centaur was a little more stretched, with liabilities of $59 million and shareholders' funds of only $35 million.) Herzog said the group hoped to be 'a major gold producer in the next six months ... We are going to remain heavily involved in the gold area — as we are in high technology through Australia Wide ...'[1]

High technology was, in fact, high on Joseph's agenda at this time. He appeared to be very excited indeed about the prospects of a revolutionary new electricity-generating process — liquid metal magneto-hydrodynamics (LMMHD) — in which he was becoming involved in Israel. 'If it comes off it will be worth hundreds of millions of dollars,' he enthused to *Australian Business*'s Trevor Sykes in August 1988. 'It will outshine all the gold things I am involved in ...'[2]

The LMMHD project was, at first sight, a strange one for Joseph to take on. He had displayed little interest in any kind of commercial enterprise in Israel, apart from his abortive oil venture with Harry Cooper in the early 1980s. But the idea of a revolutionary way of producing pollution-free electricity — a system that could potentially be used to power satellites as part of America's 'Star Wars' program — had undoubtedly fired his imagination. LMMHD was, in fact, an old idea, as old as electricity itself. The story has it that it had come to the father of electricity, Michael Faraday, as he sat on the banks of the River Thames one day in the 1830s watching the water flow by. What, he had wondered so long ago, if the river were to be filled with iron filings and two huge magnets placed on the banks of the river? Wouldn't that create a gigantic inductive electricity generator? It was as simple as that.[3] But more than a century and a half later, no one had yet found a practical way of passing a liquid metal conductor through a channel placed in a magnet that would produce electricity on a commercial scale. Anyone who did would revolutionise the generation of electricity — and make an incalculable fortune. It was just the kind of project that would appeal to someone like Joseph Gutnick. Besides, the Rebbe had asked him to become involved.

A year before the crash, in 1986, the Rebbe startled his followers by announcing during several *farbrengens* at his headquarters in Crown Heights — long before most of the world's leading Kremlinologists predicted it — that conditions in the Soviet Union were about to change dramatically, and that its three or four million Jews would finally be free to emigrate. As many of these as possible, he said, should be encouraged to go to Israel rather than scatter around the world. Among those émigrés would be professionals in highly technical fields such as engineering and medical research, and Israel — a country of fewer than five million people at the time — was ill-equipped to absorb them. Many of them would move to other countries in search of suitable work, and, the Rebbe feared, would be lost to Judaism forever. If some of them could be brought together on a major scientific project in Israel, not only would there be a good chance of rekindling their Jewish identity, which had been suppressed for almost seventy years under the Soviet regime, but they would help strengthen the embattled Jewish state.

In a private meeting at Lubavitch headquarters, attended by Professor Herman Branover (himself a former Soviet scientist who had emigrated to Israel some years before and had become one of the Rebbe's most enthusiastic followers),[4] a plan was devised whereby Soviet–Jewish émigrés in Israel would live together, work together and practise Judaism together. They would pool their rich technological skills to create a viable and self-sustaining new high-tech community. They had an ideal project: Branover had been working on LMMHD for some years, and believed that the anticipated scientists from the Soviet Union would provide just the team he needed to make the dream a reality.[5] Now they needed a wealthy benefactor.

'So the Rebbe told me to get involved,' Joseph recalls. 'Branover needed help. Could I put in some money?' Fortuitously, Joseph owned one rather peculiar asset at this time: a parcel of shares in an almost unknown US company named Bayou International Ltd — it was originally a jock-strap manufacturer based in Nevada, then an oil and gas explorer — which he had acquired in a 1986 share swap. Bayou, it seems, had been defunct for some years, and had just three part-time employees and some tenuous property and exploration leases as its only assets. Joseph took over as chairman in 1987, a few months before Bayou bought a fifty-one per cent stake in Solmecs Corporation NV, a Dutch Antilles-registered company which, like Branover, had been working on LMMHD. Joseph then used Solmecs to set up an Israeli subsidiary, Satec, as a vehicle for Branover and his Soviet émigrés to develop the LMMHD project. In less than six months, the Rebbe's vision had become a reality. Fifty-two newly emigrated Soviet–Jewish families were living in the Ramot section of Jerusalem and some two dozen scientists were engaged in research work for Satec. As Jerusalem's long-serving mayor Teddy Kollek remarked: 'Only the Lubavitcher Rebbe could have accomplished this.'[6]

The project generated a great deal of enthusiasm in its early years, despite a sceptical and sometimes hostile press. There was even an attempt, in 1988, to raise money for it on the Australian Stock Exchange. 'One of the more unusual new floats coming up, a product of the ever-convoluting Joseph Gutnick's stable, offers an exotic mix:

Russian politics stirred in with Jewish acumen, a dash of Gutnick's favourite yellow metal, and a big swab of high technology,' wrote Shirley Skeel in August of that year, noting that Joseph was 'working vigorously on the new float of Advanced Technology Engineering Ltd (Atel) with telexes and occasional bodies flying between Melbourne and Jerusalem . . .'[7] At one stage, Joseph recalls, 'we almost had the American government put in US$20 million to get it to Etgar-3, the third stage.'

That was in the early 1990s, when there was a good deal of speculation that LMMHD might be used to power President Reagan's 'Star Wars' satellites. 'But it's never got off the ground properly,' Joseph says a little regretfully. 'I have my ideas why it hasn't. I blame it more on individuals rather than the Rebbe. I'd rather not blame anyone in particular. It's still continuing. Let's hope it will be successful. At the end of the day, the Rebbe told me, it's not a charity organisation. If you can't see how it's a benefit to you, just make sure it doesn't close down, and get out.' Joseph eventually sold out of Satec, but remains 'indirectly involved' in the project although his enthusiasm for it has long since waned.

While the electrical miracle never eventuated, Joseph's involvement in the Satec LMMHD project did pay other dividends. It gave him a high profile in the growing Soviet-migrant community in Israel, which was later to prove invaluable in his political activities there (see Chapter 6). 'And it also helped me around the traps,' Joseph recalls, as he struggled to rescue his business empire in the aftermath of Black Tuesday. Bayou was, in fact, to become a key — and highly controversial — element in Joseph's survival strategy.

◊ ◊ ◊

A year after the crash, it still was not clear to contemporary observers precisely how Joseph Gutnick was faring with his rescue operation. He was still around, unlike many others similarly caught in the Black Tuesday avalanche. But beyond that, little was known. 'He is known to have been planning, but nobody knows what,' Trevor Sykes wrote in August 1988.[8] There was even some wild speculation that he might get out of mining altogether. He 'may go off on a completely different tack into an industrial endeavour,' mining analyst Peter Strachan said in March 1988.[9] There clearly was a lot of complicated restructuring going on as Joseph struggled to salvage his eight core companies — Centaur, Great Central, Mount Kersey, Johnson's Well, Astro, Quantum, Australian Gold Resources, and Australia Wide Industries.

Joseph saw off a hostile challenge to his hold on Great Central by Southern Resources Ltd; Australian Gold Resources acquired a 66.87 per cent stake in Centaur, and made a successful takeover bid for First Investors Resources; Quantum announced a Part A takeover of Johnson's Well; and Centaur announced a similar takeover of Astro. 'It has been rather like watching ripples and whorls forming on a still sea and wondering what kind of whale is eventually going to surface,' Sykes commented.[10]

What was clear was that Joseph had learned one central lesson from the crash: he was determined to establish a foundation of real assets on which to rebuild his empire. His paper-mining days were over. In April 1988 Ed Eshuys was given the go-ahead to start drilling at Great Central's Plutonic Prospect in Western Australia — with immediately encouraging results. Eshuys also managed to define a gold deposit at Great Central's Great Lady Prospect north of Kalgoorlie, and an arrangement was made for BHP to mine the site and process the ore through its nearby mill at Ora Banda. In the same area, exploration continued at Centaur's Lady Bountiful Extended; but, while findings continued to be encouraging, actual production was still some months away. Astro conducted a feasibility study on its Northern Lady deposit with a view to bringing it to production. Eshuys also continued drilling at Johnson's Well's Yalgoo and Eastern Goldfields tenements.

Time, and money, were fast running out. Although Joseph had managed to get his debt down to a sustainable level thanks to the money he had raised before the crash and by selling off his non-mining assets — including his huge chunk of FAI — his surviving companies were raking up big losses. Centaur alone lost almost $80 million in 1988 and was in danger of going under before it had a chance to realise its potential. 'Junior gold exploration companies with significant potential no longer had available through equity markets the finance to prove up gold resources,' Joseph lamented in November that year, with the result the companies foundered 'with resulting share price falls to a mere fraction of their pre-crash levels.'[11] To stay afloat, he was forced to borrow.

One of the most willing (and, as it turned out, inept) lenders at this time was the State Bank of Victoria's merchant bank subsidiary, Tricontinental. Joseph's companies had already borrowed a total of some $50 million from Tricontinental, through the good offices of Harry Cooper. But by late 1988 Tricontinental was itself under huge and mounting pressure. It was facing up to $2 billion in losses, and was beginning to totter. There was an urgent need to restructure many of its loans — including those it had recently made to Joseph.

What emerged was extraordinarily complex, and to some observers once the details became known, quite scandalous. A package was put together under which, in return for recovering its earlier loans to Gutnick-controlled companies, Tricontinental agreed to guarantee a new $72 million loan from another investment bank, Kleinwort Benson, secured against Centaur's future gold production. In essence, this meant that Tricontinental had traded its $50 million direct exposure to Joseph's companies for an indirect guarantee of a $72 million loan to be paid back over seven years from the proceeds of Centaur's Lady Bountiful Extended gold mine. It had also made Centaur the de facto banker to the other much shakier companies in the Gutnick empire. The beauty of the deal, as Tricontinental saw it, was that it 'recouped its doubtful loans from various "penny dreadfuls" in and around the Centaur group, and it did not have to find the extra money to fund the deal (or so it thought).'[12] And Joseph, for his part, hailed the exercise as 'one of the best deals that has come my way since the crash', claiming that it had saved Centaur from certain liquidation.[13]

The National Companies and Securities Commission, which was still investigating Joseph's companies in the aftermath of the 1987 stock market crash, was not impressed, and did its best to torpedo the arrangement. It failed, however, when shareholder meetings of the companies directly involved in the arrangement, Centaur and Australia Wide Industries, ratified the deal — despite an abortive last minute attempt by the NCSC to obtain a Supreme Court injunction to stop them, and at least one commentator claiming: 'It is doubtful whether shareholders in an Australian company have ever been confronted with proposals as unfair as those being put before Centaur . . .'[14]

Joseph was deeply relieved when the deal finally went through in July 1989: 'Despite bad press to the contrary, we're doing our best to make sure that the company survives. We had a $50 million debt to Tricontinental, and we look forward to new opportunities. The directors hope to restore the company to what it was before the crash. We have regrouped, restructured and planned for a sound future in gold and high technology.'[15]

Tricontinental had finally collapsed by this time, under a huge mountain of bad loans, and the State Bank of Victoria inherited the mess — including the contentious guarantee for Joseph's $72 million gold loan. When details of the deal became known and the implications for Victoria's taxpayers were understood, many in the media were outraged. One of Joseph's most trenchant critics at this time, the *Sydney Morning Herald*'s Ben Hills, was especially scathing of the $32 million of the Tricontinental loan that Centaur had paid as part of the deal to Australia Wide Industries for its forty-one per cent stake in Bayou International: 'Shares that were worth $1 million two years earlier, in a company expected to lose another $8 million plus before it ever produced one widget,' he wrote, 'had by some sudden alchemy gone up 3,000 per cent in price.'[16] Hugo Armstrong, in his book *Tricontinental: The Rise and Fall of a Merchant Bank*, was equally indignant. The chain had not stopped with Bayou, Armstrong wrote: Australia Wide had then used part of the $32 million 'to buy 25 million shares in another company, Australian Gold Resources, from a company belonging to Harry Cooper — this time for a price 10-times their market value.'

Joseph, however, rejected such carping. 'People have said that the Bayou deal was just a fraud, pie-in-the-sky,' he told Hills. 'I am just waiting for the day when I see them with egg all over their faces.'[17] It would be a long wait, however, and the Tricontinental–Centaur saga was to take a few more tortuous twists and turns before it ran its sorry course.

◊ ◊ ◊

While all this wheeling and dealing was going on, and Joseph was still struggling to keep afloat, the Rebbe suddenly summoned him to New York at the end of August 1988. This was a highly unusual occurrence.

The ageing, sickly Rebbe had, by this time, long stopped giving private audiences. In early 1974 he had told his dismayed followers: 'Our movement has grown a thousandfold since the early 1950s. I cannot possibly perform the same services as I did when I began.'[18] And the audiences did all but cease entirely in 1977, when the Rebbe suffered a serious heart attack and was told by his doctors that he would have to guard his health more carefully. After that, his followers had to seek his advice, or his blessings, almost exclusively by mail and fax, or by telephone through the Rebbe's secretaries. The secretaries would relay his answers, often months later. Sometimes he would reply not directly at all, but through prayer.[19]

Then, in 1986, the Rebbe introduced the custom of bestowing dollar bills for charity every Sunday morning, when hundreds of his followers would line up at the Lubavitcher headquarters in Crown Heights for the precious notes and, if they were lucky, a brief word of blessing. Joseph has videos of these 'dollars' encounters — and they are quite fascinating to watch. Every word, every whisper, every gesture, every sign the Rebbe gave his disciples as they filed past to receive their

precious dollars was loaded with significance. Every mumbled blessing — for a successful marriage, or childbirth, or career move, or business venture — would be greeted with a fervent 'Amen'. His followers
made life decisions, and based their most precious hopes, on just such
gestures. And Joseph, when his turn came, would engage the Rebbe in
a sharply focussed exchange, usually asking for some very specific
advice or blessing, almost invariably about his mining and business
activities, which he would then — like the simplest Lubavitcher
mother receiving a blessing for her daughter's marriage — cherish and
follow to the letter. But apart from these brief encounters, there was
little or no opportunity for Lubavitchers to engage personally with
their Rebbe for much of the last two decades of his life.

So for the Rebbe to summon Joseph, all the way from Australia, for
a private audience was quite unheard of. Joseph was stunned: 'It was
unique in the annals of Chabad that the Rebbe should call someone to
come to New York, invite him to his home and have a personal audience.' Moreover, the call came less than six months after the Rebbe's
wife, Rebbetzin Chaya Mushka, had died, and he was secluded in his
home, in deep mourning. There is a tone of awe, pride, and reverence
in Joseph's voice when he recalls it:

That was the year his wife passed away, 1988. I was going through difficult
times. It was after the crash. The Rebbe told me to come to New York. He
only saw two or three people in private audiences in his home while he was
sitting *shiva* [the seven-day mourning period]. And he called me to come
from Australia, he wanted to see me. I went up to his private library in his
house. I don't think there would be more than two or three people in the
world who ever had an audience in his home, upstairs in his library. He
called me suddenly to come.

He gave me a blessing that I would be very successful. He said that it's
time that Lubavitch should have its own wealthy people, *gvirim*, and
amongst them should be a *Cohen* [a descendent of the priestly caste]. I'm a
Cohen . . . And then he mentioned to me that I would be very successful
within five years or more . . . And he gave me certain instructions . . .

There were a number of private things he said that I have never dis-
closed. I will one day . . . He said that he was also depressed and unhappy
because his wife had just passed away. He said in Yiddish, 'I am also
lacking joy.' And if I would tell him good news, that my activities in gold
were successful, it would brighten up his life, make him happy as well. So
the sooner I had the good news the better . . . He spoke to me for about six,
seven minutes straight . . .

It is difficult to believe, given the immense influence it had on Joseph's life, that this encounter lasted a mere six or seven minutes. Joseph's father, Chaim, had spent hours on end in private conversation with the Rebbe, before he had curtailed his audiences. Yet the impact of that meeting was such that Joseph continues to celebrate it on its Hebrew anniversary, *Tet b'Elul*, each year. One recalls what Elie Wiesel had said of his own encounters with the Rebbe in the early 1960s: 'Time in his presence began running at a different pace . . .'

Much of what the deeply unhappy, recently widowed, childless Rebbe told Joseph during the minutes that he spent with him remains a mystery. And Joseph, plainly, is reluctant to talk about it. But he dropped a hint, perhaps, when he was quoted as saying, in an interview with Ian Verrender in the *Sydney Morning Herald*, on 4 June 1994, just days before the Rebbe's death: 'He adopted me almost as his son.' Joseph is a little uncomfortable when reminded of that quote:

> I don't remember saying it . . . The Rebbe was on another plane. I was nowhere near his calibre, yet he took such an interest in what I was doing, and the fact that he called me into his home and took me upstairs for a personal audience. And there are other reasons I say that, which I can't really disclose. But there are reasons . . . I had a very close relationship with the Rebbe . . . The Rebbe once wrote to me that his involvement with me is out of friendship and closeness — '*Yedidut u-kiruv*'.

◊ ◊ ◊

It was not long after his meeting with the bereaved Rebbe in New York that Joseph was able to 'brighten up his life' with some genuinely good news. In November 1988, Ed Eshuys and his exploration team announced that they had made a major gold discovery at Great Central's Plutonic site. Prospectors had passed over this desolate area, 200 kilometres north of Meekatharra, without finding anything of significance. But an innovative geologist at the Commonwealth Scientific and Industrial Research Organisation (CSIRO), Dr Jim Wright, had come up with the idea of testing pebbles for their gold content and then chasing that down at depth. 'And that was how we discovered Plutonic,' Joseph relates. 'We only had about $100,000 left in the kitty to spend, and we had to take up an option for $50,000. We had one drilling program, which Ed pushed to do. And with the help of Jim Wright and the CSIRO we made that big discovery . . . It was one of the last places that we had, and we started drilling and we got great results. We proved up about 600,000 ounces of gold.'

Plutonic was a godsend for Joseph. Although most of their debt had been repaid through asset sales, or reconsolidated through the controversial $72 million Tricontinental gold loan, his companies were still raking up huge losses and producing little or nothing by way of cash flow. Centaur's operation at Mount Pleasant continued to be encouraging, but production was still some time off. And Australian Gold Resources — which just before the 1987 crash had raised $75 million in working capital for gold exploration and investment in gold mining companies — was scraping the bottom of the barrel. By March 1989, 'it had $5.64 million left, and not one ounce of gold out of the ground'.[20] Joseph clearly needed some breathing space. And to get this, he decided to sell his most promising asset — Plutonic.

'I needed the money to keep on going,' Joseph explains. And this time, the Rebbe — remorseful, perhaps, after what had happened the last time he had advised Joseph not to sell a gold asset — did not stand in his way. Joseph did, of course consult with him. 'But the Rebbe didn't give me a direct answer. He smiled, and said I should discuss it with God. What my *mazel* (luck) is. He never gave me the green light to sell it . . .' Later, Joseph notes, he had told the Rebbe: 'I can't discuss it with God, the Rebbe's the only person I can really communicate with. He never answered me. He said he was reluctant about me selling it . . .' But, unlike when he had vetoed Joseph's sale of Centaur to Larry Adler in 1986, the Rebbe did not say 'no'.

Joseph sold Plutonic, in two stages, to a company called Pioneer Mineral Exploration. In May 1989 he sold a fifty-one per cent stake in the discovery for some $25 million. Six months later, in November, he sold the remaining forty-nine per cent to Pioneer for $23.63 million. Great Central retained a 24.5 per cent entitlement to the net profits from Plutonic after the production of a million ounces of gold (it later sold that entitlement for a further $4.8 million, bringing its total proceeds from the sale to some $53 million). It also retained full control over exploration in the Nabberu region outside the Plutonic deposit, where, in its enthusiasm after discovering Plutonic in November 1988, it had protectively pegged thousands of square kilometres outside the leases that had already been taken up.

The price paid by Pioneer was considered high at the time, as little more than 600,000 ounces of gold had been proven up. But Plutonic turned out to be one of the most stunning Australian gold discoveries of the century, and was to go on to become a major gold province. Joseph later came to regret having sold it. 'Afterwards, I was upset that I sold it, because it turned out to be a lot better than

I had thought. But the Rebbe said it would work out to my good fortune . . .'

Plutonic did, in fact, turn out to be a boon for Great Central and its lucky shareholders. The company's share price had risen dramatically since hitting a low of 20c in November 1988, about the time the Plutonic find was made. It rocketed to a stunning $7.50 in August 1989 before settling back to $6.70 in November, when the final sale of the mine to Pioneer went ahead. At the beginning of 1990, it was able to offer a $14.24 million cash dividend to its shareholders — with Joseph, who now had a stake of just over 40 per cent in the company, receiving an estimated $5.7 million. It was a welcome windfall, after all the gloom and doom of the two years since the stock market crash.

The tide was beginning to turn for Joseph on the mining front as well. The renegotiated Tricontinental gold loan had enabled Centaur's Lady Bountiful Mine to move towards commercial production, which it did in August 1989, when its first load of ore was taken for processing to the nearby Golden Kilometre plant at Mount Pleasant. 'I was an orphan in those days,' Joseph recalls, noting that he was forced to use BHP's facility at Ora Banda and the Golden Kilometre facility at Mount Pleasant to process his gold because he didn't have his own plant. By June 1990, at the end of its first year of production, Lady Bountiful Extended had produced 109,000 ounces of gold.

Joseph was a bona fide gold miner at last. Derided for years as a paper shuffler, he took immense satisfaction from this — as well as from the fact that Lady Bountiful Extended had turned out to be a much better prospect than Consolidated Exploration's original Lady Bountiful mine nearby, which he had sold out of in 1986. 'Lady Bountiful, in the end, was a lot of hot air,' Joseph recalls: 'It only produced about 50 or 100 thousand ounces. It was nothing. Our mine, Lady Bountiful Extended, produced about 350,000 ounces . . .' He was pleased, too, to have beaten his two former partners in Consolidated Exploration, Jeff Banks and Duncan Purcell, at their own game. 'Their stock went down to nothing . . . they never made it. I made the big time, those two never made it.'

Gold had also come on line at Astro's Northern Lady mine, which produced almost 15,000 ounces of gold to the year ending June 1990. This, too, was sent to BHP's Ora Banda plant for processing. Gold continued to trickle out from Great Central's nearby Great Lady Project as well, but only came to a disappointing 3300 ounces by June 1990 after an initial production of almost twice that the previous year. The company's gold focus was beginning to shift elsewhere, however: to the

Lake Violet–Yandal greenstone belt 400 kilometres north of Kalgoorlie — which, in future years, was to emerge as one of Australia's most important gold provinces and the foundation stone of Joseph's mining empire.

The other mining companies that Joseph had managed to salvage from the crash — Johnson's Well, Mount Kersey, Australian Gold Resources, Quantum and Australia Wide Industries — also continued to explore, under Ed Eshuys's guidance. But with little success.

Johnson's Well abandoned its Yalgoo and Eastern Goldfields tenements and transferred its focus to a joint venture in the Copper Hills area, 40 kilometres north-east of Great Central's Plutonic discovery. The most interesting aspect of that venture, which never came to anything, was that it brought Joseph into his first collaboration with a remarkable prospector by the name of Mark Creasy, who was to become a central figure in his future gold fortunes (see Chapter 10).

Mount Kersey spent much of the period reviewing its tenements, abandoning those in Yalgoo and entering into joint ventures with Hallmark Minerals Ltd to explore a tenement north-east of Great Central's Marymia Project, and with Selmac Partners to search for gold in the Eastern Goldfields.

Australian Gold Resources was active mainly through the 63 per cent stake it had acquired in Centaur as part of the repackaged Tricontinental loan, but entered into a number of small joint ventures on its own account. These included a deal with Selmac to explore for mineral sands north of Geraldton in Western Australia.

Quantum ceased all exploration in 1989, and disposed of its fifty-one per cent holding in Ando Minerals, going into virtual hibernation until it was revived in the mid-1990s as Joseph's main vehicle for diamond exploration in China (see Chapter 8).

Finally, Australia Wide, which continued to play a major financing role in Joseph's group of companies, continued with its Torrington topaz joint venture in north-eastern New South Wales.

◊ ◊ ◊

With gold coming out of the ground at Centaur's Lady Bountiful Extended, and starting to come on stream at Astro's Northern Lady; with Ed Eshuys on the threshold of some major discoveries in the Yandal belt; and with Joseph, although still strapped for cash, in better shape financially than he had been since the crash, having received the money for Plutonic — the storm had apparently been weathered. October 20, 1987 was beginning to look like a bad memory. But then, in August 1990, just as it seemed things were beginning to come good, Iraq invaded Kuwait.

The world went into panic. And, as usually happens in times of global crisis, there was intense speculation that the price of gold would soar. Under normal circumstances, Joseph would have welcomed this. After all, he was now a gold producer. But there was the small problem of his $72 million gold loan, negotiated as part of his deal with Tricontinental the year before. The loan — which in the meantime had been taken over from Kleinwort Benson by another hedging group, Security Pacific — had acted effectively as a hedge against falls in the price of gold. But it provided no protection against rises.

Security Pacific began margin-calling Centaur to cover the gap between the price at which its gold production had been hedged and the rising bullion price. Joseph was unable to meet the calls, and Security Pacific invoked the guarantee that Tricontinental had provided for the loan under its deal with Joseph. The State Bank — which had assumed direct responsibility for running the affairs of the now defunct merchant banker — met the margin calls and covered the short-fall. But seeing a chance to recoup some of its own losses by cashing in on Joseph's predicament, the State Bank immediately appointed receivers and managers to Centaur. It was quite entitled to do this, as, under the deal, Tricontinental had held security over the company — which, now that it had a commercially productive gold mine, was a prime asset. As one analyst at the time noted, 'Trico, struggling to recover its own punting losses, and holding security over Centaur's producing mine, simply took its chance.'[21]

Joseph was taken completely by surprise. 'I know they were trying to sell the bank and so on . . . and for reasons unknown to us they simply stopped supporting us,' he said in some bewilderment. Characteristically, he remained optimistic: 'I've been going through a tough situation over the past three years and we have survived better than many people after the crash and we will keep on surviving.'[22] He said he was confident he could trade out of his difficulties and that he had spoken to a number of financiers including Rodney Adler at FAI. Rodney had taken over the reins at FAI from his father Larry, who had died the year before, leaving the company in some disarray, and had been forced to sell down its equity investments — including large stakes in two of Joseph's struggling companies, Australia Wide Industries and Australian Gold Resources. But he did lend Joseph his moral support: Joseph's greatest mistake, he told a finance journalist, had been to be conservative. 'He had been hedging his exposure and the gold price moved against him. If he hadn't been hedging everybody would have been criticising him.'[23] Joseph just couldn't win. Meanwhile, shares in Centaur plunged to a pitiful 5 cents before the company was suspended, along with several other flailing Gutnick companies. It was a devastating blow.

Reflecting on the whole fiasco almost a decade later, Joseph is still angry. Centaur, he believes, would easily have managed to pay back the debt. 'We only had to produce 160,000 ounces of gold — we had it, hedged at $650 [Australian],' he points out.

> If they would have stuck with us, then at the end of the day we would have paid back everything, they would have had no losses. It was just an absolute disaster. When the Iraqi war broke out they thought the gold price was going to rocket and everyone got cold feet and called in the margins . . . All our hedging fell to pieces, we lost tens of millions of dollars. It was a very unjustified move. It still angers me . . .

Joseph is nothing if not a fighter, and he fought tooth and nail over the following year to regain control of Centaur. He had a number of good reasons to fight. Not only was Centaur the first gold mining company he acquired, and the one that had given him his first big break, but it was only now beginning to pay dividends, with gold coming out of Lady Bountiful Extended at a rate of more than 100,000 ounces a year. He had worked hard for that and, naturally enough, wanted to reap his reward. There was also his pride and credibility as a businessman: he was mortified that a key company of his had failed, defaulted on a debt, and gone into receivership. Then there was his responsibility to the other shareholders, who had supported his decision not to sell out to Larry Adler, at a huge profit, just before the 1987 crash, and who were now left with nothing. Finally there was the matter of the Rebbe. It was the Rebbe who had prevented him from selling Centaur to Adler, so to lose the company in this manner, for nothing, was not only a blow to his own ambitions and to his own self-esteem — but was a further indictment on the Rebbe's judgement. He had to get it back, and make it succeed.

It was a tough fight. First, Joseph managed to get Britain's NatWest Bank to refinance his Tricontinental loan, paying the State Bank of Victoria out at what was believed to have been about 20 cents in the dollar.[24] And then, helped by a slump in gold prices, which significantly reduced the valuation the receivers placed on Centaur, he put in a bid for his old company. The State Bank, Joseph recalls, was not amused:

Even though I won the tender, they [the State Bank] still weren't happy with it. They didn't want to give it back to me, so I had to give them 10 per cent of the company. They were very tough negotiations, but I was determined and challenged them. I fought like a lion . . . And in the end I got it . . .

So, in August 1991, exactly a year after it went into receivership, Centaur was back in Joseph's hands. Tricontinental still had a 10 per cent stake in the company, but was left wearing a loss of some $55 million on its dealings with Joseph — something that was to haunt Joseph in the years ahead, after he had finally recovered and was riding high, in the mid-1990s, with critics querying why he had not made good on his debt to the Victorian taxpayer. 'Banks and shareholders alike have lost tens of millions of dollars in Diamond Joe's complex web of companies over the years,' the *Herald Sun*'s 'Insider' commented bitterly years later, in August 1994.[25] 'And while taxpayers lick their wounds, Gutnick has become a multi-millionaire.'

Such barbs could not but have hurt Joseph. He had tried repeatedly to demonstrate to his critics that the main blame lay not with him but with Tricontinental and the State Bank of Victoria. They had erred in their handling of the Centaur loan, and Centaur, with gold just beginning to come on stream at its Lady Bountiful Extended mine, should have been left to trade out of its difficulties in order to repay the debt rather than be placed in receivership. 'As it turned out,' Joseph noted in October 1994, 'Lady Bountiful has produced over 300,000 ounces and we would have been able to meet all debts.' He conceded that Tricontinental, as bankers, had every right to appoint the receivers — 'but do I feel guilty about the $55 million? No!'[26]

Five years later, he felt no differently:

It's business. When you borrow from a bank you don't look at taxpayers. I didn't look at Tricontinental as the taxpayers' funds. It was a State-owned bank. The bank was there to lend money, to take the risks. And they had to assess those risks. Often, if things go bad in business, you have to work it through with the customer. And if the State Bank had given us the opportunity to work it through, they would have got all their money back. It was bad management by the State Bank, not by Joseph Gutnick . . . I didn't even get to the Royal Commission [into the collapse of Tricontinental]. To this day I don't know why. I would have very much liked to have had my say . . . Perhaps they were scared of the [scale of the] irresponsibility. It was their fault that they lost the money. I don't bear any conscience for Tricontinental.

For all that, Joseph must have known that the only way he would ever be able to lay such criticism to rest would be to make Centaur thrive and show that it did, indeed, have the capacity to repay most if not all of its debt — even through the 10 per cent stake Tricontinental still retained in the company. By 1996, Joseph was, in fact, about to do just that when Tricontinental committed yet another monumental error of timing and/or judgement.

In January 1996, with Centaur's outstanding debt still about $50 million, the foundering merchant banker decided to cut its losses and sell its 10 per cent share. Joseph was again taken by surprise. Barely two weeks earlier, he had told Centaur's annual meeting that the company was 'poised for growth and an exciting year in 1996', adding: 'If Tricontinental's smart, they'll stick with us.'[27] But Tricontinental was not smart. It received just $13.2 million for its shares — which were snapped up by Joseph — leaving the Victorian taxpayer still out of pocket by some $37 million. Just four months later Centaur's shares had more than doubled in value. Had Tricontinental listened to Joseph, it would have saved the taxpayer a further $16 million. By September 1996, the shares were worth a whopping $34 million. When it came to Joseph, it seems, the failed merchant banker just couldn't take a trick. But banker John Sambell, who was second in charge of the Tricontinental clean-up, had no regrets, and no reproaches: 'We did a deal based on commercial realities,' he said nine months later — before conceding that Joseph Gutnick had 'nothing to answer'.[28]

◊ ◊ ◊

By the end of 1991, with Centaur firmly back in his grasp and producing gold, Joseph could look back on the three years since the crash and take comfort in the fact that he had defied the odds, and was still around. Many others weren't. And he could, and did, take considerable pride in the fact that not one of the listed companies under his direct control had folded.

Some of them, including Centaur, had come perilously close and had needed what Ian McIlwraith, writing in the *Financial Review*, once called 'the financial equivalent of heart massage and artificial respiration'.[29] But they had all pulled through. Others, including all his finance services companies, had been sold off. But his eight core companies had remained solvent and in his hands. It was quite an achievement.

Joseph could now turn his attention to some serious gold exploration. 'That was on the Rebbe's encouragement,' Joseph insists, 'to keep drilling, drilling. The Rebbe told Professor Branover in November 1990 that there are millions waiting in the depths of the earth, gold, and that he should make sure I keep on drilling. *"Nicht papiereneh gelt, goldeneh gelt"* — "Not paper money, but gold money" . . ' Joseph did keep drilling. And, as we shall see, he did find the *'goldeneh gelt'* — lots of it. But first there was the matter of a special job he had to do for the Rebbe — in Israel.

The Rebbe's Man in Israel

'I have been entrusted with a clear mission: That there will be a right-wing government, and that this right-wing government will stand firm and will not give away land. This is the goal I have worked for. And this is the goal, with the help of God, I will continue to work to achieve.'

Joseph Gutnick to Rabbi Aharon Dov Halperin, editor-in-chief of
Kfar Chabad, 14 January 1999

IN EARLY 1990, while he was slowly starting to work his way back from the 1987 Black Tuesday stock market crash, Joseph acquired a major new focus in life — and a new title. He became the Lubavitcher Rebbe's Special Emissary for the Integrity of the Land of Israel. Although it sounded like something out of an obscure Gilbert and Sullivan operetta, this was not just another of the facetious 'Golden Joe' or 'Midas of St Kilda' sobriquets that attached themselves to Joseph every time he did anything seen to be outrageous or out of the ordinary. It was an official title, approved by the Rebbe himself, for the man he had personally entrusted with a sacred mission — one that was to preoccupy him and command his total commitment for the next decade and beyond.

The call came at a time of high political drama in Israel. In a move his opponents called the 'stinking strategem' (*hatargil hamasriach*), Israel's Labour leader Shimon Peres had just brought down Yitzhak Shamir's right-wing Likud-led government, which had been strongly resisting mounting international pressure to do a land-for-peace deal with the Palestinians.

Peres was about to form a left-wing government of his own that was prepared to negotiate just such a deal, with the support of two important religious parties, Agudat Yisrael and Shas. The spiritual leader

The Biblical Land of Israel

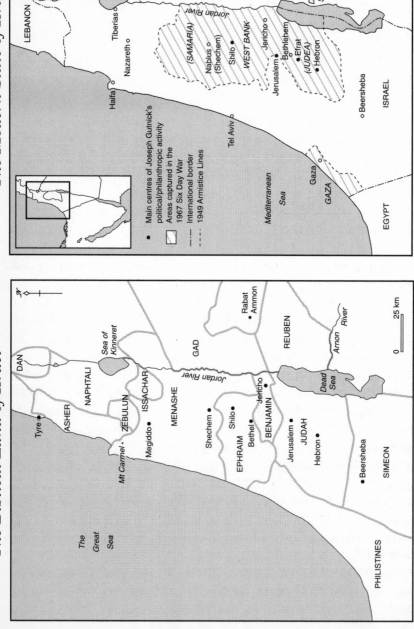

The Modern State of Israel

- Main centres of Joseph Gutnick's political/philanthropic activity
- Areas captured in the 1967 Six Day War
- — · — International border
- —··— 1949 Armistice Lines

of one of these parties, Shas, had gone on national television a few weeks earlier to announce that he would no longer be able to face God or his conscience if he continued to support Shamir's 'extremist, war-mongering government', and instructed his followers in the Knesset (the Israeli parliament) to support Peres.[1] Some years before, this same rabbi — Rabbi Ovadiah Yosef, one of Israel's most influential and highly respected religious sages — had caused a major stir when he stated quite unequivocally:

> To hold or conquer territories in the Land of Israel by force, in our time, against the will of the nations of the world, is a sin. If we can give back the territories and thereby avoid war and bloodshed, we are obligated to do so, under the Rule of Saving Life.[2]

This, of course, was anathema to the Rebbe, who, as we saw earlier (in Chapter 2) had stated no less unequivocally:

> The Land of Israel in its entirety was given by God to the eternal people for eternity, and no one has the authority to give back a single inch — especially as this involves a grave security risk and endangers life.

And he resolved to stop Rabbi Yosef and Peres in their tracks. The integrity of the Land of Israel — and, the Rebbe believed, the safety of millions of Jews — were at stake. It was time for a 'strategem' of his own.

Enter Joseph.

Joseph had not only been in constant touch with the Rebbe since 1986 and grown very close to him; he also had a long family and personal association with the Land of Israel (his grandfather having gone there from Russia in the early 1920s when he lived in the holy city of Hebron). And Joseph himself, although he had never lived in Israel, had good contacts there. He was a generous supporter of several religious institutions, both Lubavitcher and non-Lubavitcher, over which he would be able to exert some influence. He was also very involved with the Russian Jews who had started to flow into Israel in increasing numbers as the Soviet Union began to disintegrate.

Above all, Joseph was an avowed Zionist — having inherited, it seems, the same 'dangerous Zionist leanings' which, some sixty years earlier, had earned his paternal grandfather, Reb Mordechai Ze'ev, a ticking-off from the Rebbe's predecessor. He had grown up in a strongly Zionist home, where both his father and mother had been very actively involved in Zionist activities, long before this was common or even accepted in Lubavitch circles.

Joseph's Zionism is founded on three closely interrelated premises. Like the Rebbe, and all religious Jews, he stresses the Jews' fundamental religious claim to the Land of Israel:

The first passage in the Bible states that 'God created the Heaven and earth', and, our Sages say, he gave the Land of Israel to the Jewish people. It's our Holy Land, and he gave it to who he wanted . . . It's the Promised Land of the Jewish People. That's the basic premise . . . Our justification to the Land of Israel is the Old Testament, the Bible.

Then there is the historical premise:

Our history is there, in Judea and Samaria. Jerusalem . . . Shilo . . . Bethel . . . Hebron . . . We're in Israel because it's our homeland . . . Every stone is full of Jewish history, and Jewish blood that's been spilt there . . . Every rock is filled with sacrifice and love and blood and tears . . . So much Jewish history . . .

Finally, there is the political premise, irrespective of history and religion — the need for a strong, secure, sovereign Jewish state in the contemporary world, especially after the Holocaust:

It doesn't matter if you are religious, not religious. The establishment of the State of Israel is one of the greatest things to have happened in thousands of years to the Jewish people. We have our own homeland . . . In 1948, the Jews were a besieged, persecuted people. And in order that we should survive now, in 1999, in Australia, we had to have a Jewish state . . . If you secure Israel, you secure people in Australia.

For all his involvement with and passion for the Jewish state, Joseph had not, up to this point, been directly involved in Israeli politics. And, at first glance, it does seem odd that the Rebbe should have chosen someone from far-off Australia for such an important mission, when there would have been a number of at least equally well-connected Lubavitchers closer to the action in Israel itself.

'I was also surprised,' Joseph concedes. 'There were people in Israel working all their lives in politics, and here was this rich young *shmekl* ('little prick') from Australia, a *gvir*, suddenly become's the Rebbe's emissary!' The Rebbe, however, appears to have wanted someone he knew well and could trust, with contacts and influence in Israel — but not, it would seem, part of the local Lubavitcher hierarchy. He wanted someone who would be directly answerable to him, who would be able to act covertly if need be and would not openly involve or implicate the local Lubavitchers in his actions. He also wanted someone who could

The Gutnicks of Elwood, 1961. Seated (from left): Mordechai, Chaim (holding
Moshe) and Joseph. Standing (from left): Chana, Rose, and Pnina. 'We were a
Lubavitcher family, but my father was a modern, Orthodox rabbi in the Elwood
Synagogue. He didn't have a beard . . . It wasn't a typical Lubavitcher family.'

Yeshivah Bocher (Yeshivah student). Joseph at the Rebbe's yeshivah in Crown Heights, New York, circa 1971. While Joseph was a solid and competent student, and graduated at the end of his four years as a qualified rabbi, he did not stand out as an '*ilui*', or prodigy of Torah study. 'I didn't have the *zitzfleish* (backside) for that.'

Shidduch (marriage-match). Joseph and Stera (née New) on their wedding day in 1974, flanked by Joseph's mother, Rose, and father Chaim — by this time sporting a beard, in the accepted Lubavitcher fashion.

hold his own in the world of Israeli political horse-trading — someone who would be able to act pragmatically behind the scenes, and engage in 'Realpolitik', without compromising the Rebbe's own integrity on important matters of principle. In short, he wanted a kind of Lubavitcher Henry Kissinger.[3] Joseph, it seems, fitted the bill.

Joseph spent several weeks in Israel in the early part of 1990, wheeling and dealing behind the scenes. In particular, he put strong pressure on two members of the Ultra-Orthodox Agudat Yisrael party to drop their support for Shimon Peres and join a 'strong, narrow-based, right-wing government' led by Shamir. And, just hours before Peres was about to present his government to the Knesset, these two men — Avraham Werdiger and Eliezer Mizrachi — announced they were reneging on their earlier agreement with him, and swung their support behind the embattled Likud leader. Without those two votes, Peres did not have the numbers. He conceded defeat. And Shamir formed a right-wing government that was to rule Israel for the next two years, resolutely stonewalling the growing international pressure being exerted on Israel to withdraw from the West Bank and Golan Heights. For the moment, the integrity of the Land of Israel was secured.

In a remarkable interview many years later with Rabbi Aharon Dov Halperin, editor-in-chief of the official Lubavitcher magazine *Kfar Chabad*, Joseph explained, in broad terms, how he and the Rebbe had worked together to thwart Peres's 'stinking strategem' — and then, once Shamir had been reinstated, how to keep him on track:

> In the first instance, the instruction was to exert all contacts and influence on the religious and right-wing parties to join the right-wing government. Later came clear guidelines and instructions, which included how to brief each of them on the dangers of a left-wing government and of the crucial importance of joining a right-wing government. Later still, long after the government had already been formed, came instructions on how to remain vigilant that the government remained strong, what to say and what to explain . . . the Rebbe would direct me every step and every inch of the way. I would say, without the slightest exaggeration, that there were literally hundreds of questions and answers from the Rebbe concerning this mission.
>
> Most of the instructions were secret. On a number of matters the Rebbe instructed me to act as I saw fit. There were also many actions on this matter where the Rebbe instructed me to act ostensibly according to my own judgement, and not in his name. On several occasions, the Rebbe wanted his own involvement in these matters to remain secret, for obvious reasons . . . [4]

The Rebbe's grasp of, and keen interest in, the political machinations in Israel were quite remarkable, as was the detail of the instructions he gave to his emissary. This emerges from the thousands of questions and replies Joseph received from the Rebbe, all carefully preserved in the twenty-four bound volumes in Joseph's study. For example, when Shamir was struggling to establish his government, Joseph reported to the Rebbe on a meeting he had had with Geulah Cohen, one of the leaders of the small right-wing Tehiya ('Revival') Party. This was the party closest to Israel's settler movement, and vehemently opposed to any territorial compromise in the Land of Israel. It was a natural ally of Shamir's, but was driving a hard bargain to join his government. Cohen wanted Joseph to intercede on her behalf. Joseph reads out what he had written to the Rebbe:

> I had a very pleasant meeting with Geulah Cohen. She is a warm and good-natured lady. She holds and respects the Rebbe with the greatest esteem. ... Her problem with Shamir is not one of policy but the fact that he is mistreating her and offering her party nothing because he takes her for granted ... She wants to be in [the Government] but Shamir is treating her with contempt. She can't believe that my Rebbe would want her to be so compromising [concerning the portfolios she was demanding], and she wants me to pressure Shamir on her behalf. She greatly treasures the Rebbe, and wanted to know how I became his emissary ... In the end she will listen to all that the Rebbe wants. She requested that I keep in touch with her, and wants to know what she should do. I told her that whatever happens she should be in [Shamir's government] and not merely support it from the outside, and that I would do my best for her. I felt she badly needs encouragement ...

The Rebbe, however, did not believe that Shamir should give in to Cohen's demands, and instructed Joseph accordingly. While appreciating her enthusiasm and commitment to the Land of Israel, going back to her days in the pre-state struggle against the British in Palestine, the Rebbe said she should be told to compromise on her demands; the only matters where no compromise is possible, the Rebbe reminded Joseph, 'are matters of *pikuach nefesh* (sanctity of life) affecting the people dwelling in Zion, as I have declared time and again'.

Joseph would report to the Rebbe every week about what was happening in Israel, along with what was happening with his mining and business activities. These included reports on cabinet meetings, which Joseph would receive from one of his political allies in Israel and summarise for the Rebbe, as well as reports on his own dealings with Shamir and others. At one point, Joseph notes, the Rebbe appeared to be concerned that Joseph was getting a little too involved with his role as Special Emissary, and reminded him that he had other business to attend to as well: 'I wrote a report saying I hoped I would be able to tell the Rebbe the good news about what's happening in Israel. And the Rebbe replied, through one of his secretaries: "And also in his business, because *gam zeh ikar* — that's also important." So he equated the news in Israel with my business, which I found quite surprising.'

Joseph had a good relationship with Shamir, a doughty little man who, while he was not especially pious or God-fearing, had an iron-willed, dogged determination to hang on to every inch of the Land of Israel. His devotion to the Land sprang from secular, nationalistic motives rather than the religious, Torah-based fundamentalism that drove the Rebbe, but he could be relied on to do the right thing by the Land of Israel — even if not necessarily for precisely the right reasons. 'I was very close to Shamir,' Joseph recalls.

> Very close. Letters, telephone . . . Any time I would ring, he would pick up the phone and ring me back . . . Any time I came to Israel I would meet with him, spend hours talking to him . . . I had absolute access to him. I'd pass on a lot of messages to the Rebbe from him, and warned him that the Russian vote was going to bring him down in 1992. But he didn't listen . . .

The hundreds of thousands of Jews who flooded into Israel from the collapsing Soviet Union in the early 1990s were, in fact, a crucial factor in the Likud's defeat in Israel's 1992 election. They voted about 60:40 against Shamir, delivering victory to his Labour rival, Yitzhak Rabin.

Joseph, somewhat surprisingly, played no part in the run-up to the 1992 election. He didn't even visit Israel during the campaign. His mind was elsewhere. The Rebbe had recently suffered a massive stroke which left him paralysed and without speech. 'I was pretty devastated at that time,' Joseph recalls. Besides, he was disillusioned with the political scene in Israel. The religious Right was splintered, and he was at odds with some of the Lubavitcher leaders in Israel, who resented his mission on the Rebbe's behalf. 'I didn't think we were going to win in 1992.' So he stayed away.

Rabin's victory was a major blow to the Right in Israel. A life-long soldier who had been Israel's army chief-of-staff at the time of the Six Day War, Rabin had little sentimental and no religious attachment to the Land of Israel. His prime concern was Israel's security — and if he believed this could best be served by giving back the land he had captured in 1967 in return for peace, he was prepared to do so. And he had little time for the Jewish settlers who had established themselves in those territories, with the blessing and the active encouragement of the right-wing governments that had led Israel for most of the previous fifteen years. He regarded them as 'parasites', referring to them contemptuously as 'propellers spinning in the wind' — people who were expendable in his search for a 'peace with security' with Israel's Arab neighbours.

The Rebbe had met Rabin on at least one occasion, while the former general was serving in Washington as Israel's ambassador in the early 1970s. And while he greatly respected him as a soldier — after all, Rabin had devoted his life to defending Jews in the Land of Israel — the Rebbe was not impressed with his politics: 'The Rebbe said on numerous occasions that the danger of Peres and Rabin was the same,' Joseph recalls. 'Peres–Rabin, it's the same philosophy, it's the same ideology . . .' Accordingly, he specifically instructed Joseph to have no dealings with Rabin in carrying out his mission. Even after Rabin was elected, the Rebbe told Joseph not to go to Israel to meet him. 'The Rebbe said I should keep my contacts on with the Likud . . .'

Shamir had given up the leadership of the Likud party soon after his defeat in 1992, handing over the reins to the rising star of the Israeli Right — Binyamin Netanyahu. Netanyahu — or 'Bibi' as he is universally known in Israel — came from a staunchly patriotic, right-wing family that was totally and utterly committed to upholding Israel's right to the Land of Israel. His late brother Yonathan was a national hero, who had fallen while leading the Israeli commando team in the famous 1976 Entebbe hostage rescue, while he himself had later served in the same elite commando unit. Joseph saw him as the ideal candidate, under the terms of the brief he had received from the Rebbe, to lead 'a strong, right-wing government that would resist pressure to give away parts of the Land of Israel'.

Moreover, Joseph — who had been introduced to Netanyahu by Shamir some years earlier — immediately hit it off with the charismatic young leader. In the first place, he was much closer in age than Shamir had been: 'Bibi, I'd talk and joke around with,' Joseph recalls, 'whereas Shamir was a different generation.' The fact that Netanyahu had spent much of his life growing up and studying in the United States, and was in many ways more American by temperament than he was Israeli, also helped: 'Well, an American and an Australian — the same world, rather than the world of Israel . . .'

Joseph clearly regards Netanyahu as a friend — but not without some ambivalence:

I'm a good friend of Bibi's. But he's very hard to be a close friend [of], he's quite aloof . . . Especially when he was Prime Minister of Israel. He thinks the world of himself. If Bibi was not the Prime Minister of Israel and if Bibi was not in politics, and Joseph Gutnick and Bibi were to meet would they become friends? — I don't know. A talented guy, Bibi. He was fantastic in the Iraqi war in 1991, on CNN. He's got a lot of very good qualities . . .

He also had at least one serious drawback. He was thrice married and had openly confessed to having an affair while married to his third and current wife, Sarah. Joseph is surprisingly broad-minded about this:

In this day and age, most people don't even get married, and most people have affairs. We're living in a morally decadent society. I wouldn't categorise Bibi at such a level. He's not a guy who runs to brothels. He's had an affair. Now I don't justify that for one minute. And he regrets it. And his wife was angry at him. It's his third marriage. He's a good-looking fellow, and he's had temptations in front of him. So in this day and age we don't say because someone has had an affair he can't be the leader of a country . . .

But, Joseph concedes, Netanyahu's infidelity was a major issue for the highly moralistic Ultra-Orthodox electorate he sought to represent and to win over for Netanyahu:

The electorate questioned the fact that someone who was not loyal to his wife, could he be loyal to the Land of Israel? . . . But I'm not a psychologist or a psychiatrist that I can necessarily reflect that someone who was not loyal to his wife that he will not necessarily be loyal to *Am Yisrael* and *Eretz Yisrael* [the People of Israel and the Land of Israel]. There's definitely a question, but we overlooked it . . .

Besides, Joseph points out: 'The Rebbe had endorsed Bibi, and had been friendly with him . . . He was a conduit for my *shlichut* [mission] . . . He was the person at the time that was the best to champion our cause, therefore we backed him . . .'

So Joseph went about building a close working relationship with Netanyahu, who was, if anything, even more accessible to the Rebbe's Special Emissary than Shamir had been. The task for now was to impede as far as possible the handover of any land to the Palestinians and work for the return of a right-wing government in Israel as soon as possible.

It was not long before Joseph's worst fears about the Rabin government came to pass. Soon after taking office, Rabin gave the go-ahead to Shimon Peres, his foreign minister, to engage in secret negotiations with the Palestinians over a land-for-peace deal. The negotiations, which took place in Norway, yielded the so-called 'Oslo Accords', under which Israel would stage a phased withdrawal from most of the territories it had occupied in 1967. The deal was sealed on 13 September 1993, on the lawn of the White House in Washington, where Rabin did the unthinkable: he shook hands with Israel's arch enemy, the Palestinian leader Yasser Arafat, under the gaze of a beaming President Bill Clinton. It was a devastating blow to the right wing in Israel — and a bitter setback for the Rebbe's Special Emissary for the Integrity of the Land of Israel.

◊ ◊ ◊

Nine months later, Joseph was dealt another savage blow. On 12 June 1994, the Lubavitcher Rebbe succumbed to a second stroke and died in New York, at the age of ninety-two. Childless, he had left no designated successor. For the briefest of moments, as the Lubavitcher world reeled, there was even speculation in at least one respectable Australian newspaper, the *Sydney Morning Herald*, that Joseph might be his potential successor. This was, of course, quite absurd and was immediately quashed by Joseph's younger brother, Rabbi Moshe Gutnick, who told the journalist who had asked the question: 'Not a chance. Not in a million years. There will be no successor from Australia, as far as we know.' Joseph's sister, Pnina Feldman, concurred: 'I don't think so. Let him do what the Rebbe wanted him to do and find gold and diamonds.'[5]

The Rebbe's death shook the world of Lubavitch in much the same way as Black Tuesday had shaken the business world in October 1987. Thousands of Lubavitchers around the globe — including many here in Australia — had come to believe, in all sincerity, that the Rebbe was none other than the Messiah himself. Belief in the Messiah is an article of faith for all believing Jews,[6] and the Rebbe incessantly urged his followers to work for the coming of the Messiah by performing good deeds. He also led them to believe that they were living in a pre-Messianic epoch, and that the coming of the Messiah was imminent. Lubavitcher children would lay out their best clothes at the foot of their beds before they went to sleep, so they would be properly dressed should the Messiah arrive.[7] And the Rebbe, while he did not promote it, did little openly to discourage the idea that he himself might, potentially, be the Messiah. This was fully in keeping with Jewish tradition, which has it that there is, in every generation, a great sage who might be the Messiah — and who would be revealed as the Messiah if God considered the world ready for him.

The Rebbe was, of course, caught in a bit of a double bind on the Messiah issue. He could not deny that he was the Messiah, because, theoretically, he might be. On the other hand, he certainly could not say he was; Judaism had had a bad run with false Messiahs over the centuries. Only God could know for sure, one way or the other. But many of the Rebbe's followers — the so-called 'Messianists' who were sure he was the Messiah — appeared to interpret his silence on the issue as a sign of modesty, or even coyness, and argued that 'you had to force him into being crowned Messiah'.

In the event, the Rebbe died without having been revealed to be the Messiah. For many thousands of Lubavitchers around the world this was a calamity. They could not conceive of a future without the Rebbe/Messiah, and clung desperately to the belief that he would soon rise from the dead and declare himself. But for most Lubavitchers, deeply shocked and saddened as they were by the Rebbe's death, that was the end of the story — at least for the moment. The Rebbe had been a great and wise sage, perhaps even a potential Messiah in waiting; but God, in his infinite wisdom, had decreed that this was not to be the Messianic generation. It was up to the next generation to work even harder, to do more good deeds, and in this way hasten the Messiah's coming.

Joseph was as shocked and as saddened by the Rebbe's death as anyone. Perhaps more than most, given the intense personal relationship that had evolved between them in the last decade of the Rebbe's life. But, from the outset, he kept the event in perspective. He believed fervently in the coming of the Messiah, and that the Messianic era might be imminent. He had even sponsored a series of full-page advertisements in the *New York Times* and other publications in the early 1990s heralding the dawning of that era — until the Rebbe instructed him not to. 'The Rebbe told me to stay out of it,' Joseph revealed in a 1995 interview with *Australian Jewish News* editor Sam Lipski. 'The Rebbe was upset because it focused on him as a person. I don't care what anyone says. I know he was upset. When the campaign came to him as a person being *Moshiach* [the Messiah], he was upset. He was interested in the Messiah coming. He never declared himself as *Moshiach* . . .'[8]

Like all Lubavitchers, Joseph believed that the Rebbe could possibly have been the Messiah while he was alive. And he was not prepared to rule out the possibility that the Rebbe could yet turn out to be the Messiah — even after his death:[9] 'The Rebbe was definitely capable of being *Moshiach*, if anyone was, if God would have chosen him. But now that he's passed away the likelihood of the Rebbe being *Moshiach* coming from the dead is possible, but not probable.' He has strongly opposed those Lubavitchers who were continuing to push the Rebbe-as-Messiah line, believing this was deeply divisive and damaging to the movement: 'The Messianic fervour — I understand it, I'm not actively fighting it — but I think it doesn't bring any honour to the Rebbe.' He has advocated, instead, 'promoting that the Rebbe said we had to do acts of kindness' — and, in this way, hasten the coming of the Messiah. Meanwhile, the Lubavitcher movement would go on without another Rebbe. 'I lost my mother in a tragic accident three years ago,' Joseph said in an interview a couple of years later.[10] 'Can I replace my mother? That's how we look upon the Rebbe. He was different to most. The Rebbe is not like the chairman of a public company like Great Central, where shareholders elect you. We don't have to replace him. We're happy to wait till the Messiah comes.'

In this, Joseph was strongly allied with the majority camp in the Lubavitcher movement, headed by Rabbi Yehudah Krinsky — one of the Rebbe's secretaries — whose son, Shmaya, had married Joseph's eighteen-year-old daughter Rivka in New York just days before the Rebbe's death. The wedding, which took place while the Rebbe was hooked to a life support machine in a hospital just a few miles away, was hailed by Lubavitchers as the 'wedding of the century' and a 'wedding made in Heaven'. But, while Joseph's political and family alliance with Rabbi Krinsky had firmly cemented Joseph's position of influence in Lubavitch, it brought him into open conflict with his old Yeshivah College mentor, Rabbi Yitzchok Dovid Groner.

Rabbi Groner, unlike Joseph, was then perceived to be close to the 'Messianist' camp. 'We pray and we hope that he [the Rebbe] will be resurrected,' he told Melbourne's *Herald Sun* the day after the Rebbe's death — 'we are praying and hoping that it will be in the immediate future.'[11] Moreover, Rabbi Groner's younger brother Laibl was a strong rival of Joseph's daughter's new father-in-law, Rabbi Krinsky, in the post-Rebbe struggle for power in the Lubavitcher movement. The stage was set for an almighty blue.

While he has always claimed to respect Rabbi Groner as the Rebbe's hand-picked leader of the Lubavitcher community in Melbourne, Joseph felt that, as he became closer to the Rebbe and his influence in the world Lubavitcher movement grew, he was increasingly viewed as a threat by his former mentor. 'I think it was hard for some of my former teachers to discuss things with me as a peer because they saw me as little Yossele whom they had brought up and taught,' Joseph told Sam Lipski in his February 1995 *Australian Jewish News* interview. 'But I had become prominent and successful and acted for the Rebbe in Israel. Maybe they saw me as a threat, which I wasn't.' And it was especially hard for Rabbi Groner, Joseph claims: 'Here was this young guy who's put Australia on the map ... A lot of people in Israel knew Chabad and Lubavitch through me rather than Rabbi Groner.'

The large Chabad House Joseph had set up in 1992, on the Rebbe's instructions, at his swish Kimberley Gardens Hotel just around the corner from Melbourne's main Lubavitcher complex hadn't helped matters. It sowed suspicions in the minds of some that he was attempting to create an independent centre of his own that would rival and perhaps even eclipse the original Yeshivah Centre in Hotham Street. Joseph tried to allay any fears Rabbi Groner might have had by pointing out that he had the Rebbe's approval and was not, in any case, interested in setting himself up as a rival rabbi. His operation at Kimberley complemented rather than competed with Rabbi Groner's, he explained. But the suspicions lingered, even deepening after Joseph refused to help rescue the Yeshivah Centre when it ran into serious financial difficulties in 1994.

Matters came to a head soon after the Rebbe died, when the growing resentments and frustrations that had been building between Joseph and Rabbi Groner burst into the open — on ABC TV's *7.30 Report*. Interviewed for the program, Joseph justified his refusal to help bail out the Yeshivah Centre by referring to Rabbi Groner's involvement on the side of the Messianists in the political struggle taking place in New York. He said he could do 'a lot more positive' things for the cash-strapped institution if Rabbi Groner butted out of the struggle and stopped 'promoting the idea that the late Rabbi Menachem Mendel Schneerson could possibly return from the dead to be the Messiah.' Joseph later told the *Australian Jewish News*, in an interview that added fuel to the flames, that 'if the Rebbe had wanted him [Groner] involved in politics, he would have involved him directly.' He vowed that he would 'fight on' if Rabbi Groner 'goes on with his extremism about the Messiah.' There was a lot of sympathy for the Lubavitcher movement in the community at large, Joseph pointed out — but all this 'radical talk that the Rebbe will come back as the Messiah and the infighting is doing no good.'[12]

In the end, the two men made their peace. 'Rabbi Groner doesn't think much differently than I do,' Joseph now says — 'but Rabbi

Groner's got to contend with a community part of [which] is very *Meshichisti* [Messianic].' The Messiah and leadership issues receded into the background, and Joseph contributed generously to the multimillion-dollar rescue package organised to save the Yeshivah Centre and its sister institution in Sydney, which had both run up huge debts. In a token of gratitude, the main campus of his old school in Hotham Street was named the 'Joseph and Stera Gutnick Campus'.

Meanwhile, the Lubavitcher movement gradually came to terms with life in the post-Rebbe era. There were still some Lubavitchers who continued to believe that the late Rebbe would return soon as the Messiah. But, while this remained a potentially divisive issue, flaring into the open from time to time, the danger of a serious split over the Messiah — both in Australia and worldwide — appeared to have passed as a new century approached. 'The Messianic fervour, and Messianic movement that existed in Melbourne is a lot less now than it was three years ago,' Joseph proclaimed.

> Worldwide it's got less. There are some groups that are still fervently Messianically orientated; there are times when they're stronger and more vocal, and times when they're not. I think it's important that the Rebbe's message of doing good deeds and bringing the Messianic era closer is still very relevant. But the Rebbe's my Rebbe — and my personal *Moshiach* because he was so important in my life ... But whether the Rebbe is *The Moshiach* or not — that's God's decision ...

As for the leadership of the Lubavitch movement, Joseph still feels very strongly that no attempt should be made to find a successor to the Rebbe — after all, the Breslever Chassidim had made do without a Rebbe for over 180 years, and had still seen themselves as 'bound to the soul' of their last Rebbe, Rabbi Nachman. 'They never had another Rebbe in that community because they could never find anyone like him. The Rebbe was such a personality — there's no one who could fill his shoes.' There were, of course, many good, talented people in Lubavitch around the world, he said — including Rabbi Groner and Joseph's own father, Chaim. But the Rebbe was 'a holy man' — and 'Rabbi Groner, with all respect to him, and my father, with all respect to him, are very respected; but they are not holy people.'[13]

Joseph, for his part, continued to play a major role in the Rebbe-less movement, placing increasing emphasis on his role as the Rebbe's Special Emissary for the Integrity of the Land of Israel. It was a task he accepted in perpetuity, and pursued with added vigour after the Rebbe's death.

◊ ◊ ◊

Although most Israelis had greeted the Oslo Accords with great enthusiasm, convinced that these heralded the end of their bitter conflict
with the Palestinians and their Arab neighbours, public sentiment
began to turn against Rabin and the peace process after a series of devastating terrorist attacks in early 1995 left scores of Israelis dead.
Ironically, these attacks were carried out by Islamic fundamentalists of
the extreme Hamas organisation who were no less determined than
Joseph or Netanyahu to stop the Oslo agreement from being implemented. Israelis, however, were finding it increasingly difficult to
accept the logic that the casualties were not the result of the peace
process, but rather the price exacted by those who wanted to stop it.
Netanyahu began to soar in the polls, and Rabin appeared headed for
a landslide loss in the election scheduled for the following year. Then,
on 4 November 1995, a religious Jewish fanatic, Yigal Amir, acting on
what he claimed was rabbinical sanction to protect the integrity of the
Land of Israel, gunned Rabin down at a peace rally in Tel Aviv.

Rabin's assassination stunned Israel, and unleashed a backlash of
remorse and anger against the right wing and religious parties, which
many Israelis felt had helped create the atmosphere that led to the
Prime Minister's death. As May 1996 approached, it seemed that
Rabin's successor, Shimon Peres, was headed for a comfortable victory.

This time, unlike in 1992, Joseph had spent several months in Israel
in the lead-up to the election, during which time he worked incessantly
to rally Orthodox religious and Russian migrant groups behind
Netanyahu. There were angry mutterings in Israel that he was
'bribing' these groups to vote for Netanyahu, that he was 'buying' their
votes. Peres was so concerned, Joseph recalls, that he even initiated a
meeting with him, at the Holiday Inn in Jerusalem:

> He warned me, in Hebrew: '*Al techashed anashim*' — don't bribe people. So
> I said I don't bribe people . . . I give *tsedakah* [charity] all the time to reli-
> gious institutions . . . His response was, you can do what you like, only
> don't bribe anyone. It's against the law, blah, blah, blah. He carried on
> about bribing. He was scared I was bribing the rabbis. Those were the
> rumours. Giving them money so they should vote for Netanyahu. The
> *Charedi* [Ultra-Orthodox] vote was important for the elections.

Admittedly Joseph, as he explained to Peres, did generously support
several important Ultra-Orthodox institutions in Israel, not all of them
Lubavitcher. He had been doing this for years. And, naturally enough,

he did try to persuade the heads of these same institutions to vote for Netanyahu in the coming election.

> My role was to lobby and explain the concept of *shlemut ha-aretz* [the integrity of the Land of Israel] and the Rebbe's view and why the security of Israel [is endangered]. I lobby that constantly. I can't help it that I have given money to institutions. No one will ever say that I gave them money so that they should vote for Netanyahu. I've never done that, and never will do that. I don't bribe people . . .

There was, in fact, no motive for Joseph to bribe these groups. He had every reason to expect that they would do his bidding — if not out of simple gratitude for his past generosity, then because they would be keeping a prudent weather-eye on the prospect of future largesse. In any case, Joseph says bitterly, 'Shimon Peres, when he accuses someone, he's looking at himself in the mirror.' Pork-barrelling (or whatever the kosher equivalent might be) is part and parcel of Israeli politics — and Peres himself was no more averse to the practice than anyone else.

What Joseph did do, by his own admission, was help bankroll a massive and highly successful propaganda campaign on Netanyahu's behalf, targeted, in the first instance, at religious voters. Contrary to popular assumptions, the Ultra-Orthodox Jews in Israel were not in Netanyahu's pocket. They would certainly not be voting for Peres, but many would be no less reluctant to vote for a man who was not only a secular Zionist but was of dubious moral character, had been thrice married, and publicly admitted to cheating on his third wife. Joseph, as we have seen, conceded that Bibi was not the most God-fearing or morally upright man in the world; but, he pointed out, 'we endorsed him for what he represented, not as an individual'. And it was necessary to persuade other religious voters to do the same. To this end, Joseph compiled a collection of the Rebbe's statements on the integrity of the Land of Israel and 50,000 copies of these were distributed to all the country's leading rabbis, Knesset members, religious journalists and opinion-makers. He argued incessantly that while Netanyahu might not be perfect, he was the best man available to uphold the Rebbe's position on the Land of Israel.

Joseph also worked energetically to persuade the tens of thousands of Russians who had flooded into Israel since the collapse of the Soviet Union, many of whom would be voting for the first time, that Bibi was their man. A few weeks before the election, the mass bar mitzvah ceremony for children of Russian immigrants — which Joseph had been sponsoring each year — took place at the Western (Wailing) Wall in Jerusalem. That year there were over a thousand children taking part, all graduates of the Gutnick Centre that Joseph had established for the education of Russian Jews in Israel. Joseph addressed the gathering, recalling how the Rebbe had predicted the fall of the Soviet Union and the freedom of its Jews — and stressed the Rebbe's concern for the integrity of the Land of Israel. The message was clear. And in the days before the election, Joseph, at the invitation of the local Chabad leadership, helped organise an army of 5000 Israeli Lubavitchers who went from house to house throughout Israel, explaining to the Russians why they should vote for a strong 'nationalist' candidate.

Finally, Joseph made an audacious play for the broader Israeli vote, by helping organise and bankroll the controversial 'Bibi is good for the Jews' advertising blitz. Although it has been widely assumed that it was Joseph who came up with the phrase, this was not strictly accurate. Right-wing strategists were concerned that Israel's 800,000 Arab citizens might determine the outcome of the election in favour of the Left, so decided to run a scare campaign aimed at uncommitted Jewish voters. They went to a public relations professional for help, and it was he who came up with the words, while Joseph helped fund the exercise. The highly contentious slogan was plastered on posters and billboards all around the country in the weeks leading up to the election, and outraged many Israelis who condemned it as discriminatory towards Israel's Arab citizens, if not blatantly racist. Joseph was unrepentant. He categorically denied that the slogan was either racist or discriminatory: 'Our slogan was in no way meant to deride or denigrate the Arabs,' he told the *Australian Jewish News* immediately after the election. 'We happen to believe that Israel is a Jewish state for Jews. We have Arabs living in Israel. They have all their rights, including the right to vote, and they have to be looked after. But it's not an Arab–Israeli country; it's a Jewish country that has Arab citizens.'[14]

Joseph is reluctant to put a figure on what all this had cost him: 'I don't want to talk about it. I assisted in ways that I wanted to.' Reports at the time suggested that he had spent as much as $10 million to get Netanyahu elected — a figure Joseph rejects as absurd. In any case, he argues, money wasn't the issue:

Helping Chabad in Israel — Rabbi Yosef Aronov and his assistant, Rabbi Chaim Yankel Leibovitch — get thousands of Lubavitchers out on the streets was worth more than $10 million. The Likudniks paid $30–40 an hour to guys working for them. We had 5000 Lubavitchers on every corner and street in the country, who voluntarily put in 72 hours' work — 5000 × 72 × 40 is many millions. The voluntary army of Chabad was worth a fortune. More than $10 million. I didn't give anything near $10 million. Hogwash. They thought that 5000 Lubavitchers out on the street, and paid $40 an hour — it was all done voluntarily. We didn't have to pay anything.

◊ ◊ ◊

More than a few people in the Chabad movement were unhappy about what Joseph was doing, and resented the fact that he was getting Israeli Lubavitchers so actively involved in the pro-Netanyahu campaign. The Israeli newspaper *Ha'aretz* reported from New York at the time that rabbis at Lubavitcher headquarters had accused Joseph of 'taking over the movement and trying to impose his own agenda on it', claiming that he was 'behaving as if he is the Rebbe's heir'. As to Joseph's claim to have been delegated by the Rebbe to prevent Israeli territorial concessions, the paper quoted a central figure in the Chabad movement as saying: 'I don't recall the Rebbe ever saying that publicly, and no one who was close to [the Rebbe] recalls ever hearing it.'[15]

Joseph calmly rejects the criticism. He opens his folder, and takes out a note, in the Rebbe's own handwriting, which states quite specifically: '*Harei hu shaliach*' — 'Behold he is my emissary.' The note was written in response to a concern raised by one of the Rebbe's secretaries, Rabbi Benyomin Klein, in 1990, when Joseph was in Israel struggling to save Shamir's government. Awed by the immensity of his responsibility, Joseph was close to exhaustion, and Rabbi Klein was worried about his physical and spiritual health. He brought this to the attention of the Rebbe, and asked for the Rebbe's blessing, that Joseph be granted 'long and good days, rest for his soul and rest for his body, and success (in his mission).' The Rebbe replied: '*Harei hu shaliach, velo efshari chas veshalom ha-nal clal*' — 'Behold he is (my) emissary, and the above [that Joseph appeared to be heading for some kind of breakdown], Heaven forbid, is not possible at all.'

'Do you know how precious this handwriting from the Rebbe is?' Joseph asks. If all he had were those three words — '*Harei hu shaliach*' — it would more than suffice to deflate his most stringent critics.[16] But he has very much more to substantiate his claim. He pulls out another note from the folder, again in the Rebbe's own handwriting. 'I'm writing to the Rebbe, before leaving for Israel,' he explains:

I write: 'I am leaving next Sunday, 25 Nisan 5750 [April 1990]. I request a blessing that I will succeed in my *shlichut* [mission].' The Rebbe replies that

I should ask the *Moetzet Gedolei Hatora* [Council of Ultra-Orthodox Rabbis in Israel] who were against joining the Government — remember I'm asking the top Ultra-Orthodox rabbis in Israel — how many of them are experts in regards to the military dangers to Israel? Secondly, the Rebbe wrote, I should ask them if it were merely a question of their children's health and not *pikuach nefesh* — would they also act in the same manner in which they're acting now? These are two questions he told me to ask them. The Rebbe told me exactly what to ask them. That's his handwriting . . .

So Joseph couldn't care less if people query his mission. 'If I had his handwriting, if I had these instructions, if the Rebbe asked me to ask these two questions? What would you say if you were me? Tell them to jump in the lake!' Most of the criticism directed against him, Joseph argues, has stemmed from simple jealousy:

> You can imagine some of the people in Israel would have been absolutely disgusted that the Rebbe chose me and not them. People who'd worked there for 10 years, 15 years. Comes along a young fellow — how old was I then, 37? — and there I am speaking to the Chief Rabbis of all the Ultra-Orthodox communities and asking them questions on behalf of the Rebbe about their authority to pass judgement on these vital matters in Israel. It was quite an audacity . . . And they couldn't challenge the Rebbe. You can't challenge the Rebbe! I was sent by the Rebbe's Secretariat — here I have the secretaries, both Laibl [Groner] and Benyomin [Klein], who were giving me answers the whole time. How could people possibly query it? Now they query it because the Rebbe's not around!

If any more 'proof' were needed of the validity and authenticity of his mission, Joseph points out the obvious: he had consistently and publicly used the title 'The Lubavitcher Rebbe's Special Emissary for the Integrity of the Land of Israel' ever since he was given his mission in 1990 — long before the Rebbe's debilitating stroke in 1992 and his death two years later — including in articles and interviews which appeared in the official Lubavitch organ, *Kfar Chabad*.

> The Rebbe saw all the articles in *Kfar Chabad* . . . in 1990, 91, 92. Do you think that he wouldn't have objected if I was signing myself as his emissary if I wasn't? That the Rebbe would have let someone, on such an important issue, just walk around and say he's his personal *shaliach*? For three years? *Kfar Chabad* was the official mouthpiece of the Chabad organisation. The Rebbe would read it every single week. So the Rebbe would see all these interviews. If it wasn't the case, the Rebbe wouldn't have objected? He even saw some of those interviews before they were published. And checked

them. I referred to myself as his emissary all the time. Only after the Rebbe died did they start questioning.

For the moment, those challenging Joseph were a small minority, and their criticisms reflected the increasingly bitter power struggle taking place behind the scenes in Lubavitch following the Rebbe's death two years earlier, and he could afford to ignore them.

Whatever the controversy over Joseph's activities in Israel in the weeks before the election, they were certainly effective. The Russian vote went 58–42 to Netanyahu, compared with 60–40 to Rabin when he had run against Shamir four years earlier. And there were record turnouts at the polls in Ultra-Orthodox areas, where voting participation was traditionally low, with the vote going overwhelmingly to Netanyahu. In the end, Netanyahu just got up over Peres, by less than one per cent of the vote. One of Israel's most seasoned political observers, Abraham Rabinovich, writing ten months later in the *Australian,* had no doubt that this was largely due to Joseph's last-ditch efforts to swing the Ultra-Orthodox vote behind the right-wing candidate: 'It was a massive turnout of Ultra-Orthodox Jews that gave Netanyahu his hair's breadth victory,' he wrote — 'and Gutnick was a principal figure behind the mobilisation of that vote.'[17] This was a big call, but Rabinovich was not alone in making it.

Joseph was elated. He had carried out the Rebbe's brief, and Israel now had a right-wing government which he hoped would prove to be strong and which would not give back land. In an interview headlined 'Yossel Gutnick enjoys the sweetest victory of them all', Joseph told the *Australian Jewish News* that, by backing Netanyahu, and being instrumental in his election, he had saved Israel from nothing short of disaster. Under Peres, he said, 'Israel would have faced catastrophe, with a Palestinian state alongside it.'[18]

Stopping Peres from becoming prime minister in 1996, Joseph says, was 'one of the greatest things I've done in my life':

> Peres was a horrific danger . . . He had ideas of grandeur, the Nobel Prize, recognition from the non-Jewish world . . . This fellow, he can't look himself in the mirror and be proud of what his Jewish history is. He believes in a new Middle East. Well I believe in the old Middle East, the history . . . Our friend Shimon Peres doesn't appreciate Jewish history. He wanted to create a New Era in which Jews lose respect for themselves in order to gain the respect of the non-Jewish world . . .

A few months after his victory, in September 1996, Netanyahu acknowledged his political debt to the Rebbe's Special Emissary by accompanying him on a visit to the late Rebbe's grave in New York. Joseph referred to his companion as 'beloved and esteemed Prime Minister', while Netanyahu referred to 'my friend Gutnick' and recalled that the Rebbe 'was a great teacher and a great hero who served as a source of inspiration to me'.[19]

However, the Joseph–Bibi honeymoon began to sour at the beginning of 1997, when Netanyahu was forced to withdraw from eighty per cent of Hebron in the West Bank, reluctantly honouring an agreement concluded by the previous Labour Government. Although the withdrawal from Hebron ran counter to Joseph's expectations that Netanyahu would stand firm, he recognised that the Israeli Prime Minister had little choice, given the great pressure the Americans were exerting on him, but to implement a 'bad agreement' he had inherited. He was bitterly disappointed, and did not conceal this from Netanyahu.

Meanwhile, Joseph continued to help the 450 Jewish settlers who lived among the more than 100,000 Arabs in Hebron. He had already funded several projects in the town, including the Gutnick Centre across the road from the Tomb of the Patriarchs. His latest plan involved building more housing for Jewish settlers — but nothing dramatic or outrageous, Joseph pointed out at the time: 'We are not building thousands of apartments. We are talking about . . . six apartments, 10 apartments, expansions of certain places. I think the world would understand it. I think that the sensible Arab communities would understand it. If you want to survive in Hebron without agitation and confrontation, then both sides should be allowed to expand.'[20] Moreover, Joseph claimed, he was acting as a 'moderating influence' on the Jews in Hebron — 'because they know if they do anything out of line and against the peace process, I'll withdraw my support.'[21]

These explanations did not satisfy Joseph's critics. 'Gutnick, he comes to pass out funds in order to spread evil and hatred,' Shimon Peres (who, it seems, never forgave Joseph for his role in his 1996 defeat) told Israeli university students in February 1997. Joseph, for his part, dismissed Peres's outbursts: 'I think he's probably lost the plot. I respect him as a past Prime Minister of Israel, but this is sour grapes. He hasn't recovered from the loss. I'm sad he has made it a personal issue . . . I think he is just frustrated.'[22] In the final analysis, Joseph says, 'Peres hates my guts.'

The fuss over Hebron eventually died down, and Joseph was

satisfied that there would be no further handing back of land by the Netanyahu government. But a combination of internal squabbles and in-fighting in the governing coalition, unhappiness over Netanyahu's handling of a wide range of important domestic issues, and growing domestic and international pressure to move forward on the peace process eventually took their toll. The crunch came in October 1998, when Netanyahu, under immense pressure from the Americans, was forced to agree to hand a further thirteen per cent of the West Bank over to the Palestinians. Joseph's man had let him down again. 'Bibi is good for the Arabs,' he retorted contemptuously — an ironic para-phrase of the slogan he had abetted for Netanyahu in 1996.[23] The so-called Wye agreement (negotiated at the Wye Plantation in the United States) was also condemned as a 'sell-out' by Netanyahu's right-wing ministers, who refused to endorse it. And in January 1999 his govern-ment finally collapsed.

New elections were called for May 1999, and Joseph had to decide whom he was going to support. Would it be Netanyahu, who had proven to be something of a hollow reed? Or someone more resolute? Benjamin Begin, perhaps — son of Israel's first right-wing prime min-ister, Menachem Begin — who had quit Bibi's government a year earlier, in protest at his capitulation over Hebron? There was little doubt that is who he would have preferred. But he had to be realistic. Begin didn't have a chance; nor did the fire-breathing former general Ariel Sharon, or anyone else on the hard nationalist Right. 'I've got to back a winner,' he told the *Australian Jewish News* soon after a new election was announced. 'It's not Realpolitik' to support anyone else. 'In my mind, there is no one on the right who has the potential to win the election more than Netanyahu.'[24]

So, reluctantly, Joseph once again swung his full weight behind Netanyahu. Only this time, stung by Joseph's stunning effectiveness in getting Bibi across the line in 1996, the Left in Israel mounted an extraordinary vilification campaign against him. A Labour Party spokesman, speaking to the *Sydney Morning Herald*'s Ross Dunn in Jerusalem, went so far as to describe Joseph as 'a lunatic extremist' who had held Netanyahu 'hostage' for three years, forcing him to channel 'hundreds of millions of shekels to Gutnick and his special interests.'[25] The Israeli media had a field day with the story. 'Netanyahu asks, Gutnick pays,' screamed a banner headline in the mass-circulation *Yediot Achronot* tabloid, which ran a major expose accusing Netanyahu and members of his inner staff of receiving money from Joseph for favoured right-wing institutions, private charitable causes, and publicity campaigns in the United States. The paper also charged that, in return, the government would channel a 'large coffer' of funds to Lubavitch institutions in Israel — and that two of Joseph's Lubavitch aides were permanently ensconced in Netanyahu's office, with direct access to the Prime Minister, his daily schedule and senior staff. The Labour Party said it was 'unacceptable that the Prime Minister's Office should become a branch of the Chabad Movement ... or act as a broker of gifts for services rendered', and there were calls for a police investigation into possible breaches of Israel's political party funding laws.

'A lot of hot air, stupid, ridiculous and baseless accusations,' Joseph responded angrily. *Yediot Achronot* was conducting a 'typical left-wing oriented campaign by Mr Netanyahu's political opponents to besmirch the Prime Minister and his wife in every possible way.' Netanyahu's response was even more forthright: 'A load of bullshit,' he said, 'whose sole purpose is to attack me politically. Thousands and thousands of words, personal jibes and defamation, an army of reporters mobilised for [the new Labour leader Ehud] Barak and the Left.' As for the accusations of criminal breaches of the law, Joseph was unperturbed — much as he had been when facing all those probes from the Securities Commission in Australia over the years: 'I am quite happy for the Attorney-General to investigate ... but they won't turn up anything improper about my conduct or relationship with the Prime Minister.'[26] And a few months later it was, in fact, officially announced that Joseph had done nothing untoward and that no further action would be taken.

It was not only the Left that was ganging up on Joseph. No less serious was the unease that his high-profile political activities were causing within Chabad. The Chabad movement had only reluctantly become involved in Israeli politics, traditionally preferring to work at grass-roots level, winning over ordinary Israelis through outreach work rather than trying to influence government directly. By becoming too closely aligned with the right wing — even if the Right was much closer to them ideologically, especially on the question of the Land of Israel — many Lubavitchers feared they were alienating themselves from large sections of Israeli society. Cheerful groups of Lubavitchers had once been a common sight in Israel's army camps and schools, spreading their non-threatening, user-friendly message of joy in Judaism. But now they were seen by many Israelis as members of a fanatical fundamentalist sect bent on wrecking the peace process, and were no longer welcome in many places.

However, as long as Netanyahu was seen to be holding the line on the Land of Israel, members of the Chabad leadership in Israel held their peace. When they began to suspect that Netanyahu was not as resolute as they had been led to believe, and had in fact deceived them, they began to distance themselves — and to attack Joseph for creating an unwelcome political nexus that was doing little to safeguard the integrity of the Land of Israel, while at the same time undermining their outreach efforts by painting Lubavitchers as a bunch of 'radicals' in the public mind.

The bitterness boiled over at the end of 1998. It became clear that Netanyahu would be forced to withdraw from further parts of the Land of Israel, under the terms of the Wye agreement. Posters sprang up in religious neighbourhoods just before Joseph was due to arrive in Israel: 'The imposter, Joseph Gutnick, arrives in Israel . . . to rescue the Netanyahu Government and, at the same time, to try to rescue his collapsing businesses in the forests [*sic*] of Australia,' they read. 'The impudent fellow is again cynically using the name of the Rebbe and besmirching the Chassidim of Chabad . . .'[27] And, in a departure from Lubavitcher custom not to wash its dirty linen in the secular 'Zionist' press, a senior Lubavitcher rabbi told an Israeli newspaper a few months earlier that 'the "Bibi is good for the Jews" campaign and Gutnick are a big punishment that has been decreed in Heaven.' He complained that the Chabad movement had 'lost its standing and direction when it permitted Gutnick to drag it into the political arena'.[28]

Joseph accused his first cousin Meir Gutnick — son of Melbourne's Rabbi Sholem Gutnick, who had made his fortune on Wall Street — of funding the campaign against him. He shrugged off his critics as a 'bunch of radical Messianists', a minority in the movement who did not represent the official position. The official Lubavitcher spokesman in Israel, Joseph insisted, was the secretary general of the Chabad Rabbinical Court in the Holy Land — who, he claimed, fully endorsed the way in which he was carrying out his mission as the Rebbe's Special Emissary. Moreover, Joseph strongly denied that he was in any way compromising Chabad. 'Ever since 1990 until today, I have acted in a private, personal capacity as the Rebbe's special emissary in this matter,' he told *Kfar Chabad*. 'It has nothing at all to do with Chabad. I have never attempted to involve Chabad . . . That was not the mission the Rebbe had entrusted me with, to get Chabad involved . . .'[29]

Joseph did his best to keep Netanyahu in line, berating him both in private and publicly for continuing to implement the Oslo and Wye agreements. Bibi was 'still a prisoner of this historic blunder, shackled to an accord that threatens to drain the lifeblood of Israel,' he wrote in a scathing attack on the Oslo agreement in the *Jerusalem Post*, urging Bibi to 'return to the path of strength, as taught by the Lubavitcher Rebbe'.[30] As for the Wye agreement, 'I believe he made a grave blunder,' Joseph says. 'And I told him, unequivocally.' Netanyahu's reply, he recalls, was that he had no choice: 'This was the only way, otherwise the government would fall . . . If the left got in they'd give away a lot more . . . we'll only give away 50 per cent, or 40 per cent, they'll give away 90 per cent . . . He had all the answers . . .'

Joseph was far from convinced, yet he continued to support Netanyahu. In a January 1999 interview with *Kfar Chabad* he explained his reasons:

> The danger of *pikuach nefesh* that brought about this mission in 1990 has not lessened — it is much more real and apparent than it was then. Today land is being given away in practice . . . There is no doubt that we have to protest with the utmost vehemence against Prime Minister Netanyahu and his government which has given away land and has placed in danger the lives of millions of Jews. But precisely because this is the case, the mission becomes even more urgent, to work for a right-wing government that does not continue to give away land . . .

Hence, he concluded, there was no choice but to continue supporting Netanyahu as the only realistic candidate of the Right, and then to bring every pressure to bear on him once he was returned to office — even if this would not always prove successful.

There is a certain irony in the fact that Joseph was seen and berated — both in Israel and in Australia — as the 'hard-line radical' in the Lubavitcher movement for supporting Netanyahu, while those Lubavitchers who refused to back Bibi tended to be seen as the 'moderates'. From the perspective of the Lubavitcher movement, it is clear that Joseph was the pragmatic 'moderate', prepared to give ground even on matters of highest principle to achieve the best political result possible in any given circumstance, and his opponents in Chabad were the 'hard-line radicals' who would not budge from the fundamentalist 'not an inch' position.

In the event, the debate over whether or not Chabad should support Bibi became academic. Netanyahu lost the May 1999 election in a landslide. Joseph had believed, until the last minute, that he was in with a chance. He was in Israel, keeping his powder dry for when the race for prime minister went to the crucial second round, when he intended to throw his full weight behind Netanyahu in a last minute blitz just as he had done three years earlier.[31] But his man didn't even make it that far, KO'd when three of the five other candidates pulled out, leaving Netanyahu in an unwinnable head-to-head contest with Labour's Ehud Barak. Joseph was bitterly disappointed, and angry with Netanyahu's right-wing colleagues who had pulled the rug out from under him and paved the way for a government of the Left. But he remained stoical. 'I accept the democratic decision of the Israeli people,' he said. As for his future course, it was time to lie low and reassess. 'There is a time to be quiet and a time to act,' he observed, echoing Leviticus. 'Now is not the time to act.'[32]

There should be no illusions, however, that Joseph had abandoned his mission. As he told *Kfar Chabad* a few months earlier, nothing would deter him from carrying out the Rebbe's will:

> I have been entrusted with a clear mission: That there will be a right-wing government, and that this right-wing government will stand firm and will not give away land. This is the goal I have worked for. And this is the goal, with the help of God, I will continue to work to achieve. Sometimes with greater success, sometimes with only partial success. And often there are great disappointments. But that is the mission I have been entrusted with, and I am not permitted, under any circumstances, to abandon it . . . [33]

The Rebbe's Special Emissary for the Integrity of the Land of Israel was not about to give it away. But he was, it seems, taking time out.

A Reluctant Radical

'I'm not really a hardliner. A lot of people think I'm an extremist, but I'm not. You shouldn't get the idea that I'm a belligerent, non-tolerant person.'

Joseph Gutnick to *Age* writer Peter Ellingsen, 12 December 1998

JOSEPH'S ROLE AS the Rebbe's Special Emissary for the Integrity of the Land of Israel has been the cause of great angst and controversy in the Australian Jewish community. Like their co-religionists everywhere, Australian Jews are deeply divided on and very passionate about Israel. There is strong support, especially but not only among religious Jews, for the hard-line position taken by the right wing in Israel. But there is at least equally strong support in the Jewish community for the more conciliatory line taken by the Left. It is difficult to gauge with any degree of accuracy the relative strengths of the two camps — and their battles are waged with equal vigour and passion in the columns of the community newspaper, the *Australian Jewish News*, which sometimes finds itself caught in the cross-fire. So it is hardly surprising that Joseph's high-profile political activities in Israel should generate considerable heat in the community, with his supporters and detractors falling into two predictable camps.

In June 1996, for instance, several readers wrote in to the *Jewish News*, expressing their concern and distress at Joseph's involvement in the electoral process that had brought victory to Binyamin Netanyahu. Many in the Jewish community felt uneasy about Joseph using his wealth to interfere in the electoral process of a country in which he was not a citizen. A few months later, in February 1997, at the time of the furore in Israel over Joseph's support for the Hebron settlers, there was another spate of letters to the paper from both sides of the barricades. Some, from the Right, praised him for his commitment to the settlers, who were seen as the courageous flag-bearers of the Jewish right to the Land of Israel and deserved every support. Others, from the Left, were appalled at his support for people they viewed as dangerous fanatics who were undermining the peace process with the Palestinians — and they resented the impression they felt was being created that Joseph represented the views of most, if not all, Australian Jews. Even the normally mild and conciliatory editor of the *Australian Jewish News* at the time, Sam Lipski, was moved to write an uncharacteristically heated editorial in which he drew a distinction between Joseph's support for Netanyahu in the 1996 election and his support for the Hebron settlers:

> The Gutnick who campaigned for Netanyahu last May was campaigning for a mainstream political candidate for the prime ministership. Agree or disagree with his political orientation, Gutnick was then operating within the broad camp of Israeli and Diaspora Jewish opinion. By contrast, the Gutnick who is now campaigning . . . for the fanatics of Hebron . . . is beating the drum for a handful of discredited and isolated rejectionists. It is the surest way, no matter how much money he pours into Hebron, for Gutnick to lose his influence in the mainstream. For unless he reconsiders and moderates, Gutnick risks putting himself beyond the pale, just as the Hebron zealots are, and deserve to be . . . He must surely know, therefore, that this is not the way. *Lo zu haderech*.[1]

Lipski's editorial deeply offended some of his readers: 'When I read your editorial "Against the Hebronists", I looked to see if it was not a PLO paper I had received by mistake,' wrote one. 'I can see Arafat rubbing his hands in glee.'[2] Another reader made a similar point: 'While reading your editorial . . . I had to stop several times to check whether these were the words of the editor of a Jewish newspaper or whether they were from *Al Aharam*, or some other Arab paper.'[3] Joseph was also stung by Lipski's attack, and demanded, and received, the right of reply in the next issue of the *Jewish News*. Chiding Lipski for passing judgement on the 'idealistic, peace-seeking, God-fearing' Jews of Hebron without ever having met them, and pointing out that he himself had the full support of Prime Minister Netanyahu, he defended his support for the Hebron settlers on political, religious, and compassionate grounds. 'Sorry Sam', he wrote, '*Lo zu haderech*, this is not the way. To write misinformed editorials — not all Hebronites are radicals (guilt by association) . . . Please Sam, a little bit of compassion for our fellow brethren in Hebron. Or are you so full of prejudice like some extreme radicals within the left?'[4]

Joseph had, in fact, long been unhappy with Lipski and the

Australian Jewish News, which had consistently supported the Oslo 'land-for-peace' formula, and had been openly critical of the Netanyahu Government. There had been persistent rumours that he wanted to buy the paper, to make it more 'balanced' on the Israel/Palestine issue. He publicly confirmed this, shortly after Lipski's retirement as editor of the paper in November 1998, in an interview with the *Age*'s Peter Ellingsen:[5] 'If the opportunity came up, I'd buy it and get rid of [acting editor David] Bernstein. I want a more balanced view.'[6] Some saw this as an example of Joseph's intolerance towards anyone in the Jewish community holding views on Israel contrary to his own[7] — a perception Joseph himself did something to create when he 'got rid of' another political dissident, Rabbi Hershy Worch, in a celebrated incident a few years before.

Worch was a strange character, an exotically garbed rabbi who had come to Australia from the United States in 1995 to head Hillel, the organisation catering to the spiritual needs of Jewish tertiary students on campus. Born into an Ultra-Orthodox family in Manchester, England, he eventually became a follower of Rabbi Shlomo Carlebach, who was something of a cult figure among Jewish students in the United States, where he was known as the 'Singing Rabbi'. Worch was no mean singer himself, and Joseph, who was a keen fan of Carlebach's songs, employed him as a part-time cantor in his synagogue at Kimberley Gardens. He had been there only a couple of months when one of Joseph's close political allies, Professor Herman Branover, came out from Israel as Joseph's guest and addressed a public meeting at Kimberley. Worch, who was at the meeting with a group of his Hillel students, took issue with Branover's extreme right-wing views on Israel and the Palestinians, and challenged him openly. Retribution was swift. Joseph fired him from Kimberley. Joseph strongly disputes that he was being either intolerant or mean-spirited in his handling of Worch. He was clearly incensed that a man he had befriended and helped out financially should be so ungracious as to insult his guest in this way:

> Branover may be even further to the Right than me in his views. I don't necessarily agree with everything Professor Branover says . . . But I thought it was offensive in my presence to speak in such a manner . . . It was an evening of myself and Professor Branover, not of Hershy Worch's absurd views . . . I'd like him to be praying for the settlers and for the safekeeping of the Jews in Israel rather than to be praying for the Palestinians who were going to claim their houses back in Haifa . . . It's my own home. I'm entitled

to have in Kimberley, my own Chabad House, my own *shaliach tsibur* [public functionary] representing the Orthodox right-wing people who were there. A cantor has to be acceptable to everyone. He wasn't . . .

Gutsy as he was in taking on Branover, Worch must have known he was courting trouble when he chose to challenge his employer's guest, in front of his employer, at a public forum sponsored by his employer, in his employer's own hotel. It was a classic case of biting the feeding hand.

But that was not the end of the matter. Two years later, when the cash-strapped Hillel organisation was on the point of collapse, Joseph offered to bail it out — provided that the troublesome rabbi was removed as its director. Here again, Joseph fully justifies his action, and rejects charges that he was attempting to stifle dissent:

I didn't think Hershy Worch was the right person . . . I'm entitled to give money to a cause and a person that I believe is right for the job . . . I wasn't forcing him out. All I said was that if they wanted my money, it wasn't going to him. It's not as though I was forcing my candidate on them . . . There are plenty of other wealthy people in the community, and he could have continued.

A few months later Worch, unable to make a living in Melbourne, left for the United States.

Joseph's treatment of Worch remains an isolated incident. And, although he makes no secret of the fact that he would still like to control the *Australian Jewish News* one day if the opportunity arose, he has not done so yet. It is even doubtful whether, if Joseph were to acquire the paper, he would, in fact, turn it into an exclusive, radical mouthpiece for his own Ultra-Orthodox religious and hard-line right-wing political views. He himself is very firm on this:

No, I would be very balanced. I thought that the *Jewish News* was run both by yourself and Sam [Lipski] too much to the Left and not enough representation of the Right. It was not a balanced approach. And if I would get control of the *Jewish News* it would be a balanced newspaper for all Jews in Melbourne. It would be much more balanced. A strong Orthodox point of view, but also a counter view.

That, of course, would remain to be seen. One suspects Joseph is savvy enough to realise that there is only so far he would be able to go without totally destroying whatever credibility the paper might have, and hence its effectiveness, in the broader Jewish community. Why should he, after all, spend millions of dollars on what would end up being little more than just another Lubavitcher newsletter? Unless, as is quite possible, the prime goal were not to influence or shape opinion, but simply to halt the dissemination of all opposing views. Meanwhile, the impression endures in significant sections of the Jewish community, rightly or wrongly, that when it comes to Israel, Joseph has been, and would be, prepared to use his wealth to stifle dissent.

◊ ◊ ◊

In contrast to the Jewish community, the broader Australian community has shown only a passing interest in the activities of the Lubavitcher Rebbe's Special Emissary for the Integrity of the Land of Israel, being far more intrigued by the dramatic business exploits of 'Diamond Joe' and 'Golden Joe' — and the high profile football derring-do of 'Demon Joe'.

There has been the occasional eyebrow raised over some of Joseph's more contentious activities in the Holy Land. 'Imagine the outcry if the Coalition had based its federal election campaign around the slogan "John Howard is good for the Protestants",' John Masanauskas wrote in the *Herald Sun*, referring to Joseph's contentious 'Bibi is good for the Jews' slogan in the 1996 Israeli election. 'Quite rightly, all sorts of groups and individuals would have jumped up and condemned this example of religious discrimination. You could just see former PM Paul Keating, a Catholic, applying the blowtorch to Mr Howard's white, Protestant belly.'[8]

A call by the Palestinian representative in Canberra, Ali Kazak, on the Australian Government to intervene and stop one of its citizens from 'undermining the peace process' through his activities in Hebron also got a fair run in the Australian media at about this time. Joseph responded by noting that he was acting neither against the law nor against the wishes of the elected government in Israel in supporting the Hebron settlers. 'The Israeli Prime Minister believes in the rights of the Jewish people to live there,' he said, 'and he wants me to help them. I will not do anything in Hebron without the Israeli Government's approval.'[9]

Nor, moreover, was he acting against the law, the interests, or the spirit of multicultural Australia: 'You don't tell Greeks not to send money to Greece,' he pointed out. 'I've earned this money and I've got a right to give it away ... But if the Australian Government tells me not to give money to Hebron, I won't, because I live in Australia, and I abide by the rules.'[10] And the Australian Government agreed: 'Mr Gutnick is a private Australian citizen,' Prime Minister Howard told

Channel Nine's *Sunday* program. 'It is his decision where and how he spends his money. He is breaking no law.' The Foreign Minister, Alexander Downer, made a similar statement in Parliament, following a formal complaint by Kazak.

Few Australians, in fact, appear overly concerned that a fellow Australian citizen has been engaged so energetically in the politics of a small Middle Eastern country thousands of miles away on the other side of the world. This is, after all, just another aspect of turn of the century multicultural Australia, where millions of citizens maintain strong emotional and other sorts of ties with the countries of their forebears.

Joseph, for his part, has pointed out on numerous occasions that it is largely because there is a strong, sovereign Jewish state in Israel that Jewish Australians like himself can feel secure and confident in Australia, in a way they might not otherwise have done: 'We stand up and voice our opinions. I suppose I wouldn't have this pride if the state of Israel today wouldn't exist,' he told the *Sunday Age*'s Larry Schwartz on 3 November 1996. Joseph wasn't yet born when Israel was created in 1948. But what he calls the proudest moment in his life as a Jew was in July 1976, when a crack Israeli swat-team led by Binyamin Netanyahu's brother Yonathan flew over 5000 kilometres to Entebbe in Uganda and rescued dozens of Jewish hostages held by Palestinian terrorists on a hijacked Air France airliner.

> The fact that Jews were being persecuted and under siege in Uganda, and Jewish soldiers could fly in a plane and save them in such a miraculous way — it was a great moment in Jewish history . . . Here was a far-flung corner in Africa, where we could send our army and save Jewish lives. The only reason they had been attacked was because they were Jews. . . . Here was a moment when Jews could take up weapons. It was like the Hasmoneans against the Romans, like the fighters in the Warsaw Ghetto. Jews taking up arms to defend themselves.

It was from this perspective — somewhat bizarrely — that, in May 1998, Joseph responded to former Australian cricketer David Hookes's ill-considered warning that members of the Melbourne Football Club should 'beware of the Jew bearing gifts'. Joseph, who had pumped almost $3 million into the club since becoming its president in late 1996, was outraged: 'We have our own army and we have our own country and we have nuclear weaponry and we won't take any of this rubbish any more,' he told broadcaster Neil Mitchell in an angry interview on Melbourne's Radio 3AW. He was undoubtedly over-reacting somewhat, not to say committing an indiscretion by publicly revealing Israel's nuclear secrets (the Jewish state had not yet owned up to having nuclear bombs!). But Hookes promptly apologised. (See Chapter 13.)

Joseph had once considered actually moving to Israel, or at least dividing his time between Australia and Israel, and had even thought of broaching the idea with the Rebbe. This was in 1992, shortly before the Rebbe suffered his stroke. Joseph was in New York at the time, and had lined up, with thousands of others, for the precious Sunday morning dollar.

> I'd been thinking about it for months, living part of the time in Israel and part in Australia . . . I feel guilty about it, a lot of times, why I'm so involved in Israeli politics, and here I am living in Australia. But past [Israeli] prime ministers who have met with me say: 'Joseph, you stay in Australia, you can do a lot more by being successful in Australia and giving money to Israel. So they don't want to encourage me to go to Israel.' But I myself wanted to. I remember thinking about it when I lined up for the dollars . . . I went by, and the Rebbe gave me a look and said: 'Here's an extra dollar for all of Australia.' So I thought to myself: 'Just forget it Joseph, the Rebbe would give you a dirty look if you said you wanted to go and live in Israel.' He had encouraged me to explore here, and he always used to give me two dollars: 'This is for your family, this is for Australia.' He didn't give me a dollar and say, 'here's for Israel'. He gave me a dollar, 'here's for Australia'. So my place is in Australia . . .

At the end of the day, Joseph has always made it plain that, for all his political involvement in Israel, his great pride in the Jewish state, and even his hankering to spend more time there, he is a loyal Australian, and he still calls Australia home.

> I'm a proud Australian. I love it. I was born here. I'm president of the Melbourne Football Club. There's all this happening with my mining in Western Australia. It's exciting . . . Our homeland is in Israel, that's where the Temple was. We hope that the Messiah will come and we'll go and live in Israel. But I live here. I'm grateful to Australia, I'm an Australian, my loyalties are to Australia. And I don't see any conflict or contradiction between my citizenship in Australia and my love for Israel, my spiritual home . . .

Nor, it seems, do most Australians.

If there is one thing about his political activity in Israel that Joseph is touchy about, it is the perception — especially in the wider Australian community — that he is a political extremist. In his December 1998 interview with Peter Ellingsen, he initially described himself as a 'hardline right-winger'.[11] But he was clearly uneasy with this, and a few days later, he called Ellingsen back to say: 'I'm not really a hard-liner. A lot of people think I'm an extremist, but I'm not. You shouldn't get the idea that I'm a belligerent, non-tolerant person.' Ellingsen took this on board, but with something of a raised eyebrow. He noted that Joseph had answered his question 'How many Palestinians are there in Israel?' with a flip but non-too-tolerant: 'Too many!' And when asked about the Gypsies, who, like the Jews, had been the target of Hitler's extermination program in Europe, he replied: 'We have a message for the world. I don't know what message the Gypsies have.' As Ellingsen went on to note, this was 'a pretty unforgiving line'.

Joseph claims that both the statements cited by Ellingsen were 'taken out of context', and had been given an edge he had not intended. 'I would never condone the horrors and the brutality inflicted by the Nazi regime on any human being,' he says. 'It is quite false to infer that I do.' But it should be recognised, nonetheless, that Joseph does come from a 'pretty unforgiving' religious tradition, going back thousands of years, and his views ought perhaps to be seen in that context. This is a tradition that insists God gave the Land of Israel to the Jews as their exclusive and inalienable birthright, leaving little room for compassion for anyone else who happened to be living there before or since. Thus, for example, God tells the ancient Hebrews as they are about to enter a Canaan already inhabited by other nations: 'Of the cities of these peoples, which the Lord thy God gives thee for an inheritance, thou shalt save nothing alive that breathes; but thou shalt utterly destroy them' (Deuteronomy 20:16–18). The biblical book of Joshua is, essentially, a chronicle of divinely ordered 'ethnic cleansing' of the Promised Land. Joseph acknowledges that this might be seen, by non-believers, to be a 'barbaric edict'. But, he explains:

> We believe that this was given from God, and given by the Torah, which is divinely inspired. So therefore I don't question it. But it's not a problem that I face today. It is something I have to explain in the past. It's not like the fundamentalists in Iran today who are saying 'kill the Americans' and 'kill the Israelis' because they believe that Muhammad has told them to do it, in the name of religion.

There are, however, religious Jews who have no qualms at all about applying the same harsh fundamentalist logic to present-day Arabs living in Israel. The late, unlamented Rabbi Meir Kahane, for instance — an American right-wing religious extremist (not, however, a Lubavitcher) who established the virulently anti-Arab 'Kach' party in Israel. 'There is no such thing as an Arab village in the Land of Israel,' he once said during an infamous visit to the Israeli–Arab village of Umm Fahm — 'only a Jewish village temporarily inhabited by Arabs.' Joseph, of course, is no Meir Kahane, who was not averse to advocating and even using violence to 'cleanse' modern-day Israel of its Arab inhabitants. But, like Kahane, he too would prefer to see the Palestinians living in one or another of the surrounding Arab countries. They are, Joseph believes, 'part of the Arab world', and have no place in the Land of Israel. 'They've got Saudi Arabia, Egypt, Jordan, Turkey, Syria, Iran, Iraq. They've got their — United Emirates, Morocco — they've got their states. There's this one little bit of land. It's a Jewish state . . . It's ours. We were there. God gave it to us . . .' He recalls a program about Hebron shown on Australian television in 1997, in which an Arab resident of the city says: 'Tell Mr Gutnick to come and see how we live in Hebron, and he'll understand why we're complaining.' But, Joseph retorts, 'Who says he should live in Hebron? Let him go and live in [the Jordanian capital] Amman. It's our homeland . . . We should look after them [the Palestinians]. They should be compensated, financially. But you can't have [both of us] living in the same home.' He elaborates:

> I say the Land of Israel is ours, but I want the Palestinians to have a good life. And they deserve a good life. But not at our expense . . . The Arabs, Hamas, say kill, destroy all the Jews. Throw them into the sea. Kill them all. I'm not saying that about the Palestinians. I'm not saying kill the Arabs, God forbid. I wish them well. But it's a big problem. A big problem for our survival. We've got no choice. You can't expel them now. You could have expelled them in 1967 . . . But that's history. You can't change history . . .

Meanwhile, Joseph insists, the Arabs in the Land of Israel have to be treated 'with respect'. They, for their part, 'have to understand that this is a *Jewish* homeland. It's not an Arab–Israeli state . . . Just as Egypt is an Egyptian–Arab country where Jews can live if they want to, so Israel is a Jewish state where Arabs can live if they want to and follow the law of the land.' And woe betide any Palestinian who sought to challenge the Jews' eternal, exclusive right to the Land of Israel, by word or by deed. Any concession on this issue, Joseph once wrote, citing the Rebbe, 'would be interpreted as a sign of weakness. Instead of being accepted as overtures towards co-operation, they would invite more rigid demands and more violence'. It is only 'unflinching resolve, expressed by a clear declaration — backed by deed — that *Eretz Yisrael* [the Land of Israel] belongs to *Am Yisrael* [the People of Israel]' that would persuade the Arabs of the righteousness of the Jews' cause, Joseph wrote in an article in the *Australian Jewish News*. 'When the Arabs see firm determination, they will respect it . . . Once they realise that the Jews do not accept the possibility of territorial compromise, it will cease to be a relevant aspect of any negotiations.'[12]

These are unquestioningly hard-line positions. Joseph acknowledges this, noting he has questioned them himself on occasion: 'I have had my doubts, from time to time. You think, from time to time, that the peace process is great, isn't it? . . . Everyone thinks, even a hard-liner like myself, that maybe this is the way, this will lead to peace and utopia will come.' And when Israeli Prime Minister Yitzhak Shamir was coming under immense domestic and international pressure to make concessions to the Syrians and the Palestinians in the early 1990s, Joseph recalls, he went so far as to try to persuade the Rebbe to soften his position, to give peace a chance. 'I copped it once or twice for that — probably the only time I ever copped it from the Rebbe':

'Maybe we should compromise,' I told him. 'Maybe it will help the situation.' . . . And the Rebbe replied: 'How can you suggest such a thing to me? After 40 years, that's all I've been saying, it will endanger the security of all the Jews living in Israel, and every concession leads to another concession! How could such a possibility even enter your mind?'

Ultimately, Joseph points out, whatever he himself might think is of little importance:

The Rebbe is a lot wiser than me . . . What do you say about a prophet? He sees. He sees beyond what I see . . . I would probably be, as an individual, more compromising and more moderate. But I'm representing the Rebbe. I'm not representing what I might think. And the Rebbe's views were hard-line. Any compromise leads to another compromise. I'm a businessman, I compromise . . . I'm a risk-taker. Let's give away a little bit of land. But that's Joseph Gutnick. Not the view of the Torah, not the view of the Rebbe.

The only reason, in fact, that he has had the audacity to participate in the Israeli political debate at all, Joseph argues, is because he represented the Rebbe:

Otherwise I wouldn't have the chutzpah [audacity] to stand up to a man like [Israel's Labour leader Ehud] Barak. He was the Chief of Staff of the

Israeli Army, who was prepared to give his life for Israel. What have I given? A bit of money? But the Rebbe does have the right. The Rebbe was a Jewish leader, who sent his people to Israel, who sent his people to the army. In the 1967 Six Day War he told people not to leave Israel. During the 1991 Gulf War he told people to go to Israel. He was a fighter for Israel. And I represent him.

In taking on his mission as the Rebbe's Special Emissary for the Integrity of the Land of Israel, Joseph concludes, 'I took on the Rebbe's hard-line view.' And it was an extremely hard-line view. 'Rabbi Schneerson was an extreme right-winger and he had a tremendous influence,' according to one of Israel's leading authorities on Ultra-Orthodox Judaism, Professor Menachem Friedman of the religiously oriented Bar-Ilan University. Joseph, he noted, was 'continuing Schneerson's efforts with other means — money'.[13]

Fortunately, the Rebbe confined his political instructions to the Land of Israel, and Joseph's more moderate instincts were able to be given much freer rein when it came to politics in Australia, where his liberal stance on the Aborigines stands in stark contrast to his hard line on the Palestinians. He broke ranks with his fellow miners at the end of 1997, for instance, refusing to be part of an industry 'bully' campaign in support of the Howard Government's Wik Bill, which all but extinguished Aboriginal land rights in Australia. 'I will not take part in bullying Aborigines, even if it affects my business,' he proclaimed. It was 'no use big business coming out, slamming their foot on the ground, and trying to bully a resolution,' he said, and called for a negotiated compromise on native title: 'Not everyone will be 100 per cent happy, but we must make sure that the Aboriginal interests are taken care of.'[14]

In explaining his position on Aboriginal land rights, Joseph stressed that, because he was a Jew, he was especially sensitive to the rights of minority groups. 'We Jews are a minority in Australia and Australia has looked after the rights of minority groups such as the Jews, the Greeks and Italians. Aboriginals also have rights, and I believe their rights too have to be looked at and considered. I can feel for them and I believe we have to listen to them.'[15] So strongly did he feel on this issue that he even threatened to withdraw his financial support for the Liberal Party (he had donated $150,000 to the Liberals in 1996) if it refused to compromise on the Aboriginal land rights issue and insisted on forcing a double dissolution over its controversial Wik legislation which sought to curtail those rights severely. 'Even though I am a

staunch Liberal supporter, I wouldn't like it to come to a double dissolution because it would put a lot of people in a very strange position,'
he told the *Age* in December 1997. 'I would have a very difficult moral
decision to make . . . Wik is a very strong moral issue.'[16] In the event,
there was no double dissolution over Wik after the government struck
a compromise with Tasmanian Independent Senator Brian Harradine.
Joseph did, however, withdraw his support for the Liberals nine
months later, in response to what he saw as the Howard Government's
'wishy-washy' handling of Pauline Hanson and her racist One Nation
Party. 'I will be significantly increasing my support for the Labor Party,'
Joseph announced in September 1998. 'As a Jew, from a minority
group, and knowing the damage Hanson has caused overseas and in
the general view of Australia, this is the most important issue to me,'
he said.[17]

Inevitably, Joseph found himself open to charges of hypocrisy, of
applying double standards when it came to Aboriginal rights in
Australia and Palestinian rights in Israel/Palestine. 'Congratulations
Joseph Gutnick for refusing to sign a statement supporting the Native
Title Amendment Bill,' an *Age* reader wrote in a letter to the editor
after he had broken ranks with the miners: 'You are a good man.' This
elicited a response from another reader a couple of days later, charging
that the first correspondent 'does not know that Joseph Gutnick is
personally responsible for dispossessing aboriginal Palestinians of their
land now. He is a bad man.' About a year later, yet another *Age* reader
asked: 'If Aborigines make a land claim on one of Joseph Gutnick's
gold mines, will he send in troops and bulldoze their houses, as Israelis
do to Palestinians? . . . Gutnick wants freedom from intolerance in
Australia, but freedom for intolerance in Israel. It took us more than
200 years to have a National Sorry Day. How long will it take Israel?'[18]

Joseph bristles at such criticism, and refuses to accept that the situation of the Aborigines and that of the Palestinians are in any way
comparable:

> The Aborigines don't threaten and blow up people at Flinders Street
> Station. They fight for their rights democratically. There are discussions.
> They get aid. We look at ways of educating them. We look at ways of rec-
> onciliation, and I'm in the forefront of those who think the Prime Minister
> should say sorry . . . There's no question of land, and there's no question
> of rights . . . Their problem is that they don't turn up to school, and they're
> not educated properly. But, in my football, I love [Aboriginal players]
> Jeffrey Farmer and Scott Chisholm. They're part of the team. I don't look

at their colour, I look at whether they're good footballers or not. They can integrate into society, and they can have their customs and we can have our customs . . .

The Israeli–Arab conflict, he points out, is an entirely different matter:

It's gone on for thousands of years. We're talking about Jerusalem. We're talking about major religions in the world. We're talking about disputes that have haunted mankind in the past, and will haunt mankind into the future, for eternity. About who have got the rights to Jerusalem, who have got rights to the Land of Israel. This didn't start today. It's been going on for thousands of years . . . In the end you're talking about religions, and you're talking about life and death. If you lower your guard in Israel, Arafat says in the mosques 'let's throw them all into the sea, let's kill them all.' You haven't got Aborigines coming and saying we're going to kill Joseph Gutnick, or we're going to kill John Howard. It's a different type of battle. Here you're talking about a religious battle, and another Holocaust, God forbid. The Arabs want to wipe Israel off the planet . . .

Joseph's political mindset, certainly when it comes to domestic Australian politics, appears to be a rather old-fashioned mixture of 'small-l' liberalism and enlightened self-interest — what, in more colonial times and places, used to be called 'paternalism'. As long as the 'natives' behaved themselves — refrained from throwing bombs and killing innocent people in pursuit of their political goals — they could expect to be treated decently, and even generously. Thus, Joseph had managed to resolve a sensitive Aboriginal land-rights claim over his $250 million nickel project at Cawse in Western Australia by negotiating what he believed to be a generous and enlightened settlement with the original owners that involved money, educational scholarships and jobs. When it comes to Israel and the Palestinians, though, it seems that the ultimate determinant has not been Joseph's well-meaning paternalism, as has been the case with the Aborigines, but rather his hard-line brand of right-wing Zionist nationalism coupled — courtesy of the Rebbe — with a strong fundamentalist religious commitment to the Land of Israel. And the Palestinians, for their part, have consistently spurned the kind of paternalistic generosity the Aborigines have been prepared to accept in Australia. They have responded to the challenge of the Jewish return to the Land of Israel with a nationalism of their own that is often no less uncompromising than Joseph's — and, in the case of the Hamas rejectionists, with a religious fundamentalism that is no less rigorous, and a great deal more violent, than the Rebbe's.

Joseph does concede that, at some distant point in the future (in 50 or even 100 years, when the Arabs might finally have abandoned what he sees as their genocidal designs against Israel and the Jews), the Palestinians might conceivably have some of their political aspirations met in part of the Land of Israel. Even the Rebbe did not rule this out, he says — if it could be demonstrated, beyond all doubt, that such a solution would not endanger Israel and would save Jewish lives. 'The Rebbe's position was not based on the sanctity of the Land of Israel,' Joseph claims. 'He never said keep Judea and Samaria because it's Greater Israel. He said keep Judea and Samaria because those are more secure borders.' But while he acknowledged that, according to Jewish religious law (*Halachah*), the sanctity of life (*pikuach nefesh*) took precedence even over the integrity of the Land of Israel, the Rebbe made it clear that there would have to be a unanimous and unambiguous assessment by all the top army generals, devoid of all political considerations or any outside pressure, that giving back parts of the Land of Israel would indeed save Jewish lives. In the absence of such certitude — which would be a miracle if it were ever to eventuate, and which, as Joseph points out, 'is all theoretical' anyway — maintaining the integrity of the Land of Israel must be paramount.

That was Joseph's mission, as the Rebbe's special emissary. But it was a mission that looked increasingly impossible and increasingly irrelevant as the Israelis themselves moved into the new millennium with a centre-left government which did appear ready to take the kinds of risks the Rebbe had forbidden, and to trade parts of the Land of Israel in return for the chance of peace. 'We sort of lost the battle for *shlemut ha'aretz* [the integrity of the Land of Israel],' Joseph concedes. 'Although I'll still carry, wave the flag . . .'

Diamond Joe

'We will find a diamond mine because I am confident the Rebbe's prophesy will come true. There won't be a stone unturned . . . '

Joseph Gutnick on *Four Corners*, ABC TV, 25 May 1993

JOSEPH BECAME VERY excited in April 1991. The cause of his excitement was the discovery of a tiny sliver of highly compressed carbon the size of a flea's egg, so small that it could only be seen under a powerful microscope. It was a micro diamond, found embedded in a rock in the same Plutonic–Marymia region 830 kilometres north-east of Perth where Joseph had made his first major gold strike two years earlier. 'It could be a beauty,' he said in announcing the discovery — which, he later revealed, had occurred almost by accident. After making the Plutonic find in 1989, Joseph's Great Central Mines had taken out further land around the area with the intention of looking for gold deposits and had stumbled, quite by chance, on what he now hoped would turn out to be a major diamond region. The fact that the microscopic sliver, measuring no more than 350 by 530 microns, was embedded in rock rather than found in an alluvial stream meant that they were exploring in the source area — an area, what's more, where Great Central Mines had tied up some eighty per cent of the exploring rights. And adding further sparkle to the find, as well as further grounds for Joseph's enthusiasm, was the fact that he had struck a joint-venture deal with international diamond giant De Beers to press ahead with the exploration. Under the deal, De Beers's Australian exploration subsidiary, Stockdale Prospecting Ltd, had the option of earning a fifty-one per cent interest in Great Central's Nabberu tenements. 'If we can find [diamonds] in commercial quantities De Beers will back us,' he announced. 'That's the agreement.'[1] By December 1991, after further promising exploration, Great Central and Stockdale had declared the discovery of a major new kimberlite province extending 120 kilometres along the northern margin of the Yilgarn Craton.

If Joseph was excited by the discovery of this microscopic 'flea's egg' in the northern deserts of Western Australia, the stock market remained unmoved. Great Central shares remained static, and untraded, at about $6. The press was a little more enthusiastic, but not much. 'Sharemarket boom entrepreneur Mr Joseph "The Man with the Midas Touch" Gutnick may have to change his nickname to "Diamond Joe",' one commentator, Ian McIlwraith, wrote in the *Financial Review*[2] — if, that is, the discovery were to be supported by further exploration. The *Sydney Morning Herald* ran a very big caricature of a grinning Joseph peering through a microscope, accompanied by a very short article under a large headline: 'Joe sees stars shining in a flea's egg.'[3] While the author of the article, Bruce Hextall, was not exactly blown away by news of the find, he did draw attention to something significant: that Joseph believed not just luck, but 'a measure of divine providence' may also have been involved. 'There's no doubt about it, we have been lucky,' Joseph was quoted as saying, adding cryptically: 'but I would like to think there's more to it than that.' This was probably the first time Joseph had publicly hinted, however obliquely, that his enthusiasm as an explorer in his post-1987 reincarnation was driven more by his faith in the Lubavitcher Rebbe in New York than by rational geological analysis.

◊ ◊ ◊

Joseph had, by this time, come to rely heavily on the Rebbe for encouragement, inspiration and even direction in his business activities. This started, as we saw, in May 1987, when he had taken the Rebbe's advice over that of his business guru, Larry Adler, concerning the sale of Centaur. And his dependence on the Rebbe became even more pronounced after the 1987 stock market crash, when the two discussed every detail of Joseph's business in a unique weekly correspondence. Every word, every sign, every blessing Joseph received from the Rebbe was holy — even the brief exchanges he had with him at his Sunday morning 'dollars' ceremonies at Crown Heights. Joseph had dozens of these encounters with the Rebbe, and he has many of them recorded on video. It is illuminating to spend half an hour with Joseph, watching those clips, seeing his reaction and listening to his comments, as the Rebbe speaks to him and to others, about the gold and the diamonds awaiting him in the bowels of the earth:

18 November 1990. This is a very important one now . . . '*Nicht papiereneh gelt, goldeneh gelt.*' He's talking to Professor Branover. You hear: 'It's waiting, gold in the sockets of the earth — not paper money, gold money' . . . I'll let you hear it again. I'd like to hear it again also . . . He says: 'I have faith, I don't know about him.' He says: 'For me is waiting the money, the gold in the ground. Make sure that I continue to drill' . . . It's the first time he ever said it so clear like that! I'd like to see that again. 'Make sure he keeps on drilling', the Rebbe tells him. 'I have faith. Gold is ready for him' . . .

There's my mother. She's asking that 'Joseph will find gold, and a blessing for me and my husband that we'll be spared for our old age' . . .

Here's Levi Mochkin. They're talking about me. . . . The Rebbe's saying, 'I hope he'll have good news. A day earlier or a day later. And the time when he has good news it will be big news . . . I hope that he'll find gold or diamonds. Whatever way it is he will find a big expansion in his business and his shares and there'll be good news' . . . That was in 1991. That's the first time diamonds are mentioned. Now listen, you'll hear the Rebbe say *avanim tovos* [literally 'good stones' in Hebrew]; he says diamonds. Listen. He's smiling. Did you see he said it: 'He should have *parnosseh* [a livelihood]. I don't know what he'll find, gold or diamonds.' Gold or diamonds. The first time he's mentioned the word diamonds . . .

2 June 1991. The Rebbe is saying: 'A blessing for all of Australia. This is for finding all types of gem quality diamonds.'

9 June 1991. Here I'm with the Rebbe. 'Keep searching. Not just for diamonds, but also for gold,' he says. [Gives two dollars.] That's for finding gold, that's for finding diamonds . . .

16 June 1991. The Rebbe is telling me: 'You're probably preparing to be a High Priest as well. Every Jew has got the ability to be a High Priest. You don't have to know all the explanations, you're going to find it. Find not only gold, but also diamonds.'

Most poignant of all is the clip of Joseph's last encounter with the Rebbe. This was early in 1994, a few months before the Rebbe's death, on 12 June. He had not been seen in public since his massive stroke two years before. He was seated behind a table, with his hand propped up in front of him. 'They say he was blind by then,' Joseph observes. One of his secretaries placed dollar bills between the Rebbe's all but lifeless fingers as his followers filed past to receive their last precious relic. It's an excruciating parody of the 'dollars' ceremony, and painful to watch. Then Joseph's turn comes. The Rebbe nods. Joseph stares intently at the Rebbe and asks that he should 'have success in my search for gold and diamonds.' The Rebbe gives an all but imperceptible second nod. 'You see, he nodded his head!' Joseph enthuses. 'He nodded twice!' He is absolutely convinced that the Rebbe had recognised him, had registered his words, and had given his blessing.

These are the precious words, blessings and gestures from the Rebbe which, Joseph believes, are behind his success and, he says, will continue to inspire him to look for the Rebbe's gold and diamonds for the rest of his life. They are augmented by literally thousands of written comments and even specific instructions from the Rebbe about how to go about his business. On 25 October 1991, for example, Joseph wrote to the Rebbe that Ed Eshuys had found diamond traces 'in a sheet area where water runs in a wide sheet rather than a narrow stream only after it rains'. The word *rain* appears to have excited the Rebbe. Joseph opens the folder containing the Rebbe's original handwritten responses:

> Here's the Rebbe's handwriting. The Rebbe wrote, in Hebrew, 'after it rains' and that's his arrow. That's the important thing, after it rains. Earlier on, he writes: 'Here it's written about rain . . . Maybe that will help, make it easier to find *avanim tovos* [diamonds] and *zahav* [gold].' He kept on saying this . . . He asked me to ask the geologists if the rain helps, and I wrote back to the Rebbe, that if the diamonds are on the surface it makes it easier because it washes off the diamonds. But if they're further down it makes no difference. So the Rebbe's response is: 'Don't they know that the diamonds are on the surface, and not deeper down?' So when we find, it's going to be easy. . . . Here it is again. Look how many times he's marked it.

Joseph even wrote to the Rebbe, on 20 February 1992, seeking his advice, and his blessing, in his negotiations with De Beers over the Nabberu find:

> I wrote that I was going to say to De Beers tomorrow that we're serious, that they should buy 10–20 per cent of each of the companies . . . and that when we find economic [diamond-bearing] pipes they should give us $1 billion in advance for the sales and also for every year after that, five years, $1 billion each year. We wanted immediate development of the ground, otherwise I'll go to . . . I was also going to propose they give us $15 million in advance and it's obvious I won't make a partnership with them and I won't give up my control. And I asked the Rebbe's blessing if what I'm writing there is the right way, or if I'm being totally absurd.

In his reply, the Rebbe instructed Joseph not to go into a partnership with De Beers, although he did not rule out collaboration with them, and predicted that Joseph would find gold and diamond deposits 'bigger than South Africa'.

What the Rebbe did *not* do was tell Joseph precisely where to search for the gold and diamonds, or how to go about finding them. Not that Joseph didn't ask him. 'But he always told me to rely on the experts when I asked him questions where to drill, what to drill . . .' Joseph explains. The Rebbe had actually met Joseph's leading expert, his exploration chief Ed Eshuys, who is not Jewish; Joseph had brought him along to one of the Sunday 'dollars', in January 1991. The encounter is captured on one of Joseph's videos:

Joseph, to the Rebbe: 'This is Ed Eshuys. He's our senior geologist.'

The Rebbe (in English): 'He searches for you?'

Joseph: 'Yes.'

Eshuys (opening a map): 'This is a map of Western Australia. Plutonic is there. Here is Argyle, which is the largest diamond mine in the world. Here is Kalgoorlie, which is one of the big gold mines . . .'

The Rebbe: 'Kalgoorlie's for the gold, or the diamonds?'

Eshuys: 'Kalgoorlie's for gold . . . We're looking in the right area . . . [spreads out another map] Here's a plan that shows all our areas. Plutonic is the big gold discovery that we made two years ago. We are now finding gold here, and are looking for a lot more. We're finding diamonds through here, and we're hoping to find gold up through there.'

The Rebbe: 'That means that you have two places where you are searching for gold, and one place for searching for diamonds?'

Eshuys: 'Yes. Thank you.'

The Rebbe's secretary: 'You must take these dollars and put them in these three places.'

The Rebbe (to Eshuys): 'May you have good news, and success even if you are working for other people also . . .'

It is clear from this exchange that the Rebbe, while giving his blessing to Eshuys, has deferred entirely to the geologist's expertise. And, Joseph insists, 'any statements I make about exploration or results or mining or production are all based on expert advice and professional commentary.' Paradoxically, while Joseph was prepared to invest huge sums of money in the most modern exploration techniques, and to use the skills of the best and most innovative geologists he could find, it was still the Rebbe's word that counted when the chips were down. 'If there's anyone who I'd follow whether it's a geologist or the Rebbe,' Joseph once said when asked about the Rebbe's predictions, 'I'd follow first the Rebbe.'[4] Even Ed Eshuys, the man most closely identified with his mining success over the years, was seen by Joseph to be just a bit player in a much bigger drama where the Rebbe had star billing. The Rebbe 'has certain divine powers as you could say comparable to the prophets of old. He is able to see things we can't see.' It is not easy for non-believers to understand, or accept, this kind of faith. For someone like Joseph, as he was increasingly to demonstrate, it came quite naturally. 'It is not blind faith,' he insisted, 'it's heeding the advice of a very righteous man, a very responsible man.' The Rebbe was respected across the world, Joseph pointed out — and 'he hasn't gained that respect because of irresponsible statements, he makes very responsible statements.'[5]

It was to be another two years, however, before market analysts, investors or the press were seriously to consider the 'Rebbe factor' in Joseph's quest for diamonds in Western Australia. And Joseph, apart from the cryptic reference to the possibility of 'divine providence' in Hextall's *Sydney Morning Herald* article, was not inclined to draw public attention to it. There can be little doubt, nevertheless, that it was both the prime motivating factor behind his relentless search for diamonds, and the reason for the immense importance he was to attach to even the most minor or insignificant discovery.

◊ ◊ ◊

After its initial flurry of curiosity the press soon lost interest in Joseph's diamond activities, shifting its attention, as we shall see, to his far more promising gold exploration at Bronzewing. But Joseph was encouraged. He saw the find as the first concrete sign that the Rebbe's prediction about the diamonds was on track. He pressed ahead with his search in co-operation with De Beers, working closely with its Australian exploration arm, Stockdale Prospecting. There were several more minor finds in the Nabberu area, which were briefly reported in the media. And from time to time these would cause a bit of a stir on the stock market, precipitating an occasional 'please explain' from the Stock Exchange. Joseph, it seems, was finding it hard to shake his pre-crash reputation for 'mining the market' rather than the ground.

In November 1991, for instance, after a three-millimetre 'macro diamond' was found on one of Great Central's leases (Two Pools), there was a run on the prices of several Gutnick companies which had adjacent leases — the so-called 'proximity effect'. There was a query from the ASX, but Joseph denied the run was evidence that he had returned to his old ways. 'I have been a good boy since 1987,' he insisted.[6]

The ASX wasn't convinced. Two months later a report that Great Central had found weathered kimberlite bodies in one of its leases — a promising sign of diamonds — led to another dramatic rise in the share price of several of Joseph's companies, again earning him a query from the Stock Exchange. He was also the subject of a critical article in the *Sydney Morning Herald*, noting that the share prices of at least three of his companies had doubled in just four trading days, and that he was now bestriding a stable of companies capitalised at almost $500 million on the share market. The article was accompanied by an enormous caricature of Joseph sporting a grotesquely large beard with its fringes woven into dollar signs.[7] Meanwhile, a spokesman for the ASX said he was 'very concerned' about the rapid and unexplained escalation in the prices of Joseph's companies, and was particularly worried that small shareholders might get caught up in the excitement. Joseph could not give any specific explanation for the rises, suggesting that the market had probably reassessed the area around Great Central's tenements as a 'major diamond kimberlitic province'. He also strongly denied that he or anyone associated with him had bought or sold any shares in any of the companies concerned. 'That was a pre-1989 phenomenon,' he said.[8]

At about this time Joseph began to woo foreign investors for his companies, especially in the United States, where he believed there was a better understanding of the diamond industry than there was in Australia. In his first attempt, he raised some $9 million, which he announced would be used for further exploration in the Nabberu area, where Great Central had applied for additional leases. But he was finding it difficult to spark any major interest in this potentially lucrative market, and it wasn't for want of trying. One trader in New York complained that he had been pestered by an 'infuriatingly persistent man named Levy',[9] who had been touting Joseph's stock in the United States. The reference was to Levi Mochkin, the 31-year-old Brooklyn-born stockbroker and son-in-law of Joseph's old pre-crash business associate, Henry Herzog. A fellow Lubavitcher, Mochkin was on the cusp of an extraordinarily lucrative career as Joseph's favourite stockbroker.[10]

Joseph was eventually persuaded that the only way he was going to attract American investors in a big way would be by listing on the New

York Stock Exchange. Joseph acted on the advice, and in December 1992 was in New York working to have Great Central listed on the Nasdaq (the small-capital index of the National Association of Security Dealers Automated Quotation system) by early the following year. Joseph's timing could not have been better. New York was caught up in a diamond frenzy, sparked by a major find at Lac de Gras in Canada's frozen north west where a joint Dia Met–BHP venture had recovered diamonds of high gem count in several kimberlite pipes. Expectations were high that a major new diamond province had been discovered. Great Central's results in Western Australia, while promising, were nowhere near as spectacular — although just two months earlier, in October, the company announced that it had discovered four kimberlite pipes of its own at its Nabberu joint venture with De Beers–Stockdale. Joseph was elated with the discovery, which he said displayed 'the classic indicator minerals close to a kimberlitic pipe'. He declared himself to be 'pretty confident about the area' — and he was also confident the find would make it much easier to convince American investors that he had something to offer them in the hot deserts of Western Australia that was no less worth pursuing than was the Dia Met–BHP project in the frozen wastes of Canada.

Back in Australia, sceptical mining analysts, the press and investors failed to share Joseph's enthusiasm for diamonds. While a growing number of analysts were now acknowledging Great Central's remarkable gold discovery record, at Plutonic in the late 1980s and now at Bronzewing, most still had difficulty valuing the company, which was capitalised at nearly $365 million at the end of 1992 — almost double its value twelve months earlier. Great Central had net assets of only $10 million, mainly capitalised exploration expenditure. But if analysts were already having difficulty valuing Great Central in December, this was nothing compared with what was about to hit them in the new year.

It all started relatively slowly. At the beginning of February 1992, Great Central reported a fifth kimberlite find at its Nabberu joint venture with Stockdale, and the company's shares moved up 30c to $7. By mid-March they were trading for around $8. And then, on 22 March, a week after Great Central Mines was listed on the Nasdaq, the flood gates opened. Great Central shares rocketed an astonishing 37.5 per cent in a single day. While only 289,000 shares changed hands, the day's $3 leap to $11 a share was the largest single-day rise in the history of the company. It ended the day with a market capitalisation of $625.8 million — compared with $256 million a year earlier, when its shares were worth just $4.50.

Perhaps a little taken aback at the speed at which things were moving, Joseph cautioned from New York that while the diamond indications in Western Australia were very encouraging, 'we haven't got a diamond mine yet'.[11] But he denied that the price surge could not be justified on fundamentals: 'The fact is that we have a good track record when it comes to discoveries and we have a large kimberlitic province tied up. Diamonds have the potential to generate huge earnings, and this is recognised by the market.' He also noted that Great Central had gained enormously from its listing on the Nasdaq: Punters 'look at Dia Met, which is trading at CN$45 ($50) and they look at us with a larger kimberlitic province and De Beers as a partner' — and they see a bargain.[12]

And that was only the beginning. Four days later, as overseas buyers continued to snap up whatever of the tightly held scrip was available, Great Central shares were trading for $13, and the company was capitalised at $740 million. This was an astonishing seventy per cent more than the market valuation of Ashton Mining — Australia's largest diamond producer. To put this in perspective, while Great Central, to date, had uncovered only a minute sprinkling of non-commercial micro diamonds and perhaps a couple of pretty but tiny visible stones — all up, hardly enough to make a respectable engagement ring for an ant, as one wag put it — Ashton produced from its Argyle diamond mine in the Kimberley region of Western Australia some 38.9 million carats in 1992, worth about $200 million. Even though only ten per cent of its production was rated gem quality, the disparity in market valuation was nonsensical.

And still the price continued to rise. It peaked at an amazing $18 in offshore trade on 30 March 1993, making Great Central's total gain for the month a staggering $10.20, or a rise of 150 per cent! And the company was worth, on paper, $1.03 billion, or $400 million more than a week before, when Joseph had hit New York. Disbelieving brokers said it was difficult to put any tangible value on Great Central as few people could comment on the stock with any degree of confidence or expertise. Michael Heffernan, research head at Sydney's BOS Stockbroking, which handled much of the Australian trade in Great Central shares, said the next day that he knew of no new information that could explain the share run. Quoted in Melbourne's *Age*, Heffernan said: 'It's purely being bought up overnight by US buyers. Someone's getting very sexy about diamonds.'

While most analysts and brokers were rubbing their eyes in disbelief, some writers were beginning to warm up their wordprocessors. Stephen Bartholemeusz wrote a scathing piece, published in the same issue of the *Age* (31 March 1993), under the heading 'Mining the market'. He noted that while Joseph hadn't demonstrated any remarkable capacity to make money out of conventional mining operations, he had 'a breathtaking ability to mine the sharemarket . . . the fact that Mr Gutnick's Great Central Mines, an exploration company with a couple of moderately interesting diamond and gold prospects, should be capitalised at more than $1 billion — a Top 50 company, no less — is staggering and says something about the degree to which the mug punter (and not just the local mug) has returned to the most speculative end of the market'. Others were not quite so contemptuous. The *Financial Review*'s Ivor Ries (31 March 1993) acknowledged that Great Central was 'clearly a serious exploration company' which had discovered 'very promising gold and diamond-bearing ores in two separate patches of WA'. But even he cautioned that 'those gold and diamond prospects had better turn up trumps or there will be a lot of small punters left wondering how $900 million can evaporate overnight'.

On 31 March 1993 the bubble eventually burst. It was the Australian Stock Exchange that provided the prick, ordering an inquiry into the Great Central price surge from $7.40 on 18 March to its high of $18 on 30 March. The company's share price immediately plummeted more than $5 to a low of $13, ending a twelve-day rising streak, before recovering slightly to end the day $3.10 lower, at $14.90. This wiped some $150 million off its market value, leaving it valued at a still grossly inflated $847.7 million. Great Central Mines had been a billion dollar company — for a day.

Joseph responded by requesting a suspension in trading, pending the release of an exploration report on the findings at Nabberu. These had been sent to South Africa by his joint exploration partner, Stockdale, for analysis by its parent company De Beers. Stockdale reluctantly agreed to release the reports by 8 April, in what it described as an extraordinary departure from its customary policy of exploration confidentiality. Meanwhile, Joseph decided to release his own assessment report on the potential at Nabberu, prepared earlier in the year by American mining analyst Ronald Shorr, which contained some extraordinarily positive statements on the Stockdale–De Beers view of their joint venture. Shorr claimed that De Beers saw this as one of their top priorities in Australia, if not worldwide, and had stated there was 'a significant chance' that some of the kimberlites found had 'the potential to become a mine'. He also claimed that 'virtually all' the diamonds found at Nabberu so far had been 'gem quality', but he did not give quantities.[13] The report was immediately savaged by critics, who pointed out that Shorr had been paid with 6500 Great Central shares to prepare it.[14]

On Monday 5 April 1993, Joseph went still further, and had Great Central release what it described as 'some detail' from the Stockdale report on the joint venture. According to Great Central, the report showed that latest results from Nabberu included the recovery of 'four "fine" diamonds from drill cuttings from the ME22 kimberlite body'. It said sixteen samples of drill hole cuttings had been examined for 'fine' diamonds, while 160 samples from four kimberlites and other targets remained to be examined. Great Central also claimed that Stockdale had recovered a significant number of good-quality white diamonds on its own adjacent leases, and that De Beers regarded the joint-venture area as more prospective than its own. The company said its consulting geologist considered the results as 'further evidence for the area being part of a major diamondiferous kimberlite province'. On the basis of this, Joseph claimed that the market was now 'fully informed' on Great Central's joint venture with Stockdale, and called for the suspension of the company's shares to be lifted.[15]

Stockdale begged to differ. It responded the following day, 6 April, by releasing its technical report — two days earlier than it had been asked to — in an obvious move to counter what it saw as the overly positive 'spin' Joseph was putting on it. Its report was, to put it mildly, much less bullish about the prospects at Nabberu than Great Central had made it out to be, stating quite categorically that 'none of the kimberlites found has thus far been found to have economic potential'. It noted that exploration within the Nabberu joint-venture area had resulted in 'the discovery of kimberlites all of which appear to be magmatic', and that 'Kimberlite ME22 contains some micro diamonds'. But it warned that interpretation of the geological characteristics of the four kimberlites drilled and identified petrographically was difficult, as the rocks were 'sheared and altered'.[16]

Joseph was flabbergasted by Stockdale's report. 'The report comes out as if the whole area is just a fizzer,' he said angrily. 'But we know there have been numerous macro-diamonds found. It would be interesting to know how many diamondiferous kimberlites they have on their adjacent areas.' He queried how Stockdale could make a 'conclusive' statement when only ten per cent of samples had been tested, and said his company stood by 'every single point' it had made about the joint venture, and had written evidence for everything it had claimed. 'We don't say we have found a mine yet but there is a good chance we will find a mine.'[17] Joseph's exploration chief, Ed Eshuys, was less heated than his boss: 'Stockdale have told us there is a significant chance of making a diamond discovery and that is our view.' He agreed with the Stockdale report that nothing of economic value had yet been dug up. 'There is still a mountain of work to be done ... Great Central has never given any indication we are close to making an economic diamond find. What we have said is a new kimberlite province which is diamond bearing has been found ... There is a significant chance for an economic discovery.'[18]

The more he thought about it, the more suspicious Joseph became of De Beers's motives in releasing such a lukewarm report. 'If they continue the way they do I'll have to speak to my lawyers and see what legal rights I have,' he told Channel Nine's *Business Sunday* program. 'I certainly have the legal rights to audit their exploration and find out if they are merely delaying tactics, if they've really got all the results.' He denied Stockdale's claims that none of the four kimberlite sections they had tested had economic potential. 'I want to stress and squash the myth that only micro diamonds have been discovered in the area,' he said. 'There have been scores of macro diamonds discovered by De Beers on adjacent areas to our joint venture, and there are five macro diamonds discovered on our own areas adjacent to the Nabberu joint venture.' He went on to claim that the Stockdale report might have been a deliberate attempt to discredit him and cut him down to size: 'I believe that when they started to realise I wasn't signing a marketing agreement with them and I was independent and I was successful in the United States, and they saw I was building a big support base, they started to worry that maybe I was going to be a threat to their monopoly and it's in their interest to discredit me.'[19]

Joseph never forgave De Beers for pulling the pin in the way it did over Nabberu. Nor did he ever cease to be suspicious of their motives. Four years later, his anger and resentment were still palpable: 'Look at them. Like vultures,' he told BRW's Mark Davis in a 1997 interview. 'Look how they have come wherever we have gone. Here, here, here,' he said, jabbing a finger at a map of his mining tenements. 'Wherever we have gone, they have moved in. They must be frightened of us.'[20] While there was a fair bit of paranoia in this, it was by no means totally unfounded. Even the *Herald Sun*'s Terry McCrann, no great fan of Joseph over the years, had noted that too many successful diamond discoveries would pose a very real threat to the De Beers hold on the market: 'We have had a near-seventy-year selling cartel which has delivered ever-rising prices,' he wrote. 'If we got sufficient rogue product to crack that fundamental financial mystique of the gem that it always rises in value through inflationary thick and recessionary thin, the short and longer term impact could be dramatic. Once you did pull the rug out from under the diamond price, where it would end nobody could possibly guess.'[21] McCrann was referring specifically to the threat of rogue diamonds from the crumbling former Soviet Union and parts of an increasingly anarchic Africa — but the principle held, in theory at least, for someone like Joseph as well, should he ever find his diamond bonanza in Australia.

For the moment, however, De Beers indicated that it was not about to end its relationship with Joseph. They were 'disappointed' at his threat of legal action but insisted their joint venture was unaffected. That, if anything, lent some substance to Joseph's claim that De Beers was rather more optimistic about prospects at Nabberu than it had made out in the Stockdale report.[22] Joseph, for his part, cautioned that the Stockdale report did not augur well for the joint venture or for the relationship he had with De Beers — 'but let everyone remember that we've only joint ventured 10 per cent of our land with De Beers, we've got the bulk of the province'.[23]

Meanwhile, as Joseph and De Beers slugged it out in public, the Australian Securities Commission launched an inquiry into the Great Central roller coaster. 'The warning bells are there, the price has sky-rocketed and there have been conflicting reports from various geologists,' ASC director Peter Chapman told the *Herald Sun*.[24] The Commission wanted to know why the discrepancies had arisen, and whether they were reasonable. Joseph was unfazed. 'It's not the first time,' he said laconically. 'As I've said in the past, we stand by every comment we've made.'[25] A few days later the ASC upgraded its inquiry into a formal investigation, enabling it to gain access to documents and subpoena witnesses. 'They came to our offices and asked us to put our side of the story across, which we did,' Joseph said. 'We believe for the moment that is the end of it.'[26]

Simultaneously, the Australian Stock Exchange, shaken by the discrepancies in the reporting by De Beers and Great Central, initiated a long-term review of its listing rules. This was completed the following January, when it announced it would adopt the 'world's first standardised system for reporting details of diamond exploration results, resources and reserves'. The new code required companies to get professional valuations for any gem quality diamonds recovered from exploration, and dramatically broadened the data a company must report when making an exchange announcement. It stressed that valuations should be considered reliable only on parcels of at least 2000 carats of diamonds from a single deposit, noting that 'the reliability of valuations of parcels of smaller than 2000 carats decreases as the size of the parcels decreases to a point where valuations placed on a small number of diamonds from exploration samples become meaningless and are likely to be misleading'.[27] The party was over. Once the new rules were put in place, there would be no more 'flea's eggs' or 'engagement rings for ants' passing themselves off to punters as potentially major diamond finds.

Great Central's shares were re-listed on 8 April 1993, a week after they were suspended. 'We have sought and received from Mr Gutnick a statement that he agrees with the findings of the De Beers–Stockdale report that there is no demonstrated economic potential,' ASX director Ray Schoer said on lifting the suspension.[28] Within minutes, the company's shares tumbled $3.90 to $11.

The most significant change in the company's share register was noticed on 16 April, when a search showed that a holding in the name of 'Colel Chabad Inc.' — previously listed as totalling 1.5 million shares, was no longer listed. At the peak of the market the stake was worth $27 million. Asked about this years later, Joseph smiles: 'Yes, they were one of the lucky ones.' He noted that he liked to help Colel Chabad, one of the oldest and most important Lubavitch institutions. Now based in New York, it was established by the *Alter Rebbe*, the original Lubavitcher Rebbe, to support and help members of the movement who settled in the Land of Israel — supporting poor people, running a soup kitchen, and subsidising those who were learning in yeshivahs. One of the ways it could raise money was to invest in stocks. And with Joseph's Rebbe-blessed Great Central stocks going through the roof, these were an obvious, and very lucrative, investment. 'Like the Catholic Church, who invest in different things, so we're also entitled to invest,' Joseph explains. 'Rabbi Duchman, who runs the Colel, invested in some of my companies in the early days. They made a lot of money out of it ... Since then he lost money ... He re-invested some of his gains with Astro. Because of the diamonds ... He left his money there ...'

A rather better known punter, at least in Melbourne, was Carlton footballer and former Stock Exchange operator Stephen Kernahan, who offloaded his 1000-share stake in Great Central at $13.50 each. It was 'getting too hard', he explained. He had bought the shares the previous June for $5.40 on the advice of a work colleague. 'He was always saying they were going to find gold and diamonds,' Kernahan said, noting that 'obviously a lot of guys are very religious and a few believe it is going to come true'. As for himself: 'Who knows whether it will, but you've got to take a profit some time.'[29] He made $8100 on his investment.

With some of the heat gone out of the market, analysts and commentators managed to catch their breath and take a more sober look at what had occurred. Most acknowledged the obvious. The astronomical rise in Great Central's share price had been primarily the result of a shrewdly timed launch on the Nasdaq of an attractive, well-priced speculative diamond stock when the American market was primed for just such a stock following the spectacular success of the Dia Met–BHP joint venture in northern Canada. All agreed it had been driven by off-shore buying among American investors — Australian punters, burned by Joseph in the 1980s, had displayed a healthy scepticism and had stood back to watch the US players scramble for the scrip — and that it was the diamonds at Nabberu rather than Great Central's somewhat more solid gold prospects at Bronzewing that had excited them. All also agreed that it had been a market 'in heat', and that the stellar rise in Great Central stock could not, by any stretch of the imagination, be justified on fundamentals. There was broad agreement, too, that the structure of Great Central's share register — Joseph himself held around half the capital and the top twenty shareholders between them close to ninety-five per cent of the shares — was another major factor. One final, and quite crucial factor, was Joseph's American 'roadshow' just before Great Central's launch on the Nasdaq. This hugely successful operation — which went relatively unremarked at the time — now began to attract the attention of commentators, in both the United States and Australia.

American brokers and investment managers, it seems, had been bowled over by Joseph when he toured the United States in March touting his company. 'I can assure you,' one West Coast money manager was quoted as saying, 'Joe casts a giant shadow.' Herbert Lanzet, one of two New York investor relations specialists hired by Joseph to set up meetings with US brokers and money managers and to organise his roadshow, concurred: Joseph 'is a very charming, convincing little man — he has incredible charisma.' Lanzet said no one who had met Joseph 'regarded him as a sure thing' but 'everyone who met him said he was worth a shot', adding that he had introduced him only to people who liked 'really speculative situations'. Joseph's other US consultant, Michelle Roth, related how she personally had been blown away by his pitch: 'He said, "We have four million acres, we have these kimberlite pipes of three-millimetre diamonds." And then to hear that De Beers has an interest, well, I thought: "Jeez, this is really interesting."' Some of the people Joseph met were also deeply impressed by his personal piety, and one broker couldn't believe how he had turned up for a business lunch at a luxury hotel carrying a pre-packaged kosher meal and a set of plastic knives and forks.

Interestingly, despite reports that his Lubavitcher connection had opened doors for him in the United States, in his talks with brokers and investors Joseph had apparently kept the Rebbe out of his discussions. When asked about this, Joseph said that although the Rebbe's prediction after the 1987 crash that he would make 'two huge gold and diamond discoveries in the next five years' had given him the personal confidence to keep battling through, he believed the prophecy had been a 'side issue' in promoting his company in the United States. 'It's quite unusual for the Rebbe to comment about matters of business — we're in the middle of the story and we'll see if it comes true,' he said. 'While it certainly adds confidence, I don't know that investors would buy shares solely on that basis.'[30]

This was the first time Joseph had mentioned a specific deadline for the Rebbe's diamond prophecy — and he would come to regret it. The truth is that the Rebbe never did tell Joseph — not in so many words — that he would find diamonds by a certain date. What he had done, at their famous audience in Crown Heights at the end of August 1988, was give his young protégé a blessing that he would 'be very successful within five years or more'. No mention of diamonds. That came much later, in 1991, when the Rebbe had told Levi Mochkin that Joseph would find 'gold or diamonds'. But Joseph, convinced that he was on the verge of making his big discovery at Nabberu, simply 'spliced' the Rebbe's August 1988 blessing with his 1991 prophecy and concluded that the Rebbe had meant he would 'find diamonds within five years'.

Joseph was aware that he could not just do this without the Rebbe's acquiescence; and, he claims, the Rebbe did in fact confirm his interpretation. The Rebbe, however, had suffered his stroke by this time, and was unable to speak. Joseph was always concerned that he might not be fully aware of what he was being asked — which was a major problem for him, relying as he did on the Rebbe's blessings and advice to make major business decisions. The Rebbe's doctors had assured him, however, that while the Rebbe might not *always* be lucid, he was most of the time — and was able to respond reliably to questions. On important matters such as this, Joseph would ask the Rebbe's secretaries to put the question several times, just to be certain:

> I asked the Rebbe afterwards, when he said five years or more, did that mean I'll find the diamonds. And according to the Rebbe's secretaries, he nodded his head 'yes'. ... I must have asked the Rebbe fifteen times, through the secretaries — that's why I'm allowed to say in five years. And the Rebbe said 'yes' ... We created the situation — but we had the Rebbe's acquiescence.

While all the evidence suggests that Joseph did sincerely believe the Rebbe's prophecy was about to come true, that he was on the verge of a major diamond discovery, it was probably no coincidence that talk about the Rebbe's deadline began to emerge precisely when Joseph was making his big diamond play on Wall Street. *The Wall Street Journal* published an article at about this time suggesting that Joseph might have exploited his contacts with 'a purported Messiah' as a 'gimmick' to raise the value of his stock.[31] Joseph was not, in fact, beyond publicising the Rebbe's prophecies to his advantage on the stock market; but, he points out, this, too, was with the Rebbe's express approval. The Rebbe had not only encouraged his activities on the stock market — but 'he answered me twenty-five times that I should publicise his views that I would have massive discoveries. He said I shouldn't publicise his views about the *Moshiach* [Messiah], but that I should publicise [his] prophecy about diamonds and gold ...'

It was not long before the press got hold of the 'Rebbe factor' in Joseph's diamond play and ran it for all it was worth. The *Bulletin* published a full-page article, titled 'Drilling for the Rabbi', which said Joseph was 'working hard to vindicate his mentor, Rabbi Menachem Schneerson'.[32] A few days later, in New York, *The Wall Street Journal* ran a rather sensational story claiming that some stockbrokers 'became believers' when they heard about the Rebbe's prophecies concerning the diamonds.[33] The *Herald Sun* in Melbourne managed to view a ten-minute video, prepared for Joseph's US roadshow, in which the Rebbe and his prophecies about the diamonds were strongly promoted, and published an extensive report on its contents. 'Rebbe [*sic*] Menachem Mendel Schneerson — considered by some to be the Messiah — is the central figure in a 10-minute video promotion, used by Great Central in its recent US roadshow,' the paper reported, noting that the video showed the Rebbe on six occasions between September 1990 and July 1991 saying Joseph would 'find all types of "gem quality diamonds" and it will be "a blessing for all of Australia" ...' Joseph said on the video: 'There is a potential economic diamond find worth hundreds of millions of dollars and I am confident we will make a major discovery.' Later in the video, Joseph said that the Rebbe had indicated a discovery 'worth billions of dollars'.[34]

Joseph confirmed all this a few days later in Australia, when he said on Channel Nine's *Business Sunday* program that there was 'a religious aspect' to the whole affair: 'I have a rabbi in New York . . . who has predicted many years ago that I would be very successful and that I'd be involved in a major gold discovery and a major diamond discovery,' he said, adding that the rabbi was never wrong. 'I will find those diamonds.'[35]

All this was becoming just too much for some media commentators. Terry McCrann was at his sardonic best when he observed: 'Something's not quite right when you have to read Revelations to decide whether or not the time is quite literally on your side for investing in a listed stock — in this case Joe Gutnick's Great Central Mines.' And even then, he continued, 'you couldn't be sure whether you had the right data, as the Book of Revelations detailing the events of the final Apocalypse is in the New Testament — not the Old on which much of Mr Gutnick's exploration inspiration is apparently based.' But he did raise a serious question: 'The religious dynamic detailed in Mr Gutnick's otherwise hi-tech and quite extraordinary electronic roadshow in the US for Great Central Mines raises some major and difficult questions for the Australian Stock Exchange and the Australian Securities Commission. How exactly do you regulate this?'[36] McCrann's colleague on the *Sunday Age*, Stephen Bartholemeusz, argued that while 'neither the law nor the regulator should act on the basis that people should be saved from the consequences of their own foolishness,' investors should nevertheless be entitled to believe that 'it isn't possible to go out and make the sorts of claims Mr Gutnick is making without being called on by the regulators to produce evidence to support them.' But he too conceded it was probably not a criminal offence to make misleading or deceptive statements if there was a genuine belief that the statement was true, noting: 'A legal test of whether a New York rabbi's prediction of a diamond discovery and a few micro diamonds were reasonable grounds for a belief that the claims Mr Gutnick made were true would make for a bizarre but fascinating hearing.'[37]

It seemed that the 'Rebbe factor' and Joseph's unorthodox exploration and promotion strategies were also beginning to disturb his De Beers exploration partners. It didn't sit well with their own ultra-conservative image, and they appear to have wanted to put some distance between themselves and Joseph's operation. Speaking on ABC's *Four Corners* on 25 May 1993, the exploration manager of Stockdale, Dr Bobby Danchin, said Stockdale was in the process of winding down its diamond search in the Nabberu region. He suggested that Joseph's 'very considerable optimism' about possible diamond discoveries in the area was based not on any geology so much as on his belief in the Rebbe's prediction of a major diamond find in the desert. This infuriates Joseph:

> De Beers played funny games with me in the Nabberu Basin. One moment you had Bobby Danchin writing a letter to the Lubavitcher Rebbe saying it had great potential, and telling me the chromites we found and the indicator minerals indicated we had gem-quality diamonds, that it would be a big, massive diamond field. They were the ones who were exciting me and telling me that we've got something special here, that we'll find a pipe, that they'd found a pipe, and that there were great chances of a new field. They were just as much egging me on with regards to the potential that existed. And I'll show you the letter that Danchin wrote to the Rebbe. Then suddenly they turned negative. Maybe they found it wasn't as good as they thought it was. But why did they let out their own frustration on me?

Danchin went on to tell *Four Corners* that the total weight of the seventy-five diamonds discovered on the Stockdale ground adjoining its joint operation with Great Central was just under a carat, 'which collectively means they are just under the size of a pea'. There was 'no way in the world that Nabberu One would ever be able to be mined economically by De Beers or anyone else,' he concluded. Accordingly, Stockdale would be moving out of its wholly owned acreage north of the joint tenements it was exploring with Great Central and heading for 'greener pastures' to the east. Significantly, Danchin stressed that it was 'business as usual' within the joint-venture permits — which would seem to suggest that Stockdale was still hedging its bets on the Rebbe. At least for the moment.[38]

Joseph, for his part, remained as defiantly upbeat as ever, telling *Four Corners* that Great Central would 'easily and without a doubt' uncover enough diamonds to equal the $1 billion value the stock market ascribed to the company. 'We will find a diamond mine because I am confident that the Rebbe's prophecy will come true,' he declared. 'There won't be a stone left unturned in the Nabberu region.'[39]

With the ill-conceived 30 September 1993 deadline fast approaching, Joseph intensified his search for the elusive gems. Great Central announced in mid-July that it would 'dramatically' step up its $500,000-a-month exploration program at Nabberu in an attempt to meet the deadline. Joseph was not the only one looking for diamonds. The Lac de Gras discovery in Canada, and a surge in demand for diamonds, had sparked a new rush of Australian diamond exploration. Two prospects, one in the Northern Territory and the other in Western Australia, were already shaping up as having commercial potential. Triad Minerals' bulk-sampling program in Western Australia was yielding gem-quality stones that, according to one report, made 'Ashton Mining's Argyle mine look positively pedestrian'.[40] And these were just two of some thirty-eight listed companies, most of them juniors, lining up to conduct diamond exploration programs from Victoria to Western Australia. Joseph, it seems, began to eye some of them as his own search at Nabberu failed to yield the hoped-for bonanza.

In August he struck a deal with Colonial Resources to explore another diamond prospect at Walgidgee Hills prospect in the Western Kimberley. Ed Eshuys said Great Central would use the expertise it had gained at Nabberu to good effect in Walgidgee Hills, claimed to be 'the largest lamproite pipe in the world'. Could this be the one? 'I can't say too much at the moment,' Eshuys said, 'but we think it is a good prospect.'[41]

It would need to be, because a few days later, on 8 August 1993, De Beers finally concluded that exploration at Nabberu had run its course and its exploration company, Stockdale, withdrew from its joint venture with Joseph. It had been a partnership of incompatibles — a super conservative, coldly calculating international mining giant and an independently minded, religiously inspired maverick.

Meanwhile, the media wags and gossip columnists were having a field day at Joseph's expense. 'Talk around the bars of Perth frequented by mining types suggests that Joe is not prepared to let the prophecy made by his 92-year-old New York rabbi slip by,' wrote Emiliya Mychasuk ('CBD') in the *Sydney Morning Herald*.[42] 'If necessary a contingency plan will be put into action, according to our spies, which centres on the fundamental belief that "if you haven't got it, you can always buy it".' One possible target was John Byrne's Black Hill Minerals, one of the partners in Western Australia's Philips Range joint venture. 'A new security fence had just been knocked up around the gem-studded paddock's perimeter,' Mychasuk wrote, 'but a bit of religious fervour and some cold hard cash could easily knock it down, according to punters out in the West.'

Robert Weatherdon ('Bourse Sauce') in the *Financial Review*[43] came up with another juicy rumour, under the heading 'Kimberlite relief'. According to Weatherdon, the 'latest word doing the rounds of the penny hopeful index is [that] Diamond Joe Gutnick is negotiating a farm-in deal with Sydney's Double Bay miner John Merity . . . somewhere in the deep west of Western Australia'. Joseph, he noted, 'has the clock ticking, having had word from his New York religious adviser that he will strike it big before a certain date looming very soon.'

Joseph, understandably enough, was getting more than a little tetchy about it all. 'Do you think it is going to happen to the day, the day before or the day after?' he snapped as 'D-Day' approached, pledging to continue his diamond search, 'deadline or no deadline'.[44] He was overseas when the 'deadline' passed — his office in Melbourne declined to say whether 'in New York with the Rebbe', or in Jerusalem. The story made it onto page one of the *Financial Review*'s fateful 30 September issue, under the headline 'Diamond Joe yet to land the promised'. Great Central shares lost a further 20 cents on the bad news, closing the day at $8.30.

Although Joseph is not certain that the final word has been spoken on Nabberu, he acknowledges that both his own credibility and the Rebbe's had been called into question when the 30 September 1993 deadline came and went without the promised bonanza. Stipulating a time frame for the discovery had been a mistake, he now concedes — but 'a joint mistake . . . The Rebbe acquiesced to the situation. In retrospect, it's no good putting time limits on anything . . .'

If Joseph had thought that, with the September deadline out of the way, the media would look elsewhere for their titillation, he was wrong. Before the 1987 stock market crash he had acquired a small 7.6 per cent stake, now worth about $7 million, in a company called Cambridge Gulf Exploration NL. This was engaged in dredging for alluvial diamonds off the Western Australian coast, a process that involved sucking up huge quantities of gravel from the ocean floor and screening this for diamonds. In December 1993 Cambridge burst into the headlines. It had found its diamonds — all six carats of them, worth about $810. Yet, in a play that recalled the hype earlier in the year over Joseph's micro diamonds at Nabberu, the company's 'consulting geologist' was talking about spewing out diamonds worth as much as $US2.2 billion a year. 'That certainly puts a modern spin on the old saying about mighty oaks growing from tiny acorns,' the *Herald Sun*'s Terry McCrann observed, using the opportunity to take another small dig at Joseph by noting that it was also 'a little more than Joe was flashing earlier in the year, but only just. Approaching an engagement ring for Liz Taylor'.[45]

Ten months later, however, in October 1994, the *Financial Review* reported that Cambridge Gulf appeared 'unlikely to deliver colourful mining entrepreneur "Diamond Joe" Gutnick the major diamond discovery that the late Rebbe Menachem Schneerson prophesied he would find'. Joseph, while not about to shed his stake in the disappointing explorer, which had found few more diamonds in the intervening period and had incurred the wrath of the regulators, said he would not be increasing his share: 'I believe in onshore diamond exploration, not offshore exploration.'[46]

◊ ◊ ◊

With this distraction out of the way, Joseph's hunt for the Rebbe's diamonds dropped out of the headlines as the media and the markets focussed their attention on the astonishing success of his gold activities at Bronzewing and Jundee in the Yandal belt 400 kilometres north of Kalgoorlie. Both sites were turning out to be among the most exciting finds for years, with the potential to surpass even the fabulous Plutonic mine Joseph had been forced to dispose of so cheaply in 1989. And, as Joseph made the transition from 'paper king' to bona fide gold miner, AMP and the other large institutions, which until now had been shunning his stocks, began to come on board, buying up significant holdings in Great Central. This had a double effect. It forced Joseph to dilute his personal holding in Great Central, from over forty per cent to just twenty-five per cent by mid-1995, freeing up tens of millions of dollars that he could divert to other purposes. And he was forced to restructure his mining empire, to leave Great Central as a pure gold explorer and producer. There had been speculation about this for over a year, ever since the institutions started buying up the company's stock and made it plain that what was attracting them was the real gold at Bronzewing and Jundee, not Joseph's obsession with the elusive diamonds.

The restructure was eventually implemented in March 1995, when all of Great Central's diamond interests were transferred to Joseph's Astro Mining. Astro was to be the exclusive vehicle for Joseph's diamond hunt in Australia, and, using part of the money he was freeing up by diluting his holding in Great Central, he could push on with this highly speculative quest at his own pace. This earned Joseph yet another nickname to add to his collection — 'Astro-Boy'.[47] Dr Stephan Meyer was appointed exploration manager to lead the diamond hunt, and exploration began at several sites in Western Australia, including Leonora, Barlee and Sandstone in the Yilgarn and a tenement bloc in the Central Kimberley.

Joseph was determined to find the diamonds the Rebbe had promised he would find — not merely for their own sake but even more importantly, it would seem, to vindicate the Rebbe and venerate his memory. And he gave the clear impression at the time — although he was reluctant to concede this, claiming he was only responding to pressure from his institutional investors — that he was quite prepared to run down his own holding in his spectacularly successful gold producer in order to raise the money needed to finance a very expensive and highly speculative search for the diamonds. While this was not consistent with the behaviour of a hard-headed, rational businessman, it was consistent with that of a man to whom the importance of vindicating the Rebbe took precedence over more conventional business considerations. Joseph was to invest, over the years, many millions of dollars, his own as well as those of his fellow true believers, in the quest for the Rebbe's diamonds.

A series of technical difficulties prevented Astro from re-listing on the Stock Exchange until 13 September 1996, a year later than originally envisaged. But when it did list, its shares were snapped up, soaring to over $4 from their last close at just 62 cents when the company had been suspended from trading two years earlier. 'I am delighted . . . it was a great start,' Joseph enthused. 'It took us a long time to get started . . . now we can get on with exploring and find some diamonds.'[48] He personally held a 24.5 per cent stake in the restructured company, and made a $70 million paper profit on his package on the first day of trading. Even hardened analysts, used to the spectacular when it came to Joseph's companies, were surprised. A company owning just $7 million in cash and a bundle of old leases was suddenly worth just under $300 million. One senior resources analyst, John McDonald of the Perth-based Eyres Reed, a long-term watcher of speculative plays, simply shrugged his shoulders. Gutnick stocks had 'a certain cult following', he suggested, which made them hard to analyse.[49] Others, however, suggested that one of the factors responsible for the surge was the difficulty of acquiring shares. As in all Gutnick companies, the shares were tightly held by a small and easily identifiable group — and 'within the inner circle buyers are welcome but sellers for short-term gains could be likened to traitors'.[50] Astro, for its part, was up front about the fact that it was unable to make a profit forecast — basically because it had yet to find any diamonds in the tenements it held in the Yilgarn and the Kimberley. 'The company is currently in the exploration phase for diamonds and there can be no assurance that a commercially viable ore reserve exists on any of its tenements,' the company's prospectus stated.

That did not deter the punters. They would undoubtedly have been reassured by Joseph's own confident assessment that 'the risk is immense but the reward for those who stick with us will be great.'[51] By November 1996 Astro had shot to $559 million, and its shares were worth $7.82. It hadn't discovered a single diamond, yet like Great Central at Nabberu in early 1993, it was already worth more than Ashton with its forty per cent stake in Argyle, a mine then producing 40 million carats a year.[52] Joseph's personal stake in the company, for which he had paid just $3.6 million three months earlier, was now worth over $140 million. Bizarre as this might seem, Joseph had a simple explanation:

> There is no excitement in Ashton. The excitement that exists [in Astro] is the potential . . . There is an excitement and anticipation of a discovery. The market gets bored with things unless they see there is an upside . . . If we discover something, it will go through the roof. If we don't, over a few years, it will halve . . . Everyone should know that when they are buying . . . It is speculative.[53]

Joseph pledged he would be spending some $5 million a year searching for the Rebbe's diamonds, both on his own account and in joint ventures with others. Astro already had holdings totalling some 32,000 square kilometres, including new tenements in the Yilgarn, and had signed an agreement with CSIRO to explore a patch of desert near the Argyle mine. CSIRO head Dr Malcolm McIntosh appeared to have caught some of Joseph's enthusiasm, and was already speaking about this being a 'billion dollar project'. He said the venture would be using the same kind of technology that had proven so successful at Bronzewing and Jundee, and was confident they would find the gems: 'There is every reason to believe there are diamonds there and the Argyle mine proves they are in the general vicinity.'[54]

There was, in fact, considerable optimism at this time about the prospects of finding diamonds in Australia, not so much in the Argyle region, but further south, in the Yilgarn, where both Astro and — to Joseph's chagrin — De Beers were actively exploring. According to prevailing theories, the region was not especially promising. But, as one industry observer noted at the time, Joseph and his team were 'disregarding the dogma and existing science' and were going to 'places where diamonds shouldn't be'. It was that kind of philosophy, he suggested, that led to discovery. 'It may not be diamonds, but it is that inquiring mind and going to places where others haven't gone.'[55] However Dr Stephan Meyer, Astro's exploration manager, told the third annual Paydirt Diamond Conference, held in Perth in September 1996, that up to sixty-six per cent, or 4.5 million square kilometres, of Australia could be regarded as prospective for diamonds, with the Yilgarn Craton offering the best chance for economic discoveries.[56] Meyer also told the conference that because of the size and difficult nature of the terrain at Yilgarn, it required an explorer with 'a strong geological and conceptual focus' — something that Astro, with Ed Eshuys overseeing its exploration, undoubtedly possessed. So if anyone was going to find the diamonds at Yilgarn, Joseph's company was seen as having a better chance than most — at least as good as his old foe De Beers, which had refocussed its exploration effort on the same area and was prepared to spend some $10 million. Some promising findings were made in the region — where by 1998 Astro had six project areas (Narryer, Sandstone, West Leonora, Menzies, Barlee, Merredin) covering some 31,000 square kilometres — including some new kimberlites in the central part of the Yilgarn. These turned out to be barren, according to the 1998 Astro prospectus, but there were sufficient diamond traces to 'confirm the diamond prospectivity' of the Yilgarn.

While the Yilgarn remained the main focus of Astro's diamond exploration in Western Australia, Joseph went into a number of joint-venture deals with other explorers. One of these was Diamin Resources, which held some potentially promising tenements 290 kilometres east of Carnarvon — an area where De Beers had discovered kimberlite several years earlier. If the initial probe went well, Joseph said Astro would spend $10 million on further exploration, lifting its stake in the joint venture to seventy-five per cent. Neither company had yet made a commercial diamond find, yet the market valued Astro at some $140 million, compared with Diamin which was valued at a mere $4 million. While this was dramatically down on the absurdly unrealistic $560 million value the market had placed on Astro a year earlier, it still reflected the extraordinary faith Astro's investors, first and foremost Joseph himself, continued to have that the company would eventually come up with the goods. But time was ticking by, and the pressure was growing on Astro to come up with something that would justify that kind of market valuation.

In May 1998 Joseph announced Astro was buying Normandy's

alluvial diamond operation at Bow River in the north of Western Australia. Production at Bow had stopped in 1995, but Joseph was confident he could turn it around. 'It's a diamond field we feel is good,' he said. 'There's lots of potential.'[57] Two months later, in July 1998, it was announced that Astro was re-evaluating another old site, the Philips Range. This was one of Australia's most intensely explored diamond prospects, about 200 kilometres to the east of Argyle, the world's biggest diamond mine. Almost 2000 carats of gem quality diamonds had been recovered in the area, and Joseph's joint-venture partner and once-upon-a-time foe in the battle for Great Central, veteran Western Australian explorer Phil Crabb, was confident of finding more. 'I thought, well, how could they get such good quality diamonds and not find any more?' Crabb said. 'We put it all together and attracted Gutnick into the venture. He has started exploration right now ... they are going to pursue it very vigorously.'[58]

Diamond exploration in Australia, as one old hand in the industry, Ewen Tyler, has put it, is 'a tough, gut-wrenching business'. Tyler, who had been involved in Australian diamond exploration since the early 1970s, said in a 1993 interview that diamond exploration in this country had soaked up about $1 billion over the previous twenty years — and had precious little to show for it. In that time, he pointed out, hundreds of pipes had been found, some of them diamond bearing, and thousands of stones. Only one discovery to date had proven to be commercially viable: Argyle.[59] So it is hardly surprising that Joseph eventually decided to depart somewhat from the Rebbe's brief — either that, or he had begun to query the late sage's geography. He began to look further afield.

At the end of 1996 Joseph announced that Astro, in partnership with one of his other companies, Quantum Resources, had picked up the diamond exploration rights to one-sixth of mainland China. This covered an astonishing 1.6 million square kilometres in the far western province of Xin Jiang, immediately to the south of the gold- and diamond-rich Russian Siberian shield, which his two companies intended exploring in a joint venture with the Xin Jiang Bureau of Geology and Mineral Resources. 'It's a very exciting play for us which you will be hearing lots about in coming years,' Joseph enthused.[60] He had recently recruited Bob Hawke[61] to be a non-executive director of Quantum, which he was developing specifically as a vehicle for investment in Asia, hoping that the former prime minister would be able to 'open doors' for him in the region. The two companies, Astro and Quantum, later went into joint ventures with the Bureaus of Geology in four other Chinese provinces — Liaoning, Shandong, Jiangsu, and Anhui, covering a total area of some 118,000 square kilometres. Under the joint-venture agreements, the Chinese undertook to carry out the field explorations, with Joseph's companies providing the technical direction and controlling the overall exploration programs.

Little came of Joseph's Chinese diamond hunt, however, and that, along with his still fruitless search in Western Australia, soon dropped from the headlines. The world, as it prepared to end the second millennium, appeared to have lost interest in Joseph's seemingly futile obsession, and although he was reminded from time to time about the Rebbe's 'failed' prediction, that too was beginning to be forgotten. Joseph, if asked, would reaffirm his unshakeable faith in the Rebbe's prophecy, as well as his confidence that it would be fulfilled. A large picture of the Rebbe, along with his prophecy about the diamonds, continues to occupy a prominent place in the glossy prospectus put out each year by Astro.

Sister Act

'If an Orthodox Jewish woman with 11 kids finds diamonds, it's got to be the blessing of the Rebbe — it can't be anything else, right?'

Pnina Feldman, the *Sydney Morning Herald*, 6 December 1997.

IN APRIL 1997, with Joseph's hunt for the Rebbe's elusive diamonds going nowhere, an intriguing new exploration company launched itself on the stock market. Called Diamond Rose, the company stated in its prospectus that its goal was 'to find the 12 gemstones of the Breastplate (*Hoshen*) worn by the High Priest in the Temple of Jerusalem over 3,000 years ago as described in the Bible.' According to Talmudic sources, the prospectus said, 'this breastplate will be reconstructed again at the time of the Messianic Era'. And it claimed that the tenements already owned by the company in Western Australia, the Northern Territory and New South Wales 'arguably contain five definite and possibly two of the Hoshen gemstones . . .' The company hoped to sell 50 million shares at 20 cents each, raising $10 million, in a float underwritten by Pembroke Securities, a subsidiary of Rodney Adler's FAI. And to maximise its chances, the float was timed to coincide with the birthday of the late Lubavitcher Rebbe.[1]

It exceeded all expectations. The shares opened at $1.51 — more than seven-times their 20 cent issue price — and within an hour reached a staggering high of $1.75. Some of the disbelieving punters took their profits, and the shares closed the day at $1.29. Diamond Rose found itself capitalised at $156 million — not quite so impressive a performance as Joseph's Astro had recorded when it was re-listed six months earlier and its shares soared twenty-fold on its first day of trade, from an issue price of 20 cents to over $4. But impressive, nonetheless. It had all the signs of another stunning Gutnick stock market coup.

'*Pru u'rvu*' — 'be fruitful and multiply'. Joseph and Stera with their 11 children, daughter-in-law, son-in-law, and three grandchildren.
From left: Mordechai (Mordi), 22; Chana, 11; Naomi (Mordi's wife); Israel (one of the twins), 9; Chaya, 18; the Patriarch, Joseph, holding his youngest son Yochanan, 2; Zahava (from the Hebrew word for gold), 13; Raizel (named after Joseph's late mother, Rose), 6; The Matriarch, Stera; Zalman (the potential *ilui*, behind Stera), 20; Rafael (the other twin), 9; Isser ('the little Yossi'), 15; Rivka, 24, holding her baby Etti; Shmaya Krinsky (Rivka's husband); Rivka's two older children, Rosie, 4, and Chaya Mushka, 3. [Photo: Arnold Szmerling]

The Coup. Joseph with his early sidekick Harry Cooper (also bearded), flanked by Jeff Banks (left) and Duncan Purcell. The four were involved in Joseph's first major incursion into mining, when Joseph and Harry seized control of Centaur Mining — still one of the mainstays of the Gutnick empire — in 1980.

Sale of the Century. Joseph hands prospector Mark Creasy a cheque for $117 million — probably the biggest ever paid to a prospector in Australia — for his holdings in Western Australia's Yandal Belt.

The Odd Couple. Robert Champion de Crespigny and Joseph Isaac Gutnick — two of the most successful gold miners in Australia, and unlikely partners in one of the country's biggest mining companies, Great Central.

Golden Joe. Joseph in one of his early explorations with Ed Eshuys (left), at Yalgoo in Western Australia in 1986.

The One that Got Away. Joseph at the site of his first major strike, Plutonic, in 1989. With him is Ron Hawkes of Pioneer Mineral Exploration, who bought Plutonic from Joseph for some $53 million and developed it into one of Western Australia's richest gold provinces.

Diamond Joe. Joseph with Ed Eshuys (left) and Dr Jim Wright (right), hunting for diamonds at Nabberu in the early 1990s.

The Dream Team. Joseph with Ed Eshuys underground at Bronzewing, the first of Joseph's hugely successful mines in the Yandal Belt. The *Financial Review's* Ivor Ries described the two as 'clearly one of the most creative capital–intellect combinations at work in the share market.'

Reporting to the boss. Ed Eshuys shows the deeply interested Rebbe a map of Joseph's mines in Western Australia as Joseph looks on. Ultimately, Joseph insists, his success as a gold miner has not been due to Eshuys or any other single geologist: 'It's a joint effort; geologists and God's blessings'. '

Only, Joseph had nothing whatsoever to do with it. Diamond Rose, named in honour of his late mother who had died in a tragic road accident in New York five years before, was the brainchild and sole initiative of his sister Pnina Feldman. Joseph insisted that there was absolutely no connection between Diamond Rose and his companies, that he had 'no interest' in his sister's company and would 'never have' any interest. 'It would be a conflict of interest. I am only interested in my own companies.' That Joseph was 'not exactly happy' about his sister's decision to become a diamond hunter was an understatement — but, he said a few weeks before the float, 'she is my elder sister and I can't say too much'.[2]

Pnina, it emerged, had been dabbling in mining for some three years. The principal of the Lubavitcher girls' school in Sydney and mother of eleven, she was primarily motivated to enter the field, it seems, by her desire to help her husband, Rabbi Pinchos Feldman. The Rebbe had sent Rabbi Feldman out from the United States thirty years before to set up the Yeshivah Centre in Bondi Junction. It had been a great success, expanding to include two synagogues, a kindergarten, and primary and high schools with more than 700 students. But in the process it had run up a huge debt, and by 1994 was teetering on the edge of bankruptcy, owing the Commonwealth Bank some $22 million. The bank agreed to write the debt down to $10 million, which was raised by a group of wealthy benefactors — including Joseph, who generously put up half the sum as a loan. That solved the immediate problem, but not the chronic problem of finding the money to cover the institution's $8-million-a-year operating costs. It had an annual revenue of about $5 million, leaving a deficit of some $3 million. Pnina related how she asked Joseph if he could help cover the shortfall: 'I said "Listen, Yosl, it's not that much. We're not asking you to contribute the whole $3 million every year that we run a deficit, but if you gave $1 million it would be an enormous help." He said, "I've given my money, and that's what I can do, and if you don't want to have debts don't spend."'[3]

Rebuffed, Pnina decided to try to raise the money herself. Her opportunity came, she explained, quite by chance: 'Someone I knew wanted to [sell] a lease to my brother and couldn't get through to him and asked if I could give him an introduction. My brother was in Perth and said he had so many new projects he couldn't look at it but if it was interesting I should look at it myself.'[4] She did. Before long, she had formed a company called Vageta which took up this and other tenements that Joseph was either not interested in or had already explored without success — such as the Walgidgee Hills in the West Kimberley. And now, three years later, she decided to go to the market to raise $10 million with the stated aim of exploring prospective ground in the Kimberley and Pilbara regions of Western Australia and near the Orange district of New South Wales.

It took some chutzpah. Not every day did a 52-year-old Orthodox Jewish woman, the wife of a rabbi with eleven children, float a mining company on the Australian Stock Exchange. Pnina made no secret of the fact that she had no special experience or qualifications. When challenged, she replied airily: 'If you have 11 kids, you can do everything.' Besides, she added, 'the family has been so involved for years [in mining] that I instinctively understand what to do'.[5] She went out of her way to stress her relationship with Joseph, and the part this had played in her decision to look for diamonds and other gemstones herself: 'It was my mother's wish before she died in a car crash five years ago that she help Joseph in his diamond explorations . . . After she died I said to Joseph that I was so much like our mother, I would help. Now her name lives on . . .'[6]

Try as he might to distance himself from his sister's project, Joseph was inevitably perceived to be somehow involved, giving the enterprise a credibility it might not otherwise have had. The same effect was achieved by Pnina's appointment of Peter Temby as Diamond Rose's executive director of resources. Temby had been looking for diamonds for fourteen years, and was involved in the discovery of the world's biggest diamond mine, Argyle.

Even so, the pundits were taken by surprise by the enthusiasm with which the float was received — including by such heavyweight investors as the American billionaire George Soros, the GIO, BT Australia, and Permanent Trustees. FAI also received options in return for underwriting the issue. As for Pnina — she found herself suddenly worth $91.6 million, the paper value of her own 57.5 per cent stake in the company.

This catapulted her into Business Review Weekly's 1997 'Rich 200' list, which estimated her worth at $80 million. Of course, she couldn't touch the money: under Stock Exchange rules it was placed in escrow for two years. 'I thought that was pretty mean, actually,' she said of the ruling. Still, it did enable her to afford a new $2 million cliff-top 'getaway' in Sydney's Dover Heights. And the $300,000-plus a year annual salary she received from Diamond Rose would certainly have been a vast improvement on whatever she was earning as headmistress of Yeshivah Girls' High.[7]

While it was all very well being one of Australia's richest women — on paper, at least — Pnina's company had to start showing it was serious about exploration. 'I don't want to hang around,' she said. 'I want to get on with it. Instead of using one geologist to look at one prospect at a time I want to use a team to look at it all. I want to stand on the accelerator.'[8] Pnina's gung-ho enthusiasm and optimism were worthy of Joseph himself — and were just as infectious, especially among American investors. 'Everyone in New York feels it is fantastic,' she enthused. 'We have attracted some top investors.' Once again, she shrewdly doffed her hat to brother Joseph: 'He says get in the money and put it to work. Don't worry about the share price because it will look after itself . . . The company aims to have an economic diamond find within twelve months.'[9] Joseph could have told her she was dreaming. He had been looking for diamonds for the best part of a decade with nothing significant to show. And predicting a diamond discovery in twelve months was just the sort of statement that, as Trevor Sykes pointed out in the *Financial Review*, would erode Diamond Rose's credibility.[10]

So, too, did Pnina's extraordinary claim at the company's first annual meeting in November, just seven months after it was floated: that the first sale had been made of something she identified as 'pittado' — one of the gemstones referred to in the Bible as adorning the High Priest's Breastplate — to an American home-shopping TV channel called QVC, for about $3000. 'We have 119,000 tonnes of it,' she told the meeting. 'We tried to work it out and I think it was [worth] $30,000 million, or something to that effect. If we sell half of that, we'll all be laughing.'[11] She was being inadvertently conservative: she had forgotten a zero in her calculation, and was actually sitting on deposits of pittado — a green jade-like stone — worth some $350 billion. Enough to keep Sydney's Yeshivah Centre in the black for eternity.

It was at about this time that Pnina parted company with her highly experienced exploration manager Peter Temby, who had begun to wonder just what he had let himself in for. He certainly did not share his Biblically-inspired boss's enthusiasm for the High Priest's pittado, which, he pointed out, was 'a type of chalcedony with green chrome mica colouration' — a fairly common kind of quartz not hitherto used as a gemstone. As for Pnina's stated hope of finding diamonds within twelve months, Temby commented: 'She doesn't realise the amount of work required — exploration is 99 per cent hard work. It took me 30 years to get where I am — I don't think anyone can leap in cold like she has and say you'll get something viable in 12 months.'[12]

While Temby's departure would have done little to enhance Diamond Rose's credibility, Pnina's enthusiasm and optimism was unaffected. Within days, she announced the discovery of a small quantity of diamonds (0.066 carats in a 509 kilogram sample) near the King George River in the Kimberley, in a joint venture with Striker Resources and Dioro Exploration. It was the kind of discovery that, properly hyped, might once have made headlines and sent share prices soaring, much as Joseph's Nabberu 'find' had four years before — but not under the much more stringent reporting rules the Stock Exchange had since adopted. Such finds had become quite commonplace in the Kimberley, without leading to anything commercial, and no longer excited anyone.

Meanwhile, displaying an entrepreneurial flair that even Joseph would have difficulty matching, Pnina pressed ahead with her marketing of several other of the High Priest's gemstones. In addition to the pittado, her 'Diamond Rose Collection' now included gems such as red jasper and white chalcedony, also identified as being among the twelve gemstones on the High Priest's Breastplate. And, in just twenty minutes one night in July 1998, she managed to sell some $500,000 worth of the gems to TV shoppers in New York. It was reported that buyers among an estimated audience of 50 million people rang up and ordered the gems at the rate of 500 a minute — apparently an American home-shopping record.[13]

The following month, August, news arrived that a little sister for Diamond Rose was in the works: Silver Rose Mining. Its prospectus claimed the company had interests in 'an exciting group of silver and other exploration leases, some covering over 80 old mines with high silver levels.'[14] It hoped to raise $8 million when it was floated later in the year. With familiar Gutnick bravado, Pnina announced that she wanted to be 'the number 1 silver producer in the country'.[15] Whether the new venture would evoke the same enthusiasm as Diamond Rose had on its debut the previous year was highly doubtful, with the older company's shares trading by this time for a mere fraction of the prices they were fetching when they were first released.

In the end, little came of Pnina's grandiose dreams. Her heady reign among *Business Review Weekly*'s 'Rich 200' proved short-lived, and she disappeared from the list in 1998, after a single year. By 1999, she had fallen out with one of her major American backers, George Soros, and her future as a credible explorer looked bleak. Pnina had, however, managed to raise a not inconsiderable $4 million to help out her husband and the Yeshivah Centre. This had apparently come from a complex share trade she had done with an Argentinian investor, Eduardo Elstain, said to be one of Soros's fund managers. 'He is a lovely man,' Pnina told the *Sydney Morning Herald*'s Ben Hills by way of explanation. 'My son-in-law's friend is this man's rabbi.'[16] Four million dollars was no mean achievement for this enterprising novice, even though it fell far short of what she might have hoped for when she started out.

◊ ◊ ◊

For Joseph, it had been an uncomfortable, and discomforting, experience — one he is unwilling to discuss in detail, in the interests of family harmony. There can be little doubt, however, that he had not enjoyed Pnina's encroachment on his turf. Not, it seems, because he begrudged her any success that might come her way or perceived her as being in any sense a serious threat or rival. But he would inevitably have resented the fact that she appeared to be riding on his coat-tails. It is unlikely that Pnina and her project would have aroused anything like the interest it did from investors had it not been for the fact that she was Joseph's sister; that Joseph, by this time, had an outstanding record as an explorer; and the perception that Joseph — despite his vehement denials — might have been in some way involved.

More seriously, perhaps, Pnina's claim that she was searching for the twelve gemstones of the High Priest's Breastplate might have had the unfortunate effect of undermining the seriousness of Joseph's own search for diamonds — an enterprise he had spent many millions of dollars on over the past decade as an act of faith in the personal blessing he had received from the Rebbe. Ben Hills — whose comprehensive December 1997 feature on Pnina in the *Sydney Morning Herald* was titled 'God is a girl's best friend' — had the definite impression that she, too, was 'inspired by the prophecy of the bearded, stern-looking man whose photo adorns her home and business offices, the late Rabbi Menachem Schneerson . . . who forecast a decade ago that gold and the hoshen jewels would be found in Australia.' And Pnina did little to counter the impression, telling Hills: 'I think I'm going to bring credit to the Rebbe . . . If an Orthodox Jewish woman with 11 kids finds diamonds, it's got to be the blessing of the Rebbe — it can't be anything else, right?'[17]

The media, inevitably, had a field day with Pnina and the High Priest's gemstones. It was a marvellously bizarre story, and provoked some quite entertaining, and sometimes quite witty, comment — such as Sydney journalist P D Jack's ingenious mathematical analysis in the

Financial Review of Pnina's chances of finding the twelve *Hoshen* stones. Noting that various authorities had identified at least 22 gems that might fit the Biblical description, he wrote that Pnina would have to reduce the 22 possibilities to 12 — and that she had 646,646 variations from which to choose. But that was not all: 'It is possible that the jewels in the High Priest's breastplate must be placed in the specific order as laid down by His Wondrousness to Moses on Mt Sinai,' he wrote. 'If so, and we have 22 to choose from, the combinations available total more than 309 trillion.'[18] This might have been a little irreverent, but it was a bit of clever good fun. The *Sydney Morning Herald* business gossip writer Emiliya Mychasuk was more acerbic, and had a dig at Joseph: 'Yossel can be forgiven for feeling hard done by,' she wrote in one of her 'CBD' columns soon after Diamond Rose's float. Gold prices were down, his football team was on the bottom of the ladder — and then there was 'the harsh story doing the rounds that the Rebbe — who Yossel has credited, in part at least, for his good fortune — is no longer looking after his disciple because he went looking for gold when the Rebbe told him his mission was to look for diamonds. Instead, to add to his hurt pride, older sister Pnina Feldman is having all the good fortune . . .'[19]

Joseph was, of course, well accustomed to this kind of treatment in the gossip columns of the business press. For most of the previous decade, he had endured such 'spears and arrows' — and worse — from writers and commentators either jealous of his success or simply paid for the acerbity of their words. But for the Rebbe's blessing, which Joseph took with the utmost seriousness, to be associated in the public mind in this way with Pnina's much more frivolous and opportunistic search for the High Priest's gemstones was clearly a problem for him.

As if to underscore just how vulnerable Joseph and his Rebbe-driven treasure hunt were to perceptions of 'Lubavitcher crackpottery', the *Herald Sun* reported, in March 1999, how an American-born Melbourne businessman, evidently a Lubavitcher Jew, had embarked on a 'copy-cat' search of his own for the Rebbe's diamonds — in the Melbourne suburb of Footscray, where two 700 metre-deep holes were drilled in work carried out between January and July 1998. The man, identified as a Mr Israel Teleshevsky, said he was acting on the advice of the Rebbe, the paper reported, explaining that this was 'the guru whose visions led mining magnate Joseph Gutnick to vast wealth'. The bemused workers on the site explained how, each morning, they had to pay homage to a portrait of the Rebbe. 'A bag of dollar coins was provided so workers could deposit one every day in a moneybox by the picture of the rabbi,' one of them explained. And Mr Teleshevsky would occasionally halt drilling so that he could bless the operation: 'We'd have to pull our core tube out and wait for him to pour this holy water or whatever down inside the drill rig, and away he'd go . . . That was his religion and we just sort of went along with it. We knew from the geologist that he had Buckley's chance of finding diamonds, but it was work.' Eight months later the drilling company was still waiting to be paid, and lodged a claim for $166,000 from Mr Teleshevsky through the County Court.[20]

This was, of course, a gross parody of Joseph's own diamond search. But incidents like this, and his sister Pnina's *Hoshen* quest, would inevitably have raised discomforting questions about Joseph's activities and his faith in the Rebbe, and there can be little doubt that they had the potential to undermine seriously Joseph's own credibility. They were, from Joseph's perspective, unwanted and possibly harmful distractions.

Fortunately for Joseph, he had by this time established his bona fides as one of Australia's biggest and most successful gold miners . . .

Joseph Gutnick's Mining Activities

Bow River Diamond Project
Tanami Gold Projects
Rand Project
Cloncurry Project
Plutonic
Nabberu
Wiluna Gold Operation
Jundee Gold Operation
Youanmi Vanadium Project
Bronzewing Gold Operation
Astro projects
Rosemont Project – Duketon
South Laverton Tectonic Zone
Fraser Range Project
Cawse Nickel Operation
Perth
Mt Pleasant Gold Operation
Kalgoorlie
Melbourne Head Office

Going for Gold

*'Money is waiting for him, buried in the depths of the earth —
not paper currency but actual gold.'*
Rabbi Menachem Mendel Schneerson, 19 November 1990

IT IS PROBABLY only in a country like Australia that a devoutly Orthodox Jew, inspired by a venerable rabbi in New York, and a knock-about English adventurer, inspired by the stories of Jack London, could cross paths in the desert — and find a fortune in gold.

Mark Creasy had arrived in Australia from England in 1968 as a penniless twenty-four year old. He started off working as a mining engineer in Broken Hill, but soon gave that up for gold prospecting. Prospecting was a mug's game, and he only got into it, he once admitted, because he had read 'one too many of Jack London's adventure novels'. For most of the next twenty years he kicked around the inhospitable terrain of Western Australia's gold country, turning up the odd nugget, just enough to keep hunger at bay, his battered old four-wheel-drive LandCruiser going, and the age-old prospectors' dream of 'finding the big one' alive. He was 'very, very poor for very, very long periods of time', he told an interviewer many years later, after 'the big one' finally came in.[1] 'I was bloody well on the bones of my arse in 1975 and I owed considerable sums of money, and it was hard again in 1983.' As far as he was concerned, Thomas Edison didn't know what he was talking about — at least when it came to looking for gold. One per cent inspiration and 99 per cent perspiration? 'Well, I reckon in prospecting it's 0.001 per cent inspiration and 99.999 per cent perspiration.'

One of the more promising areas Creasy came across was the Lake Violet–Yandal greenstone belt 400 kilometres north of Kalgoorlie, in some of the most desolate, inhospitable terrain in Western Australia. He discovered his first 'fresh gold' there in 1978, eventually finding some forty ounces of gold nuggets at a place called Jundee, in the northern part of the belt, and encouraging signs of gold at Bronzewing, 120 kilometres to the south. The area had been lightly explored for over twenty years and much of it was still tied up by mining groups through temporary reserve licences. After they dropped out Creasy was able to move in and buy up the leases in the mid-1980s. He had been associated with many small gold deposits in the past, but nothing with anything like the potential of Bronzewing or Jundee. These, he was certain, were once-in-a-lifetime finds. They had been overlooked because previous explorers had quite simply not known what to look for. 'Because of long periods of tropical weathering,' he once explained, 'Western Australia has big areas where wind and sand [have] obscured the signs of mineralisation. Unlike South Africa, where the rocks are well exposed, weathering over here has caused the gold to be dissolved and to spread out in a mushrooming effect, rather like a "geochemical halo".' He went on to note that recent technological advances now enabled prospectors to detect these gold deposits 'not by looking for the obvious signs, but by looking for outcrops of mineralisation which had escaped previous detection.'[2]

Next came the hard part. He had to persuade the mining companies that, despite the failures of past exploration, there was gold there. Lots of it. They needed only to spend money, keep drilling — and have faith. Creasy claims he spoke to twenty separate mining groups about joint venturing his tenements. But none was interested, all displaying 'a complete lack of technical, geological and entrepreneurial ability'.[3] Then, some time in December 1990, he approached Joseph Gutnick's Great Central Mines.

Joseph had already proven himself, in his post-1987 reincarnation as a miner of the ground rather than of the stock market, to be a bold, unconventional and lucky gold explorer. His Plutonic strike almost two years earlier had turned out to be one of the most promising in living memory, more than most miners could reasonably hope for in a lifetime. And although he had been forced to sell Plutonic prematurely to keep afloat in the aftermath of the 1987 stock market crash, this alone would have more than vindicated the first part of the Rebbe's prediction that he would find huge quantities of gold and diamonds in the desert. This is possibly why Joseph appears to have been more interested at this time in 'proving up' the second part of the Rebbe's prediction, about the diamonds. Nevertheless, unlike all the other miners Creasy had approached, Joseph had the imagination (and perhaps even shared something of the weather-beaten adventurer's maverick faith in the extraordinary and the unconventional) to appreciate that his Yandal tenements might be something special. Joseph remembers his first meeting with Creasy, quite vividly:

> I liked Mark. I believed in him. My strategy always was to get big blocks of land and if you hit it you had the whole area. And Mark Creasy had these Yandal belt tenements which he was hawking around. He was a struggler, a fighter. He'd be out on the fields six months, nine months at a time. He knew the Yandal area. He didn't want to drill it because he was scared he would ruin it. He met up with me. I'd just sold Plutonic and I had some money and I wanted to look for a new area. I met him in Perth. We sat and negotiated over lots of bottles of beer. I'm more a vodka drinker. I get *shicker* [drunk] on *Simchas Torah* [a joyous Jewish festival, when it is customary to get a bit tipsy]. But I had a few drinks with Mark . . . And we did this deal on the Yandal belt . . . He was a tough negotiator.

If Joseph needed any persuasion to go with Creasy, he received it from the Rebbe. On 18 November 1990 — just before he met Creasy in Perth — the Rebbe had prophesied that gold was waiting for Joseph: 'Gold in the sockets of the earth — not paper money, gold money.' And then, on 9 June 1991, the Rebbe urged Joseph to 'keep searching. Not just for diamonds, but also for gold,' giving him the two dollar bills. Six months later, on 4 December 1991, a deal was cut. Joseph bought into 70 per cent of Bronzewing and 51 per cent of Jundee, and obtained first call over Creasy's remaining Yandal interests. In return, Creasy got 20,000 Great Central shares, $50,000 to cover his costs and a further $3 million to be paid after twelve months. It was probably the best deal these two unlikely bedfellows had made in their lives. For Joseph, it would more than make up for any regret he might have had that Plutonic had slipped through his hands so cheaply. For Creasy, it was to bring paydirt beyond his wildest dreams when, two and a half years later, Joseph exercised his option and bought out his remaining interest for $117 million.

Joseph and his mining chief, Ed Eshuys, then set about exploring the area with a commitment, energy and technical innovation that had Creasy rubbing his eyes. Eshuys's method was to 'frontal attack with the drill rig', and he was not afraid to drill often, and drill deep. 'I've no idea what happened to them before 1987, but Great Central is absolutely the top prospector in the country these days, bar none,' Creasy said. 'Joe tells his geos [geologists] to go out and spend money, and Ed Eshuys directs the spending properly. They're so much better than anyone else I've met.'[4]

Eshuys started drilling at Jundee in February 1992, but extreme wet weather forced him to transfer his focus to Bronzewing and Mount Joel, 120 kilometres to the south. In July 1992 he struck his first gold at Bronzewing. The results were low grade and some explorers may have shunned them but, Eshuys explained at a Diggers & Dealers Forum in Kalgoorlie a year later, Great Central's commitment to explain every gold occurrence and its preference to explore through drilling encouraged the company to press on. Reverse circulation drilling began a month later and core drilling began in December 1993, with Great Central spending some $1 million a month drilling out the area. Once the targets were selected — often quite arbitrarily: the first drillings simply followed the line of the perimeter fence! — they were drilled to 200 metres or more. By comparison, most other explorers went down to just forty metres, or at most fifty metres. On that basis, Eshuys pointed out, the gold at Bronzewing would have been missed. 'The old-timers' techniques weren't appropriate here.'[5] So rapid was the progress, and so spectacular the results — 'we never got intersections like this at Plutonic — never!' Eshuys marvelled[6] — that the first gold from Bronzewing was expected to be poured in the second quarter of 1994, barely two years after exploration began.

While the press and the mining community followed what was taking place at Bronzewing, events were overshadowed for much of this period by the more dramatic, if less productive, happenings at Nabberu. Joseph himself was more excited about the virtually non-existent diamonds at Nabberu than he was about the gold bonanza that Eshuys and the Great Central team were unearthing at Bronzewing. It was not that Joseph was indifferent to what was taking place at Bronzewing, or even that he had lost any of his intrinsic enthusiasm for gold. It seems, rather, that his determination to redeem the second leg of the Rebbe's 1987 diamond–gold quinella dominated his thinking — and this was reflected in the media coverage. Nevertheless, the press did acknowledge, albeit a little reluctantly, that for all the titillation they were getting out of his diamond follies, the man they liked to call 'Goldfinger' was seriously back in business. The *Financial Review*'s 'Chanticleer' even awarded Joseph his 1992 'Lazarus Award' — 'for coming back from beyond'.[7]

The markets, too, were beginning to sit up and take notice. By the beginning of 1993 — just before the American-generated diamond frenzy took the company briefly past the $1 billion mark — Great Central was capitalised at not much less than $400 million, making it the 85th-largest company on the register. Given the roller-coaster history of Joseph's business empire, and the heavy losses investors had suffered in the past, many analysts and brokers still adopted a 'wait and see' attitude — despite Joseph's insistence that there was 'no more paper shuffling, just exploration'.[8] Typical of Joseph's companies, with the top twenty shareholders in Great Central controlling most of the shares (some 96.2 per cent in September 1992, with Joseph himself holding 46 per cent), there was very little floating scrip available for trading. But it was plain to all that Bronzewing was shaping up to be a major discovery, enabling Great Central to retain much of its market credibility even after the Nabberu diamond fiasco in March. This was underscored when, at the height of Joseph's fight with De Beers over Nabberu, Rothschild Australia put up a $4 million loan in April 1993 to finance the resource definition drilling at Bronzewing. Rothschild had been interested in providing full funding, but while Joseph welcomed this as a gesture of confidence in his company, he said he did not want any joint-venture partners. His fracas with De Beers had clearly made him wary.

A major breakthrough for Joseph came about seven months later, in November 1993, when AMP became Great Central's first big institutional investor, buying up 2.8 million shares for some $16.8 million dollars. That one of Australia's largest and most solid institutional investors, which had up until now shunned him as a sharp, high-risk speculative market operator rather than a serious gold miner, was now buying into his companies was the vote of confidence Joseph needed: recognition that the pre-1987 paper king was dead.[9] It was not just a matter of ego, although Joseph did undoubtedly enjoy and perhaps even crave the acceptance and respect of the Big End of Town. He admitted he had serious reservations about both his performance and his image as a paper-shuffler in the 1980s. 'I am like a reformed alcoholic,' he confessed once, looking back on that period. 'I used to be on the phone every 10 seconds buying shares, selling shares. I much prefer exploration and mining gold to trading the stockmarket.'[10] But there was another, much more important dimension to it all, which his father, Chaim, points to when discussing Joseph's reputation as a businessman:

> I don't know all the details of his transactions and so on and so forth. I only can judge by what I hear, what he tells me, and what I read in the press. Sometimes the press has been critical. And that has upset me of course, because ethical standards are more important than anything. The whole idea of him going into business was in order to be as an example. That is

why the Rebbe gave him his blessing. If it creates the opposite, then what is the object of it?

Joseph, from this perspective, was doing what was, in essence, the Rebbe's business. He would have been aware that his public activities had an ethical, quasi-religious dimension and had to be above reproach. To be seen as other than a solid, reputable, bona fide businessman would reflect badly, not just on himself but also on his religion — and, ultimately, on the Rebbe. It was an awesome responsibility.

Changing perceptions of himself, however, was always going to be an uphill battle for Joseph, whose business performance continued to attract the constant attention not only of his many knockers in the media but also of the market regulators. His companies had been the targets of umpteen inquiries over the years, none of which had ever found him blameworthy. It was not for want of trying. Joseph, for his part, accepted the constant probes into his activities with an almost stoical indifference, confident in his own mind that he had done nothing wrong.

◊ ◊ ◊

The gold-bearing potential at Bronzewing, meanwhile, was being updated almost daily. By the end of July 1993, the site had already proven up reserves of over a million ounces; by December, this had more than doubled to 2.5 million ounces. By comparison, Plutonic had proven up just 600,000 ounces of gold when Joseph sold it in 1989. An aggressive drilling program was also under way at Jundee, and there were signs that this could turn out to be another Bronzewing. Joseph took the next step, raising a further $77 million from institutional investors, who were now beginning to scramble over each other for a piece of Great Central. At the end of March 1994 Joseph knew he had arrived: Great Central Mines gained recognition as a mainstream mining stock, and was included, for the first time, in the Gold and All Ordinaries indices.

The coming months saw proven gold reserves at both Bronzewing and Jundee regularly revised upwards as Ed Eshuys's aggressive drilling program uncovered more and more gold. By July 1994, he had sixteen drill rigs operating, and the total proven deposits at the combined sites totalled some 3.13 million ounces. A month later it was reassessed at 3.7 million ounces. Bronzewing alone was assessed at 3 million ounces, while Jundee, with only fifteen per cent of the site drilled, had already proven up close to 700,000 ounces. By October

1994, the combined reserves at the two sites passed 4 million ounces — and Eshuys still believed he had 'only scratched the surface'.[11]

While the Yandal belt was by far the most promising of his holdings, Joseph continued to explore for gold elsewhere as well. Mount Kersey pressed ahead with its Superchannel Project in the Eastern Goldfields, targeting fifteen sites with mineralisation characteristics similar to those found at Centaur's Lady Bountiful Extended. By 1994 it held over 2300 square kilometres of land in the Eastern Goldfields and Murchison regions, and reported encouraging results. Australian Gold Resources resumed gold exploration in 1994, entering into an agreement to explore an area in the Forrestania greenstone belt (it was to withdraw from the agreement in December that year).

The most encouraging results, however, were achieved by Johnson's Well. The company had become a major player in Joseph's push to find diamonds in the Nabberu area in 1992 and 1993, but reverted to gold exploration in 1994, entering into several joint ventures in the Duketon greenstone belt near Laverton. Promising drillings at several sites in the area prompted speculation about another Bronzewing in the making. Duketon, like Yandal, had been turned over before, yielding little of interest. But Eshuys attacked it with his customary gusto and tradition-defying techniques, and came up with findings that, while encouraging, would probably not have attracted the interest they did had it not been for his track record at Plutonic, Bronzewing and Jundee. It was not long before Johnson's Well was valued at $164 million — largely on the back of speculation that 'Golden Joe' might have lucked out yet again. Joseph was not about to dampen expectations. 'There is a possibility for multi-million ounces,' he said as Johnson's Well moved several more drilling rigs into the area at the beginning of 1995.[12]

As for gold production, Centaur's Lady Bountiful Extended remained Joseph's most successful working mine, producing 65,000 ounces of gold in 1992 (its first year back in Joseph's hands after he had recovered it from the receivers), 56,000 ounces in 1993, and 33,200 ounces in 1994. Astro produced 10,826 ounces of gold from its Northern Lady Project up to the end of June 1992, with a further 7842 ounces produced in 1993 and 12,459 ounces in 1994. Mining also began again at Great Central's Great Lady mine in 1992, but production remained modest — 2197 ounces in 1992, 5425 in 1993, and 5775 ounces in 1994.

While Joseph's exploration efforts were bringing in increasingly spectacular results at Bronzewing and Jundee, the action was reflected in the markets. By August 1994 Great Central had increased its value to $865 million, and was now ranked seventy-third on the Australian Stock Exchange. This was largely achieved by a successful 12 million share placement, much of which was snapped up by the big institutions, raising some $117 million. The money was needed to pay out Mark Creasy for the balance of his stake in Bronzewing and Jundee, on top of the $16 million he had already received in cash and shares. It was a few months before Creasy was to receive his money, and when he did, in February 1995, he generously agreed to lend $50 million back to Great Central to finance the building of the Jundee plant, which was about to come on stream. 'He's a very lucky man,' Joseph said as he handed over the huge cheque. 'He worked very hard. In fact I think that this is history that someone has been paid that amount of money as a prospector.' Joseph had no doubt that it was money well spent: 'I believe that in years to come this purchase will prove to have been very cheap.'[13]

Now that AMP and the other big institutional investors were buying into Great Central, Joseph's own personal stake in the company began to shrink, significantly altering the nature of its traditionally tightly held register. This was an important development. The 'tightness' of Great Central's register had been one of the most consistently criticised aspects of the company. By diluting his own holding, and increasing that of the big institutions, Great Central would be subject more to conventional market forces and less to the loyalty of his long-term speculative fellow travellers. With real assets on the ground, and stunning prospects for the future, a company like Great Central, and to a lesser degree Centaur as well, could now afford, and expect, to thrive on such exposure.

By August 1994, when Great Central raised the $117 million it needed to pay out Creasy, Joseph's personal holding in the company was down to 35.4 per cent, worth about $260 million. Eleven months later, in July 1995, following the sale of a further 12.5 million shares for $36 million, it was down to 25 per cent. This still left Joseph the principal shareholder in the company, with 62 million shares worth some $190 million. To say nothing of the $36 million in his pocket.

Some Gutnick-gazers began to speculate that Joseph was selling down his stake in Great Central not only because he was under pressure from the institutions to do so but in order to raise money to fund his search for the Rebbe's elusive diamonds. These were never far from Joseph's thoughts, and he would clearly need money to find them. Lots of money. He denied that this was why he was selling his Great Central shares, and was adamant that he remained as committed as ever to gold: 'There's enough room in a man's heart for two loves,' he said when asked. Others suggested that Joseph was not really interested in mature, well-established companies like Great Central. He was more interested, they argued, in 'the thrill and reward of small companies that make it big in exploration'.[14] Joseph categorically rejected this. 'I've still got a good holding,' he pointed out after the August 1996 sell-off. 'It's not as if I'm walking away. I'm only 43 years old and as eager and ambitious as I ever was about Great Central's prospects. I think the fact that I was able to sell five per cent to Australian institutions is a mark of my reputation. I've worked very hard to win back their confidence.'[15]

◊ ◊ ◊

In November 1994 another major landmark was passed. Bronzewing came on stream, marking Joseph's transition from being essentially a gold explorer to becoming a major gold producer. He had come a long, long way since 1987. The mine was officially inaugurated a few months later, in March 1995, with the Western Australian Premier Richard Court present, and Joseph spoke about how, for many years, he had 'dreamed of becoming a miner, discovering gold mines and establishing a premier mining house in Australia.' Then — quite uncharacteristically since the 1993 Nabberu diamond fiasco — he deliberately chose to highlight the role of the Rebbe, who had died in New York nine months earlier. 'There is one person without whom I would not have found Bronzewing or Jundee,' he told the assembled dignitaries. 'The Lubavitcher Rebbe of Blessed Memory. The Rebbe was an intellectual giant and a guiding spiritual force. He always told me, "Search for gold and diamonds in Australia. You will find massive amounts of gold and massive amounts of diamonds."'[16] It would have been a puzzling, perhaps even disconcerting moment for some of those present, but it was a deeply poignant one for Joseph. He had been mocked and laughed at when he expressed similar sentiments two years earlier, about the diamonds. No one was laughing now.

This was a familiar pattern, to be repeated time and again in Joseph's public life, be it in business, politics or football: first ridicule and titillation, then grudging suspicion-tinged acceptance, followed by genuine respect and even awe. Of course, resentment and envy too were never far below the surface — and the barely disguised glee and mean-spirited *Schadenfreude* waiting to erupt should he ever come a cropper. Some couldn't help themselves in reminding Joseph, even as he basked in his success at Bronzewing, about the 'one that got away' — Plutonic.

Plutonic, by this time, was well on the way to becoming one of Australia's biggest gold mines. It had just revised its proven resources to some 6.2 million ounces, and claimed there was a strong potential to double that. And Plutonic Resources (as Pioneer Mineral Exploration was now called), valued at just $25 million when it bought the mine from Joseph in 1989, was now worth over $1 billion. Asked if he had regretted letting Plutonic slip through his fingers, Joseph was philosophical: 'It's no use crying over spilt milk. You must remember we made the discovery in 1988. Today it is 1995. So of course I have mixed feelings about Plutonic. But I also have every confidence that the Yandal belt will be a world-class gold province.' Plutonic's general manager, Dr Denis Clarke, concurred. It was important to remember, Clarke pointed out, that the money from the Plutonic sale had enabled Joseph to go on and discover Bronzewing and Jundee. 'So he's recycled the money very, very well.'[17]

Joseph and Plutonic again crossed paths in October 1995. Seeing the opportunity for another lucrative deal with Joseph that might potentially give them the Bronzewing and Jundee mines as well as Plutonic, Plutonic Resources agreed to lend him $50 million, secured by an option on the bulk of his stake in Great Central. It was not long before Joseph had second thoughts, however. The gold price began to rise dramatically in the new year, lifting Joseph's personal share market fortune from $234 million to $337 million in the first six weeks of 1996. And the prospects at Bronzewing and Jundee kept getting better. So in July 1996 Joseph decided to buy back Plutonic's option at a cost of $15 million, scotching the persistent speculation that he might be interested in selling down his stake in Great Central. 'I'm in for the long haul,' he announced. 'I'm delighted to have that opportunity, although it will cost me $15 million, to commit long-term to the company.'[18] And why wouldn't he be? Great Central was fast emerging as the most exciting, and one of the most successful, gold companies in Australia. One prominent industry observer saw the Plutonic buyback as a watershed. 'That period crystallised things for Joseph. I think he was uncertain about what his future might be and he would go off and play some of his smaller companies.' But he sat back, had a look at what he had, and 'realised it was a substantial asset with a lot of upside, and that he could be a big industrialist instead of a wheeler-dealer'.[19]

Meanwhile, Joseph was coming under increasing pressure from the big institutional investors to restructure his confusing corporate stable.

Although much slimmer and less intricate than the impossible tangle of the pre-1987 crash days, this was still a cumbersome web of cross-owned companies engaged in a range of haphazard, sometimes contradictory activities. It was good enough to satisfy Joseph's need to maintain control of his companies and at the same time to keep faith with the small, loyal group of core shareholders — many of them fellow Jews in Australia and New York who had stuck with him through thick and thin over many years and would be disadvantaged by any amalgamation or other rationalisation that would dilute their shareholdings. But it was not good enough for the big institutions, which were now a crucial part of the equation.

Ever since they started buying into Great Central, AMP and the other institutions had been making it plain that what was attracting them to the company was its increasingly lucrative gold play at Bronzewing and Jundee — not its highly speculative, and expensive, wild-goose chase after the Rebbe's diamonds. That was for the true believers and/or the speculative mug punters. The institutions wanted Joseph to fund his search for the diamonds from other sources, leaving Great Central as a single-purpose gold company focussed on the two immensely attractive Yandal belt mines. Joseph, if he wanted their continuing support, had no choice but to comply. So in March 1995 he restructured his companies in such a way that, as far as was possible, each would be engaged in a single core activity with a clear regional focus. Thus, Great Central was to focus on gold in the Yandal belt, Centaur on gold and nickel in the Mount Pleasant area, Mount Kersey on gold and nickel around Silver Swan north of Kalgoorlie, Johnson's Well on gold in the Duketon area near Laverton — and, most significantly, Great Central's diamond interests were to be transferred to Astro Mining, which would henceforth be Joseph's exclusive, single-purpose diamond exploration vehicle, focussing on the Yilgarn area. Elsewhere in the Gutnick empire, Australian Gold Resources would remain an investment company (owning sixty per cent of Centaur) but would explore for gold in its own right in the Southern Cross region east of Kalgoorlie; Quantum Resources would also remain an investment vehicle, with a forty-seven per cent stake in Johnson's Well (it would eventually also be the vehicle for Joseph's diamond exploration efforts in Asia); and Australia Wide Industries would focus mostly on property investment.

The structure was still messy and betrayed its pre-1987 origins — but it was the best Joseph could come up with that would satisfy the institutions, ensure his own continued control and maintain faith with his loyal shareholders. 'It is not the ideal structure,' Joseph conceded, 'but it is the structure I was left with after the 1987 crash . . . It is like when you get married, you can't get the perfect woman — although,' he quickly added, 'some people do.' And he did not rule out further rationalisation or even amalgamation further down the track: 'If some institution suggests that, for example, some of the gold interests come together — and only that makes sense — we will consider it.' Meanwhile, the institutions could rest assured: 'They know we are good explorers. They know we don't mismanage our funds. They know there is no monkey-business between one company and another. They know there are no inter-company loans . . . It is all audited, all in our accounts. In regard to corporate governance, I have made a big step forward . . .'[20]

Back on the ground, Jundee, Joseph's second major mine in the Yandal belt, was officially opened in March 1996 — exactly a year after Bronzewing. Exploration at Jundee continued, with the significant Barton Deeps deposit of over one million ounces of gold announced in September. By the end of 1996 Great Central's total resource in the Yandal belt stood at some 6.3 million ounces. With gold sales of over 350,000 ounces for the year ending June 1996, Bronzewing's first full year of production, Great Central announced a profit of more than $46 million and paid a maiden operating dividend to its shareholders — the first such payment ever made by one of Joseph's companies. Another small piece of Gutnick history.

Ed Eshuys, meanwhile, was confident that even bigger and better things were in store. He saw both Bronzewing and Jundee as potential 400,000 to 500,000 ounce a year producers — with Centaur's Mount Pleasant/Ora Banda mines not too far behind. Ora Banda had been purchased in March 1996 from Newcrest Mining for $17 million. Six months earlier, in October 1995, Centaur had bought up a large slice of gold country — some 500 square kilometres — in the Mount Pleasant area for $28 million. All up, the deals had cost Joseph some $45 million, but they had consolidated the field under a single owner for the first time, sharply increasing the resource base of Lady Bountiful Extended. It was, perhaps, Joseph's way of rehabilitating and strengthening a company to which he had strong emotional ties. There was even speculation that Joseph was preparing to shift his allegiance from Great Central Mines to Centaur, and develop the latter as his 'flagship'– speculation that was to resurface from time to time. He made no secret of his optimism about Centaur's prospects, and after successfully raising some \$56 million on the Stock Exchange in late 1995, he announced the company was poised for take-off. Eshuys, with full backing from Joseph, 'attacked' the area with his customary go-for-broke enthusiasm, saturating the consolidated tenements with drill holes. And, as in the past, the results were spectacular — especially on the Quarters tenement, barely 500 metres from the Mount Pleasant treatment mill, which Joseph believed could be another Bronzewing or Jundee. This was 'elephant country', Joseph enthused, anticipating even more discoveries in the area.

Elsewhere in Joseph's gold-mining empire, developments were not quite so spectacular. Johnson's Well pressed ahead with its exploration in the Duketon Belt, defining several zones of economic gold. Mount Kersey's Superchannel project continued, with a number of encouraging results being returned; but by 1996 the company was concentrating most of its resources on nickel exploration in the Silver Swan area. Australian Gold Resources, which continued to hold a greatly reduced but still significant stake in Centaur (27.8 per cent in 1996), entered into a joint venture in its own right with Selmac Partners to explore three areas (Southern Cross, Eastern Goldfields–St Ives, and the Murchison region), and with Deluge Holdings to earn an 80 per cent interest in mining tenements south of the Kambalda–St Ives area. Quantum Resources sold its interest in Mount Carrington Mines to retire debt, and entered into four joint ventures to explore for gold in the Laverton–Leonora area.

Nevertheless, at the rate at which he was going, Joseph was shaping up to be a 1.4 million ounce a year producer. Asked if he expected to overtake Robert de Crespigny's Normandy Mining to become Australia's biggest gold producer in the next two years, Joseph replied modestly: 'We'll go close.'[21] The market seemed to agree. By the end of 1996, it valued Joseph's empire at an astonishing \$3.3 billion dollars. Joseph's personal share of it came to \$574 million. To put this in some kind of perspective, Joseph's entire stable of companies would have been worth just \$17 million at their post-crash low in 1989. His own share would have been barely \$3.4 million.

'Anyone brave or foolhardy enough to have bought a \$10,000 spread of Gutnick group shares in 1989 would today be sitting on just a tad under \$1.7 million worth of paper,' the *Financial Review*'s 'Chanticleer' columnist, Ivor Ries, calculated, adding that no other Australian industrial or mining group could match that.[22] Trying to explain the phenomenon, Ries ran through the now familiar 'tight share register' argument, and noted also the support of 'a group of extremely wealthy

New York investors' and 'tons of hype from the broking houses that support the group'. But, he stressed, that did not explain why Australia's largest and most respectable institutional investors — including AMP, Prudential, BT Funds Management, National Mutual Life, and Mercantile Mutual — were scrambling over each other to get their hands on Gutnick scrip. Especially in Great Central, where the institutions held fully sixty-five per cent of the shares, and Centaur, where they held thirty-five per cent — adding up to an investment of just under $1 billion in the two companies. They clearly, and with good reason, saw Joseph's two large gold-mining companies as solid, safe investments with great future potential.

National Mutual funds management specialist Paul Willis, who had told Joseph a few years earlier that he wouldn't touch his shares, now said that, with Great Central and Centaur, he had 'the best gold assets and prospects in Australia'.[23] This was recognised abroad, too. A major international research group, RBC Dominion Securities, listed Great Central at this time as the only Australian 'strong buy' among world gold stocks, and said it remained undervalued. And, to put the icing on the cake, Great Central was on the verge of becoming eligible to join Britain's prestigious FT Gold Index as a 300,000 ounce a year plus gold producer. Joseph was delighted, describing this as 'a great recognition for the company . . . and a big step forward'.[24] It was an appropriate note on which to end a golden year.

For Joseph, his success was vindication not only of the faith he had had in the Rebbe — a faith that had been severely tested in the tough times he had experienced since the 1987 stock market collapse — but of his mother's faith in the small boy clinging to her dress many years before. Having died tragically in New York in January 1992, Rose had not lived to see just how remarkably prescient she had been. The Orthodox Jewish kid from the Melbourne *shtetl* had become not only one of Australia's most brilliantly successful gold miners, but one of the country's wealthiest men and one of the Jewish world's most generous philanthropists. That he had accomplished this as a proud and deeply religious Orthodox Jew in the rough-and-tumble world of mining, rather than in the traditional Jewish areas of wealth-generation — property speculation and development, or the textile industry — equipped with a yeshivah education that better qualified him to find his way around the intricacies of the Talmud than around the vast deserts of Western Australia, made it all the more remarkable. It was both a personal success story and a tribute to Australia as a vibrant, accommodating multicultural society where anyone, irrespective of background, could aspire to just about anything — a point that Joseph has been the first to acknowledge:

> Australia is a country where Jews have had a real go . . . Look at the 'Top 100' — we're nearly 40 per cent of the wealth.[25] So we've had a really good go in Australia . . . My own experience has been very positive. I've been able to do anything I want in life . . .

If I Were a Rich Man...

'My main ambition in life is to make money, and through money do all that I want to do in life — help others, help Israel, help Lubavitch institutions, help the Rebbe's prophecy come true, live a comfortable life. A mixture of all those things ...'

Joseph Gutnick, interview, October 1999

JOSEPH, FOR MUCH of the past decade and a half, has been one of Australia's richest men. He first made the *Business Review Weekly*'s 'Rich 200' list in 1987, when he had an estimated personal net worth of $65 million. The Black Tuesday stock market crash in October that year all but wiped him out. But by 1991 he was, as *Australian Business* put it, 'visibly back from the dead',[1] with a net worth estimated at some $40 million. And in 1993 he shot to number 13 on the *Business Review Weekly* list, with a net worth of $430 million — largely as a result of the diamond frenzy early in the year. His personal fortune, as estimated by *Business Review Weekly*, fluctuated in subsequent years. It dropped dramatically to $250 million in 1994 and $230 million in 1995, before rebounding to $430 million in 1996 — when gold production at Bronzewing and Jundee came massively on stream and the Yandal belt confirmed itself as one of Australia's most significant gold provinces — and stabilised at $435 million in 1997. It was down again, to $265 million, in 1998, reflecting a huge drop in the price of gold, and lower still in 1999, to $245 million. With gold prices rebounding late in 1999, the expectation was that Joseph would see out the millennium on an upward trajectory. Meanwhile, he was drawing a substantial salary as chairman and director of his eight companies — some $1.21 million in 1997, according to the *Financial Review*.[2]

With that kind of money, Joseph has not exactly been living in poverty. But his lifestyle has not been especially ostentatious either — certainly not by the standards even of men far less wealthy. He continues to live, comfortably, in East St Kilda — not an address that has much cachet in moneyed Melbourne circles — apart from anything else, because this is where he feels comfortable, in the heart of the city's Jewish 'ghetto' and close to his synagogue and co-religionists. Besides, this is where the Rebbe told him to live. 'I think that every Jew who lives outside Israel can't be totally comfortable,' he says. 'Maybe that is why the Rebbe told me not to build a new home in Australia, a new fancy home. Because that's not our real home, even if I live my whole life here.'

That's not to say he's living rough. The family home is no shack. It's big — it has to be. The Gutnicks are a big family. And it is quite luxurious. And Joseph has several other homes, too. These include what is described as a 'palatial home' in Jerusalem's Ultra-Orthodox Geulah neighbourhood — 'a five-storey structure, with marble floors and gilded door handles, watched over by closed-circuit TV cameras and alert security guards'.[3] He also has two other homes in Australia: one, a seaside holiday home in Aspendale — 'about as far from trendy Portsea as it is possible to get and still be on the bay,' Peter Ellingsen noted in his 1998 *Good Weekend* article[4] — the other in Kalgoorlie, near his mines. The large multi-roomed bungalow in Kalgoorlie, which Joseph uses whenever he's out West visiting the mines, is also a favourite holiday home for his brood, who enjoy the camel rides, Aboriginal encounters and other desert attractions. 'Needless to say,' business-gossip columnist Emiliya Mychasuk wrote in the *Sydney Morning Herald*, the rambling home with its swimming pool is 'a far cry from the traditional fibro or weatherboard cottage typical of the architecture in the mining town'. To which Joseph retorted: 'Can you imagine me living in a weatherboard?'[5]

Joseph does, it is true, like to drive in big, expensive cars. He has a Lexus for everyday use, and a swish twelve-cylinder Rolls-Royce for smarter occasions. He gets a buzz out of driving the Rolls himself, even if it does ruin the image a bit. But he has not, as far as is known, set his sights on a Porsche or a Ferrari or other favoured toys of the rich. He also has his own executive jet — a long-range seven-seater Learjet 35. For a man who lives in Melbourne and conducts his main business in the wastes of Western Australia, that would come close to qualifying as an essential tool of his trade.[6] 'It used to take me seven hours through Perth,' he once explained to a nosy journalist. 'Now I will be able to get to Bronzewing and Kalgoorlie in three hours.'[7]

Perhaps Joseph's one real indulgence was his purchase in 1996, when he was at the peak of his fortune, of a $2.5 million yacht called

Illusion. The tabloid press had a field day with it. 'Diamond Joe Gutnick's ship came in yesterday,' chortled Peter Coster in the *Herald Sun*, and was 'tied up at the St Kilda Marina'.[8] Built in Taiwan, it had been fitted out in a Queensland boat yard — where, Coster noted, 'Christopher Skase, now a permanent Spanish resident, still owes money on his pleasure craft.' Bondy 'also liked big boats', Coster added for good measure, before going on to talk about 'the mining magnate's other forms of transport: the $2.7 million Learjet and the Rolls-Royce and Bentley for the shopping.' Joseph seemed embarrassed about the yacht, and was a little gruff when Coster — who seems to have had a thing about Joseph's wealth — quizzed him about it a year later.[9] 'That's my personal business,' he snapped, saying only that the craft was now in Brisbane, apparently with a new owner. Joseph's sister, Pnina Feldman, was a bit more forthcoming, telling Coster that her brother 'didn't like the boat anyway'. Nor, it seems, did his children, who apparently preferred terra firma when it came to holidays.

Otherwise, Joseph appears to have been be no more self-indulgent than any other very wealthy businessman — and a great deal less self-indulgent or ostentatious than most. 'You are used to the good life,' Jana Wendt suggested in her 1999 CBS interview with Joseph, noting that he had 'all the trappings that come with great wealth. . . . There must be a lot of temptations.' Joseph conceded this: 'The Talmud says the temptations and tests of being wealthy are greater than the tests of poverty. I can't go against what the Jewish sages taught. There are always things that a person is attracted to. I'm only human. But till today, I think I've been pretty good.'[10]

Joseph's father, Chaim, one of his most uncompromising critics, is not so certain. 'I can't say that Joseph has avoided all the pitfalls, that would be impossible,' Chaim told Peter Ellingsen in December 1998. 'It is very hard for a rich man to live a life of purity and honesty.'[11] Chaim, although obviously proud of his son's success, is, in fact, very ambivalent about Joseph's wealth: 'I must honestly say that deep down in my heart, I think that wealth is not a blessing. I think having money is not a blessing. You have to have enough to have a comfortable life and when you need it. But I don't think that anybody who has a lot of wealth is happy or blessed . . .'

◊ ◊ ◊

Where Joseph has been very much more than just 'pretty good' — and his father acknowledges this wholeheartedly, as do all but his most hostile detractors — has been in the area of charity and philanthropy.

'He is definitely, as one rabbi once said, a *"gaon* in *tsedakah"* — a "Genius in Charity",' Chaim says proudly. 'He is unique in the amounts that he gives away. And it doesn't matter the reason for it, whether he gets *kavod* [honour] for it or not doesn't matter. But the fact is he has helped so many institutions and people. That I'm happy with.'

There would be few contemporary Jewish businessmen anywhere who have given as much as Joseph has over the years, either in absolute terms or relative to their wealth. Joseph can't put a precise figure on it, but says it is in 'the tens of millions' — well over the ten per cent of the income Jews are required by their religion to give to charity. 'It would be more than twice that,' Joseph says. This appears to have been confirmed in a September 1999 article on Jewish philanthropy in an Israeli magazine, *Mishpachah* ('Family'), which rates Joseph as one of the top five religious Jewish philanthropists in the world — wealthy Jewish businessmen in places as far apart as Australia, Canada, Brazil, Israel and Britain — who had each given over US$30 million during the 1990s to Jewish religious institutions alone.[12] Edward Hoffman, in his book *Despite All Odds: The Story of Lubavitch*, singled him out as far back as 1991, several years before he had reached the height of his prosperity in the mid-1990s, as 'one of the principal figures in Lubavitch, not only in Australia and Israel, but worldwide. He has been instrumental in the setting up of Chabad Houses, *Mikvaos* [ritual baths] and other Jewish institutions in places as far apart as Tasmania and Tiberias.'[13] A couple of years later Gershon Jacobson, editor of the Yiddish newspaper *Algemeine Journal*, recalled how he had watched in amazement as Joseph wrote out a cheque for US$95,000 for a Lubavitcher school in Argentina. 'I'll never forget this one quote he told me,' Jacobson said. 'He said: "God entrusted me with the deserts in Australia. I buy them cheap and I find gold and diamonds there. My wealth is there, and I will share it with other people".'[14] And Abraham Rabinovich, writing from Jerusalem in 1997, noted how, whenever Joseph arrived in Israel, 'the lobby of the hotel where he happens to be staying rapidly fills with petitioners seeking contributions for causes ranging from an operation for someone destitute to the underwriting of a new religious school' — and 'he and his aides reportedly see to it that no one goes away empty handed.'[15]

Joseph, for his part, recalls that one of his main reasons for wanting to become wealthy in the first place was to give charity. 'Part of my rationale for not being a full time rabbi, a full time *shaliach* [emissary], is to use the wealth that God places with me to help others, Jewish institutions, and generally to be philanthropic.' He had always wanted to be the Rebbe's *gvir*, to bankroll Chabad. But, as the Rebbe had made plain, he was to use his fortune to help all Orthodox Jewish institutions, not just those belonging to Lubavitch — something that has earned him considerable criticism from fellow Lubavitchers:

> I've been criticised a lot by some in Chabad because I've helped universally, I've helped all types of Orthodox organisations. I don't look how much I'm giving here, how much I'm giving there. It depends on the cause at the time. People approach me. And I'm always looking around . . . I've given a lot of money to Chabad Houses around the world . . . The Rebbe once told me I should give away at least 11 per cent of the clear profit. He very rarely told me where to give away money.[16]

Much of Joseph's philanthropy is to institutions in Israel and around the world. According to the September 1999 article in the magazine *Mishpachah*:

> Tens of millions of dollars have found their way from Gutnick's bank accounts to yeshivahs and synagogues belonging to every sect and stream [of Orthodox Judaism] in the world. A long chain of Torah and Chassidic institutions has been built by him around the world. And it is to his credit that, despite his Lubavitch affiliation, he doesn't discriminate against any Orthodox group that approaches him. Even the 'Litvak' Lakewood Yeshivah in New Jersey enjoys the fruit of the Chabadnik Gutnick's empire . . .

The article went on to single out several non-Lubavitch Orthodox institutions that have received large donations from Joseph — including those belonging to the ultra-strict Ger and the more progressive Boyan Chassidim. But the key to Joseph's heart — and his pocket — the article suggested, was to propose a project in Judea and Samaria, the Biblical heartland. Joseph is extremely proud of, and enthusiastic about, the projects he supports in the West Bank. Of these, his support for the settlers in Hebron is probably the best known, and certainly the most controversial. 'I've been the major sponsor over the past number of years of the activities of the families that live there,' he says of the 400-odd religious Jewish settlers living among the more than 100,000 Palestinians in the bitterly divided city, holy to both Jew and Muslim as the burial place of the Biblical Patriarchs. 'I've helped them personally, to renovate their houses.' He has also given money to rehabilitate the old Chabad cemetery in the town — which had been an important Lubavitcher centre for scores of years before the 1929 Arab pogrom ended the Jewish presence there. Then there is the Gutnick Centre next to the Cave of the Patriarchs. 'I gave hundreds of thousands of dollars to renovate it,' Joseph recalls. 'To build a *mikveh* [ritual bath] there, to build a hall there. I've also given hundreds of thousands of dollars to the Hebron Yeshivah.'

Besides Hebron, Joseph's biggest project in the West Bank — and the one that most excites him — is the magnificent new synagogue he sponsored in Shilo, named Beit Menachem, in honour of the Rebbe. Joseph gave over US$1.3 million for its construction. 'Shilo is the place where the Tabernacle was for 365 years,' Joseph enthuses. 'It's right in the middle of Judea and Samaria. Right on a major hilltop. This massive building. Even Jordan's King Hussein when he was still alive and flew over the area wanted to know what it was. A massive synagogue. You can see it in the whole of Samaria. It's a synagogue, a centre. And the Israeli government has given a lot of money towards it . . .'

Other projects in the West Bank include Kiryat Shoshanah, a new settlement between Hebron and Jerusalem in memory of Joseph's late mother Rose (Shoshanah is the Hebrew word for Rose). The settlement is, in effect, an 'offshoot' of a large established settlement, Efrat. 'Generally, I've helped other areas as well,' Joseph confirms. 'But nothing of the magnitude of Hebron and Shilo.'

Hechal Menachem, a library and resource centre based in Jerusalem that prints and distributes the Rebbe's teachings and reproduces and disseminates tapes and videos of the Rebbe's speeches, is one of Joseph's favourite projects. It has branches in Melbourne and New York. 'I'm very big in that,' Joseph points out. 'I'm the founder of the Hechal Menachem Organisation. The Rebbe gave me permission while he was alive to call it in his name . . . That's my main, personal organisation.' There is also a religious girls' seminary that he has established in Jerusalem, Machon Shoshanat Yerushalayim, also named in memory of his late mother, and he supports several Chabad Houses around the country.

There is one final, and quite important, area of philanthropy Joseph has been involved in: the hundreds of thousands of Jews who arrived in Israel from the republics of the former Soviet Union in the early 1990s. He has spent large sums on the Gutnick Centre in Jerusalem, which was set up to cater to the religious needs of the Russian newcomers. The Gutnick Centre has now broadened its focus, and no longer caters exclusively to the Russian Jews. Migration from the former Soviet Union has fallen from its early 1990s levels. Besides, Joseph says, 'I believe the Russian Jews should integrate more into regular Israeli society.' So the Centre has started an outreach organisation called Ma'ayanot, which deals with boys and girls in Chabad Houses around the world.

With his fortunes a bit down in the late 1990s due to the fall in gold prices, Joseph had to cut back on his philanthropy, and was not giving as much to institutions in Israel as he had in previous, fatter years. Changes in the tax laws were also making it difficult to give as much to overseas charities as he had in the past. 'But as my fortunes improve, I'll increase my support,' he insists. 'I'm very committed. I very much want to help Lubavitch worldwide.'

◊ ◊ ◊

Charity, however, does begin at home. And Joseph is the major bankroller of Lubavitch activities in Australia, which include those run from his Kimberley Gardens hotel in East St Kilda. Apart from being a popular business convention centre serving the general community, Kimberley Gardens is Melbourne's only fully kosher hotel and restaurant. It is also home to the Caulfield Chabad House which Joseph established at the Rebbe's behest in 1992. This includes a synagogue, of which Joseph serves as the rabbi, a library with reputedly the largest collection of Jewish books in Australia, a Jewish Studies Centre, and a Rabbinical Seminary (Machon) that trains and certifies rabbis. The hotel and religious centre are a magnet for dozens of Orthodox Jewish visitors from around the world, many of them seeking philanthropic aid from Joseph for their institutions. He is reputed rarely to have turned away any of the many emissaries who pass through Australia each year raising donations for all manner of religious institutions in Israel. (This landed him in a spot of embarrassment in 1998, when it was discovered that the money he had given some of these emissaries — twenty-one cheques worth more than $70,000 — may have been caught up, quite inadvertently he maintains, in an alleged $50 million money laundering scam involving banks in Australia and Israel and religious charities in Israel.)

Apart from his own operation at Kimberley, Joseph is a generous supporter of several Chabad Houses and other Lubavitcher institutions around Australia. He was the biggest contributor, after the Commonwealth Bank, to the multi-million-dollar rescue packages put together in 1995 to save his old school, Yeshivah College, in Melbourne and its counterpart in Sydney. And, as in Israel and elsewhere in the Jewish world, he has supported many other Jewish causes outside the Lubavitcher movement. These include Jewish schools (Australia's largest Jewish day school, the 2000-student Mount Scopus College in

Melbourne, to which he pledged $1 million in 1997, following a similar $1 million pledge to Yavneh College, as well as Jewish schools in Perth and Adelaide and on the Gold Coast), synagogues, homes for the aged (Melbourne's Montefiore Homes being a major beneficiary), and even Jewish sporting organisations such as Ajax and Maccabi. The latter must pose a dilemma for Joseph as many of their activities are on the Sabbath. He appears to justify his support for these organisations on the grounds that, if Jews won't pray together, they should at least play together and in this way reduce the 'risk' of assimilation. At the other extreme, Joseph is also the main benefactor of the Ultra-Orthodox Adass Israel community — despite the fact that some members of the tiny, strictly Orthodox, inward-looking community look askance at much of what the Lubavitcher movement stands for. Unlike Lubavitchers, who are philosophically committed to 'reaching out' to Jews of all persuasions, and to participating actively in general society, members of the Adass community prefer to keep to themselves.[17] Joseph does, however, draw the line at supporting non-Orthodox religious institutions. He is quite happy to support Jewish community organisations used by or servicing non-Orthodox Jews, whom he says he respects as individuals. 'But would I support Temple Beth Israel [the main Progressive synagogue in Melbourne]?' he asks. 'No, I wouldn't.'[18]

Joseph's eclectic generosity is not always appreciated in the Jewish community. While he doesn't complain about this, and nor does it seem to affect his giving, his father Chaim is saddened by the fact that no matter how much his son gives, it is never enough, and this generates a great deal of unpleasantness:

> You must realise that everybody who gets money from him never gets enough. They should always get more than the other person. And the natural tendency is that instead of feeling obliged to him they get angry with him — why did he give one institution a quarter of a million dollars and we only got one hundred thousand? There's a lot of resentment . . . a lot of animosity towards him . . .

◊ ◊ ◊

Unlike some other very wealthy Australian Jewish philanthropists such as Richard Pratt, John Gandel, Harry Triguboff, or the Smorgon family, who have divided their philanthropic activities between Jewish and general community causes, the overwhelming bulk of Joseph's giving has been within the Jewish world. His name is conspicuously absent from the list of big-time Jewish philanthropists included in a 1997 *Business Review Weekly* feature, by Ali Crombie, titled 'Australia's Most Generous'.[19] That is not to say that he has not given — and given generously — to non-Jewish causes. He made a $500,000 donation to the International Diabetes Centre, and has been a generous supporter of Reach Youth, the charitable organisation that former Demons champion ruckman Jim Stynes runs to help young people at risk. He has also given money, at different times, to both the Liberal Party and, more recently, to the Australian Labor Party — which, at a pinch, might just fall into the category of 'philanthropy'.

Joseph also considers the almost $3 million he has put into the Melbourne Football Club since 1996 to have been motivated, at least in part, by a philanthropic impulse to return something to a country that has been so good to him:

> I've had a tremendous amount of criticism from Jewish religious circles of why I give to the Melbourne Football Club. Now football is such an important part of Australian society, and I feel that one of the ways besides giving to hospitals, a way that I can give back to a country that's done so much for me, is to support one of the sport activities that is so important to so many people . . . It's part of my repaying Australia . . . Others, like Richard Pratt, give money to the Arts. But I'm not an arty person. I give to football . . . I've helped a club survive . . .

Looking to the future, Joseph says he'd like to do more in the way of medical philanthropy. He has, in fact, long been interested in this area, supporting, among other things, Professor Paul Zimmet's research into obesity and diabetes. While his initial impulse was — and to a large degree, still remains — philanthropic, Joseph was quick to see the huge commercial potential in biotechnology, and, as discussed in Chapter 20, he is very actively engaged in that area. He says he would also like to do something for the mining industry. And for the Aborigines:

> I've supported individual Aborigines. And I gave $30,000 to help the Aboriginal orchestra to go to Israel. I've helped different Aboriginal groups. That's something I'll continue to do. Even though some people accuse me of doing that because of my business, rather than really wanting to do it . . . I'd like to do more. But it has to be done in a way that it's not wasted . . . And certainly I'm monitoring what's happening in the Aboriginal community . . . But a priority for me would be medical research and hospitals. If I'm ever going to give a large sum of money to non-specifically Jewish causes, it will

be in the health area. I'd enjoy doing that. It's contributing to society, something that's needed. Very much so in Australia. And that would encompass Aboriginals as well.

These are fine sentiments. And there is no reason to doubt Joseph's sincerity — or to disregard the generous contribution he has made to Australia, a country where there is not a particularly strong philanthropic culture. 'Australia's wealthy don't seem to subscribe to the idea that it is better to give than receive,' Ali Crombie observed in 1997. 'In short, compared with the Americans, they are downright stingy.' Dick Smith, one of the few exceptions who proves the rule, was quoted as saying: 'In this country, the way that wealthy people get most peer approval is to outdo each other — buying bigger boats and better waterfronts . . . If you donate to charity you have to do it secretly or you are looked down upon.'[20] Joseph, of course, comes from a very different tradition, where charity, or *tsedakah*, is very highly regarded indeed. But in the final analysis — although he repeatedly stresses that he 'calls Australia home', is openly appreciative of all Australia has done for him, and has given generously to Australian causes — charity, for Joseph, appears to have begun and ended elsewhere. If God had placed him in Australia for a purpose, that purpose, it would seem, was first and foremost to generate the wealth needed to advance the cause of the Rebbe and the Jewish people. He makes no apologies for that.

The Rabbi

'If Judaism was the sort of product you could buy off a super-market shelf, Gutnick has been responsible for millions of dollars worth of free advertising.'
Ashley Browne, 'People of the boot', the *Australian Jewish News*,
24 September 1999

EVERY DECEMBER, IN Melbourne's Caulfield Park, Rabbi Joseph Gutnick climbs into a cherry picker and is raised high into the night sky to ignite the first light in a gigantic eight-branched candelabra. It is the first night of the Jewish festival of Chanukah, and the candelabra, known as the menorah or *Chanukiya*, symbolises the successful second-century BC revolt of the Maccabees against their Syrian–Greek overlords.[1] Joseph has been sponsoring the lighting ceremony since the early 1990s, and thousands of Jewish Australians gather in the park each year for the ritual, which is followed by a huge fireworks display, singing, dancing and other fun activities. It is Australia's largest public display of Jewish piety — the Jewish answer to Christmas, and an important assertion of Jewish self-confidence and Jewish self-esteem at a time of the year when many Jews might feel alienated and perhaps even mildly threatened.

Similar ceremonies take place in public places in cities all around the world. 'From New York's Fifth Avenue to Los Angeles, from Caracas to Melbourne, from Paris to Hong Kong,' Edward Hoffman writes in *Despite All Odds: The Story of Lubavitch*, these menorah-lighting rituals 'have become almost a symbol of Lubavitch's unique — and at times controversial — worldwide Jewish outreach.' The practice started in the United States in the mid-1970s, and was strongly endorsed by the Rebbe. 'Before we began these *Menorahs*,' Rabbi Yehudah Krinsky, one of the Rebbe's chief aides and father-in-law of Joseph's eldest daughter Rivka, once explained, 'Jews would see only

Christians seemed to celebrate their holiday publicly and that Jews were somehow shy. Well, Jews are feeling more pride now . . .'[2] Today, Lubavitchers organise a menorah ceremony in every American city where there is a significant Jewish community, and the practice has been emulated in several other countries as well, making Chanukah an integral part of the festive season.[3]

Lighting the *Chanukiya* in Caulfield Park is by far Joseph's most public rabbinical role, and one he takes very seriously. He explains why it is especially important in the Australian context:

> There's nothing as big as our Chanukah event. We have over 5000 people. Jews turn up there who tell me they don't even go to synagogue on Yom Kippur. But now this has become a regular occasion, where they're proud to publicly identify with the concept of the Maccabees' revolt — when, like the modern-day Israel, we stood up for our rights, defended ourselves. That's the message of Chanukah, the Chanukiya in Caulfield Park. It shows the whole miracle of Chanukah, and the fact that you can live in Australia, that it's a multicultural community. We can demonstrate publicly that we're Jewish without antagonising anybody. It's the exact opposite of what existed in Nazi Germany. That we live in a country that's very special. We can go out and celebrate our religious event in a free manner . . .

Moreover, Chanukah is also a time when Lubavitchers are urged to reach out to the leaders of the countries they live in and promote the message of inter-religious and inter-ethnic harmony. It is in keeping with this tradition that political leaders are regularly invited to speak at Joseph's *Chanukiya*-lighting. In 1989 Joseph even went up to Canberra and presented the then Prime Minister, Bob Hawke, with a miniature *Chanukiya* and a book about the Lubavitcher Rebbe and his teachings.[4]

For the rest of the year, Joseph's rabbinical activities are strictly 'in house', in the framework of the Caulfield Chabad House he set up in a wing of the Kimberley Gardens hotel, at the behest of the Rebbe, soon after acquiring it in 1992. It is here that the other Jewish festivals are celebrated: Purim, Pesach (Passover), Succot — and Simchat Torah (literally 'Rejoicing in the Law'). This is the joyous marking of the completion of the annual cycle of Torah readings. It is a time of great rejoicing and hilarity, well lubricated in Lubavitcher congregations by the free flow of vodka, the traditional Lubavitcher *schnapps*, and other alcoholic drinks. And the party Joseph throws for the Jewish community at Kimberley Gardens each year at this time is probably the most joyous, and best lubricated, in Australia. It is a magnet for many otherwise not so observant younger members of the community, intent on having a good time. Unfortunately, things got a little out of hand one year, with under-age drinking making the event the target of widespread parental and community concern. This has resulted in much closer supervision of the event, with the flow of alcohol tightly restricted to adult revellers.

Ideally, Joseph would like to go to his synagogue at Kimberley for morning prayers each day before going on to work. Realistically, this is not always possible, and like many Orthodox Jews, his day usually begins with laying *tefillin* (phylacteries) at home. *Shabbat*, the Sabbath, though, is sacrosanct. Whatever Joseph might be doing, regardless of its importance, comes to a complete halt late on Friday afternoon. Business negotiations are left dangling, contracts unsigned, until the Sabbath ends on Saturday night. He goes home, bathes, and puts on his Sabbath finery — which includes a broad-brimmed black felt hat identical to that worn by the late Rebbe — and goes to his synagogue, where he is the official rabbi. After the Friday evening service comes the festive *Shabbat* meal at home with his family and, more often than not, several dinner guests. The dining table is a central feature of the Gutnick home; it is massive, seating as many as thirty people, and is set for the Sabbath with the finest cutlery and china. As in all Orthodox Jewish homes, the *Shabbat* meal is the highlight of the week, when families come together, the preoccupations of the working week are forgotten, and *Shabbat Hamalka* — Sabbath the Queen — is honoured.

Saturday mornings are invariably spent in synagogue, followed by a *farbrengen* or *kiddush* — the meal that follows the service and is usually light but which in Joseph's case is quite sumptuous, with the tables laden with traditional delicacies such as *gefilte* fish and chopped herring. The *pièce de résistance* is the *cholent*, the huge, heavy stew of meat, legumes, potatoes and dumplings which is prepared the day before (no cooking is permitted, of course, once the Sabbath has started) and kept warm passively. The *cholent* is Jewish 'peasant food' — rich, nutritious, and relatively cheap to prepare — and was the *Shabbat* staple in the *shtetlach* (Jewish villages) of Eastern Europe, especially in the bitterly cold winters. The *farbrengen* is a men-only affair, and the women — who attend synagogue, fully concealed behind a *mechitzah* (partition) so as not to distract their menfolk from their worship — have a separate *kiddush* of their own in an adjoining room.

When he has time to prepare a sermon or commentary on the weekly Torah reading, Joseph delivers this either in the synagogue or at the *farbrengen*. These can be quite fiery — and Joseph himself can be quite fired up, as there is always plenty of vodka on hand — and often have a strong right-wing political message. They go down well in this company; Joseph is usually preaching to the converted here — quite literally in many cases. A large part of Melbourne's rapidly growing Lubavitch community is made up of what are known as *'chozrim b't-shuva'* (literally 'penitents') — the term used for formerly secular Jews who have returned to the Orthodox fold. Outreach to disaffiliated or alienated Jews is a central tenet of the Lubavitcher ethos, and the movement has been hugely successful in re-igniting a love for and commitment to Orthodox Judaism, sometimes in the most unexpected breasts. One of Australia's better known 'returnees' is Rabbi Shimon Cowen — the Scotch College-educated son of former Governor-General Sir Zelman Cowen — who, although not a regular congregant at Kimberley, does attend services and *farbrengens* there from time to time.

The synagogue at Kimberley feels like, and is, only a stopgap. Joseph has far grander plans. A few years ago, three stones — one from Hebron, one from Jerusalem, and one from Crown Heights, New York — were dedicated by the Chief Rabbi of Great Britain and the British Commonwealth, Rabbi Jonathan Sacks, on an empty site adjoining the hotel. Nothing much has happened since. But some time early in the new millennium, Joseph says, a distinctive new building will arise on the site: a replica of 770 Eastern Parkway, the Lubavitcher headquarters in New York. Costing many millions of dollars, it will be the fifth such replica in the world — the best known is at Kfar Chabad in Israel — and will house a large Lubavitcher synagogue.

While this might appear to many, even in the Jewish community, as a whimsical folly and an ostentatious waste of money that might be put to better use in any number of other ways, it is, in fact, a project of profound symbolic significance in the Ultra-Orthodox world and affirmation of Joseph's total commitment to the Lubavitcher cause. Samuel Heilman, in his sociological study of Ultra-Orthodox Jewry, explains why such buildings are so important. They are, he writes, 'in many ways physical symbols of a group's existence and vitality. Indeed, the larger and more impressive [the building] ... the larger and more impressive is the group that calls this place home.' They represent 'the symbolic effort' by these groups 'to express and affirm their survival, even after the triple onslaught of the spiritual challenge of modern secular society, the dislocations of migration, and the destruction of the Holocaust.'[5] Heilman goes on to note that the replica of the Rebbe's headquarters in Israel was a prime example of this phenomenon, intended to project the strength and the vitality of a religious movement that had all but perished in the Holocaust.

'The Rebbe once said when they built the famous replica in Israel, at Kfar Chabad, that there will come a time when we will have to be reminded that there was such a place in New York,' Joseph says in explaining why he is building another replica in Melbourne. 'It will be a constant reminder of the Lubavitcher movement.' When completed, the new building will house Joseph's synagogue and serve as the home of the highly successful rabbinical seminary (Machon) which he currently runs out of the Kimberley Gardens hotel. This is a fully accredited yeshivah, where young Lubavitcher rabbinical students come from around the world to qualify as rabbis. The building may re-house the impressive library of Jewish books at present in a wing of Kimberley. It will also be the hub of the wide range of social and educational activities presently centred on Kimberley, which is for the time being the official home of the Caulfield Chabad House. Once the new synagogue is functioning, Joseph says he hopes to play a more active rabbinical role.

◊ ◊ ◊

The private side of Joseph's Orthodox Jewish lifestyle centres on his family. And, like many Ultra-Orthodox families, which take the Biblical injunction 'pru u'rvu' ('be fruitful and multiply') with utmost seriousness, the Gutnick family is a very large one. Joseph and Stera have eleven children, ranging in age from twenty-four to almost two; and three grandchildren — two of them older than their youngest uncle. And with the benchmark set by one of Stera's great-grandparents who had eighteen children, there is no assurance that their race is run. Asked after the birth of his eleventh child how many more children he was planning to have, Joseph replied: 'You'll have to ask my wife that. That's her decision. I just co-operate.'[6]

Economics, of course, doesn't come into it — although, as Joseph is quick to point out, 'the Talmud teaches us that every child is born with a loaf of bread in its hand. So we're told not to worry about the economics. You have faith.' Not, Stera comments dryly, that they're necessarily 'satisfied with a loaf of bread . . .'

Joseph could probably tell you, at the drop of a hat, the current price of gold and nickel — to the nearest nano-cent. He is on less sure ground, though, when you ask him about the ages of his eleven children:

Stera: 'Go on, test him!'

Joseph: 'Rivka's 24 years old.'

Stera nods her approval.

Joseph: 'Next is Mordi. He's 22.'

So far so good.

Mordi (Mordechai) and Rivka are both married. Rivka has three children. Their ages?

Stera: 'The real test!'

Joseph (thinks): 'They would range between . . . Two, 3 and 4?'

Stera (impressed): 'OK — one and a half, 3 and 4.'

Joseph: 'Our youngest is 2. He's younger than the two grand-daughters.'

Stera: 'Than the two nieces . . .'

Joseph: '*Our* grand-daughters. I get mixed up. I don't know which are my kids, which are my grand-kids!'

After Mordechai?

Joseph: 'There's Zalman. He's 18.'

Stera: 'Eighteen, but he's going to be 20 . . .'

Joseph: 'So he's 19?'

Stera (resignedly): 'He's nearly 20.'

Joseph negotiates the rest, with a little prompting from Stera: another daughter, Chaya, 18; a son, Isser, 15; then two more daughters, Zahava, 13, and Chana, 11; the twin boys, Israel and Rafael, 9; a daughter, Raizel (named after Joseph's mother), 6; and the baby, a boy, Yochanan, almost 2. Six boys and five girls.

An obvious question: 'Is there a little Yossel among them?'

Joseph finds the question hugely amusing for some reason. He cracks up laughing, and defers to Stera: 'Nu Sterrel, is there a little Yossi?'

Stera: 'My second name is Miriam, but I'm not a prophetess . . .'

Joseph: 'Each of our children is free to choose their path in life without any intimidation from my part . . . I'm very happy to have my children in my business. I've got a lot of divisions and endeavours and am building up a mining empire and I would like some of my children to help me and I would like them to continue, for generations to come. Hopefully some of them will also choose to become the Rebbe's emissaries or enter the rabbinical world.'

Mordi, the eldest son, is keen to go into his father's business. He was studying at a yeshivah in Israel but, like his father before him, does not see that as his vocation.

Zalman, the second son, on the other hand, appears destined for the rabbinate. Regarded as the studious one, always with a book in hand, he topped his year in Jewish studies at Yeshivah College and is now at the yeshivah in Crown Heights. 'I would think he's interested in a rabbinical career,' Joseph says. 'But look at my father, he first went into business and then into rabbinics. I went to rabbinics, then business, and now I've got a mixture of all worlds . . . rabbi, business . . .'

'And footy,' Stera reminds him.

The third son, Isser, like his two older brothers before him, is doing the *'mesivta'* — intensive Jewish and religious studies — program at Yeshivah College, supplemented by lessons in Maths and Science. 'He's the one that the Rebbe said, when he was a little boy, you want to help your father out in the business,' Joseph recalls. 'Meanwhile you can't, but at least you can say psalms for him. He's saying the psalms . . . Psalm 121 . . . he says it every day. And I used to write to the Rebbe that he's saying it every day . . . So maybe Isser's the little Yossi . . .'

There are no plans for any of the Gutnick children to go on to university. This is a low priority in the family, as it is for most Ultra-Orthodox Jewish families. The boys aren't even encouraged to do their VCE (the Victorian Matriculation, or school-leaving certificate) — the *'mesivta'* program is the preferred option, leading on to advanced studies at a yeshivah and ultimate rabbinical accreditation (*smichah*). For all their openness to the secular world, the Gutnicks, like all other Lubavitchers, still regard Torah study as the highest calling for an Orthodox Jewish male. As David Landau has noted in *Piety & Power*, his study of Ultra-Orthodox Judaism:

> Learning the Torah and keeping the mitzvot are the recipe for Jewish living, according to the haredi [Ultra-Orthodox] outlook on life . . . Learning itself is the greatest mitzva. It 'weighs', according to a Talmudic statement incorporated into the morning prayer-service, 'as much as all the other mitzvot together'.[7]

There is, of course, no dishonour in going into business — the Rebbe was profoundly aware of the importance of *parnosseh* (livelihood), and he encouraged many of his followers in their endeavours while making it clear to them that they would have to balance this with devotion to Torah study. One senses, however, that Joseph, for all his achievements as a businessman, would take genuine pride in one of his own sons becoming a great rabbi. Stera certainly would. Acknowledging the irony of this — 'I come from a business family, my father is a businessman, while Yossel comes from a rabbinic family' — she still admits that she would probably have preferred Joseph to have followed a rabbinic rather than business path. But she has long since come to terms with the fact that this was not to be, recognising that he has probably done infinitely greater good as a businessman–philanthropist than he would have as a rabbi: 'Now I see his business as *shlichut* [a mission] . . . I think he's very generous.'

For the girls, the priorities appear a little different. Girls in Ultra-Orthodox society, Landau points out in *Piety & Power*, 'are imbued from an early age with the belief that learning Torah is the highest goal [for men], and that their [girls'] task in life is to make it possible for their future husband and future sons to devote themselves to that end.'[8] Accordingly, they are encouraged to acquire a secular education and skills so that they can go out into the workplace and be the bread-winners while their husbands devote all their time to holy learning. This would not, of course, be a serious consideration for the Gutnick girls — but the importance of girls receiving a good secular education appears to have been acknowledged nonetheless. Hence, Joseph's daughters, unlike his sons, are encouraged to do their VCE, and, Stera concedes, it is not inconceivable that they might one day go on to university — 'but only after they are married'. She does not say so, but she emanates the fear many Orthodox Jews have that their children might be seduced by the secular culture they would encounter at university — or, more to the point, by the bright, interesting non-Jewish fellow students they might meet. Meanwhile, the girls, like the boys, are encouraged to continue with their Jewish studies after school at one of the many special girls' seminaries that have sprung up in recent years to meet the needs of bright young Orthodox girls who wish to take their Jewish education further before settling down, getting married — and having children of their own.

This is a subject very close to Stera's heart, and she and Joseph have established a new girls' seminary in Jerusalem tailored specifically to the needs of young Lubavitcher girls at the end of their schooling. 'We set it up because our girls didn't really have a place of excellence in learning, with the emphasis on Chabad philosophy, learning to love the Land of Israel and appreciate diversity in Judaism,' Stera explains. 'It's a Chabad seminary. Jerusalem didn't have an overseas program for Lubavitcher girls. This is the first.' Called Machon Shoshanat Yerushalayim in honour of Joseph's late mother, the institution is fully funded by him, and he and Stera are closely involved with its operation. Their second daughter, Chaya, who completed her VCE at Melbourne's Lubavitch-run girls' school, Beth Rivkah, in 1999, was enrolled to begin there in 2000.

Stera has a particular interest in education and is the driving force behind some of the huge sums Joseph has given to schools and other educational institutions over the years — including to Yeshivah College. He freely acknowledges her role:

Stera supported me very strongly with Yeshivah — she pushed me to prob-ably give more than I would have on my own, to Yeshivah College. It's give and take. Stera's had to agree to some of the charities I give to that she might not have supported. There are certain charities that she wants to give [to] and I acquiesce . . . But it's a joint effort, the Joseph and Stera Gutnick Foundation . . .

Another pet project of Stera's is her Woman of Valour program. This is an adult Jewish education program for women in Australia, and holds a number of encounters at the Kimberley Gardens over the year with interesting guests from abroad or locally. The encounters have been so successful that many men attend. One of the more intriguing Woman of Valour events organised by Stera in 1999 brought the worlds of Judaism and football together in a unique encounter between Rabbi Simon Jacobson, one of the late Rebbe's leading aides who was Stera's guest from New York, and former Melbourne Football Club champion Jimmy Stynes. The topic — which was inspired by Stynes's book on the subject — was 'Find your Spirit, Live your Dream'. 'They both gave a talk,' Stera recalls. 'Both the rabbi and the footballer, as we called them, said things that were compatible with each other. It went off very nicely . . .'

Stera, like the rest of the Gutnick family, is, in fact, very caught up in Joseph's involvement with the Melbourne Football Club. She and the children attend games whenever possible. The younger children are now fervent Demons supporters. The older ones, though, are dyed-in-the wool Carlton fans. They grew up in the 1980s and 1990s, when the Blues ruled, and, like Joseph forty years earlier, had gone with the winners. 'We used to make fun of him,' Mordi says of his father's life-long support for the Demons. 'They were the biggest losers. They couldn't win a thing!' Stera is less interested in the football than she is in the social side of things, and enjoys attending Joseph's President's Luncheons and other functions. She has made many new friends in the football world — including Lynne Samuel, AFL Commissioner Graeme Samuel's wife, who is a fanatical Demons supporter.

Both Stera and the Gutnick children bridge the Lubavitch and gen-eral Australian worlds with the same facility as Joseph and Joseph's father, Chaim. The older boys are bearded — and, of course, wear yarmulkas. Joseph, incidentally, strongly believes that all Jewish males — and certainly all Jewish male school pupils — should wear a yarmulka, whether they are religious or not, as a 'badge' of Jewish identity in a society where distinctions are rapidly blurring:

It may from time to time remind you who you are. Remind you that there's something higher than yourself . . . I believe by having a yarmulka it stops a person from doing what he might otherwise get away with . . . Just because someone doesn't feel the meaning behind it, it doesn't mean it's meaningless. Hopefully by wearing it, they will learn why it's meaningful, what the purpose is . . . Especially in this day and age, a sign of identification.

The girls are conservatively and demurely dressed, as demanded by the rules of modesty. And Rivka, now that she is married, keeps her hair covered in keeping with Ultra-Orthodox custom. Otherwise, they are all very much like any other young Australians of their generation — as I discovered on a stereotype-shattering few days I spent with Joseph and part of his family in Western Australia in September 1999.

Apart from the buzz of flying in Joseph's sleek little Learjet (now re-trimmed in Demon red-and-blue coachlines); wondering at the sheer magnitude of the gaping pit, and driving deep into the bowels of the earth through over twenty kilometres of cavernous tunnel at Bronzewing; and being dazzled by the gee-whiz technical gadgetry of the nickel plant at Cawse — the trip was a good opportunity to get to know some of Joseph's family at first hand.

His two eldest children, daughter Rivka and son Mordi, and their respective spouses Shmaya (Krinsky) and Naomi, were on the trip with us. Rivka is a clone of her mother, Stera, and Mordi is not unlike the 'soft, sweet boy' his grandfather Chaim remembers the young Joseph as being. Shmaya has the gravitas one might have expected from the Lubavitch 'prince' he is, and I was a little surprised to learn that he worked for Joseph, in his Autogen biotechnology company. Naomi, Mordi's wife of six months, comes from a large Lubavitcher family in Seattle, in the north-western United States. The women whiled away the four-hour flight from Melbourne to Kalgoorlie chatting. Shmaya and Mordi listened in as I interviewed Joseph, occasionally breaking in to the conversation. Apart from the recitation of *t'filat haderech* (the travellers' prayer) at the start of the flight, there was no obvious religiosity — heads buried in holy texts or *davening* (praying), or even breaking out into some holy imprecation for salvation when the little Learjet ran into some heavy turbulence on its landing approach to Kalgoorlie. Mordi, sitting diagonally opposite me, merely broke out in a sweat and gripped the seat. Joseph didn't even finger the *mezuzzah*, resting in what appears to be a cheap plastic case on the windowsill next to him. (I comforted myself with the thought, 'We'll be right — Yossel hasn't found the Rebbe's diamonds yet!')

In Kalgoorlie we stayed at the large ranch-style house Joseph bought there in the mid-1990s. When Joseph is not using it on his frequent business trips out West, Stera and the children join him there for holidays. It's a great holiday home, with its swimming pool and large games room. And the children enjoy the desert adventures it affords. The evidence is on the walls of the kitchen — a series of holiday drawings by the various members of the Gutnick brood. Another stereotype smashed. The pictures, many of them quite charming, are what you would expect from any Aussie kid — no pious texts, or Biblical heroes or religious themes. My own personal favourite was something called 'the carrot monster' . . .

Kosher food is flown in to Kalgoorlie from Melbourne or Perth, and the freezers and refrigerators in the large, fully equipped kitchen are well stocked. Observing the dietary laws in their minutest detail is a major part of Orthodox Jewish living, and no compromise is possible. Joseph insists, moreover, that just because he keeps kosher, he doesn't have to compromise on the quality of the food he eats either, or on the enjoyment he gets out of eating, wherever he might be: 'I don't have to, because I keep kosher, be at a lower standard,' he says. 'I like to have the same standard or better than anyone else who is eating non-kosher food.'

The meals in Kalgoorlie are prepared by Joseph's Man Friday. A big burly man, who describes himself as Joseph's 'valet', Steve Kelson is a former policeman with a distinguished background in VIP security. He accompanies Joseph everywhere, looking after his every need — from seeing that he has kosher food to overseeing his safety. He's an interesting bloke. Lives in Footscray. Looks tough, with his close-cropped, scarred skull. He's proud of his working-class, Catholic background and was once an avid supporter of the Fitzroy Football Club. But he has lost all interest in football since his club was, as he puts it, brutally raped by Brisbane with the connivance of the AFL; now he goes to footy only in the line of duty, accompanying Joseph to Melbourne games. Although deeply loyal to his boss, and appreciative of what he did to prevent his own team going the way of Fitzroy, it wouldn't even cross his mind to transfer his loyalty to the Dees. 'Nah,' he says. 'A few sycophants might have done that . . .' Steve can make a mean *glatt kosher* (super-kosher) schnitzel sandwich — and there was always a pile of these on hand throughout the trip to keep hunger at bay.

There can be the occasional glitch, though. Joseph's staff at Bronzewing, about a forty-minute flight from Kalgoorlie, put on a delicious spread for us when we visited the mine. Although someone did

take the trouble to put out some very smart Demon red and blue servi-
ettes, in deference to the boss's football allegiances, they were less au
fait with his dietary requirements. Aesthetically prepared meat and
cheese club sandwiches were not a good option (according to Jewish
dietary laws, meat and dairy products have to be kept strictly sep-
arated). Joseph and his family made do with some fresh fruit. Someone
had left Steve's schnitzel sandwiches on the plane . . .

It was interesting to see Joseph with his miners. He has the same
easy familiarity with his staff out here as he does in Melbourne, and
everyone knows him simply as Joseph. One senses, though, that
behind the familiarity, they have a genuine respect for him and his
mining nous. They pore over the latest findings, intricate maps and
cross-sections, which Joseph seems to understand and interpret with
the ease of a seasoned Yeshivah student studying the Holy Texts. He
asks questions, gives answers, and makes decisions on the spot, some
of them probably involving many millions of dollars. And what he
doesn't understand, he asks. He has yet to get his mind around the precise workings of the hugely complex, state-of-the-art acid-leaching
nickel plant at Cawse, and after a guided tour of the site, asks his manager, a big Scotsman called Jim Stewart, to prepare a detailed description for him and send it on to Melbourne.

Back in Kalgoorlie that night Jim and the other senior management
from Cawse and the nearby Mount Pleasant gold operation were
Joseph's guests at a staff barbecue next to the pool. The barbecue —
strictly kosher, of course — went down well. So did the wine, also
kosher, and the beer. Joseph gave his chairman's speech, outlining,
among other things, a proposed share allocation plan for staff. And
then he invited questions from his managers.

'Do you ever think of moving to Kalgoorlie?' one of the managers
asks. The question is both a reproach and a compliment.

'I'm a Melbourne boy,' Joseph replies. 'My family's there, my life's
there — my footy team's there. But I intend spending much more time
out here in the future.'

They seem reassured. They clearly like, and respect, him.

◊ ◊ ◊

In unselfconsciously bringing his and his family's strictly Orthodox
Jewish lifestyle into the mainstream of Australian public life, from
the highest echelons of the corporate world to the rough and ready
miners of Kalgoorlie, Joseph has probably done more than any other
Australian of his generation to demystify Jews and Judaism for

hundreds of thousands of ordinary Australians who may never have met or even seen an Orthodox Jew in their lives. 'If Judaism was the sort of product you could buy off the supermarket shelf,' sports writer Ashley Browne noted in the study on Jews in football he had carried out for Jewish Community Services, 'Gutnick has been responsible for millions of dollars of free advertising.' He continued:

> His religious observance has been a source of fascination with the football public still unable to fathom how a club president quite happily chooses not to go to watch his team play on a Friday night or Saturday afternoon . . . He has probably educated the football public about the basic tenets of Judaism more effectively than any school excursion to a shule [synagogue] or adult education course could possibly hope to do.[9]

Thus, readers of the sports pages soon became as familiar with the word *yarmulka* as they were with 'beanie' or even 'Akubra', and they not only came to know why Joseph couldn't attend footy games on '*Shabbes*' but why he had to eat 'kosher' when he did attend. And it won't be too long before '*mazel tov*' vies with 'Jolly good, chaps', 'You bewdy' or whatever it is the old boys in the Long Room might utter when the Dees are going well. Joseph's kosher eating regime and Sabbath observance in particular have been frequent subjects of some fascination. Typical was the following item in the *Sunday Age*'s 'Spy' column in July 1997 under the heading 'Gutnix to you: top Demon a brisket case':

> At 11.30 am last Sunday, the kosher caterer's van pulled up outside AFL Park. A microwave oven, two meals of roast beef, a cheese [*sic*] and fruit platter, glasses, napkins, cutlery and crockery were ferried up to the Hawthorn Football Club president's suite. An hour later, Melbourne Football Club president Joe Gutnick arrived, with his two minders and a guest, and tucked in to a meal that looked exactly the same as the nosh in front of the other 130 guests present at the pre-match luncheon but had been prepared according to the traditional Jewish dietary laws.[10]

Bar mitzvahs and circumcision also came in for the occasional light-hearted comment. Thus Quote of the Week in the *Herald Sun* one week in December 1996 was attributed to Olympic gold medallist Russell Mark, who, when asked on 3AW radio how Melbourne would have dealt with Collingwood legend Micky McGuane's defection to Carlton, replied: 'Mr Gutnick would have had him circumcised.'[11] Likewise, the *Herald Sun*'s Mark Knight observed that AFL Supremo Wayne Jackson's decision to shut down League headquarters over the

Christmas–New Year period and deduct the time from his employees' annual leave had 'gone down about as well as Brian Dixon at a Gutnick barmitzvah'.[12]

The cumulative effect of all this has undoubtedly been positive for the way Jews are perceived in Australia. It would not have been especially remarkable in New York, say, where Jews and elements of Jewish culture have long been part of popular culture. But this has not been the case in Australia, where Jews form a far smaller proportion of the general population and where they have, traditionally, chosen to keep a far lower profile. And in familiarising the general Australian public with many aspects of religious Jewish life, demystifying Jews and helping shatter stereotypes, Joseph has played an important role in countering the ignorance on which bigotry and anti-semitism thrive. For even Australia — a country that has always been good to its Jews — is not immune from the age-old contagion of irrational Jew-hatred.

The Oldest Hatred

'I've been called a dirty Jew from time to time, walking in the street. Teenagers in cars hurling nasty comments ... That's about the extent of it. Unless it has been behind closed doors ...'
Joseph Gutnick, the *Herald Sun*, 28 September 1996

IT WAS 12 MAY 1996. Rabbi Moshe Gutnick, Joseph's younger brother, was out shopping with his wife and children in Sydney's Rose Bay. His wife, who was driving the family car, attempted to park in what she had thought was a vacant spot. A man, who was apparently trying to save the space for someone else, accosted the Gutnicks in a rage. 'You f–ing Jews. You should all have been slaughtered,' he yelled. Rabbi Gutnick also thought he heard the man say, 'You should have been turned into lampshades' — something he took to be an obscene reference to what the Nazis are said to have done to their Jewish victims during the Holocaust. He was profoundly shaken and, deeply distressed by the incident, pressed charges. The case came to court, where the magistrate described the language the man — a fifty-year-old pensioner — had used as 'not only offensive, appalling, thoughtless, and quite asinine but ... illegal in terms of the Summary Offences Act', and fined him $400.[1]

Such incidents, though not unknown, are, in fact, quite rare in Australia, which, since the time of the first settlers 200 years ago, has been largely free of vicious or overt Jew-hatred. Jews have been present in Australia from the start of white settlement — there are believed to have been at least eight, possibly twelve, Jewish convicts on the First Fleet when it arrived at Botany Bay in January 1788 — and, for most of the past 200 years, Jews have constituted a small but constant proportion of the settler population (about 0.4 per cent).

While there have been, throughout this period, some manifestations of anti-semitism — reflected at certain periods in such publications as

Chavers (mates). Chaim Gutnick with the Rebbe, circa 1990. The two men enjoyed a uniquely warm and relaxed friendship, palpable in this photograph, which tempered the awe that the Rebbe almost invariably inspired in his followers.

The Disciple. A typical shot of Joseph with the Rebbe, taken some time in the early 1990s. Joseph's relationship with the Rebbe was unparalleled in the Lubavitcher world, both in terms of its scope and, as this photograph shows, its remarkable intensity.

No love lost. Joseph's first encounter with Shimon Peres, in 1988. The smile belies the animosity Peres later came to harbour for Joseph, who played a crucial role in the veteran Israeli labour leader electoral defeat at the hands of Binyamin Netanyahu in 1996. In the final analysis, Joseph says, 'Peres hates my guts.'

The newly anointed Rebbe's Special Emissary for the Integrity of the Land of Israel, with hard-line Israeli Prime Minister Yitzhak Shamir in 1990. 'Any time I came to Israel I would meet with him, spend hours talking to him ... I had absolute access to him. I'd pass on a lot of messages to the Rebbe from him ...'

Hebron. Joseph with Ariel Sharon, the controversial former Israeli general and strident Land of Israel activist, in the volatile West Bank city where 450 Jewish settlers live uneasily among more than 100,000 Palestinians. Joseph's extensive aid to the settlers has earned him widespread criticism from the Left — and praise from the Right..

The Golan Heights. An Israeli military expert briefs Joseph on the strategic importance of the plateau that Israel captured from Syria in the 1967 Six Day War.

The 'Aussie' and the 'Yank'. Joseph and American-raised Binyamin (Bibi) Netanyahu, soon after he became Prime Minister of Israel — with Joseph's help — in 1996. 'Bibi, I'd talk and joke around with,' Joseph recalls. 'An American and an Australian — the same world, rather than the world of Israel...'

Netanyahu with Joseph and Israel's leading rabbis at the mass bar mitzvah ceremony for Russian children that Joseph sponsors at the Western (Wailing) Wall in Jerusalem each year.

Pilgrimage. Netanyahu accompanies Joseph to the Rebbe's grave in New York after his 1996 election triumph. Note the thousands of *kvitels* (notes) sent by Lubavitchers from around the world — including Joseph — scattered on the grave in the belief that the dead Rebbe will intercede on their behalf from beyond the grave.

Smith's Weekly and the *Bulletin*, and the blackballing of Jews in such establishment strongholds as the Melbourne Club — the general consensus has been that Jews, by and large, have been, and have been felt to be, welcome in Australia. It has been suggested that the general goodwill towards Jews in Australia in the first half of the twentieth century, when anti-semitism was rife in many other countries, may have owed something to the fact that Australia's highest ranking World War I soldier, General John Monash, was a Jew. He was revered by his men, many of whom would never have met a Jew before, and presented them with an image of the Jew that would have shattered any negative stereotypical images in the minds of the hundreds of thousands of Diggers who served under him. As a consequence, perhaps, few Australians appear to have had any difficulty accepting, as their first native-born Governor-General, a Jew by the name of Sir Isaac Isaacs, or later, a second Jewish Governor-General, Sir Zelman Cowen.

The large influx of Jewish survivors from the Holocaust in Europe undoubtedly raised the level of suspicion, distrust, and occasionally paranoia in certain sections of the post-World War II Jewish community. Jewish institutions such as the B'nai B'rith Anti-Defamation Commission assiduously record every reported incident of anti-semitism — from graffiti, hate-mail, offensive phone and radio talk-back calls, slurs in the street, prejudiced reporting and media comment, to more serious incidents such as a spate of synagogue desecrations in the mid-1990s. Physical violence against Jews, however, has been virtually unknown, and few Jews would dissent from the proposition that Australia remains one of the world's least threatening and most comfortable places to be a Jew. Even if, from time to time, Jewish Australians are reminded by some ignorant lout or fifty-year-old pensioner succumbing to a fit of road rage that vestiges of the age-old hatred persist beneath the benign surface.

Joseph — with his great wealth, extremely high public profile and assertively Jewish persona — is an obvious lightning rod for whatever anti-Jewish sentiment might be around. He has, in fact, encountered remarkably little — certainly nothing, in public, to compare with the violence or the ferocity of what his brother Moshe experienced in Sydney in 1996. 'I've been called a dirty Jew from time to time, walking in the street,' he told the *Herald Sun*'s Ross Brundrett a few months after that incident. 'Teenagers in cars hurling nasty comments . . . That's about the extent of it. Unless it has been behind closed doors, I've never suffered any other racism in this country.'[2]

There has, of course, been a good deal of critical, sometimes quite snide comment about Joseph, his wealth, his lifestyle, and his business practices in the media, and he has been the butt of numerous cartoons and caricatures, some of which might have had a thinner-skinned or more litigious person talking to his lawyers. The caricature (mentioned in an earlier chapter) which appeared in the *Sydney Morning Herald* on 18 February 1992 — depicting a grinning Joseph sporting a grotesque beard with dollar signs woven into its fringes — was especially offensive, and bordered on the anti-semitic. Even Joseph's generally tolerant and broad-minded father complained to the newspaper, which apologised for any hurt but denied there had been any anti-semitic intent. Joseph, by contrast, took it in his stride. 'I disliked that one,' he admits. 'But I'll only complain when I really think it's below the belt. I've seen similar things done with non-Jews as well. You've got to know where to draw the line . . . If I get offended I'll send a solicitor's letter. If I feel something's very offensive and anti-Jewish, I'll let them know . . .'

Joseph has dispatched surprisingly few solicitor's letters. Unlike many of his fellow Jews in a notoriously prickly community that can sometimes be hypersensitive to the most trivial of slurs, Joseph, by and large, has kept things in perspective. In this respect, he is very much like his father, Chaim, whose own easy, comfortable interaction with the non-Jewish world would have helped form his own attitudes from an early age.

For instance, Joseph appears quite regularly on Channel Nine's *Footy Show*, where he is often the butt of good-natured but sometimes quite outrageously politically incorrect allusions to his Jewishness (one program had Sam Newman, the show's chief dwarf-thrower, wearing a red-and-blue Demons jockstrap in parody of the trademark red-and-blue yarmulka Joseph dons in his capacity as president of the Melbourne Football Club). This has, on occasion, undoubtedly upset or offended some Jewish viewers, especially in the Orthodox religious community. But Joseph takes it all in good spirit:

Some people have said *The Footy Show* has crossed the line. But I take it in the spirit of what the show is. I think of all my appearances on the show, I haven't been offended. Some people ask, 'Nu Yossel, why haven't you been upset?' I reply: 'That's the show!' If it would only be me, it would be one thing. But anyone who goes on the show cops it. So it's not anti-Jewish. That's the show. So if you want to go on the show, you have to be prepared to face the music.

In general, Joseph doesn't have 'a complex about being Jewish':

Just like someone's Christian, someone's Catholic, someone's a Moslem. It just doesn't worry me. I don't walk around with antennae out waiting for somebody to say something . . . Maybe I'm born in a different era. I was born after the establishment of Israel. So I'm proud to be Jewish . . . I've got something to be proud about.

But he can be pushed too far on occasion. In May 1998, for instance, former Australian Test cricketer David Hookes criticised him for being photographed in the Melbourne Football Club's locker room with his arms around his players singing the club song following a nail-biting win. 'I'm happy for Joe to be there,' Hookes said on Melbourne's popular 3AW radio station. 'But make sure he's got his arms around the players when they lose. Now he may well do that, to be fair . . . But just, you know, beware of the Jew bearing gifts.'[3]

When Joseph heard about the comment, he was incensed. He protested to both the radio station and the Australian Football League, demanding an explanation and an apology. Hookes, who has his own segment on 3AW, apologised personally to Joseph within hours, and promised to make a public apology on air the following morning. 'By saying beware of Jews bearing gifts,' he explained, 'I was just saying that because they have a multimillionaire at the club now, in eight years' time Joe might decide to do something else. He won't be there in a hundred years, but hopefully the club will be . . .' It was a lame, not particularly convincing explanation for what had clearly been a foolish, ill-considered comment. Although it is quite possible that Hookes, by all accounts a decent man, had genuinely not thought through the sinister implications of his classical allusion: the original 'Beware of Greeks bearing gifts' refers to an act of treachery, when the ancient Greeks presented their Trojan foes with a huge wooden horse concealing scores of Greek warriors who then emerged to slaughter them. It is possible that Joseph wasn't fully aware of this either. At all events, he took Hookes at his word, and told him that once he had made a public apology the following morning on 3AW, 'the issue would be dead and buried'.[4]

There the matter might have rested — except that some hours later the Melbourne Football Club issued a formal statement, signed by chief executive Cameron Schwab and vice-presidents Ian Johnson and Bill Guest, branding the former cricketer's remark about their president as 'racist', 'bigoted' and 'anti-semitic'. The gesture was undoubtedly well intentioned, but it added fuel to the flames. Radio 3AW's general manager Graham Mott, who had hoped that Hookes's prompt apology and

Joseph's acceptance would have put an end to the affair, was staggered
by what he felt was the club's 'quite unbelievable over-reaction'.[5] In a
bid to prevent the incident from escalating further, Joseph was invited
on to Neil Mitchell's 3AW drive-time program the following morning,
when he publicly confirmed that he accepted Hookes's apology. But
then he went on:

> We are celebrating now the fiftieth anniversary of the establishment of the
> State of Israel. We have our own army and we have our own country and
> we have nuclear weaponry and we won't take any of this rubbish any more.
> We will fight for our rights and if it means suing the Prime Minister of
> Australia . . . whoever it is that says anti-semitic comments . . . then we will
> fight it to the end.

'You can taste centuries of persecution in that,' Mitchell observed in a
subsequent newspaper article defending Hookes, suggesting that
Joseph had grossly over-reacted to something that was 'at worst crude
and stupid' for which Hookes had already apologised. 'Racism and
anti-Semitism are abhorrent,' Mitchell concluded. 'But those who over-
state their complaint often undermine their cause.'[6]

The incident had clearly escalated far beyond what anyone, Joseph
included, would have liked. Joseph, looking back at the incident some
eighteen months later, was still angry about it — but he made the following quite revealing comment:

> Why shouldn't I sing with the players after a game? Why should Hookes
> care what Joseph Gutnick was doing there? I was very proud of our players
> after that game . . . I was offended, besides the Jewish comment, because he
> was just having a go . . . Why does 'Jew' have to come into it . . . What was
> the relevance? Did he complain about Carlton president John Elliott
> putting his arms around the players? What was David Hookes' problem? If
> you watch TV, you'll see all the presidents join their players in the rooms
> after a game. So why did he single me out?

What really upset Joseph, it seems, had been Hookes's challenge to his
legitimacy as president of the Melbourne Football Club, rather than the
throwaway line about Jews bearing gifts. 'I'm very sensitive about my
football,' he concedes, agreeing that his reaction to the Hookes incident
may have reflected the fact that he feels rather less secure about his
place in the football world than he does about his place as a Jew in
Australia. 'That may be a better explanation,' he laughs.

◊ ◊ ◊

Much more serious was an incident involving Joseph just a few months later. The *Age,* in a front-page story on 6 August 1998, reported that one of Australia's leading stockbroking firms, J B Were & Son, had been forced to issue a public apology to Joseph and to the Jewish community for 'disparaging' remarks, allegedly about Joseph and his Jewish associates, made by one of its senior traders. The remarks had emerged in the course of a committal hearing into an alleged insider-trading case involving shares in Joseph's Mount Kersey Mining, dating back to the time of the dramatic 1995 Silver Swan nickel discovery in Western Australia. The dealer in question, Gregory James Doyle, had been involved in discussions with Dr Peter Woodforde, a Were director of corporate services, allegedly about keeping Joseph in the dark over its dealings in the Mount Kersey shares at the time of the discovery. In the course of these discussions, according to transcripts presented to the Melbourne Magistrate's Court, 'words to the effect of "beating them at their own game" were allegedly used'. The report also mentioned that Doyle had said 'I can't go near the Jews' — the prosecution alleging these references were to Joseph and his associates. It was not clear, the *Age* concluded, 'whether the transcripts contain further references to Jews'.

Matters became a bit clearer a couple of weeks later, on 18 August, when the paper printed another front-page story, reporting that Joseph's lawyers had obtained access to previously unreleased transcripts 'containing "repugnant and abhorrent" statements and mimicry that were "a damning indictment on the culture, propriety, ethics and professional standards of J.B. Were & Son"'. There was still little detail, beyond reference to a research note stating that the relationship between Joseph's Great Central Mines and Robert de Crespigny's Normandy Mining was similar to the relationship of a pig and a chicken to a meal of bacon and eggs — where the chicken makes a mere contribution, while for the pig it is a total commitment. It was an old joke, familiar to many in the Jewish community, and hardly offensive enough, if offensive at all, to warrant yet another front-page story in the *Age.*[7]

The next day, however, a few more details began to emerge. Reporting that J B Were chairman Terry Campbell had gone to Joseph's office to apologise in person for what he acknowledged were 'offensive remarks about him and the wider Jewish community', the *Age* provided some examples of what the transcripts had contained. There had been some offensive 'mimicry' of Joseph, the paper reported, as well as references to a 'Jewish Mafia' and references to Joseph himself as 'the rabbi'. In one conversation, the *Age* reported, Doyle 'mimics Mr Gutnick and says to an unidentified person, "We're all bergs and steins around here now".'[8] Things were becoming clearer. It was understandable why Joseph was so upset — and why J B Were had been so quick to apologise. A broking house with as many big Jewish clients as J B Were could not afford to do otherwise.

Two days later, on 21 August, the *Age* felt the need to publish an editorial explaining why it had given the incident such prominent coverage:

> In recent days . . . the *Age* has published a number of reports relating to comments about the Jewish businessman Mr Joseph Gutnick . . . We have given the reports of these conversations prominence because we believe they raise important — and disturbing — questions about the extent to which some old, supposedly discredited racist attitudes still linger . . . It is not possible to know how widespread are the attitudes revealed in the transcripts. However, it is a cause for dismay that supposedly intelligent and educated people can not only hold such attitudes, but can express them with confidence within the walls of one of the nation's oldest and most respected brokerage firms. Comments that generalise disparagingly about any group of people, whether they are made on the basis of race, religion, age or gender, are hurtful, unfair and invalid. The remarks quoted in this case must cause Jews, who have been part of Australian society since the First Fleet, to wonder how long it might take for some Jews to be accepted.[9]

And the following day, 22 August, the *Age* finally published extensive excerpts of the Were transcripts — including the following, of a conversation between Doyle and a client, identified as 'Sam':

> Doyle: Hello. Greg.
> Sam: Jews are buying Croesus.
> Doyle: I couldn't give a s–t about f–in' Jews. I'm, I'm going to become a good Catholic boy.
> Sam: Doylestein.
> Doyle: I know. I know.
> Sam: Have you seen Joseph? Are you meeting him?
> Doyle: I can't. No, I haven't got time.
> Sam: He said he's got a lot of time for you, Doyley. He's going to say, 'Who bought my million shares that day?'
> Doyle: Yeah.
> Sam: 'Who bought my shares?'
> Doyle: 'Who bought my shares?' (laughs), yeah. 'Who bought my shares?'

Sam: 'My million shares. You f–in' gentile.'

Doyle: (Laughs) You can see him doing that, too.

Sam: Oh, little curly bearded little c–t.

Doyle: You can actually see him doing that, too.

Sam: (laughs)

Joseph was livid. 'I'm still recovering from what I've seen,' he told the *Herald Sun* soon after seeing the transcript. 'It's an indictment of what goes on in Collins Street ... It reminds me of the 1930s in Nazi Germany.'[10] He provided a more measured response in an article of his own in the 24 August issue of the *Age*:

> These transcripts contain numerous anti-Semitic statements of the grossest and most repugnant kind. Without wishing to discount the appalling personal attacks and mimicry directed at me in the transcripts ... it was the other numerous anti-Semitic statements — directed at the Jewish community generally — that were my principal concern. It was because of these statements that I publicly aired my concerns. There are so many such statements in the transcripts that it would be impractical to refer to them all ... On any objective view, the transcripts contain evidence of intolerable anti-Semitism.[11]

Harrowing as the J B Were affair had been for Joseph, and shocking as it had been for many in both the Jewish and the general community once the full details were known, it did have a salutary outcome. Two J B Were employees, Gregory Doyle and Dr Peter Woodforde, were forced to resign — and Joseph, characteristically, was prepared to put the affair behind him, once a formal apology had been tendered and he had received assurances that such attitudes would not be tolerated in the future. 'We have resolved our differences amicably,' Joseph said after meeting for a second time with Were chairman Terry Campbell on 25 August. 'I think that Were has taken the right steps, and are taking the right steps to ensure that such things are not repeated.' He added that Campbell, a Richmond supporter, would be his guest at the forthcoming Melbourne–Richmond football game.[12] Meanwhile, he told the *Herald Sun*, the affair had been an unfortunate one — 'but it may be a lesson for corporate Australia that such things won't be tolerated.'[13]

It was a lesson that J B Were, for one, took to heart, employing a high-profile Jewish consultant, Eve Mahlab, to conduct a cultural values audit of the firm. The role of the audit, Campbell explained, was to 'find out whether employee attitudes are acceptable to the broader public and, if not, what to do about it.'[14] He strongly rejected the suggestion, put by a respected management consultant, that the comments revealed in the transcripts were essentially harmless, typical of the kind of 'banter' that took place in trading rooms around the world. 'If Gutnick had been a New Zealander,' the consultant had argued, 'the same comments would have been made, except that they would have been about New Zealanders poking sheep.'[15] Campbell made the pertinent point that the comparison was invalid, if for no reason other than the fact that New Zealanders, unlike Jews, 'haven't been persecuted' as a result of such stereotyping. He revealed that he had spent hours discussing the episode with Joseph and Jewish community leaders, and after learning about the long history of Jewish persecution, conceded: 'I'm not sure that I've appreciated Jewish attitudes before.' He added that while he accepted there was 'a certain macho psychology that is part of dealing rooms', what had occurred in his own company was beyond the pale, and would not be tolerated.[16]

Closure was completed when Joseph revealed, in September 1999, that J B Were was the major broker for his Autogen biotechnology company, and would be a prominent sponsor of his revolutionary new Capital Growth Resources Fund — the ambitious new financial vehicle he launched in October 1999 to propel him into the new millennium. 'That's one of the ironies of my relationship with J B Were,' Joseph notes, not without some satisfaction.[17]

◊ ◊ ◊

Summing up his dealings with non-Jewish Australian society, Joseph concedes that while there is undoubtedly a certain level of anti-semitism in Australia, as there is in most places, it remains a wonderful country for Jews:

> I would say, mixing among non-Jews, that there is a very strong anti-Asian feeling among die-hard Aussies . . . But I don't think there's very much anti-Jewish sentiment . . . My own experience has been very positive. I've been able to do anything I want to do in life. There's the Melbourne Club, I don't think I'd get in there. And you can go through very well in life without having to deal with Upper Collins Street . . . But that is part of my challenge in life. I would like to be able to walk into those circles and point out to them that we're all equal . . . To make sure that Jews are recognised as being equals and part of society, even though we have our religious laws that restrict us in certain areas, but shouldn't in any way disadvantage us.

As is revealed by the following exchange with Jana Wendt — in a profile that went to air on CBS's *Sixty Minutes* program in the United

States in August 1999 — Joseph has always been determined to push the boundaries, to raise the ceiling, at every opportunity. And he does not flinch from the challenge; if anything, he relishes it:

> Wendt: How do you feel on your own skin that chill, that discomfort, of walking into an establishment place and feeling unwelcome?
>
> Joseph: I love it. I like to move into those places, with a yarmulka and a beard, because I like to walk into these kinds of cliques and institutions and say: 'Here I am, we're all the same, you can't make these divisions.'
>
> Wendt: And the bigger, and grander the entrance, the bigger success you are?
>
> Joseph: And the more they have to acknowledge my existence . . .

Joseph had made his biggest, grandest entrance of all into that 'closed' world three years before, in August 1996. He had donned his red-and-blue Demons yarmulka, loaded his saddle bags with gold, and charged to the rescue of one of Australia's oldest, most conservative, blue-blooded, establishment-with-a-capital-E sporting institutions: the Melbourne Football Club. This represented a quantum leap in Joseph's interaction with, and exposure to, broader Australian society. And it has not only tested the extent of Joseph's commitment to and acceptance by that society — but it has probed, questioned and challenged the possibilities, and the limitations, of multicultural Australia on the cusp of the third millennium.

His first baptism of fire came on the night of Thursday 29 August 1996, when he made his maiden appearance on Channel Nine's *Footy Show*.

Demon Joe

'In a city for which football is a defining experience, the diminutive rabbi as savior of an old club, one that carries the city's name, is a kind of symbol of what multiculturalism means, of what it can be.'

Michael Gawenda, the *Age*, 2 June 1997

THE FOOTY SHOW on Kerry Packer's Channel Nine is the top-rating sports program in Australia. A blokey, boisterous, quintessentially Ocker cross between locker-room, bucks' night and dwarf-throwing contest, the show regularly has over half a million football fanatics glued to their TV sets every Thursday night of the football season — plus sell-out crowds in the studio. Appearing on it was never going to be easy for someone like Joseph. Even seasoned veterans of the football world have found themselves hard put to match it with the show's resident Rottweiler, John 'Sammy' Newman, when he is minded, as he usually is, to insult, embarrass and roast whatever unfortunate prey comes his way. Taking on Newman requires considerable guts, an inordinately thick skin, and not a little masochism. It is a rare guest who comes away with the points.

Joseph was invited on to the show just four days after he had stunned the football world by holding a press conference in the Melbourne Football Club change rooms under the northern grandstand at the Melbourne Cricket Ground. He had announced that he was putting his weight — and his money — behind the fight to prevent a merger between the 128-year-old club he had supported ever since arriving in Melbourne as a small boy almost four decades before and another embattled football club, Hawthorn. The proposed merger was part of a long-range strategy by the Australian Football League to whittle down the number of football clubs in Melbourne, heartland of Australia's most famous indigenous game, and transform what had once been a passionate but impecunious suburban sport played mainly by semi-amateurs in the state of Victoria into a high-profile, high-income, TV-based national competition. The Melbourne clubs, however, were putting up a strong fight — none stronger than the diehard supporters of the two targeted clubs: the Hawthorn Hawks; and the Demons, as the Melbourne Football Club is known.

Before Joseph was to make his appearance, however, there was a little scene-setting to do. Joseph Gutnick was not your usual Aussie Rules Football supporter. Although he was a very prominent, high-profile figure in the business world, few outside that world would have known very much about him. People in the general community may have been vaguely familiar with his name, with the fact that he was Jewish, perhaps that he was a rabbi — and that he was very rich. Some might have had a dim recollection that he was one of the high flyers who came a gutser in the 1987 stock market crash; others may have recalled that there was some controversy involving Joseph and Tricontinental, a mess that had cost Victorian taxpayers tens of millions of dollars. He may even have been vaguely familiar to the more politically minded as someone who had been meddling controversially in Israeli politics. But few would have seen him in person, or heard him speak. Even fewer would have imagined, even in their wildest dreams, that he was a fanatical supporter of Melbourne's WASPiest football club.

Not only that — few, if any, football followers would ever have encountered a bearded, skullcap-wearing, deeply religious Orthodox Jew. Of course, Jews had long been associated with football, going back to March 1888, when a prominent Jewish businessman, Mr E Michaelis, was invited to the annual meeting of the St Kilda Football Club.[1] But in all that time — apart from the Sydney Swans' flamboyant Dr Geoffrey Edelsten in the late 1980s, with his penchant for fast cars, pretty women and pink helicopters — there had been no one who had challenged the prevailing football culture in anything even remotely like the way Joseph did when he burst onto the scene earlier that week. *The Footy Show* and its audience were in for a heavy dose of culture shock . . .

◊ ◊ ◊

'What a huge week it's been in football,' intoned the show's host Eddie McGuire, in his signature opening that Thursday night, 29 August 1996. 'Diamond Joe Gutnick! Could he be the saviour of the Melbourne Football Club? We'll soon find out because Diamond Joe is

our special guest on *The Footy Show* tonight. A big round of applause
for Diamond Joe!'

The strains of 'If I were a rich man' from the Jewish musical hit
Fiddler on the Roof wafted into the studio. A strange apparition
appeared — bearded, yarmulka on head, *tzitzis* (ritual tassels) pro-
truding from beneath a shabby waistcoat — gesticulating jerkily and
singing tunelessly, more or less to the music:

If we were a rich club
We would divvy, divvy, divvy, divvy
Divvy up the cash
All day long, we'd divvy up the cash
If we were a wealthy club
H-u-u-u-uh!
We'd never have to play hard
Divvy, divvy, divvy, divvy, divvy
Divvy up the cash
If we were a wealthy club!
Hu-u-u-uh!

'That was the new Melbourne Football Club song,' the Tevye-the-
Milkman look-alike announced proudly, in a broad Aussie accent.
'We've all jumped on the bandwagon. He's come and embraced us, the
Saviour from Bethlehem.'

'Oh come now, Sam,' McGuire laughed nervously as Newman
shaped up to outrage every Jewish viewer in Melbourne. He quickly
passed the baton to Trevor Marmalade, another *Footy Show* regular,
who announced that Telstra was appealing to 'viewers in the Caulfield
area not to overload the exchange'.

Marmalade then went on to point out 'the fantastic merchandising
opportunities' that had been opened up by Joseph's arrival on the football scene — among them, the red-and-blue 'Demons Ya-mool-ka'. This
was a new word being introduced into Australia's football lexicon —
and it wouldn't be long before 'yarmulka' was enshrined alongside
'Sherrin' and 'Yibbida, yibbida — that's all folks!' as an integral part of
Aussie footy-speak.

And then, the big moment arrived.

'Most football fans have never heard of Joseph Gutnick, unless
you are a follower of the Fortune 500 in BRW's 500 richest people,'
McGuire stated portentously. 'Yet this man could yet be the next president of the Melbourne Football Club ... The father of ten joins us
right now on *The Footy Show*. Joseph Gutnick!'

Joseph entered to loud cheers and catcalls — sporting his own beard and wearing his own spanking new red-and-blue Demons yarmulka. He looked guarded, apprehensive, not quite knowing what to expect. Like a strange bird that had flown into a cage full of chooks, finding himself encircled by curious, head-cocked onlookers, not sure whether one of them was going to take a peck at him. But he was not intimidated. Having *Business Review Weekly* tell the world you're worth well over $400 million can do wonders for the self-confidence. To say nothing of a special mateship with the man many believe was probably the number one draft pick for Messiah in the last 2000 years. And with another mate who owed him one for having helped him get elected prime minister of a country with the biggest and most powerful Jewish army the world has ever known — bigger, even, than Ben-Hur's. Joseph had had countless 'spears and arrows' hurled at him over the years. His skin was as thick as a rhinoceros's.

Joseph shook hands with Newman and McGuire. He looked carefully behind him before taking his seat, next to Newman. 'Don't worry — I'm not going to pull it out from under you!' Newman assured him. Joseph was not so sure: 'We're watching all sides.' He'd probably been forewarned about Newman, once described by the *Age*'s Patrick Smith as someone 'who wakes up each morning only so he can insult everyone with whom he comes into contact'.[2] But Newman, it would seem, had been told to go easy on the rabbi. The *Fiddler on the Roof* skit was OK, but don't push things . . . The last thing the show's executive director Harvey Silver — who happened to be Jewish — needed in his life was a risqué Newmanism with connotations that some of his more hypersensitive co-religionists might find offensive, or worse. And, if he needed a reminder, Harvey's mum, Cesia, was on the set. Just to make sure . . .

Joseph endured five or so minutes of Newman's uncharacteristically restrained, but all too characteristically facetious, questioning about his motives for coming to the rescue of the Melbourne Football Club. He then turned his back on him, and spoke directly to Garry Lyon — Melbourne's captain and a regular panellist on *The Footy Show*, whom he had never met before. He explained slowly and deliberately why he was backing the opposition to the proposed merger. It was all getting a bit earnest, and the audience a little restless.

Silver got the show back on its customary manic tack by sending his mother Cesia on to the set — another first — with a bowl of chicken and matzoh-ball soup, popularly known as 'Jewish penicillin'. She put this in front of Lyon, who had been off the field for weeks with a chronic back injury. 'Here's some soup for Garry! . . . Enjoy it!' 'I will,' Lyon responded. 'I'll share that around with the boys.' One of Lyon's football mates on the panel looked suspiciously at the matzoh balls: 'Those little bally things in it, what are they?'

Then it was back to some serious questioning of Joseph's intentions. McGuire pointed out that Melbourne would need to raise at least an extra three or four million dollars a year to stay competitive with the top interstate clubs. 'You carry that much in your fob pocket, don't you?' Newman quipped, to which Joseph responded: 'Well, it's a day's work . . .' The audience laughed appreciatively, and McGuire ended the segment by thanking Joseph for coming onto the show and 'being such a good sport'.

That was it for Joseph, but the show was not quite finished with him. Newman had taken his notorious 'Street Talk' video segment to the heart of Melbourne's Jewish 'ghetto' — Carlisle Street in East St Kilda.

'Aussie Joe Gutnick! The name on everybody's lips,' Newman announced. 'The Messiah. He's arrived at the Melbourne Football Club. I wonder what the Faithful think?' Mike in hand, he buttonholed a few of the 'faithful' in the street. One of them suggested that Yossel was going to change the name of the club, 'from the Melbourne Demons to the Melbourne Rabbis', and that it was going to be 'compulsory for all players to have beards and circumcisions'. Another was a reporter from the *Australian Jewish News*, haplessly on assignment with a disposable camera. Sam's eyes lit up: 'That's a $2 disposable camera, Madam. And that's what the *Jewish News* runs to, is it? . . . And what do they charge for the *Jewish News*?' He spotted another victim. A student from Joseph's old alma mater, Yeshivah College. His parents had been making some fortunate orthodontist very wealthy. The youth ignored Newman's predictable jibe about his dental work and declared his hero-worship of two talented young Carlton Football Club players: 'I love Scott Camporeale — and I love Anthony Koutoufides's Greekness,' he blurted out breathlessly. The youth's teachers at Yeshivah College would be tearing their hair out at the advanced *Hityavnut* (Hellenisation) their young student was displaying. But the irony was probably lost on Newman, who decided to liven up proceedings with a mildly risqué Jewish joke. (It was an old one, about a bloke who walks into a shop that has a window display of watches and asks to buy a watch. 'We don't sell watches, we do circumcisions,' the shopkeeper tells him. 'So what have you got watches in the window for, then?' the bloke asks, to which the shopkeeper replies: 'Well what would *you* put in there?')

Back on set, Sam was a little emboldened at having been allowed to get away with that one. 'Actually, a bit of news when I was down there on Carlisle Street . . .' he began. 'This isn't going to be another Jewish joke, is it?' McGuire asked anxiously. 'No Eddie,' Newman reassured him. 'I was speaking to some Scottish people down there. The MacGoldsteins . . .' Sam did manage to get another joke in, though: Hymie rings up the *Age* to put an obituary notice in the paper for his wife. He keeps it brief: 'Ruth died.' The girl taking the ad tells him he's allowed a five-word minimum, so he can add an extra three words at no extra cost. Hymie is delighted and decides to extend it to: 'Ruth died, Volvo for sale.'

McGuire cleared his throat theatrically: 'Our executive director Harvey Silver, and our producer Ralph Horowitz will be answering the phones tomorrow morning. The rest of us? . . . Oh boy! . . .'

◊ ◊ ◊

Eddie McGuire needn't have worried. Not that everyone in the Jewish community was overjoyed by Joseph's appearance on the show. There was, undoubtedly, a good deal of fairly crude stereotyping and innuendo — even if it was, by and large, good-natured — that would have offended some of the more sensitive souls. It was also a far cry from the low profile many in the old established Jewish community still preferred Jews to maintain. And Joseph came in for some quite sharp criticism from a number of his fellow religious Jews, who felt he was demeaning his religion and bringing ridicule on the religious community. Most Jews, however, appear to have recognised that any negatives were far outweighed by the positives in Joseph's exposure — both on TV and in the press — as a proud and uninhibited Orthodox Jew who shared the passions of ordinary Australians, and who could mix it with them on their own terms. That, certainly, appears to have been the view of the *Australian Jewish News* editor at the time, Sam Lipski, generally a reliable barometer of mainstream Jewish thinking in Australia, who devoted his editorial to the subject in the next issue of the paper:

> The truth is the high-profile projection into the headlines by a wealthy Jew, whether problematic or benign, wittingly or unwittingly, sets off its own waves of mixed responses among Jews. Clearly amongst many, particularly those of an older generation, such exposure causes anxiety and apprehension. They would prefer that all such Jews stayed out of the media, kept a low profile, and did not run the risk of provoking those looking for excuses to complain about 'Jewish money', the 'Jewish lobby' and 'Jewish

influence.' But many other Australian Jews have come to understand that pluralism and multiculturalism are two-way streets. This means that this country's freedom and openness which enables Jews to succeed and prosper means that Jews, as much as individuals as collectively, also have to feel free to participate fully in Australian society. Furthermore, they have to do so without fearing that some Jews might regard such high-profile activities on their part as a *shandeh far di goyim* . . . a matter of shame in the eyes of the non-Jews. In this respect what we have seen of the Gutnick–Melbourne campaign, at least so far, should make Australian Jews feel encouraged. In its own way, it represents a vindication of the best of Australian multiculturalism and its increasing maturity . . . [3]

As for Joseph himself, he has no doubt at all that his appearances on *The Footy Show*, and his involvement in football in general, have been overwhelmingly positive — both from a Jewish perspective and from that of the broader Australian community:

It hasn't done any harm promoting the fact that someone like myself who may be looked at as a black hat, beard, yarmulka, religious Jew — maybe who has had the Shylock image with some Australians — is part of the football club and enjoys the game and is as emotionally involved as they are. It humanises — I didn't want to say de-demonises, I'm a Demon! — 'de-Shylocks' the image that the religious Jew may have to an ordinary Australian. So I think that's a big positive. I enjoy that. I like to show that we as human beings, as a persecuted people for thousands of years, that we laugh about the same things, and we cry about the same things. And we enjoy football . . .

◊ ◊ ◊

Joseph's involvement in the affairs of the Melbourne Football Club had started only ten days before his remarkable maiden appearance on *The Footy Show*, on 19 August 1996. He had just arrived back from Israel, where he had basked in the glory of his triumphant coup two months earlier in helping get Bibi Netanyahu into the prime minister's office, when he received a phone call from an old friend, Izzy Herzog.

Herzog, a car dealer and property developer, was the brother of Joseph's neighbour and pre-crash business associate Henry Herzog. He was also a good friend of Brian Dixon, a former Demons champion footballer and a leader of the anti-merger fight. Dixon, or 'Dicko' as he liked to be called, had been the Liberal Party member for St Kilda in the Victorian State Parliament for many years until 1982, and had forged close ties with the large Jewish community in the electorate. After joining the Demon Alternative — the group opposed to the merger with Hawthorn — in mid-August, Dixon set about getting in touch with anyone he knew who might be in a position to help. He contacted a string of high-profile Demons supporters, including the State treasurer Alan Stockdale, WMC boss Hugh Morgan and Crown Casino chief Ron Walker. But while sympathetic, they all felt the merger was inevitable and it would be futile to try to stop it. Dixon was more successful with Herzog, who agreed that every effort should be made to save the Melbourne Football Club. They needed to find 'someone who sees the value of an icon . . . and has business clout'.[4] Herzog immediately thought of Joseph, and gave him a call. Joseph remembers it clearly:

> Izzy didn't even know I was a Melbourne Football Club supporter. He thought here's an opportunity to become involved. They needed someone, a white knight to come along and help them. The amazing thing is I had been reading in the papers about the merger, and I thought that if I could do something for the Melbourne Football Club I'd do it. My nature is when I follow something I get obsessed and passionate about it. I always was a Melbourne supporter. And I stuck with them when they've been lousy, in the 70s and 80s . . . So when Izzy called, I was interested. It was my club. And I was on top of the world then in the gold market, doing extremely well, and I thought that if I could do something to help the Melbourne Football Club, I would.

Herzog got back to Dixon, told him Joseph was interested, and that the two should meet. Dixon set up an appointment, and that same evening sped down to Joseph's office in St Kilda Road. There wasn't a moment to lose. He couldn't find the office, and was furious that he arrived at 6.12 for a 6.10 meeting. Then, he recalled, Joseph greeted him 'with a big smile, beautiful eyes, reddish cheeks, big beard, full of enthusiasm and warmth. And he said, "Come in Brian".'[5] Again, Joseph remembers it vividly:

> Brian came in, and he was very emotional about it. Crying . . . I'd never met him before. I followed him as a kid, as a winger. I knew he was a star foot-baller. And then he said they needed someone to back them . . . We had a long talk, for an hour or two. There wasn't talk about me becoming presi-dent or anything like that. Just to help out . . . There was this whole idea of the Demon Alternative, getting a group, having finances to help spread the word. They had no money. They needed publicity. They had to fight it

all in court. I said you'll get my financial backing. It was $100,000 or something, I forget how much it was exactly. So I put up money for the Demon Alternative.

And that was about the extent of Joseph's commitment — for the moment. He had become involved, quite by chance, without any clear idea of where it would all lead.

> I made maybe an irrational decision at the time. That was the motivation, the total motivation — no other, initially, no other reason, other than my love for the Melbourne Football Club ... I was never a member of the Melbourne Football Club, because I couldn't go on *Shabbes* [the Sabbath], but I was a follower. No one had ever approached me in the past to support the Melbourne Football Club, and I just decided that this was something I could do — you know, you follow a team when you are young, and if you can do something for them ... It brought out for me part of my character — something I believe in I'll fight for it.

Joseph and Dixon met twice more over the next couple of days to thrash out a strategy and to determine the nature of Joseph's involvement. That was when it was decided that Joseph's name would be put forward as the Demon Alternative candidate for president of the Melbourne Football Club, with Dixon as his deputy, should the merger be thwarted. This was, on the surface, an extremely odd decision. Joseph was a complete outsider, who had had no formal link to the Melbourne Football Club — not even ordinary membership — and was unknown to anyone in the club, from club president Ian Ridley down. He had, by his own admission, barely attended a Demons football match in his life. 'Dicko', on the other hand, was a Melbourne Football Club legend. Recruited from Melbourne High in 1954 as a sixteen year old with a mighty leap, Dixon had set a club record when he played his 238th game in 1967 and then went on to play twenty more before retiring in 1968. His career coincided with the Demons' golden years under legendary coach Norm Smith in the 1950s and 1960s; he was the club's Best and Fairest in 1960; and he was hailed, along with players like the great Ron Barassi, John Beckwith, Laurie Mithen, Ian Ridley, and Hassa Mann, as one of the outstanding players of that era. He would have seemed an obvious choice to lead the anti-merger charge.

The problem was that Dixon had squandered the goodwill he had built up in his brilliant fourteen years as a player by having nothing to do with the club once his playing career was over. 'I'm disappointed he hasn't seen fit to do anything for the club since he left,' one of his former team mates, Ian Thorogood, said in an August 1996 interview with the *Age*'s James Button. 'He's been missing in action.'[6] His sudden emergence as passionate would-be saviour of his old club generated immense animosity, and not a little contempt, on the part of his former team mates — especially people like Ian Ridley and Hassa Mann, who had remained involved and were now leading their club towards what they genuinely believed was the only way to secure its long-term survival in any form as the Australian Football League evolved inexorably into a national competition.

'How often do you sing the club song these days?' Ridley asked Dixon contemptuously when he suddenly resurfaced. Dixon wept as he recalled the slight: 'It's unbelievable he could ask that question,' he quavered. 'My mother is 92 and we held hands on her birthday and sang "It's a Grand Old Flag" . . . it's part of our family life.' That only increased Ridley's contempt. 'He's cried about 25 times so far,' he said dismissively. 'Crocodile tears.'[7]

Dixon, for his part, conceded that his absence from the club 'has been preying on my mind', but said he hadn't been made to feel welcome. He claimed he had approached coach John Northey (1986–92) and his successor Neil Balme, but 'neither were remotely interested in me talking to the players'. He also conceded that 'sometimes I rub people up the wrong way. Possibly I have spoken my mind too freely. I have tried to temper that. How successful I've been I am not sure . . .'[8] Clearly, if there was to be any chance of fighting the merger without tearing the club apart, Dixon was going to have to take a back seat. Joseph, strange as it was, would be the front man. Football culture, whatever that might mean, was being stood on its head.

On Monday 26 August 1996, Joseph fronted up, with Dixon, at a Demon Alternative press conference in the Demons' changing rooms at the MCG to announce their plans. This was hallowed ground — 'the place where,' as the poet Bruce Dawe wrote, 'when children are born, they are wrapped in the club colors, laid in beribboned cots, having already begun a lifetime's barracking . . .'[9] The incongruity of Joseph's appearance for the first time in these surroundings was patently obvious to the large media contingent. John Hamilton, writing in the *Herald Sun* the next day, described how Joseph sat at a trestle table covered with a plain white table cloth under a sign 'All fired up'. He was dressed in a dark double-breasted suit and was wearing a black skullcap on his head (his trademark red-and-blue Demons yarmulka was to make its debut on *The Footy Show* later that week). He 'clasped his hands as if in prayer and occasionally adjusted a cuff over the gold watch on his left wrist. It was a very large gold watch indeed, secured around the wrist by a gold bracelet with links the size of small ingots.' Across the bare room with the white painted walls and the worn blue carpet, Hamilton noted, almost as a reproach to Joseph's presence there, was a bronze memorial plaque to one of the club's past champions: Keith William 'Bluey' Truscott, described as 'a brilliant fighter pilot, Melbourne premiership footballer, club cricketer and superb all-round athlete. A man for all seasons.'[10] The strangeness of the situation was acknowledged by Joseph: 'If you had asked me a week ago if I would be sitting here I'd have said "that's incredibly bizarre".'[11]

Joseph took the opportunity to spell out his immense passion for the club, going back to the Demons' glory years in the 1950s and 60s when players such as Ron Barassi had fired the imagination of the small Orthodox Jewish boy in Elwood who loved winners but could never watch a live game on Saturday because of his religion. Which was why he had not become a member, until just a day or two before. He spoke a great deal about passion. And he told the assembled media that he would use some of his very considerable wealth to help ensure that the Melbourne Football Club remained a separate entity. He declined, for the moment, to put a figure on the extent of his commitment, but stressed that, while he was prepared to lend his financial support to the club, he was not contemplating any kind of takeover. He was merely a passionate, wealthy member doing his bit for his club. 'It has to be a joint effort,' he insisted. 'It has to be all members involved. You can't rely on one individual.' Joseph also revealed — to a stunned press — that he would, in fact, be running for president of the Melbourne Football Club with Brian Dixon as his deputy on the Demon Alternative ticket. 'I'll do whatever I can, I'll use all the business acumen that I have, all the passion that I have . . . to keep our old club the way it is and the way it should be in the future,' Joseph said, concluding: 'Melbourne Demons forever.'[12]

The *Herald Sun*'s John Hamilton called it 'one of the most extraordinary media conferences called in Melbourne in recent times'.[13] And it was big news. It was the lead story in the next day's papers, with a huge colour picture of Joseph under the Demons logo dominating the front pages. Neither the hundreds of millions of dollars Joseph had made — or lost — over the past decade nor his high-level political activity in Israel had brought him anything like this kind of recognition. But sport in Australia, especially in Melbourne, seizes the popular imagination as nothing else can — as Joseph was just beginning to discover. People were fascinated, and more than slightly bemused, by what had motivated an Orthodox religious Jew — and a rabbi, to boot — to rally to the cause of a club like Melbourne. This was reflected in the media in the days and weeks ahead as it sought to come to grips with the story.

Sports writer Ashley Browne was, like the rest of his colleagues, gob-smacked. 'The grizzled veterans of football journalism thought they had seen it all,' he wrote in the *Australian Jewish News* — 'but they had to pinch themselves to believe what they were seeing was true.'[14] The Gutnicks, he observed in the *Age* three days earlier, as a prominent rabbinical family, would appear 'as likely to discuss football around the family dinner table as the British royal family is to talk about kick-boxing'. And if having a Gutnick as the figurehead of an AFL club weren't bizarre enough, 'then that club being Melbourne is even harder to fathom'. Melbourne, after all, was the football club of the city's establishment; an old-moneyed group that founded institutions like the Melbourne Club, the Royal Melbourne Golf Club and the Royal South Yarra Tennis Club, notorious for having few if any Jewish members. Browne — who is himself Jewish — suggested, however, that once they were convinced that the Gutnick–Melbourne connection was no joke, members of the Jewish community would have been 'chuckling quietly to themselves . . . they enjoy socking it to the establishment every now and again . . .'[15]

Writing in the same issue of the *Age*, Paul Heinrichs wondered how Joseph had managed to maintain, for all those years, even a token interest in football when he was destined almost never to go to a game: 'How can you account for a stupendous Demon spirit that he nurtured inside himself, alongside his love of religion, his family, the stock-market, and the exciting possibilities under the red dust of the Western Australian desert?' he asked. 'It's not always explainable rationally, is it?' Joseph told him. 'It's the dedication and devotion that a person has to his club. It's innate, intrinsic, it's in the person . . . I think I may be a passionate person.' And then, Heinrichs mused, there's the matter of tradition: 'Remember, it's the name of a song in *Fiddler on the Roof*, and it's perhaps one of the most powerful traits in all of Judaism, especially Lubavitch . . .' Joseph liked that: 'That's me,' he acknowledged '– and it's translated itself into sport'.

There was some more mundane speculation: that Joseph might have been driven by commercial reasons, perhaps to lift his profile in the corporate world and garner the prestige and attention that presidency of a club like Melbourne might bring. Joseph's elder brother Mottel (Rabbi Mordechai Gutnick) suggested this might be the case: 'From his point of view it's important PR. It's good for his own image and good for his corporate image. I know my brother well enough to know he does things with a clear head and enough thought. And who am I to tell him how to spend his money?'[16]

This was certainly how seasoned football administrator Cameron Schwab saw it: 'The importance of sport in terms of increasing the profile of individuals cannot be underestimated,' he wrote in the *Age*, suggesting a simple test: 'Put up your hand if you would have recognised Joseph Gutnick if you walked past him in the street three weeks ago.' Speaking from his own experience of football 'white knights' Alan Bond and Kevin Parry at the Richmond Football Club in the mid-1980s, Schwab warned of the lack of commitment or genuine interest these image-seeking entrepreneurs from outside football had displayed. His conclusion: 'Beware white knights.'[17]

Jane Willson, writing in the *Herald Sun*, expressed a similar concern: in his attempt to rescue the Melbourne Football Club, Joseph had become just the latest in a string of prominent businessmen 'seduced by football's power and glory'. Bob Ansett, Christopher Skase, Lindsay Fox, John Elliott, Geoffrey Edelsten and Alan Bond were 'just some of Australia's more colourful entrepreneurs who have put cash into an AFL team while enjoying the kudos of taking the reins as club president,' she noted. But Joseph was perhaps the most unlikely candidate of all for the Melbourne rescue bid, 'appearing to be a classic outsider in traditional football circles'. His gaffe about where Melbourne was on the AFL ladder — Joseph wasn't sure when asked in a radio interview a few days earlier — did not augur well, Willson suggested, recalling how Alan Bond, when he first took over the Richmond Football Club in 1986, had stood before the yellow-and-black Tiger faithful and said: 'I've always loved the red and the black!'[18]

Joseph himself, when asked if he saw a business dividend for himself out of being involved in football, insists that this had not entered his mind when he first became engaged with the Melbourne Football Club. He was, however, quick to recognise that there were advantages. 'It's going to open a lot of doors for me in business,' he said barely a month later, at the end of September 1996, after he was installed as president. 'For instance, I didn't know the Treasurer of Victoria, Alan Stockdale. Now I do.'[19] Stockdale was a passionate supporter of the Melbourne Football Club, and it was not long before Joseph persuaded him to take a place on the board.

Inevitably, perhaps, there was some speculation, or innuendo, that the Lubavitcher Rebbe might in some arcane way have been behind

Joseph's latest passion. There was a hint of this — perhaps a little tongue in cheek — in an article by Damon Johnston and Jane Schulze in the *Herald Sun* at about this time. 'The *Herald Sun* has learned that Mr Gutnick — whose personal fortune was rescued by his religious mentor — had a premonition he would save the Demons,' they wrote. The 'extraordinary event' had occurred some weeks before he had been contacted by Brian Dixon — who, it appears, was 'convinced that providence had brought the Demons and the millionaire together'. And Joseph, the paper reported pointedly, 'has reaped millions after the advice of his mentor, the late Lubavitcher Rebbe Menachem Mendel Schneerson, to mine for gold and diamonds in Western Australia.'[20]

The Rebbe, of course, had been dead for over two years. That, however, had not stopped Joseph from continuing to draw inspiration from him in his other spheres of activity, in his search for gold and diamonds and in his political involvement in Israel. But football, Joseph is adamant, is a Rebbe-free zone. He wants to win a premiership for Melbourne — just as he wants to find diamonds — but he knows he is going to have to achieve that without the Rebbe's help:

> I haven't had a blessing from the Rebbe that the Melbourne Football Club is going to win a premiership. I have got a blessing from the Rebbe that I'll make a massive gold and diamond discovery. On the other hand, the passion for a premiership is something that has come from me, something that is part of my ambition and motivation. With regards to my own motivation in life, Melbourne Football Club is very important. But I can't say it's got that same significance and aura, and the same benefits that can happen to Lubavitch and society if I made a gold and diamond discovery . . . [21]

While Joseph's arrival on the football scene left the general public and the media intrigued, even if a trifle bemused, it aroused outright hostility in the football establishment. Ross Oakley, the Australian Football League supremo and driving force behind the 'rationalisation' of the League and its transformation into a national competition, was particularly hostile as he saw his well-laid plans for a Melbourne–Hawthorn merger in danger of being derailed by this wealthy alien upstart.

The AFL put out a statement saying it was against private individuals taking substantial financial positions in Victorian-based clubs: 'Private ownership in whatever guise, which puts the club in the hands of a wealthy entrepreneur or entity, is totally unacceptable to the AFL Commission.'[22] Oakley then served notice, both to Joseph and to the International Management Group which was behind a similar bid to keep the Hawthorn Football Club alive, that the AFL would block any attempt to fund the two clubs privately. 'We're delighted to have people come in and donate $2 million or $3 million, but if it's something other than that, then we would need to give it our stamp of approval, and we won't be doing that,' he warned, noting that the days of private ownership in the AFL were over. Oakley cited the unhappy experiences of Brisbane under Christopher Skase and then Reuben Pelerman, and Sydney under Geoffrey Edelsten, followed by media proprietor Mike Willessee and jeans tycoon Craig Kimberley, to illustrate the shortcomings of private ownership. 'On many occasions, the capital was used to cover operating shortfalls, which means you need to pour more and more cash in,' he said. 'Eventually, the entrepreneur gets tired and he'll make a very quick decision, because he owns it and, either way, he's off and the club collapses.'[23]

It was not a bad argument — except that it was irrelevant so far as Joseph was concerned. He had made it plain from the outset that he had no intention of taking over or privately owning the Melbourne Football Club. He was, he explained, simply a passionate supporter, like any other — only a lot wealthier than most, so could afford to tip in a lot more to help save his club:

> Clearly the current board has not explored all options and that's something I feel, given the resources at my disposal, obliged to do for club members. What I am proposing is not a buy-out or privatisation of the Melbourne Football Club ... I'm just like any other member who has paid their $80 and doesn't want to merge. The only difference is that I have the money and I am prepared to use it ... I've managed to turn a losing commercial situation around into a winning one and yes, the prospect of making Melbourne not only viable but also successful on the field is attractive.[24]

Oakley went even further in casting aspersions on the football credibility of benefactors like Joseph. 'They probably don't quite understand the culture of football and the culture of a club when they haven't been involved,' Oakley said. 'They will run it like a business, and they will cut when something's not happening, because that's the way it's run.'[25]

The disingenuousness of Oakley's position was immediately pounced on by two of the media's most highly respected sports commentators, Patrick Smith and Garry Linnell. 'Forgive us,' wrote Smith,

> but is it not the AFL Commission that constantly tells us that footy is no longer a sport but a business — a big business? Is it not the AFL

Commission that has drawn and converted businessmen to all positions in football? Then how outrageous has been the attack on Joseph Gutnick, wannabe white knight of the Melbourne Football Club, by AFL figures who query his expertise to run a club because he was merely a businessman.[26]

Linnell was equally scathing:

Excuse me? Is this the same Ross Oakley who once observed that football and business was all about doing deals? And what are mergers if not rational, cold business decisions? . . . Why is it that when a man such as Gutnick rides into town and says he wants to save the club he barracks for, he is pilloried because he doesn't know where it is placed on the ladder? Is that the criterion for saving a club? Do you need to understand the culture of football to save it, as Ross Oakley would have it?

Linnell further underscored the absurdity of Oakley's position by pointing out that his closest ally in the economic rationalisation of the League was AFL Commissioner Graeme Samuel, who had made no secret of the fact that he had a limited understanding of the game's intricacies when he was first appointed back in 1984. 'At one game he attended early on,' Linnell recounted, 'the ball flew into the stand near him. After touching it, a League official turned to him and joked along the lines of: "Do you know what that thing is?" '[27]

Samuel, it so happens, had a double problem with Joseph. Not only did he view him as an irrational threat to his very rational view of football's future in Australia, but as a fellow Jew of a very different ilk (Samuel is a proud but very acculturated Progressive Jew, who wears his Judaism lightly), he was concerned that a bearded, skullcap-wearing Ultra-Orthodox Jew had the temerity to put himself up as president of the League's most blue-blooded establishment club. And, Joseph recalls, he made this known to him in no uncertain terms:

We'd arranged to have lunch at Kimberley. I was going to speak to him about becoming a non-executive director of some of my companies. I'd never met him before. And I told him I was considering getting involved in the Melbourne Football Club and probably going with the Demon Alternative as president. And he just said: 'Are you insane? First of all you will never ever get to be president of the Melbourne Football Club. If there's any club that you won't be president of, it's the Melbourne Football Club. Just forget it. It's the most ridiculous idea!' I had a beard, a yarmulka. I'd never get there.

Samuel was soon proven quite wrong: 'Graeme doesn't admit too easily that he makes a mistake,' Joseph points out. 'But Graeme in retrospect has told me on a few occasions that he made a mistake. He wouldn't have believed that I would have got the recognition and to where I did in the club.' Not only that, but the bearded, Orthodox, Lubavitcher Joseph and the suave, opera-loving, Progressive-Jewish Samuel soon grew to be close friends. They had, it emerged, much more in common than met the eye: Graeme Samuel, Joseph discovered, was a direct descendent of the *Alter Rebbe,* the first Lubavitcher Rebbe and founder of the Chabad Movement. Joseph was thrilled at the discovery:

> So you throw an arrow up in the sky it comes back to its roots. They say that about Hagar, Abraham's wife in the Bible, she went back to her people ... So finally it took generations and generations, what brought two Chabadniks back together was football! We're worlds apart in our views on Judaism, although he's got similar views [to mine] with regards to Israel ... But we seem to have bridged the gap, and are able to mix socially. And if he comes to a Melbourne Football Club President's Luncheon, Graeme eats kosher food with me ... We have *shiurim* [religious study sessions] together once in two months. He's now a member of the Chabad House in Malvern — if you would have told somebody three years ago that Graeme Samuel would be a member of a Chabad House! ... I would consider him now one of my close friends. Just because of football ...

In addition to the hostility Joseph and the Demon Alternative were encountering from Oakley and the AFL, there was the ire they were arousing among the pro-merger Melbourne Football Club board. Club president Ian Ridley genuinely believed the merger was in the best interests of the club he had devoted the best years of his life to as champion player (he had played in five premiership sides), coach and now administrator. And while he was firmly opposed to the Demon Alternative attempt to keep the club going in its own right, he conducted himself with dignity and with respect for those opposing the merger. He met with Joseph soon after he came on board, but made it plain to him, politely but firmly, that until it was 'satisfied beyond doubt that a long-term secure, financially viable alternative is guaranteed, the board's decision will not alter.'[28] He said he would gladly hand over control if Joseph financially backed the club forever.

'If Mr Gutnick is prepared to underwrite the football club forever, well that's fine with me and I would step aside and let him run it,' he said. 'But I don't believe it would happen.'[29] To which Joseph responded: 'I would have to resign from all my boards if I made an irresponsible comment like that. But at the same time, Mr Ridley doesn't guarantee either that in 20 years' time the Melbourne Football Club is going to be viable even with this merger.'[30] Ridley also suggested that Joseph's religious beliefs, which would prevent him from attending matches on Friday night and Saturday, would make him a pseudo-president. 'It would mean that Brian [Dixon] would in actual fact be the true chairman, I guess, because he would have to do all the talking,' he said on Channel 7's *Today Tonight* program — underscoring the animosity he and others in the Melbourne Football Club establishment felt towards Dixon. Joseph had been 'thrown in at the deep end', he suggested. 'I certainly don't want the man to be made a fool of because he's obviously a very decent person.'[31]

Others on the Demons board, however, were less sensitive to Joseph's feelings. Channel Nine boss and club director Ian Johnson said that he respected Joseph as a 'smart businessman' but was 'surprised he would get himself involved in a business that he clearly knows nothing about. I doubt that he had any understanding of managing a football club in the modern AFL competition . . . I suspect he's not the type of person who likes to see his personal fortune dribble down the toilet paying football players $150,000 a year to play. And that's what will happen.' Melbourne general manager Hassa Mann — like Dixon and Ridley, another former Demons champion from the glory years of the 1950s and 60s — said Joseph's rescue bid was full of rhetoric and lacked substance. What is more, Mann carped: 'We haven't seen Mr Gutnick before and I've been around since 1964. I hadn't heard of him until this morning . . .'[32]

The criticism annoyed Joseph — especially Johnson's 'money down the toilet' comment. 'I think it's a bit of an insult, the reports in the paper this morning that I'm throwing my money down the toilet,' he said. 'There's no difference if it's $80 or a million dollars . . . The hundreds of thousands of football followers around Australia, are they throwing their money down the toilet because they are members of a football club?'[33] Apparently not. Devoted diehard Demons fans hailed Joseph as 'the saviour' of their club. Admitting they still knew little about 'Diamond Joe', the Melbourne Football Club faithful still saluted him. 'We've even learnt how to pronounce his name properly,' one of them said.[34] This was indicative of the intrinsic grassroots opposition to the merger which Joseph had intuitively sensed from the start, and which was to grow exponentially in the days and weeks ahead.

Up to this point, Joseph hadn't decided precisely how much money he would be putting up to save the Demons. When asked, he played coy: 'I have just found out that some of my colleagues in the mining industry are big supporters of other clubs, giving $6,000, $10,000, so I am certainly entitled to give how much money I want. I haven't decided how much money I'm going to give because I don't know all the facts yet.'[35] He finally revealed his hand on Monday 2 September 1996 — exactly two weeks before the Melbourne and Hawthorn members were due to vote on the merger. He announced that, should the Melbourne members vote against the merger on 16 September, he would immediately provide $1.5 million to establish the Melbourne Demons Forever Foundation. He would provide a further $500,000 up-front to assist in the development of social club, training and administrative facilities — the three areas listed as critical by Ridley and his board. He also offered to make his Kimberley Gardens hotel complex a major sponsor of the club, to the tune of $200,000 a year over five years.

All up, the package came to some $3 million — a figure, Joseph explains, that was arrived at to counter the $4–6 million the AFL was offering the two teams if they agreed to go ahead with the merger. 'Until now it's been airy, fairy talk as to what my commitment is. Now I'm giving a concrete commitment, an initial commitment,' he said, 'putting my hand in my pocket and giving it to the club without any ownership, or any takeover.'[36] He urged Melbourne fans to back his rescue bid by donating $1.5 million of their own to the Demons Forever Foundation in its first year. 'I don't want to be an owner,' he insisted. 'The owners are the members and I'll just be one of them and I call upon them to give their support. Maybe my commitment will influence others.' He was aware, however, that the lion's share would be coming from him: 'Not everyone has a goldmine in Western Australia.'[37]

Ridley described Joseph's offer as 'generous' — but said that the $3 million injection still wasn't enough to guarantee the Melbourne Football Club's long-term survival.[38] But Patrick Smith, writing in the *Age*, said it was too good for the club to pass up: 'To an outsider it is simple — accept Gutnick's money and support, encourage others to join and fight like you've never fought before.' Even if Ridley was right that Joseph's $3 million wouldn't save the club forever — and Joseph wasn't suggesting it would — it would provide the breathing space necessary for Melbourne to get its house in order while other more vulnerable clubs (Smith suggested St Kilda, Footscray or even Richmond) 'fell over' and the Victorian clubs were reduced by attrition. 'Gutnick's offer has taken the urgency out of the argument,' Smith concluded. 'If it has the soul of the Demons at heart the Melbourne board should accept Gutnick's peace offering.'[39]

Try as he might, Joseph could not persuade some of his critics that he was acting altruistically, out of a genuine commitment to Melbourne's future as an independent club. Joseph had barely made his offer when it was suggested that it was part of some clever tax dodge. All donations to the Demons Forever Foundation would be tax-deductible, it was argued, because it would be set up under the umbrella of the Federal Government-sponsored Australian Sports Foundation. Thus, it was reported, Joseph would save himself 'about $500,000 in taxation by his $1.5 million donation to establish the independent trust'.[40] This was ill-informed malicious nonsense. The Taxation Commissioner, Michael Carmody, pointed out that while donations to the ASF to use at its own discretion were tax-deductible, this obviously did not apply to donations channelled through the ASF to a designated football club or any other third party. And it was hardly likely that Joseph would be making his $1.5 million subject to the ASF's whim.

As the 16 September vote on the merger approached, the struggle between the pro- and anti-merger camps intensified. Joseph had said on *The Footy Show* that he would accept the decision of the members and would 'still be there' if the merger proceeded. Ridley apparently took this to mean that the $3 million Joseph had subsequently committed to the Demons would still be available to the merged club, and informed the members accordingly. Dixon soon disabused him: 'If the merger proceeds Gutnick's contribution lapses,' he warned. 'All he will be buying will be the club membership ticket.'[41] Joseph confirmed this a few days later: 'My financial commitment would not be there, but I'll become a member. It only costs $80!'[42] Joseph claims that Ridley had even offered him the presidency of the 'Melbourne Hawks' if he came on board — 'But I wouldn't accept that. I was interested in the Melbourne Football Club; I wasn't interested in the Melbourne Hawks.'

On Thursday 12 September, a 'Demons Forever' rally was held at the MCG. It was a bitterly cold day, but 3000 diehards showed up.[43] Joseph, who addressed the rally, said he was confident the 'no merger' vote would 'come out with an 80 per cent majority'. He noted that he had tried to reach a compromise with Ian Ridley and the Demons captain Garry Lyon — who, he was already aware, wielded an influence in the club far greater than most club captains did — suggesting that a decision be put off for a year. 'I implored and beseeched Ian Ridley that rather than dividing Melbourne we should unite and work out a compromise,' he said. This had been rejected. 'I'm disappointed that they weren't willing to compromise, and now it's gone too far,' he told the rally. 'They should have postponed it for a year to let the supporters show their determination to keep Melbourne as a separate entity. But they've refused to budge.' It was, he said, time for the old board to go: 'I don't like attacking any of the existing board — they've done a good job — but it's time for them to give over to the Demon Alternative. Their time has run out . . . If they lose they should all resign.'

Joseph declared that the $3 million package he had pledged was only an initial commitment, and hinted that there would be more to come if the merger were defeated: 'But it's not only Joseph Gutnick contributing; everyone has to do their best to contribute, to find new members, new supporters, and new sponsors.' The anti-merger camp received an important fillip when former Demons premiership player Geoff Tunbridge declared his support. He had been one of twenty-six past players who had recently signed a letter supporting a merger, but now had switched camps. 'I always said I would accept a merger if there was no other option,' he told the rally. 'But when Joseph came along, I felt his offer was something the club should seriously consider. I've now withdrawn my support for the merger.'

Joseph was later mobbed by the crowd and signed hundreds of autographs. It was his first taste of the adulation usually reserved for champion players — something he had not expected but appreciated and enjoyed immensely. To be acknowledged, accepted and liked by the club rank-and-file was at least as important to Joseph as it was to be accepted by the players and the establishment hierarchy.

Ian Ridley and the pro-merger camp were getting worried. With the rank-and-file clearly running against them, they began to take steps to shore up their proxies. Melbourne vice-president Bill Guest, for example, had sixty staff at his company Guest's Furniture take out Melbourne Football Club membership, while another major sponsor — which was not named — allegedly asked as many as thirty employees to send in proxies in favour of a merger.[44] This put Ridley in an embarrassing position. According to minutes taken by the Demon Alternative when they met the Melbourne Football Club board, Ridley had categorically opposed the garnering of memberships by club directors. But desperate times, it seems, demanded desperate measures, and Ridley found himself forced to condone the practice. He said he had received advice that nothing illegal had been done; as for the ethics — he compared the tactic to Joseph and his wife, Stera, buying

Melbourne Football Club memberships just days before the cut-off a few weeks earlier. Melbourne general manager Hassa Mann said Guest was the Demons' marketing manager and had been 'just carrying out his duties' in signing up his employees. He noted that there had been some 800 new signings in August — including Joseph and Stera Gutnick.[45]

The vote in Melbourne's Dallas Brooks Hall on 16 September was a farce.[46] Over 5000 members showed up, but the auditorium could only hold 2100. Some spilled over into a basement room, but thousands were locked out. Angry fans threatened to break down the doors. Melbourne board member Kevin Jones said the numbers at the meeting 'had exceeded expectations by about 4,000'. At one point, there were even thoughts of calling the whole thing off. Joseph arrived an hour and a quarter early, at 6.40 pm, to a hero's welcome. With his bushy beard and red-and-blue yarmulka, he was instantly recognisable, and the fans mobbed him. He was already a Demons icon. But he was appalled at the shambles and, even before the meeting started, threatened to challenge in court any decision taken under such extraordinary circumstances, saying his legal advice indicated 'an appalling failure to observe proper meeting procedures'.

The mood among the swarming members was overwhelmingly anti-merger. They had been hugely boosted by the news that the Demons' most famous living player, the legendary Ron Barassi, had just broken ranks with the pro-merger camp and was now in favour of giving 'Joseph Gutnick a chance to see if he can save the club,' wrote the *Age*'s Patrick Smith, one of several of the paper's senior sports writers covering the historic meeting. 'It seemed as though 99 per cent of the members were enraged with the decision to merge with Hawthorn.'

Proceedings got under way an hour late, at around 9.00 pm, as organisers tried to cope with the pandemonium. Joseph rose to speak, and received a standing ovation. 'This man has addressed a meeting or two in his time,' Smith wrote admiringly. He 'said nothing new but he said it with pride and determination'. Joseph repeated his commitment to the Melbourne Football Club, and his willingness to go beyond the $3 million he had already pledged. 'I've committed money and I'll commit more money . . . but only to a board that's committed to no merger.' How long would he continue to support the Demons? he was asked from the floor: 'If I discover diamonds, for eternity.' His plea: 'I believe the board hasn't explored all options . . . and I'm one of those options. It's too premature to kill the Demons. I beseech you and implore you to give us a chance to build the Demons once again.' Each statement was given rapturous applause and cheers.

Next came Brian Dixon's turn. 'He did not speak, he shouted,' Smith wrote. 'He demanded. No one had the right to sign away the heart and soul of his beloved Demons.' He whipped the already hostile crowd to fever pitch: 'Three weeks ago Ian Ridley looked me in the eye and said "Dicko, there are no options." Well there are options,' he bellowed. Dixon then returned to his seat, embraced Joseph, and the two received another standing ovation.

He was followed by Demons supporter Maree Mulcahy, who urged the members to oppose the merger. 'This cannot be just about Joseph Gutnick,' she said. 'It's got to be about us.' And Ian Ridley and his mates on the pro-merger board had 'under-estimated the power and passion of the supporters'.

Then came Ridley, the sole speaker for the pro-merger side. He asked for silence and a fair go from the crowd. 'It is fair to say he got neither,' Smith wrote, noting he looked tired and drained. 'He was hurting more than anyone could know.' Like Joseph, he, too, said nothing new, stressing that the board had looked at all the options and had concluded that the merger was the only way to secure the Melbourne Football Club's long-term viability. But, Smith noted, 'he said it with dignity'. Unlike Joseph, who had been greeted with adulation, Ridley had to maintain his dignity through constant jeers and taunts. He had become a 'target of insult, ridicule, contempt . . . and undisguised hatred,' Trevor Grant wrote in the *Herald Sun*, which also had a large team on hand to cover the event. 'Those were the feelings in the venomous eyes of a teenager in a Melbourne jumper who shouted: "You traitor! Resign!"' Grant might have been describing one of the rallies addressed by Israeli Prime Minister Yitzhak Rabin in the months before his assassination in November 1995.

The mood in the hall, and straw polls conducted by the *Herald Sun*, suggested that the anti-merger forces would win by a landslide — both at Melbourne and at Hawthorn, which was holding a parallel meeting at the Camberwell Civic Centre. Of 853 people surveyed at both venues, 718 were against while just 135 supported a merger. But despite the overwhelming grass-roots opposition to the merger in both clubs, the outcome would hinge on the thousands of proxy votes held by the club directors. And these, in the end, decided the issue. Of the 1952 members who managed to squeeze into the Dallas Brooks Hall, 1455 (75 per cent) opposed the merger — but Ridley and his pro-merger Melbourne Football Club board, armed with thousands of proxies, won the vote by 4679 (52.5 per cent) to 4229 (47.5 per cent).

It was a devastating blow to Joseph and the Demon Alternative camp, who had been convinced that they had had the numbers. In the end, it didn't matter. A few kilometres away, in the Camberwell Civic Centre, Hawthorn members voted down the merger. The vote on the floor was even more overwhelmingly against than it had been in the Dallas Brooks Hall: 2300 to 200. But, unlike the Melbourne vote, the proxies were evenly divided. 'We've won,' a jubilant Don Scott, leader of the Hawks' anti-merger Operation Payback campaign declared before the proxies had even been counted. 'From these figures we've won . . . The merger's definitely off!'[47] Even Hassa Mann had to concede defeat; they'd won the battle, but lost the war. 'Unless there are other developments within the Hawthorn camp, the merger is off,' he conceded — but added defiantly: 'I believe the merger will be revisited in two or three years' time.'[48] Joseph was relieved. 'I would have gone to court, if Hawthorn would have voted pro,' he says. 'I would have gone to court, because it was rigged.' But now was not the time for recriminations.

Joseph immediately offered an olive branch to Ian Ridley. He wanted to put the merger battle behind them, and look to the future. Ridley, for his part, was prepared to co-operate — although he could not, at first, get his mind around Joseph Gutnick as president of the Melbourne Football Club: 'I want to talk with him and ascertain his actual desire. I couldn't imagine time would allow him to be [president]. I want to talk to him to see how he sees the picture . . . We are the current board. We did win last night.'[49] The two men met — with the club captain Garry Lyon and former Demons champion Robert Flower also present — and Joseph convinced the old Melbourne veteran he was serious about leading the club, and wanted to be president. Ridley eventually accepted this, and an agreement was thrashed out whereby he would step down and serve as Joseph's deputy. At the same time, two other members of the Demon Alternative — Mark Jenkins and Garry Pearce — would be co-opted onto the Melbourne Football Club board, which would be expanded to twelve members.

'Under the present circumstances I thought it was better to stand down and let Joseph take the reins,' Ridley announced on Wednesday 18 September, less than forty-eight hours after his pyrrhic victory in the Dallas Brooks Hall. 'It was a pretty hard decision.'[50] He added, however, that it would be 'every club's desire to have a person such as him [Joseph] as the godfather, or the white knight or whatever you want to call him'. As for the merger, that was in the past. 'I doubt if anyone will ever set out to attempt a merger again,' Ridley said. 'I think the next time, the only way it would happen is if a club really is gone and ready to fall over . . . I don't think anyone would be silly enough, brave enough or sensible enough to try it again.'[51]

Joseph found himself in a position he would not even have begun to imagine a month earlier: president of the Melbourne Football Club. There had been a bitter price to pay: Ridley had insisted not only that Brian Dixon would not be Joseph's deputy, but that he would have no place on the Demons board. Not, that is, if Joseph wanted to face the future with a united front. Sticking with Dixon would have left the club in tatters, as Joseph was quick to perceive. It was a tough call for Joseph, and he took the decision with the greatest difficulty: 'We have in a way reluctantly accepted [the Melbourne offer] because Brian has been omitted,' he said, paying tribute to the part Dixon had played in fighting the merger. Dixon was deeply hurt, but surprisingly philosophical: 'I don't know why Ian's decided to exercise this particular blanket on me,' he said. 'So be it, as far as I'm concerned. Ian, you're just a mate of mine, we've played in premierships together and I don't understand. All I know is Ian Ridley didn't want me there.'[52] There was no public reproach for Joseph.

◊ ◊ ◊

Demon Joe had arrived. The Orthodox Lubavitch Jew who had barely watched a game of football in his life had not only saved, but had become president of, the country's oldest Australian Rules football club. It was a remarkable twist in a story which, in many ways, already defied belief. Sam Lipski, editorialising on Joseph's latest exploit in the *Australian Jewish News*, suggested it was so outlandish not even Hollywood would have bought it:

> The other day a film script was presented to Hollywood. It told the story of a rabbi and a Lubavitcher Chasid from Down Under known as Diamond Joe who listened to his Rebbe and found gold in the Australian desert, became a multi-millionaire, donated to many institutions and charities around the world, and ran an advertising campaign which tipped the Israeli election in favour of Bibi Netanyahu. After much discussion about the story being too fantastic to be credible even as fiction, the producers reluctantly accepted it. Unfortunately, the script was never made into a movie because, at the last minute, the writers wanted to add something. Apparently they came up with a real incredible idea. To create a lighter moment in the film, the Chasidic mining magnate would lead a campaign to save the hometown football club he had supported since childhood — rather ironically called the Demons — from merging with another club

known as the Hawks. This time the producers insisted it was all too fantastic and dropped the whole project.[53]

Senior sportswriter on the *Age*, Patrick Smith, looking at it from the perspective of Aussie Rules football, was no less amazed:

Joseph Gutnick has been president of the Melbourne Football Club for nearly as long as he has been a member. That's a couple of minutes. Takes longer to boil an egg. The club's philosophy has been turned about 180 degrees by this orthodox Jewish rabbi, who is about as tall as a fire hydrant and wears a red and dark blue yarmulka . . . Just take a deep breath and think about it. A rabbi, with a long black-grey beard that gets on the goat of Rex Hunt. Melbourne Football Club, where affectation is considered good form, the home of hyphenated names and four-wheel drives. The establishment. Football and a rabbi. It is the coming together of two religions. Gutnick's appointment to the presidency has been an ecumenical occasion. It is a fantastic story, a warm and exciting tale, but it is bizarre in its dimension and the speed with which it began and ended. Yet it is a story that is perhaps possible only in this town of such a wonderful mix. Football breaks down barriers. Sometimes slowly . . . but sometimes as quickly as it takes to say 'thank your mother for the rabbits'.[54]

Michael Gawenda, then deputy editor of the *Age*, made much the same point a few months later:

There were few stranger images of life in this city . . . than those of Mr Gutnick wearing his Demons skullcap and his footy scarf, being mobbed by hundreds of Demons supporters . . . Strange, and yet somehow appropriate in a city as multicultural as Melbourne. In a city for which football is a defining experience, the diminutive rabbi as savior of an old club, one that carries the city's name, is a kind of symbol of what multiculturalism means, of what it can be.[55]

Lipski, too, had recognised that for all the elements in the Demon Joe story 'that lend themselves to melodrama, humour and expressions of disbelief, puzzlement and wonderment', it was telling something important not just about football, but about Australia:

the key issue rises from the intersection of the Jewish community with mainstream Australia . . . if multiculturalism means anything at all it surely means that Jews, in common with all other religious and cultural minorities, can aspire to participate in the mainstream of Australian life at every level and to do so without a double standard being applied. It means, in short, that a Yeshivah boy in a blue and red beanie in Hotham Street can dream about one day sitting on the boundary line at the MCG as club chairman. Just as a Vietnamese boat kid or a Lebanese refugee can and should have the same dreams . . . [56]

It was a marvellous, and quite inspirational, instance of Australian multiculturalism at work. And, as Lipski concluded, the fact that 'an Australian Jew of Joseph Gutnick's very wealthy standing and militantly Orthodox and Chasidic commitment and style [could] be linked so dramatically to the sport of Australian Football . . . without a trace in the media or from the sporting community of the xenophobia that would have accompanied such a move even a couple of decades ago is a good sign.' All the more so, Lipski suggested, 'because it is in sport and sporting prowess that Australians define themselves and who they are as a people.'[57]

Mister President

'There is nothing more difficult to carry out, nor more doubtful of success, nor more difficult to handle, than initiate a new order of things. For the reformer has enemies in all those who profit by the old order, and only lukewarm defenders in all those who would profit by the new.'

Niccolo Machiavelli, *The Prince*

IF IAN RIDLEY or anyone else at the Melbourne Football Club had imagined their new president was going to be a mere figurehead — that he would be too preoccupied with his other business and political interests to devote much time to the club, or that he would make do with basking in the limelight and signing the cheques, and let others get on with the job of actually running the club, or that he would soon tire of the novelty and move on to other things — they were in for a rude awakening. It was not in Joseph Gutnick's nature to take a back seat to anyone. That was how it had been in his business career. Once involved in a company, his instinct was to seize control, become chairman, and call the shots. And if he was president of the Melbourne Football Club, that was what he was going to be, in practice as well as in name. He may have become involved without a great deal of forethought, but once committed, his commitment was going to be total: not just his money, but his time, his passion and his energy.

Joseph moved cautiously at first. His priority was to heal the wounds left by the merger battle, stabilise the club, restore morale and rebuild for the future, on and off the field. This, he soon discovered, meant further distancing himself from Brian Dixon, who he was well aware by now was *persona non grata* around the club. He had only reluctantly agreed to drop him as his running mate for vice-president on the Demon Alternative ticket, saying 'I think that in negotiations, Brian Dixon comes out as a hero for Melbourne.' And he promised to fight to get him involved in the club in some capacity.[1] Barely a month later, by the beginning of October 1996, he knew he would not be able to honour that pledge. Dixon had had reasonable expectations that Joseph would endorse his candidacy for one of the positions on the Melbourne Football Club board up for election in December. But this was not to be. Joseph came out openly in support of the incumbent board members standing for election. 'It is the right of any member to stand for election, but I support the present board members,' he said. Moreover, he added, biting the bullet: 'I wouldn't be happy if Brian Dixon stood for the board.'[2]

Dixon, understandably, was again deeply hurt and upset — this time by what he saw as Joseph's betrayal. 'It's fair to say I was amazed and personally hurt by Mr Gutnick's actions,' he said, noting that he had sensed, very early in their relationship, that Ian Ridley had turned Joseph against him. He conceded his weaknesses — 'in my eagerness to obtain objectives I'm perceived as being rude, abrasive, unwilling to brook opposition to my views, trying to be too domineering etcetera, etcetera' — but still felt he had a lot to offer the Melbourne Football Club. To his credit, Dixon handled his disappointment with a good deal of dignity: 'I've certainly had my share of these sorts of surprises. I've tried to absorb them and get on with my life. It's not particularly easy but that's what I'm doing now . . .'[3]

Joseph, for his part, was never comfortable with the way he had been forced to treat Dixon. He doesn't like to talk about it:

Q: 'Did you feel bad about what happened with Brian Dixon?'
A: 'Yes. He was the one I'd worked together with to fight the merger.'
Q: 'Do you feel a sense of betrayal on your part?'
A: 'Yeah . . . Yeah . . .'
Q: 'And have you discussed with him why you felt you had to do it?'
A: 'Yes. He didn't accept it. He understood it, but he didn't accept it. I wanted to keep the club united, not divided. And they said bringing in Brian would be very divisive . . .'

This was the same kind of mental toughness that had enabled Joseph to survive and succeed in the dog-eat-dog world of mining. It appears not to have come easily to him, but he knew he had no choice. 'You have to make tough decisions,' he had said of his business activities. 'You have to be ruthless, and you can't have pity . . . It really hurts. But you've just got to do it . . . If you start feeling too bad about it you won't be able to continue . . .' It was a toughness that, as we have seen, had troubled Joseph's father, Chaim — but which increasingly came to be recognised, grudgingly respected, perhaps even a little feared and, in some instances deeply resented, by people in the football world.

Although Joseph did not interfere directly in football matters, about which he acknowledged he still had a lot to learn, he ordered a review of the Melbourne Football Club's football department soon after taking over as president. The club had had a poor season on the field in 1996, with just seven wins and fifteen losses, finishing fourteenth on the sixteen-team AFL ladder, and its playing list was widely regarded as mediocre, after years of poor recruiting. The review was conducted by former club legend Robert Flower (with whom Joseph was to develop a close relationship), Greg Wells, and Stephen Newport. As a result of the review, football and recruiting manager Richard Griffiths and assistant coach Peter Russo were axed. Former Richmond general manager Cameron Schwab was recruited to head the football department, and Greg Hutchison was appointed assistant coach. The first steps had been taken, at the new president's behest, towards the club's revival.

There was a certain irony in Schwab's appointment: as already mentioned, barely a month earlier, he had publicly warned, in an article in the *Age*, against 'white knights' like Joseph coming in and taking over football clubs. 'I missed that article,' Joseph concedes. 'Had I read it, he would never have got the job.' Joseph recalls that he had already had reservations about Schwab. Schwab had left Richmond in 'unhappy circumstances' in 1993,[4] and Joseph had been warned that, despite the fact that Schwab was highly regarded by the media, he might be better advised to look elsewhere:

> Brian Dixon told me to beware, because of what happened to him in Richmond, and I should look at other opportunities. But I was pushed by a number of individuals. I can't exactly remember, but I believe Garry [Lyon] recommended it. And others. The press was very in favour. He was a football insider. There were others who warned against ... He was very impressive. Very knowledgeable about football. He'd studied, he was an MBA, he was going to turn the world upside down. And boy, did he turn things upside down ... Oh boy, did he turn things upside down!

That, however, was all in the future. For the moment, he and Joseph got along well — although, Joseph notes: 'When I look back, I just got that feeling he was a bit aloof, there was a bit of arrogance about him ... Sort of wanted to keep me out of things. Like Neil Balme and Garry Lyon. This clique. That I've just got to be told what to do. Just cough up my money.'

As the December board election approached, eleven nominations were received for the eight vacancies. Joseph, who was also standing, endorsed an eight-man slate. It was a careful balance between members of Ian Ridley's old pro-merger board and anti-merger members of the Demon Alternative. Joseph canvassed members to support his slate, in the interests of 'stability on the board' and 'unity among all members of the Melbourne Football Club'.[5] The election was held on 10 December 1996, and Joseph's ticket got up easily. He received 2825 votes — over 99 per cent of the vote — with his seven endorsed candidates not far behind. Joseph then outlined his plans for the year ahead. These included moving the club's permanent training facility and administration base to the Junction Oval, where Joseph would put up at least $500,000 of the $1 million needed for the site's development. He repeated his commitment to the club, both financially and 'with ideas'. The aim for the coming season was to field a team that could be a meaningful finals participant and to make available the resources to rebuild playing depth. Joseph's grip on the club and the extent to which he intended getting involved were now apparent. Veteran *Age* football commentator Patrick Smith described him as 'the most powerful man in Australian football', noting: 'No man holds the future of a football club more securely in his hands than the Melbourne president . . . Are they Demons or Gutnicks?'[6]

Ian Ridley, who had not been up for re-election, had by this time come to terms with the new order. It had not been easy. 'For all his business power, political clout and devout religion,' Caroline Wilson wrote in the *Age*, 'Gutnick was a savage misfit in the world of AFL football and Ridley, a former tough star player and coach, treated the strange-looking new chum as such.'[7] Ridley was still defiant that he had done the right thing in advocating the merger with Hawthorn, and was dismissive of the effort of the anti-merger camp: 'If I'd have been the person in charge of the "no" vote and I'd picked up a Joseph Gutnick, I would have won it 90 to 10,' he said mischievously. 'I think they should be ashamed of themselves. It's the easiest thing in the world to win a "no" vote.'[8] Nevertheless, he had nothing but praise for Joseph — at least as a banker. He related how, when the club had needed money for a player acquisition fund, he, general manager Hassa Mann and board member Bill Balcam went and saw Joseph. 'He wrote out a cheque to the football club for $500,000 on the spot,' Ridley said, acknowledging that 'Joseph being there certainly takes a bit of pressure off the finances . . .'[9]

While he was happy to honour his financial commitments to the club, Joseph made it plain that this did not absolve the supporters of their responsibility for the club's future. 'I'm not bankrolling the club, I'm supporting some of its projects,' he warned, expressing his disappointment that they had not embraced their club with the same fervour as Hawthorn's supporters had after the failed merger.[10] Melbourne's membership was still languishing around 15,000 — while Hawthorn's had soared to over 23,000. In 1996, their respective memberships had been 12,964 and 12,484. A poor start to the 1997 season had not helped matters. A rousing first round win (70–55) over reigning premiers North Melbourne had raised expectations for a great season. But this had been followed by a humiliating 163–56 walloping at the hands of Collingwood in the second round, which brought the club back to earth with a thump.

By round five, with the 1997 football season well under way and still only the one win over the Kangaroos in the first round, Joseph was starting to feel confident enough to speak out publicly on football matters. He was adored by the fans, and had become something of a cult figure around the club (according to Hassa Mann at this time, Joseph's autograph was as sought after as Garry Lyon's among the club's young fans).[11] 'Five games into the season is too early to be critical of anyone,' he said, expressing his full support for the coach Neil Balme. However, he warned: 'Another five weeks and things might be different.'[12]

It was to be a short five weeks. Just two days later, on Sunday 4 May 1997, Joseph attended his second game for the season — the round six clash against St Kilda at a wet and windy Waverley Park. The Demons were execrable. They were 43 points down at half time, and all the signs were that worse was to come in the second half. Joseph was horrified by what he had seen, and by what he had heard around him. 'I was sitting next to some pretty important Melbourne Football Club people,' he recalls. 'And they were carrying on "Sack the coach! Sack the coach! Sack the coach!" That's all I was hearing.' It was not the best moment for Joseph to have agreed to be interviewed by the Triple M radio station that was covering the game. But, he explains, 'we were getting such a thumping by St Kilda, that I lost the plot at half time.'

In what was seen at the time as one of the more extraordinary 'dummy spits' in recent football history, Joseph went on air and, while coach Neil Balme and his team were licking their wounds and trying to gear themselves up for the second half, gave vent to his feelings. He was president of the Melbourne Football Club, and had just witnessed a performance he would not have tolerated in any of his companies; he was in no mood to pull his punches:

This has been going on for too many years and we'll have to make some radical changes in the very near future . . . We'll get the experts together and get their opinion . . . Some people will say it's the coach, some will say we haven't got enough good recruiting, others will say injuries, but even with all the excuses change has to take place. It would be the same in any type of business or institution. When you are in the dumps for so long, you have to make radical changes just for the sake of change as well as try to improve the team. Our supporters will demand it, our members will demand it and I as president, I'm not going to stand around and watch Melbourne sit at the bottom of the ladder . . . Our supporters, that's what I'm hearing, are asking for blood . . . We're bleeding and we're going to mend that bleeding.'[13]

This was rousing stuff — the first real taste the football world had had of Demon Joe at his fiery best. As he told Triple M: 'I haven't instituted a lot of changes because I'm just a new boy to the game and I've had to rely on the views of experienced people.' That was about to change. Joseph had served his apprenticeship. 'If the Melbourne Football Club thought it was getting a benevolent multi-millionaire who would tip in money without asking a few questions about where it was going and how well it was being spent, then they now know otherwise,' Martin Blake wrote in the *Age*. 'Gutnick means business.'[14]

It is debatable that a blast from the president on commercial radio was precisely what Neil Balme or his team needed to lift themselves for the second half of a game that was already well and truly lost. The final scoreline, 121–35, was the final humiliation. Joseph concedes that he should, perhaps, have waited until after the game to speak out. But, he insists, if he had his time over, he would do it again. And once the game was over, he was even more outspoken. He told the press that his team's 86-point drubbing by St Kilda had been 'pathetic' and 'unacceptable'. Asked if Neil Balme's job as coach was safe, Joseph replied:

I don't think anybody is safe at the moment. Probably not me either. As president I will bring in changes . . . Within 24 or 48 hours we'll discuss it at board level and make what I feel should be necessary changes. I don't think it would be fair at this stage to make any comments about Neil [Balme] or Hassa [Mann] or our captains or our senior players. But change is on the way.[15]

Although stunned, Balme reacted quite coolly to his president's onslaught. He denied that he felt under any pressure, or that he was concerned about his future at the club: 'All I do is my job. It's as simple as that and I'm not concerned about that sort of speculation. I have absolutely no influence over that. I just have to do what I do and if people don't like it, that's fine.' He expressed his surprise that Joseph had spilled out his feelings to the media: 'I wouldn't think the best way to get a result was to talk to the press,' he said. 'I think he should be talking to us and sure, we'll approach it in a methodical, analytical way.' Joseph was 'a fine man', he said — but 'inexperienced' in football matters.[16]

It was true, Martin Blake wrote in the *Age*, that 'Gutnick has only been at Melbourne for five minutes.' But while he 'might not be an aficionado or an expert, he knows an insipid team when he sees one. He knows what the league ladder looks like right now and he knows where Melbourne has been in the last two years. The essence of what he said was right.'[17] The *Herald Sun*'s leading football commentator Mike Sheahan concurred: 'Gutnick may not know much about footy, as he readily admits, but he knows things are amiss in his footy club, and he has the inclination and the power to rectify the situation.'[18]

Joseph had had enough of being frozen out by a 'clique' in a club which, while happy to accept his money, refused to accept his authority, resented him as a football outsider, and wanted to have as little as possible to do with him. That, it seems, was the crux of the problem — and possibly a major cause of the frustration that had resulted in Joseph's outbursts to the media. He readily acknowledged his inexperience, and that he had a great deal to learn about football. And he was willing to learn. But he was made to feel unwelcome, he relates — especially by Balme:

> I first met Neil soon after I became president of the club. He was very unco-operative and negative. Who's this Joseph Gutnick, wanting to be president, wanting to know about football, and what does he know, and how's he going to tell me what to do? There was no rapport ... I couldn't approach him. I couldn't talk to him. I dealt with him through Cameron Schwab. I tried a few times, but I didn't get anywhere ...

Did Joseph suspect that there might be some anti-semitism behind Balme's attitude? 'I don't think so,' Joseph replies. 'I don't know. I wouldn't accuse Neil of being an anti-semite. I've got no grounds to say that. But I would say that he was negative towards me. I don't know for what reason.' Whatever the reason, it was not a recipe for a successful long-term relationship between the president and coach of a club battling to survive.

When the board met on the Monday after the St Kilda rout, it was widely anticipated that Balme would be axed. But Joseph came under tremendous pressure not to sack him, especially from football manager Cameron Schwab and club captain Garry Lyon, who were both very close to Balme. This was another instance of the remarkable influence Lyon wielded in the Melbourne Football Club — something that Joseph had to accept but was not entirely happy with. He respected Lyon as a champion player and brilliant leader, but felt his influence in other areas was less than healthy. The board was divided on the issue and, after a two-and-a-half-hour meeting, decided without taking a vote to retain Balme for the remainder of the season. 'We fully endorse Neil for the present season,' Joseph announced afterwards, 'and we will reassess at the end of the season.' In a hint that his half-time outburst at the St Kilda game had been criticised at the board meeting, Joseph added: 'I won't have any outbursts in the future at half-time.' But, he insisted, 'I haven't been gagged. I'm not easily gagged.'[19]

While it had not turned out to be the bloodletting Joseph had fore-shadowed, and which many had expected, the board meeting was not bloodless. The old club champion and general manager for the pre-vious four years, Hassa Mann, became the scapegoat, and was forced to make way for the 33-year-old Schwab, who became CEO six months earlier than originally anticipated. Although disappointed, Mann pub-licly acknowledged Joseph's contribution to the Melbourne Football Club. 'He came in with a platform of putting in $3 million and his com-mitment is already nearing that mark,' Mann said. 'I've no doubt that he will exceed that.'[20]

The crisis was over, for the moment. Joseph had made his mark, and this had been largely acknowledged by the football world. But the *Age*'s Patrick Smith, who was one of the first senior sports writers in Australia to accept Joseph as a potent, legitimate and welcome new force in the game, had a gentle word of advice: 'Joe, football is only a business in part. It remains a sport played out of a club. Tinker with the fabric to the detriment of the club's spirit and you and Bill Gates wouldn't have the money to save the place.'[21] It was sound advice — but a little gratuitous. Joseph was well aware, from the moment he had stepped into the Melbourne Football Club, just what football was about: 'Football is not only a business,' he had told Eddie McGuire when he had made his famous debut on *The Footy Show* nine months before. 'It's not about money. It's about the emotion of all the followers . . . It's the emotion, it's also skill, it's also motivation, it's a combination of everything . . .'

It was because Joseph understood precisely what football was about, rather better than Smith and others had given him credit for, that

Balme's reprieve turned out to be short-lived. Although relieved that he had survived the axe, the affable, relaxed Balme signalled that he was not about to change his ways. 'I can only do what I do and be what I am and if that's no good, well, that's OK, I'm happy to live with that. But I can't be someone else or something else . . . I'm not very confrontational in what I do . . . It's not my way to come along and try to stamp my authority on people . . .'[22] Except his way wasn't working.

The very next week, 11 May, Melbourne took its losing streak to six, going down to lowly Fremantle by 55 points. The following week was even more dismal: Melbourne was thrashed 128–49 by Geelong. Joseph was getting restless. The Demons had lost seven games in a row, the last few by huge margins. 'I'm a very impatient individual,' he said after the loss to Geelong. 'I don't like long hauls.'[23] The final straw came the following week, in round nine, when Melbourne lost to League newcomers Port Adelaide by 78–27. It was not so much the loss that upset Joseph. He knew his team had a poor playing list and that it had been decimated by injury. It was Balme's carefree, easy-going attitude, while his team was being thrashed by large margins week after week, Joseph explains, that finally got to him:

> The pits was when he just sort of gave up. I read in the *Herald Sun*, and I later got a tape of it, he said that our players, if they ever got into a race they'd never win, they'd always be last; if there were a skills test they would always be last. Those were the same players who the following year almost won the premiership. Balme lacked drive. He didn't believe in the players. It was like me telling my daughter, who's doing her VCE next month, that it doesn't matter how hard she works, she's never going to do well in the VCE. So if a coach doesn't believe in his players, doesn't believe that he can lift them, he shouldn't be coach. I don't care what they say. If I know a lot about football, or I don't know a lot about football . . .

Joseph had had enough: Balme had 'had his go; he was used goods for Melbourne'. The president got his board together in a telephone link-up on 29 May, the Thursday after the Fremantle game, and won endorsement for Balme's sacking. He fronted up to the media that night and explained the decision:

> It didn't work with Neil Balme. It's irrelevant to go into the reasons why it didn't. I've got my own views on it, other people have got other views. Other people will say it wasn't his fault. We'll hear phrases tomorrow . . . I believe we need someone to come in now and deal with the Melbourne Football Club as it is, with its players, and inspire the players to win races

and go beyond their skills ... It's a mediocre team. We've got a lot of injuries. We've got to get in someone who is really going to motivate them and really aim that they should be at the fore ... I know it's a hard controversial decision, a very difficult decision, and there will be many journalists out there that will say it was the wrong decision. Hard decisions have to be made when you want to turn around the club.[24]

Balme professed to be dumbfounded by his sacking, although just why is hard to fathom. His four-and-a-half seasons as coach at Melbourne had been a less than brilliant success. They had yielded a mediocre win:loss ratio of 41:57, with a fourth spot in 1994 the pinnacle. The Demons had won only 17 of 53 games since then, finishing ninth in 1995 and fourteenth in 1996, and were languishing at the bottom of the ladder in sixteenth spot when the axe fell midway through 1997. He had little cause to feel badly served. Coaches had lost their jobs for far better performances. True, the club was seriously undermanned, and he had been told he would serve out the season. Yet, to the bitter end, he refused to concede that Joseph Gutnick might know just a little about football — not, perhaps, the finer tactical points of the game, although he was learning fast, but the passion and spirit that drove it.

Joseph was 'probably a bit inexperienced in footy matters and like all young players we hope he keeps at it and gets better', Balme said snidely at the press conference he called the day after he was sacked. And Joseph's outburst during half-time at the St Kilda game, he said, just proved 'he knows absolutely nothing about football. I don't know how many games he's actually played but how can he comment on how you play and what you can do?' Ultimately, Balme concluded, Joseph 'may be able to judge where to find gold, he may be able to judge how to run a boardroom, but he can't judge who can and who can't play.' Balme's contempt for Joseph was palpable, observed the *Herald Sun*'s Trevor Grant, who was present at the press conference. His 'biting sarcasm reflected a genuine, deep-seated, and obviously long-held lack of respect and trust ... at every opportunity during the 30-minute question-and-answer session he continued to display his contempt for the Melbourne president.'[25]

Putting pen to paper, Balme came to the crux of his problem with Joseph in an article two days later in the *Sunday Age*. 'In the modern football environment, does the amount of influence one has depend on the amount of dollars tipped in?' he asked. He noted that 'white knights don't have a great record in league football. Used to being at or near the top of the business tree, naturally they want to be accorded the same status in football — immediately! Unfortunately, in today's football, turning around ailing fortunes isn't as simple as takeovers, acquisitions and the power of the dollar . . .'[26] To Balme, from beginning to end, Joseph was no more than a businessman who didn't understand football culture. He was an outsider, an interloper, who could put up his money if he wanted but then should butt out and leave the running of the game to those who, like himself, really 'understood' it. He wasn't the first, and he wouldn't be the last to take this view. But Joseph had had a gut-full:

> We have all heard that too many times, but I am there and the supporters elected me by an overwhelming number of votes, I think the most in the history of the Melbourne Football Club. I know enough about football and sports and it's not uncommon when a team is on the bottom of the ladder that coaches are sacked . . . People can . . . say I don't know anything about football, but I know enough to know that we need a new lease of life. There's not going to be much of a rapport between a coach and a president if the president is always told he knows nothing about football.[27]

The fallout from Balme's sacking was huge. A bearded little rabbi from East St Kilda had had the temerity to follow his own instincts and take on the football world on its own terms — and dare it to tell him he was wrong. And it did. The press was full of the incident for days afterwards, with much of the comment sympathetic to Balme and openly hostile to Joseph. 'Balme is an exceptionally talented coach,' wrote Rod Nicholson in the *Herald Sun*. 'He is innovative, active and alert and was the AFL's Coach of the Year in 1994. And he's a good bloke.' Joseph, on the other hand, was not such a good bloke: 'Gutnick may be a master of the business world, but he lacked football nous when organising Balme's exit.'[28] Over on the *Sunday Age*, Rohan Connolly's rage was bordering on the hysterical: 'Gutnick's recent actions smack disturbingly of the behavior of other "celebrated" AFL club leaders such as Paul (pick Warwick Cappa or else) Cronin during Brisbane's Carrara days, Geoffrey Edelsten, or Reuben Pelerman, who baled the Bears out of their black hole of debt, but who didn't think a day at the club was complete without a routine threat of a sacking or even winding up the place altogether,' he wrote. Noting that Joseph had told the media when he announced Balme's sacking that the Melbourne Football Club needed 'a new breath of fresh air, a new style', Connolly asked: 'Doesn't he realise Melbourne already has it? It's called uncertainty, anxiety and fear, and it's a recipe for complete disaster.'[29] Somewhat more balanced was Mike Sheahan's column in the *Herald Sun*. Sheahan conceded that 'something had to be done' at Melbourne — which had 'embarrassed not only itself and its supporters, but anyone with pride in the game of football'. But even he questioned whether Joseph had the 'right' to do it: 'Gutnick is seen to have too much influence for a man who knows far more about mining plans than game plans,' he wrote. 'Surely a man elected because of his business profile and willingness to dip into his vast fortune doesn't buy the right eight months on to decide who coaches the club?'[30]

Running against the general trend was a thoughtful article by Michael Gawenda, the then deputy editor of the *Age* and a fanatical Essendon supporter, who debunked the conventional 'wisdom' that Joseph was an interloper, a 'stranger' to 'footy culture', who didn't know what he was doing:

> it can be argued that Mr Gutnick, during the past six months or so, has clearly adapted to footy culture like a duck to water. After all, the sacking of coaches whose teams perform badly is an integral part of football culture. Coaches are required to do many things, but the main thing required of them is to be the sacrificial lamb when their team performs badly. Mr Gutnick has absorbed that central element of footy culture very quickly indeed. In fact, those who know Mr Gutnick know that he does not accept for a moment the notion that his knowledge of football is negligible. He knows, for instance, that it is incredibly painful to watch your side go down week after week. He knows now — if he did not know before — that money alone won't solve Melbourne's problems. And he knows what it means to be a football nut, prepared to spend hours discussing the game. He knows what it means because he has become one himself. That's the point. Whatever may have been Joseph Gutnick's motives when he decided to lead the charge to save the Melbourne Football Club, there can be no doubt that the club and the game have now become an obsession. And at root, obsession is what the culture of football is all about.[31]

Balme was replaced by his assistant, Greg Hutchison, until a process could be put in place to recruit a permanent coach. And, as often happens in football after a coach is replaced, the team went out the following Saturday night and notched up its first win in nine rounds — a creditable 92–67 victory over Richmond. Joseph, who was present at the game, was delighted. He came into the Demons' changing room after the game beaming. In his hands was the trophy the two old rivals traditionally play for, named in honour of the Berry Street Children's Home. 'It almost was a premiership cup,' Joseph enthused. It wasn't, of course, but the president could be forgiven the indulgence after all the club had been through. It was a marvellous result, and should have been just the morale booster the club needed to salvage something out of the second half of the season. 'It looked like the change was the catalyst for our players and it's fantastic and I'm so happy not only for ourselves but for our supporters,' Joseph said. 'They came to a game and saw Melbourne win.'[32]

Few in the changing room shared Joseph's elation. The TV cameras captured the boisterous rendition of the club song — the first time it had been sung since the round one win over North Melbourne, nine long weeks before. But afterwards, the mood turned to introspection. Many of the players' thoughts turned to Neil Balme who was a popular man around the club despite his lack of success. He must have been hurting. For the captain, Garry Lyon, it was an especially bitter–sweet moment, probably more bitter than sweet. Balme was a close friend, and Lyon had put up his hand to play that Saturday, despite the chronic back problem that had kept him out of the game for months, mainly to help him out. That was before Balme was fired. Now he found himself playing for his friend's successor — and in a winning team to boot. 'It's a strange sort of feeling,' he said after the game. 'It's obviously a great victory and much needed, but it's come at a cost and casualties along the way and that doesn't make me feel fantastic . . . I'm rapt for the boys. But at the same time it's a disappointing indictment on us as a group if this is what it takes to stir us into action.' He and fellow veteran Todd Viney took the trophy around to Balme's home, where it stayed for the night. 'It had been on our minds since Thursday,' Viney explained. 'We just felt it was appropriate that we talk to him, have a few drinks with him and a chat.'[33]

Lyon made no bones about the fact that he thought the board had treated Balme badly. The day after Balme was sacked, Lyon showed up — against his will, apparently — at a supporters' function where Joseph was present. According to Joseph, he put out his hand to Lyon and was snubbed: 'I sort of put out my hand and I didn't get a hand back,' Joseph recalls. 'Garry says he didn't notice my hand. But it was done in front of hundreds of people, and many other people saw it.' Joseph never forgot the incident, and his relations with the club captain were never the same. Critics accused him of being 'paranoid', and that he had stewed over the perceived snub when 'all he needed to do was confront Lyon about it.'[34] More than two years later, in August 1999, the matter was finally laid to rest. 'We met and Garry said he didn't mean what I thought,' Joseph relates. 'He apologised for what happened then

241

and supported the two of us working together for the sake of the Melbourne Football Club. And I accept that, if that's the case.'

The day after its victory over Richmond, and still reeling from the fallout from the Balme sacking, the Melbourne Football Club made another break with its past. The old war horse Ian Ridley finally decided to call it quits. 'It's time to mow the lawns up at Jamieson,' he told the *Age* on 3 June. 'I'm not resigning, I'm retiring. I've been involved in this club in some capacity since 1954. I've had a pretty good go at it.'[35] He had played 130 games for Melbourne between 1954 and 1961, including in five premiership sides, and had coached the team from 1971 to 1973. It had been a long and distinguished career. But the upheavals of the past year had obviously taken their toll, and Ridley decided enough was enough. The final straw was probably the handling of the Balme dismissal. He had been in Sydney at the time, and wasn't included in the telephone hook-up when the decision was taken. It was a shabby omission but there had been speculation for some weeks, ever since his old mate Hassa Mann had resigned, that it would be only a question of time before he, too, followed. It was a new era at the Demons. Dignified and gracious to the end, Ridley had this to say about Joseph: 'It's been 33 years since Melbourne last won a premiership and in that time there have been a lot of presidents, a lot of coaches and a lot of general managers who have been moved on or sacked or whatever. None of us have been able to get a premiership; perhaps Joseph can.'[36]

Whether or not Ridley believed this, Joseph, for his part, was convinced he could win a premiership for Melbourne, one day. And if he didn't, it wouldn't be for want of trying. Chasing dreams was nothing new to him — he had been doing just that for the past decade as a miner, and he was still investing millions of dollars each year in the search for the Rebbe's diamonds. 'I would be very disappointed if during my presidency we didn't win a premiership,' he says. 'On the other hand, I saved the Melbourne Football Club's independence, it survives, it's one of those clubs in Victoria that's there forever. It's a great achievement. But I still very much want to be the president of a premiership club . . .'

Meanwhile, Joseph was confident that the shock treatment he had administered the club by sacking Balme had done the trick, and that the club's fortunes were about to turn. All the talk about the players' having 'done it for Balmey' the previous Saturday was a load of hogwash: 'Why didn't they do it weeks ago?' Joseph asked. 'Why didn't they do it when he was almost challenged four weeks ago?' What had turned the club around were the changes he had made: 'While I was told nothing could be done, we saw something was done and it changed them and they performed,' he said. And he was delighted with his stand-in coach Greg Hutchison: 'Greg won the first game. I've got a great rapport with him. He looked great, he made the changes. He gave some of the younger players a go.' Joseph was already talking him up as a possible long-term candidate for the coach's job: 'I think he's done well and if he continues to do well then he'll certainly have my backing.'[37]

While Joseph's enthusiasm was understandable, it was premature — and probably showed that he really did have a lot to learn about football. He ought, perhaps, to have been more sensitive to the mixed feelings in the rooms after the victory over Richmond. Crowing about his coup, and dismissing the players' feelings about Balme was not the smartest thing Joseph could have done at this time. Nor, probably, was putting such great pressure of expectation on Hutchison. Hubris was swift. The very next game, the Demons received a 52-point belting at the hands of Adelaide. From that point on, it was a familiar tale. For the rest of the season they were to win just two more games — a good 119–100 victory over Carlton in round fifteen, and a satisfying season-ending 119–79 win over Fremantle in the final round. But just four wins and eighteen losses for the season was a dismal record, and left the club in sixteenth and last place on the ladder.

Off the field, however, the picture was brighter. At the board level, a disgruntled Sean Wight — a former Demons player and one of just three board members who had opposed Neil Balme's sacking — resigned in disgust over the handling of the affair, and was replaced by the Victorian State Treasurer, Alan Stockdale, a long-standing Melbourne supporter. Wight's departure left Stuart Spencer as the sole surviving former player on the board, and this was not ideal. But Joseph was delighted with Stockdale's appointment, which was unanimously approved by the board: 'Alan brings a host of unique skills and experiences that will be invaluable as part of the Melbourne Football Club's rebuilding program,' he said.[38]

In the football department, Joseph scored a major coup by managing to snare Danny Corcoran from Essendon to relieve Cameron Schwab as football manager. Schwab, who had replaced Hassa Mann as CEO earlier in the year, had been doing both jobs concurrently. The highly respected Corcoran was viewed as a prize catch, and his move to the Demons sent jitters through other clubs who feared that their top personnel could be subject to similar raids, funded by Joseph's seemingly bottomless kitty. Unlike players, who were subject (at least in theory) to a strict salary cap, the very best coaches and administrators could be poached at will, and there was no limit to the inducements they were offered. Not every club had a Joseph to bankroll such acquisitions, and the less well endowed clubs had good reason to worry. A strong football department was the key to long-term success on the field, and the Demons now had the wherewithal to get the best that money could buy.

The *Age*'s Patrick Smith, usually a good barometer of how Joseph was going in the eyes of the football world, was impressed. 'The best thing that has happened to Melbourne over the past 12 months is the appearance of Joseph Gutnick,' he wrote. 'He has brought with him money, diamonds, gold, vision and an undiluted demand for success. He dazzles as Melbourne's way out of the darkness.'[39] But, Smith warned, Joseph still had a perception problem: 'We should not doubt Gutnick's intentions. He wants the very best for Melbourne. But suspicions remain that Melbourne is a toy and the boardroom is his playground ... Gutnick will eventually overcome that view but until he does ... he ... should hasten slowly.'

Joseph, meanwhile, was getting along splendidly with Greg Hutchison, despite the ongoing losses on the field. 'Joseph's been good,' Hutchison said. 'He's communicated with me on a regular basis. I communicate with him also. He's the boss of the organisation, so I've got to spend some time talking to him. And we get on OK. I don't think he'd try to tell me how to coach. I wouldn't be trying to tell him how to run his diamond mines [sic].'[40] It was a far cry from the days of Neil Balme — and Joseph made it known that if it were up to him, the coach's job would be Hutchison's for the asking: 'It would have to be a very attractive and convincing argument for Greg not to keep the job,' he said at the end of July, after Hutchison had been in the hot seat for about two months. 'I think he's done a good job ... and he's injected a new spirit into the club.'[41]

The choice of a new permanent coach was not Joseph's alone. Cameron Schwab was overseeing the process, and he went about it with an efficiency and a rigor that would have done justice to the selection of a Pope. The job specification ran to fifteen pages, and listed ten professional and sixteen personal attributes that the successful applicant must possess. The latter included such qualities as leadership, intelligence, strong work ethic, commitment to winning, personal communication skills, sense of humour, well-balanced lifestyle. The professional attributes included 'the capacity to develop and implement a well-defined style of game and team rules that allow the team to be a bona fide premiership contender'. And the successful applicant must be a 'student of the game' and a 'football fanatic'.[42] Perhaps the most important criterion of all was not spelled out: the ability to respect and maintain a constructive rapport with the president of the Melbourne Football Club. Anyone without it would not be getting past first base.

There were four candidates for the position: Greg Hutchison, the incumbent acting coach, who had played 96 games with Melbourne between 1975 and 1984; Peter Schwab, who had played 171 games with Hawthorn between 1980 and 1991; Neale Daniher, who in an injury-plagued career had played 82 games with Essendon between 1979 and 1990; and Damian Drum, who had played 62 games with Geelong between 1982 and 1989. All four had had extensive coaching experience, but none, apart from Hutchison, at the most senior level (Schwab, Daniher and Drum were all assistant coaches, at Hawthorn, Fremantle and Sydney, respectively). In the end, despite Joseph's backing for Hutchison, Neale Daniher got the job. Announcing the appointment at the end of the 1997 home-and-away-season, on 12 September, Joseph signalled his disappointment for Hutchison, and said it had been a 'tough decision' not to give him the job. He was, however, offered his old position as assistant coach. As for Daniher, Joseph said it was the club's opinion that the brilliant former Essendon player, who had been unable to realise his full potential on the field because of chronic knee problems, was destined to be an outstanding AFL coach. 'His football career was cut short in its prime and immediately there was a coach in the making,' Joseph said. 'Neale, in effect, has been preparing for this day for the past 10 years.'[43]

Joseph had, of course, been intimately involved in the selection process. And the last hurdle Daniher had had to leap was an interview with the president, in his St Kilda Road offices. What, Joseph had asked him, if it were round ten, 1998, and the Demons had won only one game? What if the team were faltering and the supporters were screaming? What would Daniher, a first-year coach, do then? Daniher's answer, recalled Cameron Schwab, was: 'Joseph, don't worry about me, what will you do?'[44] It was an apt answer — frank, with a touch of humour and irreverence — and one that Joseph, apparently, appreciated.

Daniher would have had other attributes that would have appealed to someone like Joseph. Despite his rural background and easy-going country-hick appearance and drawl, he had a sharp mind and a tertiary education. This included a brief study of Old Testament theology at

Melbourne University which would have given him something extra to talk to his new president about, apart from football — although, Joseph says, he prefers to use his 'quality time with the coach to talk about football' rather than trade ideas about the Bible. He was also a football fanatic, born into one of the game's most famous playing families, and passionate about it. 'Don't be misled by that Dwight Yoakam thing,' the Fremantle coach, Gerard Neesham, said of his former assistant. 'Neale's got boundless energy when it comes to football and it's something that has consumed not just his life but his whole family's life. He's very, very passionate about coaching and doing as good a job as he possibly can.'[45] Energy, passion. These were important buzz words for Joseph — something he had perceived as having been glaringly absent in Neil Balme.

Physically, too, Daniher was poles apart from his predecessor. Thin and rangy, he projected a touch of steel beneath his laid-back country manner; the big, beefy Balme, on the other hand, projected a congenial quality that was very appealing socially but was not what a struggling, demoralised team had needed to lift itself to play beyond its capacity. Added to these attributes were Daniher's perceived hunger for the success denied him as a player because of his dodgy knees; his renowned knowledge of the game; and his highly honed organisational and computer skills (he had formal qualifications in applied science, computer science and applied finance and investment). He was, in short, almost too good to be true — and, it seemed, just what the Demons needed.

Daniher had one other thing going for him. He had coached at Fremantle, and had grown close to one of football's most promising young players — a twenty-year-old ruckman by the name of Jeff White. Melbourne was already in the box seat to snare White: as the 1997 wooden-spooners, the Demons had the pick of the crop under the AFL's policy of advantaging bottom sides in the national draft at the end of each season in a bid to balance the competition. All the out-of-contract White had to do was nominate for Melbourne, and the deal was done. Money would not be a problem — not with Joseph around — provided he could be fitted under the salary cap the League imposed on all clubs, again in the interests of a more balanced competition. But would he want to sign for a struggling club that had just gone through a year of turmoil? The presence of Daniher would be an important factor in persuading him and the new coach signalled, at his first press conference after being appointed, that snaring White would be a high recruiting priority. Less than a month later, he had landed his man.

On 7 October 1997, Jeff White signed with the Demons. His three-year contract was believed to be close to $300,000 a season — a phenomenal figure at the time, earned by only a handful of the game's elite. For a twenty year old who had made just thirty-two senior appearances for a struggling club, Fremantle, it was widely seen as not only obscene, but an unconscionably high-risk gamble by the Melbourne Football Club. There was considerable concern about the effect paying so much for a young, relatively untried player could have on morale in the club, where far more senior players were earning only a fraction of that amount. 'It's one of the stupidest things I've seen in football,' player–manager Peter Jesse said of the deal. 'It is the best wedge you can drive in a football club. Whether you like it or not, people are human. When you've got a bloke running around for $300,000 who's as soft as butter, are you going to kick it to him? I wouldn't think so.'[46]

Predictably, the football–money nexus quickly focussed on Joseph. Trevor Grant in the *Herald Sun* questioned whether Joseph would ever do anything like that in one of his own companies. 'Of course not,' Grant wrote — 'Gutnick's a smart businessman. He would never risk the relativity that exists within his company structure. He knows if he did, the potential staff problems could create major damage to the company.'[47] For all his business expertise, Grant concluded, 'Gutnick is like any other footy club president. He wants to see his team win and he's prepared to go as far as possible to achieve it.' This was a refreshing change. Whether intentional or not, accusing Joseph of acting more like a typical footy club president than a hard-headed businessman was a rare acknowledgment from the football-writing fraternity that he had fully acculturated. Joseph must have enjoyed the compliment.

◊ ◊ ◊

In the little over a year since Joseph had taken over, the Melbourne Football Club had undergone a major transformation. The old guard, symbolised in Ian Ridley and Hassa Mann, had gone. Joseph, with his beard and red-and-blue yarmulka, was the new face of the club. In all, five of the old board had been replaced, as had two coaches and an assistant coach. There was a dynamic new CEO in Cameron Schwab, a highly rated new football manager in Danny Corcoran, a coach with huge expectations resting on him in Neale Daniher and, to round out the off-field staff, a new development/reserves coach in Chris Fagan. Some twenty-eight players had been discarded, and with the talented Jeff White leading the field, steps were in place for a revamped playing list. Out-of-contract backman Jamie Shanahan was lured from St Kilda, and a number of very promising juniors were recruited — including the year's number one draft pick, Travis Johnstone, as well as two surprise packages in Guy Rigoni and Nathan Brown. Senior players such as David Schwarz and Stephen Tingay, sidelined by injury in 1997, were expected to be back in the side. Wounded captain Garry Lyon was also in training, and hopeful of a return. Morale was high, and everyone was looking forward to a much improved season in 1998. 'Getting to this point . . . has needed some difficult and unpopular decisions,' Joseph conceded looking back on his first sixteen months as Demons president. 'It's been at times traumatic making these decisions, but Melbourne needed a clean sweep.'[48]

The 1998 season got off to an inauspicious start. The Demons went down to Neale Daniher's old side Fremantle — one of just four teams they had managed to beat in 1997 — 61–84. It had all the makings of a long year. But then came three uplifting victories, over North Melbourne (125–100), Brisbane Lions (100–87), and Carlton (72–70). The mood in the Demons camp was euphoric. 'Mazel Tov. Mazel Tov. Mazel Tov. You hear it once, you hear it twenty times,' Patrick Smith wrote after visiting the Demons' changing room following their gripping two-point win over Carlton at Optus Oval in round four. 'The joint is jumping.' Smith had just added to his vocabulary another footy neologism, '*Mazel Tov*' (Yiddish for 'good luck'), to join 'yarmulka' in the standard football lexicon. The mood was infectious, Smith wrote — 'you can't help but share the buzz'.[49] Joseph believed that his club really had turned the corner. 'It's just a different Melbourne look, isn't it?' he enthused. 'Being three goals down and to come back like that and beat Carlton at Carlton, it's almost like winning a premiership, isn't it? It was a fantastic comeback. I think this game's the turning point for Melbourne.'[50]

Two more good victories followed, against Port Adelaide (102–53) in round five and against Sydney (80–61), in Sydney, in round seven. Melbourne was now one of four teams closely locked at the top of the table. The press was impressed. 'King Midas, who turned everything he touched to gold, was a mythical figure,' Ron Reed wrote in the *Herald Sun* at about this time. 'Joseph Gutnick is not. He just seems to possess the same enviable gift from the gods . . . Having made a fortune finding gold and diamonds where others saw wasteland, he is now proving — to the astonishment of most of the AFL — the same can be done with football.'[51] Joseph modestly deflected most of the credit for the Demons' revival to his new coach Neale Daniher and football manager Danny Corcoran, who had 'made the players believe in themselves'. Unlike in the bad old days, when he had felt despised and frozen out by Neil Balme and those around him, Joseph now had an excellent rapport with his football department. He was learning a lot from chats with Schwab, Daniher and Corcoran, and his capacity to absorb information, Schwab noted, was phenomenal. 'Many in football wondered who this very Jewish figure was when he appeared, and whether he knew enough about football,' Reed concluded. 'If he lacked footy cred then, he's acquired some now.'

Melbourne's round eight clash with Collingwood at the MCG marked another important milestone in Joseph's football evolution. Daniher invited him into the inner sanctum — the coach's box. He was warned, though, that he would have to sit down and shut up: 'It's a big game Melbourne and Collingwood,' Joseph said before the game, as delighted and excited as a small boy being invited into the cockpit of a jetliner for the first time. 'They'll have to handcuff me and tape my mouth.'[52] He was even more excited after the game, which Melbourne won 114–111 in a nail-biter:

> It was fantastic. It's every supporter's dream to sit with the coach, isn't it? . . . I heard what was going on, the reactions when players do well and players do badly . . . it was better than hearing [radio commentators] Sam Newman and Rex Hunt! . . . It was just great to be there together with all the coaching staff to see Melbourne win a nailbiter . . . I thought they'd swear a lot more, but it wasn't as much as I thought. It was pretty bad though . . . But it was a great experience for me to see how it works, and only confirms to me that Neale Daniher's a great coach and is a real part of the Melbourne turnaround.[53]

Much as he enjoyed the experience and appreciated the symbolism of his appearance in the coach's box during a game, Joseph made it plain that he would not be making a habit of it: 'Whenever Neale wants me to be there, I'll be there. I don't think I'll overdo it. Only once in a while. It's one of the good things in life. Otherwise you become too used to it.'[54] It was enough that he had been taken into the confidence of his football department, which had already made him welcome at planning meetings held before games and at the Monday-morning postmortems. That would never have happened under Neil Balme, and was, for Joseph, the ultimate acknowledgment that he was now accepted as part and parcel of the Melbourne Football Club family. 'Here's a fellow who is president of our football club and he should know how the people he's put in place operate,' Daniher said after the game. 'Other presidents may have more of a football background, but Joe's now an expert.'[55]

Watching the game that day was AFL commissioner Graeme Samuel — the man who had once told Joseph that he would never be accepted by the Melbourne Football Club. Now a close friend, he was with the rest of the Gutnick family in their corporate box when Joseph, wearing his red-and-blue yarmulka, strode on to the MCG after the game and followed the players up the race to the rapturous acclaim of the Melbourne supporters. 'Graeme told me afterwards that he had never felt prouder as a Jew,' Joseph relates.

Melbourne's 113–64 win over Carlton in round nineteen provided another milestone of sorts for Joseph. He had a $1000 wager on the Carlton game with his Blues counterpart, John Elliott. The sum was mere pocket money for the two multi-millionaires — but the loser would have to pay up in front of the media wearing the rival team's guernsey. Joseph, however, made a bit of a blooper. He, too, squeezed into a Melbourne jumper for the cheque-presentation ceremony — only it was the previous year's model, displaying the logo of the club's former major sponsor Tooheys. Oops! 'Isn't it nice to see a couple of tycoons having fun with footy!' the *Herald Sun*'s Scot Palmer commented in his 'Punchlines' column.[56] Clowning for the cameras with his mate 'Big John' Elliott was yet another indication of Joseph's growing comfort in the footy world.

After winning their last five home and away games of the season, the Demons, quite incredibly, found themselves part of the September finals action for the first time since 1994. It was a fairy-tale end to the season. Joseph was full of praise for the players — and especially for his football department. He described Schwab, Corcoran and Daniher as the off-field equivalent of the Demons' star forward trio of Lyon, Neitz and Schwarz. Daniher, especially, had more than met his expectations. 'I'm talking about bringing Neale Daniher into my business to inspire some of our geologists,' he quipped on Channel 7's *Talking Footy* program. 'I've sat in on a lot of his talks with the players and it's been fantastic. He's really inspirational, dedicated, sincere, committed and a workaholic, and he believes in the players. All these factors have created something very special and unique — the aura has been created.'[57]

Sadly, Joseph would not be at the MCG to see his team take on the reigning premiers, Adelaide, in the first qualifying final. It was a Saturday afternoon game, and Joseph would be spending a quiet Sabbath at home with his family. 'I have to stick to the rules just like the players,' Joseph told a reporter a few days before the game.

However, he added, 'I'll be there in spirit.'[58] And the moment the Sabbath ended after sunset, he would be glued to the video watching the replay — courtesy of a video Channel 7 had promised to have delivered to his home within an hour of the final siren. In the event, he 'cheated' a little, admitting he knew, well before the Sabbath ended at 6.40 that evening, that his team had won a stirring 42-point victory and was through to the next round. Joseph was not, of course, allowed to listen to the game on the radio — but, he explained a little coyly, 'if someone tells me this is happening, I don't have to close my ears to it . . .'[59]

Not only did Joseph not see the Demons thrash Adelaide but, he soon learned, he would be unable to watch the next game, against St Kilda the following Saturday. 'It's called footy torture,' a frustrated but delighted Joseph said when he heard his team had gone through. And, he found out, the frustration would not end there. If the Demons got up against the Saints, they would be facing North Melbourne the following Friday night — also a no-no for Joseph. Should they overcome that hurdle and make it into the Grand Final . . .'Yes, I am going to be very, very frustrated during the next three weeks,' Joseph conceded. 'I knew this could happen, but it is much harder now as you can imagine. I have always said that I am looking forward to the bad news that we will be in the grand final and that I won't be able to attend. That should be the worst news I ever had.'[60]

The 'footy torture' continued for Joseph. Melbourne duly beat St Kilda by a convincing 51 points. Joseph was now quite open about the fact that he was kept abreast of the game by his non-Jewish bodyguards. 'I heard during the day what was going on,' he said. 'I didn't have a ball-by-ball description but they let me know from time to time what was going on.' Joseph could not, of course, instruct his employees to listen to the radio and keep him updated. But they didn't need to be asked the scores. 'They know to come and tell me,' Joseph explained. 'If someone was dying of thirst wouldn't you give them some water from time to time?'[61] (There is a hallowed principle in Judaism, called *'tsa'ar ba'alei chayim'* — the obligation to avoid cruelty to animals. It is for that reason religious Jews are permitted, for example, to milk their cows on the Sabbath, to alleviate the suffering caused by painfully ingested udders — a sensation Joseph would have been experiencing acutely at this time. Metaphorically, of course.)

Joseph wasn't the only one faced with a dilemma by the Demons' unexpected success. The old champion Ian Ridley had promised himself that he would keep well away from his former club for at least a year, to give Joseph and the new regime a chance to establish themselves. So he, like Joseph, wouldn't be at the Friday night preliminary final against North Melbourne — but, he said, he would be listening to it on the wireless and, like Joseph, hoping 'like billyo Neale Daniher and the boys can bring home the bacon'.[62] (Joseph, of course, would have expressed it rather differently.) And what if the team he had played and bled for most of his adult life made it through to the Grand Final? 'Of course he would love to watch his club in a Grand Final,' Mike Sheahan wrote in the *Herald Sun* on the eve of the Melbourne–North Melbourne clash. 'But he can be a stubborn little bugger, "Tiger" Ridley . . . [He] has lived his life on the principle that you're totally in, or you're totally out.'[63]

In the event, both Joseph and Ridley were put out of their 'misery'. Melbourne went down to North Melbourne 84–114, and the dream was over. Joseph would be able to spend his next *Shabbat* quietly with his family and give his bodyguards the day off, and Ian Ridley could spend the day peacefully mowing the lawns up at Jamieson . . . But rising from wooden-spooners in 1997 to fourth in just a single year — just one win short of having a shot at its first premiership in over thirty years — was a remarkable achievement.

And Demon Joe Gutnick, president of the Melbourne Football Club, was the toast of Melbourne.

The 'Outsider'

'How long do I have to be the outsider, for me to understand football? It doesn't take the greatest talents and skills in the world to be able to understand football. It's not a big mathematical, Einstein theory that you have to be a genius to understand it . . . I have been involved for three years, and I know a little bit about football. I know a lot about football.'

Joseph Gutnick, September 1999

AFTER ALL THE euphoria of 1998, and the huge expectations this had generated for the following season, 1999 got off to the worst possible start. The Essendon Football Club was found, in February, to have been in massive breach of its players' salary cap between 1992 and 1996, and was fined $276,274 and hit with heavy drafting penalties. Joseph immediately ordered an internal review of his own club's player payments. What he discovered shocked him to the core.

Melbourne had breached its salary cap even more blatantly than Essendon had over the previous five seasons, by as much as $800,000. 'I'm very distressed and alarmed that I wasn't informed of these breaches,' he said when he found out.

> I had no idea and I was under the impression Melbourne was way under the cap . . . I'm not interested in vendettas. But I'm from a world of corporate governance and I have a duty of full disclosure . . . We're asking the AFL to come in and do an independent investigation with the full compliance of the club, clear the slate and move forward.[1]

Joseph's action — which he took quite spontaneously, without first consulting his board — came as a bombshell not only to his club but to the football world. It precipitated a *Kulturkampf*, a clash of cultures, the likes of which the football world had never seen. There had long been a great deal of cynicism about the salary cap — a sense that the cap was there to be rorted as long as you could get away with it. There seemed to be a tacit understanding that not too many questions would be asked, and if they were, and you were found out, you would stand solidly by your mates. It was the same kind of philosophy that enabled a player to claim a free kick on the field, yet swear blind at the tribunal that the offending player had done nothing untoward. 'Anything from blatant lies, vivid imagination to heat stroke, amnesia and temporary insanity were acceptable utterances at the tribunal,' former Essendon player-turned-media-commentator Gerard Healy noted — 'but honesty wouldn't wash.'[2] Similarly, it was OK to abuse an opponent in racist terms to 'gain a psychological advantage' and, until relatively recently, receive the abused player's 'understanding' that nothing racist or hostile had been intended. It was a form of good old-fashioned amoral Aussie 'mateship' of the kind Prime Minister John Howard was once so keen to have enshrined in the Constitution. For better or for worse, it was part of a culture that belonged to the past. And, for all his commitment to tradition, it was part of a culture that Joseph found alien, and alienating.

Joseph had shown, both in his business dealings and in his political activities in Israel, that he could play the game as hard as anyone. But he had always insisted that he had played by the rules. His many detractors have often claimed otherwise, yet countless inquiries into his activities, both in Australia and in Israel, had invariably failed to prove any serious impropriety. The occasional technical breach, perhaps, but never anything more. Moreover, he came from a religious tradition that — despite the stereotypes and the many exceptions that proved the rule — placed high store on ethical behaviour. 'If being president of the Melbourne Football Club helps to make the name of God beloved amongst people,' Rabbi Chaim Gutnick said of his son's involvement in football, 'then it's worthwhile. But just for the sake of showing that we are Australians, that doesn't interest me very much.'

There can be little doubt that Joseph was genuinely outraged, and distressed, that the Melbourne Football Club had rorted the salary cap while he had been president, and that people he had trusted either had been directly implicated in or had known about these rorts without informing him. 'When I first came into football, people said I didn't know anything about football,' he said. 'Well, I didn't know anything about these [deliberate salary cap breaches] . . . This has not been easy. I didn't enjoy seeing my picture on the front page with 'Demons Disgrace'. Besides the dollars, I've also given of myself since I became president. This is very distressing.'[3]

His decision to 'dob' his club in to the AFL Commission — a term Joseph loathes and rejects: 'I'm not a dobber,' he insisted when former Carlton champion Robert Walls publicly accused him of that[4] — was widely hailed in the media. 'Joseph Gutnick fessed up on behalf of his football club yesterday, and good on him,' Mike Sheahan wrote in the *Herald Sun*. 'It's novel and refreshing to hear a club president pay more than lip service to terms such as "salary cap" and "corporate governance" and "an honest game".'[5] Sheahan's counterpart on the *Age*, Patrick Smith, was equally impressed: 'Joseph Gutnick was correct and brave to investigate his new club's salary transactions,' he wrote. 'Gutnick, as always, was a class act. He would not name individuals, made it clear that nothing less than the highest probity would be acceptable at the club . . . Football's wink, wink, nudge, nudge administration era is over. May the change be irreversible.'[6] The *Age*, in an editorial on the subject, was equally convinced that Joseph had done the right thing:

> Mr Gutnick's decision was a bold one . . . and he deserves the praise of all who care about Australian football . . . From the mid-1980s the direction of Australian football has swung from a teetering state league to the most watched competition in the country, but the level of administrative excellence has failed to keep pace with the growth of the game. Mr Gutnick's brave, honest actions may be just the accelerator for which the AFL has been looking.[7]

◊ ◊ ◊

Joseph Gutnick, the 'footy outsider', was now not only seen and accepted by some of the most influential opinion-makers as an integral part of the game but hailed as the benchmark. It was a remarkable achievement by a man who had been spurned and derided by much of the football establishment when he first burst onto the football scene just two and a half years earlier.

The Melbourne Football Club, however, was in a state of shock. It had grown accustomed to, and had by now fully accepted, its unconventional president. But it was still rooted, like the rest of the competition, in the old culture. Honesty was still 'a word not often associated with AFL clubs,' Gerard Healey observed, asking a question that many in the football world would also have been asking about Joseph's action: 'Was it naivety, part of a personal agenda, panic or just plain honesty? It's a new concept in football and difficult to accept at face value.'[8] Joseph spelled out precisely where he was coming from, in a letter to all club members:

We are the oldest football club in the world, our forefathers wrote the original rules of the game and we carry the name of the town which is the heartland of Australian Rules football. We are the guardians of that tradition, which we must be loyal to and build upon. We do so with an absolute sense of responsibility, for the sake of our history, our people, ourselves and our future ... the board of the Melbourne Football Club believes that the club has a fundamental duty to its members, supporters, players and employees, and to the game itself, to ensure the club conducts itself with complete honesty and public openness.[9]

Anyone familiar with Joseph and his background would recognise the resonances in those words, and the depth of emotion behind them. But it took a while for the message to sink in, and not all in the Melbourne Football Club, including some members of his board, found it easy to absorb this strange new concept.

Joseph openly admitted that he had acted without consulting the whole of his board when he informed the AFL of the salary cap breaches. And he fully justified this: 'I have a board I couldn't fully trust,' he told the *Age*'s Caroline Wilson. 'There are too many leaks on my board and there are members who are remnants of the past at the time these breaches could have taken place. I found it my duty to remain intact. I couldn't compromise myself.'[10] This had clearly upset some members of the board, and there were widespread reports that he faced a board rebellion over his move.

Joseph was quite unfazed. Speaking to the *Herald Sun*'s Leo Schlink three days later, he said:

There are a few individuals who are stirring. That's what happens when reform is taking place. You expect that there are a few disgruntled individuals around the place ... One or two individuals want a certain culture to continue to exist at Melbourne. I can't allow that to happen ... There are some people who are angry that I went to the AFL over these breaches, but I don't regret going to the AFL. If that costs me the presidency, so be it. It would mean Melbourne would be a club, and have a culture, that I would not want to be involved with.[11]

Joseph challenged those who had grievances to come out in the open and confront him. None did. There wasn't a single resignation, or open expression of dissent. Even those in the club who might have had misgivings did not have the courage to express these openly and when they did speak to the media, it was on the condition that they remained anonymous. 'Much as Joseph has done for the renewal of Melbourne,

Chanukah gift. Joseph presents the then-Australian Prime Minister Bob Hawke with a silver *Chanukiya* (candelabra) in 1989, watched by his father Chaim. Chanukah is a time when Lubavitchers are urged to reach out to the leaders of the countries they live in and promote the message of inter-religious and inter-ethnic harmony.

Chanukah in the Park. Joseph, flanked by the recently elected Victorian Premier Steve Bracks (left) and Israel's Ambassador to Australia Gabriel Levy, at the huge *Chanukiya*-lighting ceremony Joseph sponsors in Melbourne's Caulfield Park each year.

Joseph 'Gutnickel'. Joseph with Anaconda's Andrew Forrest at Centaur's state-of-the art nickel plant at Cawse, after concluding their joint-venture deal at the end of 1999. 'The Rebbe told me I'd find a whole lot of good things – not only gold and diamonds... I stumbled upon this. Who knows where it's going to lead me...'

Joseph with his Learjet.

'Look in the North, in a place that hasn't been explored yet, there are valleys and mountains of gold.' Joseph points to the site in the Northern Territory which, he believes, could turn out to be the start of another Witwatersrand. Dr Neil Phillips (left) indicates the site of the original Witwatersrand as Jonathan Law looks on.

people won't see it all torn down again by a needless purge,' one unidentified source within the club was quoted as saying at about this time. 'There is an element of honor in what he is attempting to do but the line between good intent and serious, unnecessary harm has been reached.'[12] Those who spoke on the record fully supported him. Club vice-president Bill Guest confirmed that, even though there was some dissent, the majority of the board was solidly behind the action Joseph had taken. 'I firmly, absolutely and categorically believe we made the right decision in going to the commission,' Guest said. 'Such a decision will lead to some discontent and some people will get hurt in the process and many egos will be crushed . . . A situation like this can damage a football club, but the strength of us is how we can handle that.'[13]

As soon as he had informed the AFL of his club's salary cap breaches, Joseph set up a team to carry out the internal investigation. Headed by himself, it included a top lawyer, Peter Hayes QC; a senior accountant, Michael Perry (from the auditing firm Arthur Andersen); and two Melbourne board members, Greg Healy and Tony Rodbard-Bean. Joseph meant business.

The focus was strongly on the club's CEO, Cameron Schwab. Joseph had long harboured reservations about Schwab — whom he had viewed as part of the Balme–Lyon clique that had frozen him out of the club when he first became president. He had developed a strong working relationship with him during the heady 1998 season but the old distrust resurfaced when Joseph found out that Schwab had known about 'a series of secret deals' for some eighteen months. It appears that Joseph had wanted to fire Schwab for keeping him in the dark, but had been advised by AFL boss Wayne Jackson as well as by his coach Neale Daniher and football manager Danny Corcoran not to act hastily.[14] Schwab was an immensely popular man, both within the club and in the football fraternity, and Joseph was told the backlash would be considerable, with potentially devastating consequences for the Melbourne Football Club. Morale in the club was already fragile, with several senior players under investigation in connection with the breaches. Although Joseph was persuaded to stay his hand, and allow the investigation to take its course, he indicated his lack of faith in Schwab's ability to do his job as CEO by announcing that the salary cap fiasco had underscored the need for him to become more directly involved in the hands-on, day-to-day running of the club:

> I was relying on a lot of individuals. Now I see I have to be more involved myself. I'm not talking about the football department. I have nothing but

admiration for Neale Daniher and Danny Corcoran, and Danny and Neale are right behind me. I've got to be involved in the general administration to make sure that everything is done properly and I'm talking about all areas: membership, sponsorship, publicity and not breaching the salary cap.[15]

Over the next few months, several senior players, including Garry Lyon, Todd Viney, Jim Stynes, Stephen Tingay, David Neitz and David Schwarz, were questioned about the breaches. While there were some rumours of unrest and unhappiness, Joseph claimed he had the full support of his football department for what he was doing — as well as that of the bulk of the players. A leading Demons player, who preferred not to be named, was quoted in the *Herald Sun* as saying reports of player anger at what Joseph and the board were doing were 'total bullshit . . . We've got a lot more on our minds than worrying what's going on behind the scenes . . . and there are certainly no plans to confront Joe.'[16]

Joseph did, in fact, enjoy an excellent rapport with most of the players. Senior player Stephen Tingay, interviewed at the height of the controversy, in May 1999, described how the players had been sceptical of Joseph when he had first arrived at the club but had learned to respect and to like him: 'Initially they were cynical because he admitted he didn't understand footy. I reckon that was a feather in his cap from the start. First he didn't know you had to be a club member and the next thing he's president. He's obviously done his homework to get his position right.'[17] Veteran ruckman Jimmy Stynes was another player who liked and admired Joseph, as did his brilliant young successor, Jeff White. 'Jeff's told me he's doing a course at university on the Holocaust because he respects the fact that he has a president who's a Jew,' Joseph relates. 'I think he's a very fine fellow. Also Shane Woewodin, Andrew Leoncelli, David Neitz, and David Schwarz. I get on very well with all of them . . .'

The press, too, continued to support Joseph. 'Joseph Gutnick wants to run a clean club,' Patrick Smith wrote in the *Age*. 'How dare he?' he asked facetiously. 'He wants clear lines of communication between the administration and board. The cheek of him. And he doesn't like his officials not telling him the correct state of play. Just who in the hell does he think he is? A president?'[18]

Although he was preoccupied with the turmoil off the field, Joseph still managed to take a keen interest in his team's performance — disappointing as this was, compared with the highs of the previous season. At the end of June, he was present at one of the Demons' rare wins for the season — an 11-point victory over a struggling Collingwood at the MCG. Neale Daniher had once again invited him to watch from the coach's box. 'I've got two out of two (wins) now in the box so Neale is saying maybe you should come in again,' he said after the game. At the halfway mark of the season, with five wins and six losses, the Demons were still a chance to make the final eight come September. Sadly, this was not to be. Perhaps distracted and demoralised by what was happening off the field, they lost ten of the last eleven games — the only win coming in round thirteen, over the reigning premiers Adelaide.

The Demons were on fire that day, not least of all Joseph, who used the pre-match luncheon at the MCG, which was attended by AFL chief Wayne Jackson, to launch a blistering attack on the League's high-handed treatment of the clubs. 'We are alsatians, not French poodles, and we will not be muzzled,' Joseph thundered, demanding that club presidents be represented on the AFL Commission. He resented the fact that 'whenever the Melbourne Football Club voices its opinion we are reminded about our salary cap breaches'. His club, he declared, 'won't be intimidated, won't be threatened, won't be bullied. We will face the penalties of the salary cap breaches, but we certainly believe that they should be lenient and should take into account that it was a voluntary disclosure.'[19]

The outburst, which was widely reported, was perhaps a measure of Joseph's frustration — as much as it was of his growing confidence as an equal among equals in the football world. Although, as Patrick Smith pointed out in the *Age* a couple of months later, Joseph's demand that club presidents be appointed to the commission indicated that he still had something to learn. His only support came from the Carlton president, John Elliott — which, Smith remarked, 'is generally an indication these days that you have made an error in judgement'.[20]

The simmering crisis in the club came to a head on 6 August 1999, some three weeks before the AFL was to deliver its findings into Melbourne's salary cap breaches, when Cameron Schwab was finally forced to resign as CEO. His position had become untenable. Both Joseph and Schwab were tight lipped about the circumstances surrounding his departure, but it was no secret that Joseph, and in the end his board, had come to the conclusion that the former CEO no longer had a role to play in the Melbourne Football Club. 'My relationship with Cameron hasn't been brilliant since the salary cap saga but his resignation goes beyond the salary cap issue,' Joseph told the press a couple of days later. 'There was a breakdown not only with the president. There was a breakdown in numerous fields around the club.' Two employees — one from the marketing and one from the football department — had been called in and asked their opinions of Schwab, Patrick Smith reported, claiming — erroneously, according to Joseph — that 'the two supported Schwab'. Two days later Smith wrote, citing Joseph: 'They did exactly the opposite . . .'[21]

Schwab's demise reopened an old wound in Joseph's uneasy relationship with Garry Lyon, who although he had finally succumbed to his chronic back injury and hung up his boots in July, was still a powerful influence around the club. Both Lyon and his successor as club captain, fellow veteran Todd Viney, had been especially close to Schwab — as they had to Neil Balme two years earlier. They were the last vestiges of an old 'clique' which Joseph felt had never really come to terms with his presence at the club, and, as they had done when Balme was dismissed, they openly expressed their disapproval. Joseph was in no mood to tolerate this. He read the riot act, squarely targeting Lyon:

> It is unfortunate when individuals, this clique within the Melbourne Football Club, pass comment without knowing all the facts. The board is running the club, not ex-players or ex-coaches . . . Garry is an ex-player. An icon and hero of the club. However he is unaware of all the facts . . . he should speak to those people who are in charge. If he's still disgruntled he should call a meeting of members and get rid of the present board. But whilst the board has been elected by its members it'll do its job.[22]

Joseph had laid it on the line, just as he had to his board five months earlier. If Garry Lyon, Demons icon and ex-champion footballer in a series of mediocre Melbourne sides in the 1980s and 90s, wanted to challenge Joseph Gutnick, ex-soccer goalie at Yeshivah College, East St Kilda, saviour of the Melbourne Football Club and, God willing, president of a future premiership club in the new millennium — he was welcome to do so. But he should put up or shut up. Lyon blinked. Two days later, he met with Joseph, and emerged from the meeting contrite. 'We have agreed to disagree on a number of issues because in the end it's the club that's the most important thing,' he told the *Age*. 'I know what the players are going through and they don't need this. So Joseph understands how I feel about Cameron and we have agreed to move on because the club is bigger than the individual.'[23]

It was not immediately clear that Lyon saw a future for himself in a Melbourne Football Club where he would no longer have the stature or the clout he had once enjoyed under the old regime. There were rumours he was sounding out the possibility of a coaching or assistant coaching job elsewhere. His old mates Todd Viney and Jimmy Stynes were offered and accepted part-time coaching roles at the club. Assistant coach Greg Hutchison moved on to be assistant coach at Richmond and was replaced by Brian Royal, who moved over from the Western Bulldogs. It looked as though Lyon was being left out in the cold. In the end, he accepted a part-time coaching job with the Demons, with a special brief to work with Jeff Farmer in a bid to recapture the magic and the confidence that appeared to have deserted the brilliant young Aboriginal goal sneak in the 1998 season.

Joseph welcomed Lyon's decision. He had made it plain in September, some two months before Lyon had decided to take up the part-time position, that he believed the former champion had a role to play at Melbourne:

> Garry is, has always been, welcome to stay at the Melbourne Football Club. Garry has been anti, you know, maybe some of the moves that I have done. By sacking Balme. By forcing Cameron Schwab's resignation. By him not being part of the inner circle like he was in earlier days. But that's a fact of life. Garry is an important part of the Melbourne Football Club, and we'd like his involvement. It's a question of how far his involvement should go.

And after Lyon had made his decision in November, Joseph expressed his satisfaction with the outcome:

> Garry will help coach the forward line, especially Jeffrey Farmer. They've always had a very close relationship over the years. He'll also do some marketing work for the club . . . He's a past legend and icon for the club and he's stayed with Melbourne. We're very pleased for that. I don't know if it will be long term because Garry has said that if he would be offered a coaching job full time he could have gone elsewhere. But we're delighted that he's staying and using his talents. Especially the Garry Lyon–Jeff Farmer duo which was very successful in 1998, and hopefully he can get Farmer to perform and enthuse others in the club in the year 2000 and beyond.

It was another important landmark for Joseph as president of the Melbourne Football Club. He had stamped his authority unmistakably on the club and had set its face to the future, yet had managed to retain, on mutually acceptable terms, the services of Garry Lyon, Todd Viney and Jimmy Stynes as important links with a past that Joseph both respected and valued. Just as he had when he first became president in 1996 and had worked to build bridges with Ian Ridley and his pro-merger forces in the club, he recognised the importance of stability and

continuity. At the same time, the continued presence of three of the
club's most highly respected players of the recent past — all three of
whom had been investigated in connection with the salary cap
breaches — gave the lie to speculation about any serious unhappiness
with or opposition to what Joseph was doing, and the football department — headed by Danny Corcoran and Craig Cameron — also
remained intact. And Neale Daniher, after a wretched 1999 following
his brilliant debut as coach the year before, could look forward to a
much more tranquil season in 2000.

Quite remarkably, the departure of Cameron Schwab, popular as he
had been at the club, had left scarcely a ripple. As one fan put it in a
letter to the *Age*: 'I do not know the details of Cameron Schwab's performance as Melbourne's chief executive. However, I do know that I
prefer a chief executive to concentrate on running a multi-million
dollar business. To be mates with the players comes a fair way further
back.'[24] In the club there appeared to be tacit agreement that Schwab
had to go.

On 26 August 1999 the AFL finally handed down its report, prepared
by special investigator Michael Easy, on the Melbourne Football Club's
salary cap breaches. The club was found guilty of breaches totalling
just over one million dollars. This was apparently a compromise
between Melbourne's claim that its own investigation, conducted by
Peter Hayes QC, had uncovered breaches totalling just $600,000, and
Easy's probe, which put the figure at $1.5 million.[25] The club was fined
a total of $600,000, with $250,000 suspended for five years. There
were also various draft penalties. Joseph declared himself satisfied
with the outcome: 'We deserve the penalty,' he said at a press conference after the penalties were announced, adding that he felt the AFL
had acted wisely and fairly.[26] He also made it clear that he would not
be dipping into his own resources to cover a fine for misdemeanours
that had been deliberately kept from him. 'I've already given the club
$2.7 million,' he replied when asked.[27]

The AFL finding was almost an anti-climax. There was a general
consensus that Melbourne had got off relatively lightly because of
Joseph's decision to inform the AFL of the breaches immediately he
had learned of them. 'Gutnick's voluntary disclosure earned
Melbourne a $250,000 rebate,' Mike Sheahan wrote in the *Herald Sun*,
adding: 'That's a handsome reward for honesty.'[28] Any outrage at the
AFL's conclusions was directed not at Joseph and the Demons but at

Fremantle — which had been given Melbourne's first draft pick to 'compensate' for having lost Jeff White to Melbourne at a time when the latter was rorting the system. Even that soon ran out of steam. The whole matter dropped from the headlines it had occupied for much of the previous six months. Joseph was convinced that he had done the right thing, not only by his own club, but by football in general: 'There's no messing around these days. No one would want to go through the embarrassment of being caught breaching the salary cap any more. I don't think anyone is rorting today. At least I hope not . . .'

The one other casualty of the affair, apart from Schwab, was the club's former finance manager, Bill Balcam — one of five current board members who had held office during the period in which the worst of the salary cap breaches occurred (the other four were Ian Johnson, Bill Guest, Stuart Spencer and Kevin Jones). Balcam announced he would not be standing for re-election in December, but insisted that he was guilty of no wrongdoing: 'Peter Hayes confirmed that there was no evidence of any wrongdoing by me.'

Balcam was also adamant that there was no bad feeling between himself and Joseph, confirming that the board had been 'unified on any major decisions taken'.[29] That was not, however, how the media saw it. There was speculation that the salary cap affair and Joseph's vigorous handling of it had left a residue of deep resentment in the Melbourne Football Club that could yet unseat him, and there were persistent references to unhappiness about Joseph's 'dictatorial' style. 'The old guard says the benefactor has turned dictator,' Mike Sheahan wrote after the Schwab sacking. 'It is frustrated by his independence, by his lack of consultation.'[30]

Patrick Smith, too, alluded to Melbourne Football Club board members being 'uncomfortable with his [Joseph's] ruthless and dictatorial style'.[31] Smith, long one of Joseph's more sympathetic and perceptive critics, was concerned that Melbourne was 'no longer a club but a franchise', and intimated that that board was cowed into submission only because the club's finances were 'so fragile that without Gutnick's generous support the club would struggle to pay its bills' — something which, he wrote, gave Joseph 'enormous power'.

Caroline Wilson, also in the *Age*, wrote that 'Gutnick's style has been perceived of late as dictatorial' and that 'while the club is putting on a brave public front and insisting the board is united, serious disquiet remains over Gutnick's ability as president, his off-the-cuff judgements and his persistent media appearances.'[32] A few days later, Wilson wrote that several resentful board members could be 'plotting a campaign against him [Joseph] when his tenure on the board expires at the end of 2000'.[33]

Joseph is unperturbed by such speculation. He concedes that there is 'still some dissension out there that says just because Joseph's got money he can do what he wants and is a dictator.' But, he points out, the Melbourne Football Club board was not a bunch of patsies. 'We've got some very strong people on the board. Starting from Alan Stockdale and others.' They were not going to be just pushed around, and if they wanted to challenge him openly, they could. 'I believe I have got over-whelming support,' he insisted. 'Despite what everyone is saying, we have got a unified board, we have vision, we're a strong football club and we're moving forward.'[34] He was convinced that what he was doing was right for the club — and, moreover, that he had the vast bulk of the membership behind him. 'I believe people want to have a clean club, strongly administered, and that we can win games cleanly,' he had said soon after launching the inquiry into the salary cap rorts.[35] He was still prepared to stake his presidency on that: 'Whatever the mem-bers say is what happens. If they want me out, I'm out, if they want me in, I'm in.'[36]

Joseph's faith in the broad-based support he was convinced he enjoyed at the grass-roots level in the club was largely vindicated a few months later, in December, when four of the five candidates he had endorsed and canvassed for were elected to the board of the Melbourne Football Club with overwhelming majorities. The four included a former player, Stephen Bickford, and popular ABC TV sports pre-senter Beverley O'Connor — believed to be only the second woman ever appointed to the board of an AFL club. The only endorsed candi-date not to gain re-election was Mark Rothfield, a member of the old pre-Gutnick board, who was narrowly defeated by the immensely pop-ular former Demon champion Gary Hardeman. Joseph was disap-pointed for Rothfield, but delighted at the overall result. Not only had four of his five candidates (Bickford, O'Connor, Peter Hayes QC and George Szondy) been enthusiastically accepted, but the addition of two high-profile former players in Bickford and Hardeman redressed an imbalance on the board that had been causing some concern. It was a resounding vote of confidence in Joseph's leadership, all the more sig-nificant for coming, as it did, after a year of unprecedented turmoil which many of his detractors had tried to blame on Joseph.

There were, of course, members who did want Joseph out — espe-cially after the break with Schwab. One of them, a member of one of the Demons' coterie groups, the Redlegs, even launched a short-lived

'Joe Please Go' campaign at the beginning of August 1999. The disgruntled member, an accountant by the name of John Pollock, called in
to one of Melbourne's commercial radio talk-back shows after it was
announced that Schwab was leaving, and asked like-minded members
to contact his office for a 'Joe Please Go' kit. This included a proxy
form to vote Joseph out and a poster they were meant to hold up and
point at the president's box 'at the appropriate football match'.[37] The
response was underwhelming. Nothing came of the initiative, and all
the indications were that the vast majority of Demons supporters were
solidly behind Joseph and what he had done — despite the fact that
many believed the salary cap scandal and the controversy over Schwab
had distracted the club and may have contributed to its poor showing
on the field.

The 1999 season was, in fact, deeply disappointing, especially given
the great expectations generated by the club's performance the year
before. The team won just six games, lost sixteen and finished fourteenth on the ladder. It was as though 1998 had been no more than a
false ray of light for a once-proud team that remained bogged down in
the mediocrity that had denied it the glory of a flag for the past three
decades. The Demons appeared to have taken a step backwards in 1999.

In the space of little over three years, Joseph, the quintessential outsider, had turned the world of football on its head — paradoxically in
the name of tradition. The old culture of footy mateship — that
amoral, mildly cynical, larrikin culture that evolved when football was
still basically a working-class suburban game played hard and tough by
semi-professional players who would do anything to win a game as
long as they could get away with it — had given way to a new culture,
better suited to the glitzy, high-profile, money-laden, TV-driven form of
mass entertainment Australian Rules football had become. This was
the culture of the boardroom, with its strange new mantras and alien
concepts like 'due diligence', 'fiscal probity' and 'corporate governance', a world that Joseph understood far better than had people like
Ian Ridley and Hassa Mann, the traditional custodians of the old culture. At the same time, Joseph had fought tooth and nail to preserve a
proud old football club even when it seemed obvious that, in cold
rational economic terms, its days were numbered — something that
Ridley and Mann, for all the courage and commitment they had shown
for the red and the blue as players, had not found the stomach or the
passion to do as administrators.

No less remarkable is the fact that Joseph managed, from the very beginning, to win over the rank-and-file Demons membership. They appreciated the fact that he was ready, from the start, to put his money where his mouth was. Joseph was seen as the man for the moment, and, for all his superficial strangeness, was embraced with a warmth and affection usually reserved for club champions. Since he was lionised by members at Dallas Brooks Hall in August 1996, his popularity appears not to have waned significantly. Strangers still come up to him with an 'Onya Joe! How're the Dees going?' And a little doll complete with greying beard, red-and-blue yarmulka and a sparkling rhinestone diamond on its chest — sent to him by a fan in the country — has pride of place among the collection of photographs and memorabilia behind the huge curved desk in Joseph's office. Joseph admits that he gets just as much of a buzz from his acceptance by the fans as he does from walking through the MCG's Long Room as president: 'I love that part of it,' he says. 'I'd like to portray that more as time goes on. I'd like to be the "people's president". There's the challenge of mixing with the MCC and the Long Room at the MCG — I enjoy that, it wouldn't have happened twenty years ago — but I like to represent the people out there. I like and respect them.' And he was quite prepared, after all the turmoil the club had endured, to place his future as president squarely in their hands.

As for the charges, constantly heard from his detractors, that he was riding rough-shod over the Melbourne Football Club's 'culture' and 'traditions', Joseph has this to say:

> What do you mean by tradition? The Melbourne Football Club, the Demons, the oldest club, its association with the Melbourne Cricket Ground? I don't want to change that. But the culture of the 1980s and 90s was not necessarily the culture of the 1950s and 60s. . . . We're thirty-five years in the wilderness. Melbourne used to be the envy of every club. In the 1950s and 60s.

Joseph claims that he is all about trying to recreate the winning culture of the 1950s and 60s — the culture that had first attracted him to the Demons and had kept him loyal ever since. 'The old mateship cliques that afflict football can't succeed now because we have got to run it and be disciplined and professional,' he has explained.[38] 'Otherwise you won't survive to see the new millennium.' Ian Ridley and Hassa Mann, as administrators, had not managed to win a premiership for the club in the 1980s and 90s. And neither had a champion and icon like Garry Lyon. Perhaps, in the 2000s, Joseph Gutnick would . . . In practical terms, Joseph explains, this means going back to basics. The successes of 1998 had been a false dawn, concealing the fundamental flaws that remained to be corrected if Melbourne were ever to be a genuine contender:

> We're rebuilding at the Melbourne Football Club. What should have taken place in 1998 is taking place in the year 2000. Two years later. And I'm very excited about it. Even when I became president, there was still a half board pro-merger, a compromise with Ian Ridley — I didn't have the freedom and the board together to work to rebuild the Melbourne Football Club. There were a lot of constraints. And Cameron Schwab was very overbearing, and did a lot of things on his own . . . I want a five-year period. Either I'll be successful or I won't be . . . We'll see if Joseph will win a premiership over the next five years . . .

The appointment of John Anderson as CEO in place of Schwab has, Joseph believes, been an important step in the right direction. A former cricketer for the Melbourne Cricket Club, Anderson has a strong emotional commitment to the MCG, which Joseph wants to reclaim for the Melbourne Football Club as its natural home. Joseph sees him as a first-rate administrator — and, perhaps most importantly of all, he was not part of the football mateship cliques that bedevilled the Demons for too long. He is 'the right man, in the right place, to take the Melbourne Football Club into the new millennium'.

Yet no matter what he did — good, bad or indifferent — to some he would always be the outsider. 'Little Joe Gutnick knows what it is to be an outsider,' wrote Ian Verrender in the *Sydney Morning Herald* in June 1999 at the height of the salary cap/Cameron Schwab brouhaha. 'The long beard, greying at the margins, and the yarmulka — even if it is blue and red at AFL matches — mark him as such . . . in the blue-blood world of Melbourne private schools and corporate directorships, Joseph Gutnick, while striving for acceptance, has never been part of the main game.'[39] And, asked Garry Linnell, author of *Football Ltd: The Inside Story of the AFL*, a few weeks after Cameron Schwab had been forced to quit: 'If Gutnick is not an outsider, what is he doing here?' The reference was to Joseph's office building off Kings Way in South Melbourne, an area which Linnell described as a 'no man's land of panel-beating shops and small industries on the outskirts of the city' — from where he could see in the distance 'the glass and concrete cathedrals that line Collins Street, the heart of the city's business establishment'. No, Linnell wrote: 'You're not part of that town, Joe.'[40] Talk like this angers Joseph — especially the inference that he knows nothing about football:

I've been president of the Demons for three years. How long do I have to be the outsider, for me to understand football? It doesn't take the greatest talents and skills in the world to be able to understand football. It's not a big mathematical, Einstein theory that you have to be a genius to understand it. There are also some quite ordinary individuals who follow football and have strong opinions. I wouldn't say that Sam Newman, and Dermott Brereton, and — who's the guy who's down on the ground always with the long moustache? Dipper [Robert DiPierdomenico] — and Shane Crawford, and Billy Brownless, and what's his name, Dougie Hawkins, are the greatest geniuses that the world has known. I have been involved for three years, and I know a little bit about football. I know a lot about football.

There have been others, like respected *Sunday Age* writer Rohan Connolly, who has continued to suspect Joseph's motives, who has continued to see him as, first and foremost, a businessman. Someone who didn't really understand or appreciate 'footy culture', who, like other tycoons who had become involved with football clubs, was mainly in it for what he could get out of it. 'While no one doubts Gutnick's commitment to the Demons,' Connolly wrote after Schwab's dismissal, 'his role with the club has been very good for him on other fronts as well . . . And will anyone except Gutnick ever really know how much his admission of the Demons salary cap breaches was due to his concerns for the club, and how much to the scarring of his business reputation?'[41] It was a reasonable enough question to ask; Joseph would quite rightly have been concerned about what condoning such conduct would do for his reputation as a businessman. But it indicated an unwillingness on Connolly's part to accept or acknowledge the depth of the passion Joseph felt for the Melbourne Football Club — or the genuineness of the moral outrage he felt at the deception.

Joseph is not, in fact, sure that his involvement in football has any significant impact on his business activities, one way or another. When asked, he seems to find the question genuinely puzzling:

I don't know . . . I'm trying to think . . . It may have portrayed me in a better light in relation to my business activities. That this is a normal guy, not the Shylock image that I may have had earlier. It's certainly been from that point of view positive. Business people talk to me about footy when they come to see me. . . . I'm not saying I haven't brought some business people to football. And I don't know what the future will bring. I must say it hasn't been negative . . . It may have improved my image. I'd say you become more of a celebrity status because of this football thing. But has it helped my business? It hasn't been negative. How positive it's been I can't tell . . .

Business advantage was plainly not a major motivating factor when Joseph first rallied to the Demons' cause in August 1996 — even though, as he conceded at the time, it did bring him into contact with people like Alan Stockdale; and it appears to have been, at best, only the most peripheral incentive for him to have remained involved since. If anything, the greatest 'business' benefit Joseph might have derived from his involvement in football lay in the psychological release it provided. 'Psychologists, psychiatrists whom I have met say if you concentrate on one thing and you haven't got any outlets to take your mind off work from time to time, it's very bad for your performance,' he explained in a January 1997 interview, about four months after he had become president of the Melbourne Football Club. That was why, he said, 'you will find any big businessman having other activities and other involvements'.[42]

Far more significant than what his involvement in football may or may not have done for Joseph as a businessman, however, has been the opportunity it has given him to help change the perception of Jews in Australia, and to repay part of a debt he owes to a country that has treated him well: 'Someone Jewish becoming president of the Melbourne Football Club!' Joseph had told the *Bulletin* in October 1996, barely two months after he had assumed the role. 'It shows how much Australia has changed. For me it's not only the fulfilment of a dream, but the opportunity to put back something into Australia that allowed me to become wealthy, to be free and to practise my religion.'[43] Three years later he felt much the same way:

> The fact that I was able to save the Melbourne Football Club, the establishment club, is quite a feather in the cap of the Jewish community. It may not be important in some people's eyes, but football is important in Victoria, in Australia. It's a very important part of our lives. . . . I was able to save a club, I was very proud of it. Someone else may be very proud setting up an art centre. For me, it's been football . . .

Moreover, Joseph points out proudly, he has been able to achieve this without in any way compromising his religious beliefs:

> I make sure I have kosher food. I have my yarmulka there. I don't attend on *Shabbes*. So as much as I can, within the framework of my beliefs, be part of it, I am. And I gain respect for it, so I'm happy about that. This year [2000] I'm more delighted than ever that I'll be able to attend sixteen

games. They really took me into account. The AFL took into account a religious Jew that he should be able to attend games! I'm sure some people will complain, why should Gutnick get his way. But the club wants me there, and I want to be there. As president of the Melbourne Football Club . . .

◊ ◊ ◊

The significance of all this is immense, and goes beyond football, to the very core of what it is to be Australian at the turn of the century. Jews, like other ethnic minorities, have long been able to participate fully and at every level in the public life of the country. And many had — most prominently, Sir John Monash and Sir Isaac Isaacs before World War II, and Sir Zelman Cowen since. But it had always been accepted that such participation would be on the majority's terms. Jews like Monash, Isaacs and Cowen, while not in any way denying or concealing their Jewishness, deliberately chose to 'de-emphasise' this in their public lives. They were indistinguishable in their appearance, demeanour, and cultural identity from their fellow non-Jewish Australians. The same has been true of Jews like AFL Commissioner Graeme Samuel and Western Bulldogs president David Smorgon in the world of football. Joseph Gutnick, on the other hand, has demanded, and fought, to be accepted *on his own terms*. He has not only forced the prevailing culture (specifically the prevailing football culture) to recognise and accommodate his right to participate fully without having in any significant way to compromise his beliefs or his cultural identity as a Jew; but, what is perhaps even more remarkable, he has helped to alter materially the very fabric of that culture by bringing to it values from his own corporate *and* ethical Jewish world.

Whatever might happen in the future, however many people in the football world and in the media still have difficulty swallowing him, Joseph Gutnick's evolution as president of the Melbourne Football Club has been a remarkable story of late-twentieth-century Australian multiculturalism, full of paradox and stereotype-shattering contradiction. Nothing, perhaps, encapsulated this more graphically than when the Jewish 'outsider', Joseph Isaac Gutnick, soon after becoming president, invited the establishment aristocrat Robert Champion de Crespigny to become the number one ticket holder of Australia's oldest and most conservative football club — in the hope and expectation that he would kick in some money. It was a marvellous inversion of classic ethnic stereotypes. Joseph's relationship with de Crespigny, a fellow gold miner from a background vastly different from his own, is an intriguing story in its own right, going back to the black days just after 1987 stock market crash . . .

The Odd Couple

'Joe can't make himself rich (and get out of debt) without making Robert rich too. It's the perfect marriage.'
Trevor Sykes, the *Australian Financial Review*, 15–16 May 1999

'SOME PEOPLE ARE out to get you,' the voice at the other end of the line said. 'If you want a friend, give me a call.'[1] That was back in 1988. Joseph was struggling to keep his head above water in the aftermath of the Black Tuesday stock market crash the year before. Friends were few and far between. 'I was a good friend of Solly,' he recalled more than a decade later, referring to Coles Myer's Solomon Lew. 'And of John Gandel' — then ranked twelfth on *Business Review Weekly*'s 'Rich 200' list. But, he reflected wryly, 'not good enough for them to put their hands in their pockets.' In fact, none of the wealthy Jewish businessmen he had approached, including Australia's second-richest man, Westfield shopping centre tycoon Frank Lowy, was prepared to help, 'Their excuse was that they didn't understand resources. It wasn't real estate.'[2]

The friendly caller that day in 1988 was Robert Champion de Crespigny. A man Joseph had never met, or even so much as spoken to. An old Melbourne Grammar boy, de Crespigny had worked for more than a decade as a chartered accountant at KPMG. And then — not unlike Joseph's adventurous prospecting sidekick Mark Creasy — packed it all in and set off in search of something rather more challenging. Like Creasy before him, he found himself drawn to the gold country of Western Australia where, 'armed only with his accountant's eye for costs and returns', he made it big among the 'adventurers, cranks and cowboys of Kalgoorlie's Golden Mile'.[3] He was, even then, well on his way to becoming Australia's most brilliantly successful gold miner.

It is a bit of a mystery why this reputedly somewhat cool, ruthless operator should suddenly have felt a pang of compassion for Joseph. 'I rang him up because I heard someone was trying to shaft him,' is about as close as he has come to giving an explanation on the public record. While Joseph appreciated the gesture, he did nothing to follow it up at the time. Three years later, he had reason to be grateful to de Crespigny once again. He was battling to retrieve his Centaur mining company from the receivers, and de Crespigny could easily have sunk him once and for all by tendering against him. 'Robert could have tendered but he didn't,' Joseph reflected. 'I think it was because he was not going to tender against someone who was down.'

Apart from these two incidents — cited by Trevor Sykes in an insightful article on Joseph and de Crespigny[4] — the two men appear to have had little to do with each other for the next few years, during which they were engaged in a healthy rivalry. Joseph, after his luck turned dramatically for the better with his discoveries at Bronzewing, Jundee and Mount Pleasant in the mid-1990s, made no secret of his ambition to challenge and perhaps even surpass de Crespigny's Normandy Mining as the country's premier gold miner. And he appeared well on his way to doing just that when, quite suddenly, in the first half of 1997, the bottom dropped out of the gold price, the Australian Reserve Bank dumped two-thirds of the country's gold reserves, and the gold industry plunged into deep crisis. Gold miners needed every friend they could get.

Joseph picked up the phone . . .

◊ ◊ ◊

Eight months earlier, at the beginning of 1997, Joseph had been on a high. The gold resources in his group had passed the 10-million-ounce mark — over 6 million ounces at Great Central's Bronzewing and Jundee, and almost 4 million at Centaur's Mount Pleasant and Ora Banda. But this was not enough for Joseph, and by March he was openly talking about his ambition to find an Australian version of Busang, the fabulously rich 70-million-ounce gold deposit said recently to have been found in Indonesia. 'They say we won't find a Busang in Australia,' he told the Australian Gold Conference in Kalgoorlie. But 'I tell the managers in my company that we are after one of those big deposits. We may slip a number of times in that endeavour but we are not going to fall and we are going to find one of them.'[5] He appeared to think Mount Pleasant–Ora Banda might possibly be it, announcing that Centaur would be spending $30 million in 1997 on intensive exploration there.

It might have been hubris, but within days of Joseph's Busang-dreaming in Kalgoorlie, the share market turned on him, wiping

$106 million dollars from Great Central in less than a week.[6] Joseph shrugged it off at first, blaming weak bullion prices and moves by Western Australian Premier Richard Court to impose a gold royalty. 'The general market has taken a hiding and we're part of it,' he said. Analysts pointed out, however, that Great Central had been savaged far more than most, its share price falling almost 30 per cent in the previous six months compared with just a 7 per cent decline in the Gold Index. And they noted that doubts had arisen over Great Central's ability to meet its 1997 production target of 550,000 ounces — essential if the company was to stay on course for its medium-term target of 750,000 ounces. Great Central confirmed this in May 1997, revising its production forecast down to under 480,000 ounces because of unexpected difficulties that had arisen in Bronzewing's underground operation. Joseph acknowledged that the company had been 'slaughtered' on the market — but, characteristically, he pointed to the positive: even the revised production target was significantly up on the 362,000 ounces the Great Central mines had produced in fiscal 1996. In the end, Great Central produced 436,209 ounces in the year to June 1997 — which, with Centaur producing 146,000 ounces, gave Joseph's companies an aggregate of 583,209 ounces for the period.

Meanwhile, Joseph insisted, despite the setback at Bronzewing, his luck as an explorer was still holding. He was spending over $1 million a week on exploration, and was, he maintained, still coming up with the goods. Centaur had just made another major gold discovery at a site called Federal, in a well-worked but hitherto fruitless area just north of Kalgoorlie. 'This is unbelievable,' Joseph enthused. His exploration team had taken up 'wildcat drilling' at Federal, on ground old-timers had walked over for the past 100 years, and had come up trumps. 'This is a one or two or possibly a five million ounce discovery!'[7] Johnson's Well also announced an important gold discovery, of some one million ounces, at Rosemont, in the Duketon Belt. Mount Kersey and Australian Gold Resources pressed on with their gold exploration programs around Kalgoorlie and in the Yilgarn Craton, respectively.

The markets remained sceptical, and Joseph was puzzled. 'Our market capitalisation is actually less than it was before we discovered Bronzewing,' he mused. Part of the problem was the bear market in gold but, he conceded, his companies might have done themselves some damage by 'overcooking' their forecasts. Yet he continued to insist that both the Mount Pleasant area and the Yandal belt were 'elephant country', containing potentially huge finds that could rival Indonesia's fabulous Busang. Large tracts in both regions remained 'highly prospective', he claimed. 'They are also highly under-explored, they have the right structure and they have never been drilled. You normally find the big deposits in elephant country.'[8] A couple of weeks later, it was revealed that Busang had been a monstrous hoax, and no more was heard of 70-million-ounce gold strikes, either in Indonesia or in Australia.

This was probably just the splash of cold water Joseph needed. He had been living in a state of something approaching self-denial for the past five months as gold prices plummeted and, along with them, the value of his empire. The markets would take care of themselves, he kept insisting. 'It takes time for people to realise the story. The thing is to get the runs on the board and then the institutions have to support you.'[9] But for all the runs he and his geo-whizz Ed Eshuys were getting on the board, at Yandal and at Mount Pleasant, the markets were not coming around. By mid-year Great Central's shares were trading for just $2.40, another $1.10 down on their already depressed level six months earlier. A frustrated Joseph turned on local stock market analysts, accusing them of destructive 'negativism' that was driving down his companies' prices. 'We haven't got enough patriotism here,' he told an Australia–Israel Chamber of Commerce luncheon. 'We should be more proud of the resources that we possess and we should talk it up and that will help the economy.'[10] Reaffirming his own faith in gold, he cited recent comments from the Japanese Prime Minister, Ryutaro Hashimoto, who threatened to jettison United States Treasury paper for gold, as proof of the metal's enduring appeal.

But if anyone was listening, it certainly was not the Australian Reserve Bank. Barely a month later, in July 1997, the Reserve dropped a bombshell that shook the country's gold industry to its foundations. It revealed it had decided to dump more than two-thirds of Australia's gold reserves, some 167 tonnes, and had secretly been selling this on the international market since the start of the year. Joseph was flummoxed. Had the Reserve taken leave of its senses? Gold was Australia's second major mineral export, after coal, earning some $5.6 billion in export revenue in 1995–96. Gold prices — and gold stocks — went into free-fall. 'For a couple of billion dollars [the amount raised by the sale] to affect a multi-billion-dollar industry like that,' he declared, 'is quite bizarre.'[11]

However angry and bewildered Joseph and his fellow miners were at the move, both the Reserve Bank and the government were unrepentant. The Reserve Bank governor, Ian McFarlane, said the sale had been taken 'in the national interest' and would boost the Reserve's earnings by $150 million. The impact on the gold miners was 'unfortunate', he said, noting that all the Reserve's decisions had 'a sectoral impact'.[12] He was backed by the Prime Minister, John Howard: 'At a time of low inflation, and where the expectations are that inflation will remain low for a long time, it plainly makes a lot of sense to get out of gold.' Howard said the miners themselves had caused the fall in gold prices by forward-selling gold still in the ground, and told them to 'stop whingeing'. But 'how can he expect us not to whinge when $2 billion has been knocked off the market?' Joseph whinged. 'The industry has been shot in the back.' And he suggested to the Federal Treasurer, Peter Costello, when they met at the Melbourne–Essendon football match at the weekend, that if the government 'truly had the Australian gold industry at heart, they would go back to the market and buy it back'. But, he conceded a little wistfully, 'it's not going to happen'.[13]

Joseph, finally, had come back to earth. Yet he remained as bullish as ever about the future of gold. 'I don't think human nature has changed that much,' he said. 'I can't envisage a billion people in China all wanting paper issued by Wall Street in preference to gold.'[14] For the moment, the gold industry worldwide was in crisis, and Joseph realised that the immediate challenge was simply to survive. Joseph tried to secure his position by restructuring Great Central's debt with the help of a $150 million facility managed by Chase Manhattan. He also paid off the last $25 million he owed to Mark Creasy. It was plain by now that only the biggest, strongest players were going to make it in the dangerous new environment. The predators were already beginning to circle, hoping to swallow the minnows at bargain prices. Even Joseph was vulnerable. While he was a big enough fish in the Australian pond, he was still a very small fish compared with North American mining giants such as Barrick, Newmont and Homestake.

The Canadian giant Barrick, in particular, was on the acquisition trail, looking for bargains around the world, and rumour was rife that it had Joseph's Great Central firmly in its sights. There was considerable speculation at this time that Joseph might, in fact, be a willing seller — if the price were right. It was calculated Joseph would pocket in the region of $175 million for his 24.7 per cent stake in Great Central — on top of the $74 million he had realised by selling down his stake in the company over the previous two years. Again the idea was raised that Joseph might welcome the chance 'to shed the sometimes troublesome and tedious burden of running a large-scale production company and return to the fun of exploration.'[15] When asked about the rumours concerning Barrick, Joseph played a little coy, merely agreeing that Great Central would be an ideal takeover target at the current depressed prices. 'I think that the high-quality, low-cost companies will stand out,' he said, 'and one of those is Great Central.'[16] But Barrick, it would seem, was driving a hard bargain. And this finally prompted Joseph to pick up the phone and call a friend. Robert de Crespigny.

On a personal level, Joseph Isaac Gutnick and Robert Champion de Crespigny made the oddest of odd couples. On the one side, there was the aristocratic de Crespigny — 'tall, clean-shaven, proud of his Norman heritage, born into a medical family and an accountant by training.' On the other side, Joseph — 'short, sporting an explosively anarchic beard, proud of his Jewish heritage, born into a religious family, and a rabbi by training.'[17] And that was just the start. The two men had a diametrically opposed approach to mining. Joseph, as we have seen, was a gung-ho, go-for-broke, up-and-at-'em miner who would throw everything at a project in the profound belief that it would come up trumps. After all, he had the Rebbe in his corner, and a track record that proved his approach worked, spectacularly. De Crespigny had none of this passion or reckless abandon. He saw himself as still being essentially a book-keeper rather than a miner. And he had built up his empire — which he liked to describe as 'the Woolworths of the gold industry'[18] — not through adventurous, high-risk exploration, but through the shrewd, carefully calculated acquisition of proven gold mines. Both men had, in their own ways, been remarkably successful, completely dominating the Australian gold mining scene for a decade. Now they were driven into each other's arms by necessity.

At first, it seems, Joseph may simply have been trying to shore up his position vis-à-vis Barrick, perhaps even seeking to pit Normandy against the giant predator in a bid to drive up his asking price for Great Central. De Crespigny told him he wasn't interested in being drawn into an auction — but he should call back once Barrick was out of the picture. De Crespigny could, of course, have put in a bid of his own for control of Great Central. But as he explained at the time, Normandy didn't want to dominate the whole Australian gold industry. Instead, he preferred to enter into a 'strategic alliance' with Joseph.

Towards the end of August 1997 the two men shook hands on just such an arrangement. De Crespigny agreed to bankroll a takeover by Great Central of two smaller mining companies operating in the Yandal belt — Eagle Mining Corp and Wiluna Mines — in a move that would consolidate virtually the entire belt under Great Central's exclusive control. In return, de Crespigny would have the option of acquiring a 25 per cent stake in Great Central, making him the largest shareholder in the company, with the possibility to 'creep' even higher.

This would give de Crespigny a strong position in what was emerging as possibly Australia's most valuable new gold region, and bring the combined potential gold output of the Normandy–Great Central alliance to well over 2 million ounces a year. De Crespigny also agreed to make a huge loan (eventually revealed to be $165 million) to Joseph's perennially cash-strapped private holding company, Edensor, which needed the money to repay his $30 million debt to Plutonic, bankroll exploration activities in his other money-hungry but as yet unproductive companies, and meet his philanthropic and other commitments. This was to be repaid after five years — by August 2002 — and was secured against Joseph's holdings in five of his eight publicly listed companies.[19]

With his customary ebullience Joseph saw himself and de Crespigny as a winning combination. 'He's the ruckman,' he enthused — and 'I'm the rover!'[20] Others were not so certain. 'Make no mistake about it, this is not an alliance,' wrote Ivor Ries ('Chanticleer'), usually one of the more astute and sympathetic of the media's professional Gutnick-gazers. 'It's a prelude to a takeover . . .'[21] Some observers were already licking their chops. They were about to witness, they thought, a typically ruthless de Crespigny-style coup: 'Normandy's de Crespigny has embraced smaller allies in the past, each resulting in the slow but remorseless ingestion of the weaker party,' wrote the *Financial Review*'s resources editor, Ian Howarth. 'His track record says that when de Crespigny has you in his grip, corporate life expectancy is short.'[22] And Kate Askew, writing in the *Sydney Morning Herald* three months after the deal was concluded, was all but drooling as falling gold prices tightened the squeeze on Joseph: 'Gutnick hasn't quite lost his shirt to Robert Champion de Crespigny yet, but it is being slowly unravelled . . . The lower the gold price goes, and the lower the value of the shares in his plethora of companies, then the more shares Gutnick hands over to de Crespigny's Normandy.'[23] Joseph Gutnick was going to be swallowed alive. And they all watched, in fascinated anticipation, as Normandy's stake in Great Central gradually rose, from 10 per cent in August, through 14.6 per cent in September, 19.3 per cent in January 1998, to the agreed 25 per cent in March. It didn't stop there, as, through the 'creep provisions' in the Corporations Law, Normandy was able to raise its stake to 27.5 per cent by October. Normandy's interest in Great Central was now more than double Joseph's, which by this time had shrunk to just 12.6 per cent — down from the 24.7 per cent he had held before doing his deal with de Crespigny.

Joseph was unfazed. 'Everyone's writing that de Crespigny's going to control, de Crespigny's going to sneak up,' he noted at the time of the deal, claiming that the doomsayers had failed to understand the nature of his agreement with the Normandy chief. 'Do you think I'm just going to pass over to Robert de Crespigny my empire?' he asked. 'It's quite obvious I wouldn't do a stupid deal with de Crespigny that will allow him within two years to send me up the gurgler for something I built for ten years.' Besides, they had got de Crespigny all wrong. 'I like him,' Joseph told the sceptics. 'I know a lot of you dislike him, but I like him . . . He's worked very hard. He's very diligent . . . I have a very good rapport with him.' If, however, it were to emerge that de Crespigny did have a hidden agenda, Joseph warned, he was going to be no pushover. 'I know all the reputations, everything that has been said about Robert de Crespigny . . . But you can be sure that he's going to get the battle of his life if ever he thinks that he's going to get control of Great Central or he's going to get control of any of my companies just because of a default on our loan or anything of that nature.'[24] The Gentile Shylock was not going to get his pound of flesh from the Jewish Antonio quite that easily.

But if the pundits had indeed misunderstood the nature of his deal with de Crespigny, Joseph himself gave the impression that he too was a bit fuzzy about what it all meant — at least, initially. For while Joseph did speak about 'strategic alliances' and the need to 'rationalise' the Australian gold mining industry 'after the stupid sale of Australia's gold reserves by the Reserve Bank',[25] he simultaneously signalled that his main aim in striking the deal with de Crespigny was not so much strategic as tactical — to strengthen his hand ahead of a sell-out to a third party. If there were a predator — such as Barrick — lurking, he said on the day the deal was announced, 'they are going to have to pay top price. Normandy's presence strengthens us. Great Central is talking from a much stronger platform now.'[26]

De Crespigny, on the other hand, was adamant from the outset that he viewed the deal as at least a medium-term strategic alliance between two natural allies. He did not deny that Normandy could eventually take over Great Central. 'It's possible,' he conceded. 'But I don't want people to think it is imminent. We have agreed to take up to 25 per cent, and that's the stake we're comfortable with at the moment.' He also confirmed that the deal had been conditional on Joseph and his highly successful exploration team headed by Ed Eshuys remaining on board. 'He's agreed to stay around for an extended period,' de Crespigny said, in a statement that should have quashed all speculation that he wanted to 'shaft' Joseph.[27] Nine months later, de Crespigny indicated that a takeover was no closer. The relationship with Joseph was 'working very, very well' — both on a professional and, it seems, on a personal basis. 'We are both very, very independent people and want that independence. That's probably why it works. And we have enjoyed spending time together,' he said. 'We are comfortable with [the arrangement], and . . . that surprises people. If they look more and more there is some real logic in it.'[28]

There was a great deal of logic in it, as many analysts — although by no means all — were beginning to discover. Essentially, de Crespigny, who was brilliant at making money but not so good at finding gold, and Joseph, who was brilliant at finding gold but was chronically short of cash, complemented each other perfectly. Normandy had, in effect, become Great Central's (and Joseph's) banker — and Great Central, Normandy's de facto exploration arm. The arrangement gave de Crespigny dominant position in Australia's most exciting new gold region, which was being successfully developed by Australia's most dynamic and successful exploration team. And it gave Joseph the money he and Ed Eshuys needed to consolidate and continue developing the region — as well as the personal loan Joseph needed to bankroll his other interests. Moreover, as Joseph's major creditor, de Crespigny did not have to carry Great Central's, or Joseph's, huge debt. Servicing that would be Joseph's problem — and a compelling incentive for him to continue developing Great Central's Yandal mines. That, in turn, would not only make Joseph rich and enable him to repay his debt — but it would make de Crespigny, with the major stake in Great Central, even richer. If things went well, they were all laughing. But, should the wheels fall off, and Joseph find himself defaulting on his huge debt to Normandy, de Crespigny could foreclose on Joseph's stake in Great Central and several of his other companies and end up with control of the Gutnick empire anyway. It was a fiendishly simple and brilliant strategy. De Crespigny undoubtedly held the whip handle — but that did not necessarily mean, which many analysts continued to have difficulty accepting, that he saw Joseph as his 'bunny'.

Armed with de Crespigny's backing, Joseph set about successfully consolidating Great Central's stranglehold on the Yandal belt by acquiring both Eagle Mining and Wiluna Mines — although not without a struggle. There was strong pressure on Joseph to raise his bid for both mines, as shareholders dug in their heels. Eagle eventually capitulated in October 1997, when the company's chairman reluctantly advised shareholders to accept Joseph's $3-a-share offer. The deal cost Joseph $230 million. Wiluna, however, proved a tougher nut to crack. The Wiluna board played hard ball, and even sought the intervention of the Australian Securities Commission. But it, too, finally gave in. Spooked by rumours at the end of October that the Swiss Government had decided to sell off half its gold reserves, panicky shareholders came to the conclusion that Joseph's final offer of 75 cents a share (5 cents up on his original offer of 70 cents) in the hand was worth more than whatever it was the Wiluna board seemed to feel was out there in the bush. Plutonic Resources sold out of its 19.9 per cent stake in November, and Great Central moved to compulsory acquisition of the remaining shares in January 1998.

With the entire Yandal belt effectively controlled by Great Central, gold production rose substantially and totalled 651,102 ounces by the end of June 1998 — compared with 436,209 ounces in the previous year. 'To control the Yandal belt was our aim,' Joseph commented. But 'the results haven't exceeded our ambitions yet — because we were very ambitious. In time we'd like to prove the existence of something as significant as Nevada's Carlin trend.'[29] Ed Eshuys, in fact, began talking in terms of a 'super pit' at Jundee/Nimary, to rival that at Kalgoorlie. He envisaged a huge open cut four kilometres long and a kilometre wide, combining the existing pits at Jundee and Nimary. This would make it Australia's third-largest mine, with an annual production of up to half a million ounces.

Centaur's gold operations north of Kalgoorlie were also consolidated into a single entity midway through 1998, based at Mount Pleasant. Exploration there focussed on converting existing resources — some 2.6 million ounces — to mineable-reserve status. Production for the year to June 1998 was 194,955 ounces — not quite in the Bronzewing/Jundee league, but still highly respectable. With the 651,102 ounces produced by Great Central, Joseph's gold production for the year totalled some 846,057 ounces. He was rapidly advancing towards becoming a million-ounce-a-year producer.

Elsewhere in Joseph's empire, Johnson's Well acquired more land in the Duketon Belt north-east of Kalgoorlie and began a feasibility study on its Rosemont deposit. In November 1998 Johnson's Well joined with Mount Kersey and applied for 63,000 square kilometres of ground in Central Australia, where they hoped to find a massive Witwatersrand-type deposit — a project that Joseph saw as potentially dwarfing all he had achieved so far. Mount Kersey also acquired ground in the South Laverton Tectonic Zone and the Fraser Range during 1998, while Australian Gold Resources continued accumulating holdings in the Yilgarn Craton, with a focus on gold, nickel/cobalt and vanadium. Astro and Quantum pressed on with their so-far fruitless diamond hunt, in Western Australia and, increasingly, in China.

◊ ◊ ◊

At the end of 1998 speculation was rife once again that de Crespigny was poised to pounce. 'I saw in the paper that we're going to be out Rambo-ing next week,' the Normandy chief told a Security Institute briefing in Brisbane in late November. 'I think the papers will be disappointed. We don't have an intention to make some kind of takeover . . . The relationship with Joseph Gutnick is such that we are delighted with the way things are, so I think it's funny the way people jump to it. It's logical, but it's too big a conclusion to jump to.'[30] As if to underscore how well the relationship was working, de Crespigny announced in December that he would be taking an interest of up to 50 per cent in Johnson's Well's Rosemont discovery. The $43 million deal served to further emphasise Normandy's growing role as Joseph's main banker, and Joseph's role as Normandy's principal explorer.

In January 1999 Joseph and de Crespigny further entrenched their alliance. In a dramatic move that took the industry completely by surprise, the two men announced the formation of a new joint-venture company called Yandal Gold, jointly owned by Joseph's Edensor (50.1 per cent) and de Crespigny's Normandy (49.9 per cent). The objective of the new company was to buy out the 60 per cent of Great Central not already held by Normandy (27.8 per cent) and Edensor (12.6 per cent). This would leave Normandy and Edensor as the sole owners of a privatised Great Central, with Joseph's stake, through Yandal and Edensor, rising dramatically to some 42.5 per cent. The $276 million needed for the buyout — set at $1.50 a share — was to be provided by Chase Manhattan and secured by Normandy.

The Odd Couple had, or so they believed, pulled off a stunning coup. There was a hiccup, however, when the Australian Securities and Investments Commission stepped in and belatedly attempted to block the deal, claiming it was in breach of the Corporations Law. Under the law, a party and its associates could not become entitled to more than 20 per cent of a company without first making a bid to all shareholders — which, ASIC claimed, Joseph and de Crespigny had not done. ASIC failed to obtain the necessary interim injunctions to halt the bid, however, and it was allowed to proceed, with the overwhelming majority of the minority shareholders taking up the $1.50-a-share offer.

But just three months later, the Federal Court dropped a bombshell. In a shock ruling, the Court declared the Yandal takeover bid had indeed 'amounted to a deceptive and misleading breach of the Corporations Law'. This, Justice Ron Merkel ruled, had enabled Yandal, Normandy and Edensor to make a 'highly successful bid for Great Central Mines shares at a significantly lower price than would have had to be paid at the time', resulting in a significant detriment to shareholders who were 'effectively and permanently deprived of the opportunity of a higher bid price.'[31] Justice Merkel stopped short of unravelling the deal — but he ordered Joseph's Edensor Holdings to pay some $28.5 million in compensation to the shareholders whom he deemed had been dudded. Although he regarded Normandy's culpability as 'no different to Edensor's', Justice Merkel said in his ruling that he had decided against Normandy having to pay half of the compensation as the effect of his order would be 'to redirect the "price" the Normandy group paid to Edensor to the shareholders.'[32]

De Crespigny stuck by his mate once again and offered to split the penalty payment with Joseph. 'That's the morally right thing to do,' he said.[33] It was a generous gesture, which yet again defied speculation that de Crespigny would take advantage of Joseph's vulnerability to grab control of his mining empire. De Crespigny not only believed that it had been unfair for Joseph to be singled out for punishment when both parties had 'enjoyed "benefits" implied by the offer structure', but he was adamant that the matter 'should not have resulted in a trial, and certainly not in an adverse finding'.[34] He was, however, prepared to 'cop it sweet', pay out the Great Central shareholders as ordered by the court, and get on with the business of developing Yandal. A protracted, and very expensive, litigation process would not be in the best interests of his company or its shareholders. Also, he had an unshakeable belief in his own integrity — and the aristocrat's indifference to the opinion of others — which enabled him to live with the indignity of an adverse finding that he himself knew was unfair.

That was not an option open to Joseph. He had worked too hard for too many years to win the acceptance and the respect of his peers in the business world — an acceptance and a respect he appeared to sense was always conditional. One false move, he knew, and all the old suspicions would be resurrected. Besides, there was the matter of the Rebbe. Joseph could never forget, could never afford to forget, that his search for gold was for a higher purpose, carried out at the Rebbe's behest with the Rebbe's blessing. It followed that any public dishonour would besmirch not just his own name but the Rebbe's as well. Justice Merkel's finding, that he had been party to 'a deceptive and misleading breach of the Corporations Law', could not go unchallenged.

Regardless of the cost. So Joseph, independently of de Crespigny and against de Crespigny's better judgement, appealed against all of Justice Merkel's rulings against him.

Joseph's appeal was heard by a full bench of the Federal Court in the last week of August 1999; just over three months later, on 10 December, it ruled in Joseph's favour. The Federal Court, the judges ruled, did not have jurisdiction to hear cases dealing with important parts of the Corporations Law, and they reversed Justice Merkel's order that Edensor pay $28.5 million to the former Great Central shareholders.

The press hailed the Court's ruling as 'a stunning victory' for Joseph[35] and 'a blow to the Australian Securities and Investments Commission which mounted the case.'[36] As for Joseph, he was both relieved and delighted by the Court's ruling, which it handed down on the last day of the Jewish festival of Chanukah — something that Joseph found highly auspicious:

> No wrongs were ever committed. It's been very traumatic for me. I followed it through because I was very determined to clear my name . . . For me, it was very important to clear my reputation . . . I have stated many times that I always acted honorably and on the best legal advice in the country. It is a great Hannukah present for me. The last Friday is always the happiest . . . [37]

Although the Court had ruled only on the matter of jurisdiction, Joseph says he is confident he would have won — and if the ASIC chose to pursue the case, would win — on merits as well:

> I'm very confident I'd win it on merits. It (Justice Merkel's original ruling) was an unjust decision . . . I don't know if it's over with, or whether ASIC are mortally wounded now after this decision, or are going to follow it through and appeal. I can't predict what ASIC are going to do . . . We won on jurisdiction, and we will win on merits. And if it comes to it and they [ASIC] appeal, we will appeal again. Whatever I need to do I will do . . . Our lawyers are very confident that the worst-case scenario would be the decision would come back to stage one again before the judgement was ever put to me, then maybe they'll appeal and chase the case again with the Supreme Court or the High Court. I doubt it. It would be wasting taxpayers' money. How much have they lost already?

◊ ◊ ◊

Joseph and de Crespigny ended the millennium as the dominant force in Australian gold. Joseph was still highly vulnerable to de Crespigny, as industry watchers were always ready to point out. And Joseph was well aware of this. 'Robert has a reputation for being very ruthless,' he told the *Financial Review*'s Trevor Sykes. 'However, I haven't seen that aspect of his character . . . I certainly have a vested interest to make sure our exploration is successful, so why wouldn't he want us there, especially given our track record? Normandy are not exactly a great success in exploration. I believe that is how it will be for the future. There is no reason for any hostility between us.' And that, Sykes concluded, was the bottom line: 'Joe can't make himself rich (and get out of debt) without making Robert rich, too. It's the perfect marriage.'[38] Perhaps the penny had finally dropped.

For all that, Joseph realised that nothing could be taken for granted — by either side. 'He tells me that people tell him, watch Joseph, he'll screw you in the end,' Joseph noted a few months later, at the end of 1999 — 'and I tell him that people tell me that he's going to screw me at the end!' But Joseph remained optimistic that their arrangement suited both of them well, for the moment. And he acknowledged a debt of gratitude to de Crespigny:

> I will be forever grateful to Robert, no matter what happens in the future. It was my decision to get into bed with him, and he helped me get through a very difficult time . . . He didn't do it out of commercial philanthropism. He did it because he saw Great Central as a prize. As a big prize. And Robert will do the best for Normandy. And I'll do the best for Edensor and Joseph Gutnick . . .

Joseph made no secret of his interest in retaining a long-term stake in Great Central, the company on which he has based his fortune:

> My intention is to have a long-term involvement with Great Central . . . I'm the founder of Great Central, I was part of the driving force to make these big discoveries. We have a gold province that is going to produce gold for the next hundred years. Wiluna, Bronzewing, Jundee . . . I would like to remain with 30–40 per cent in Great Central. At the moment it's in Robert's favour, 53:47. I owe him money, so at the end of the day he'll have a larger portion than myself. I'd like to be 50:50. But he'd like to be 60:40 . . . I hope Robert will give me every opportunity in the world to keep my percentage . . .

He didn't. Just three months later, in early April 2000, de Crespigny moved to end Joseph's involvement in Great Central as part of a long-awaited corporate restructure forced on Normandy by the market. While the deal with Joseph was shrouded in confidentiality, media reports suggested that it would cost Normandy some $1.1 billion. Not only would Normandy be taking on more than $750 million in associated debt for the Yandal gold interests but, it was reported, in return for Joseph's 42 per cent stake in the company, the more than $165 million he owed de Crespigny had been written down to $100 million — which Joseph was given another 10 years to repay. Moreover, it appeared that while Joseph would be relinquishing his direct stake in Great Central, he retained a major interest in its future exploration prospects in the Yandal belt, with his exploration team retained on an ad hoc basis for the period of the loan, until the year 2010.

Difficult as it must have been to hand over his stake in Great Central to de Crespigny, Joseph declared himself 'delighted' with the deal — especially the opportunities it held out for the future:

> Not only has Normandy taken responsibility for Great Central's huge debt, but it has paid me X amount of dollars and given me an important stake in future discoveries that will more than amply compensate me for the years of effort and commitment I have put into the company. I am absolutely delighted . . .

Whether this was mere bravado, or a case of Joseph's irrepressible optimism, only time would tell. But, clearly, an era had ended. For despite the 'blue-skies' deal he had struck with de Crespigny, Joseph had finally been forced to give up his direct stake in one of the oldest, and to date by far the most successful of his companies. It must, at some level, have been a sad moment. Meanwhile, the Odd Couple would be going their largely separate ways. Joseph — while he was determined to pursue his new exploration deal with Normandy with the utmost vigour — had several other irons in the fire. Including an intriguing nickel play just north of Kalgoorlie, which showed great promise at a time when gold appeared to be losing much of its glitter.

All that Glitters . . .

'The Rebbe told me I'd find a whole lot of good things — not only gold and diamonds.'

Joseph Gutnick, September 1999

ABOUT FORTY-FIVE kilometres north-west of Kalgoorlie, rising out of the bleak scrub just past Joseph's Mount Pleasant and Ora Banda gold mines at a place called Cawse, one comes across a collection of pipes, tanks and futuristic buildings. It is Australia's first commercially operating laterite nickel plant, and one of Joseph's lesser known but potentially most significant projects. Centaur had spent over $270 million on this plant, and Joseph had high hopes that it would provide much of the momentum that would propel him into the new millennium.

Joseph's nickel play had started in earnest four years earlier, towards the end of 1995, when an Australian–Finnish consortium made a freakish nickel find on its Silver Swan tenements, not far to the east of Cawse. 'Here we go again,' said one old-timer in Kalgoorlie, Geoff Stokes, recalling the stupendous boom-and-bust of the late 1960s, when the shares in a small company called Poseidon rocketed from a few cents to $280 on the back of a nickel find at Mount Windarra. 'This is '68 and '69 all over.'[1]

It so happened that Joseph's Mount Kersey company held a series of tenements adjacent to the Silver Swan discovery — and was immediately caught up in the frenzy. So too was Joseph's sentimental favourite Centaur, which had already made a promising nickel find two years earlier, quite by accident, in the Cawse area to the west. 'Nickel kindles the excitement of everyone,' Joseph noted at the time. 'Its price has the ability to go high and analysts say demand for stainless steel, especially in Asia, will rise. Whether it's the start of another nickel boom I don't know, but it certainly looks like it.'[2]

The share prices of both Centaur and Mount Kersey began to soar —

and Joseph acquired a new nickname to add to his growing collection: 'Joe Gutnickel'.[3] Mount Kersey's price more than tripled in a week. By the end of the month, it was capitalised at $180 million, up from just $30 million less than two weeks earlier. All this without having found a thing in the ground. It was *déjà vu* for Joseph — and for the market surveillance authorities, which were reputed to have paid more attention over the past decade to the various Gutnick companies than to any other corporate group. Only this time it was not Joseph who was targeted, as the Australian Securities Commission launched an insider-trading probe into the circumstances surrounding the trade in Mount Kersey shares. It was to prove a messy investigation — the most celebrated result of which was, as we have seen, the release, in August 1998, of taped phone calls made by senior brokers at Melbourne's J B Were & Sons in which a number of scurrilously anti-semitic references to Joseph were made.

While nothing of significance was discovered on Mount Kersey's Silver Swan tenements, Centaur was much luckier at Cawse. This was to prove an unexpected bonanza for Joseph. 'We were drilling for gold and found nickel,' Joseph explained at the time. 'We got lucky.'[4] So lucky, in fact, that AMP bought up $40.6 million worth of stock in the company at the end of March 1996, sending its share price into orbit and taking its market value over $500 million. Centaur was back in town, in a very big way. And at this point, Joseph was sitting on a publicly listed empire worth some $2.3 billion, with investors, including the big institutions, tripping over themselves to get their hands on his stock. A further $102 million was raised in under two hours when another batch of Centaur shares were put on the market on 21 August, and yet another $34 million's worth were snapped up the next day. Many Jewish investors, apparently, climbed on the bandwagon.[5] 'Maybe I should get more involved in football and my companies will do better,' Joseph quipped, alluding to his sudden eruption onto the scene as saviour of the Melbourne Football Club a few days earlier when asked to explain the phenomenal performance of Centaur. 'I've got no other explanation.'[6] By this time, though, it was clear that Cawse was on track to become a significant nickel and cobalt producer, possibly within the next twelve months. The site was estimated to contain 1.5 million tonnes of nickel and 80,000 tonnes of cobalt. In December, Centaur joined forces with Belgian giant Sogem NV, which undertook to market any nickel and cobalt mined at the site.

Cawse was one of the new-age so-called 'lateritic nickel' projects. Nickel ore occurs in two main types — sulphides and laterites. Until quite recently, it had been assumed that only sulphide nickel ores could be mined profitably, and exploration companies that found nickel laterites tended to ignore them. But developments in nickel refining technologies, especially the invention of large-scale, high-pressure acid leaching, had raised the prospect of mining and processing lateritic nickel at a fraction of the cost of conventional nickel sulphides. It was too early to say whether the new nickel plants — including Joseph's at Cawse — would deliver the dreams of their owners. But if the new methods did work, the global nickel industry would never be the same — and those, like Joseph, who had gambled on the new technology could find themselves in the box seat of the $5-billion-a-year world nickel industry as the old sulphide nickel producers were priced out of the market.

There were three Australian companies in the field: Centaur, Anaconda and Preston. Joseph was first out of the blocks, and by the end of 1999 Centaur had stolen the march on its much larger competitor, Anaconda, opting for a relatively small operation that could be scaled up once it was running smoothly. Anaconda, on the other hand, with massive backing from the international mining giant Anglo American, had gone for a much larger operation from the start — and found itself in a spot of bother. There were serious structural problems with its plant at Murrin Murrin, and it was way behind target. The Centaur plant, meanwhile, was already running at an operating profit by late 1999, with nickel and cobalt production well on track.

The plant manager at Cawse, Jim Stewart, was very upbeat when Joseph paid one of his regular visits to the site in September 1999. There were still some bugs in the system that needed to be ironed out, he told Joseph, and some further fine tuning remained to be done before the plant was producing at full capacity. But things were going well, and the buzz around the place was unmistakable.

The Cawse plant comprises an intricate system of pipes and tanks which, through a revolutionary process of high-pressure acid leaching, decantation and precipitation, is able to produce a rich solution of nickel and cobalt. The cobalt is precipitated out before the remaining nickel-rich solution, purified of all residual impediments, is passed into a huge electrowinning building where, in a seemingly endless series of tanks, large plates of almost 100 per cent pure nickel are 'grown' on starter sheets immersed in the solution as electricity is passed through them.

The heart of the entire operation is the $25 million autoclave, in which the crucial high-pressure, high-temperature acid-leaching

All the President's Men. Joseph with senior Melbourne Football staff and players. Back, left to right: Stephen Newport, Anthony McDonald, Daniel Ward, Joseph Gutnick, John Anderson, Darren Kowel; front, left to right: Todd Viney, Neale Daniher, Greg Hutchison, Danny Corcoran.

Footy Mates. Joseph and a famous football colleague, Carlton President John Elliott, who had to go through the indignity of wearing a Demons guernsey after his team lost to Joseph's.

'It's a Grand Old Flag': Joseph sings the club song with David Neitz and the rest of the boys after their stirring Round 22 win against Richmond, which propelled the Demons into the 1998 finals for the first time since 1994.

Mr President. Demon Joe in
a pensive mood at one of the
games he was able to attend in
a troubled 1999.

Facing the future. Joseph with former
Demons champion Gary Hardeman,
who, along with another former player
Stephen Bickford, added much needed
hands-on football experience to the
Melbourne board when they were
elected in December 1999.

Joseph and Stera with their first grandchild, Rose — named for Joseph's mother,
who was tragically killed in a car accident in January 1992. [Photo: Yankel Samuel]

process takes place. From the outside, the huge, bright silver capsule looks for all the world like a giant bomb or small submarine. It was, in fact, built by a submarine company, using the same technology as that used to build high-pressure submarine hulls. The technological break-through that made it all possible, Stewart explained, was a French-developed technique that enabled platinum to be blast-bonded onto steel to produce a durable platinum-steel 'sandwich' capable of with-standing the immense pressures and temperatures that would be generated in the autoclave. After some initial teething problems, the autoclave was now running beautifully.

The only serious glitch was the desalination plant, ironically imported from Israel, which is supposed to be a world leader in desali-nation. It plays a crucial part in the process, as the local water is very brackish and has to be purified before it can be used. 'Don't talk to me about your f–ing Israelis,' Stewart tells Joseph irreverently when asked how the plant is going. 'Not mine — his,' Joseph shoots back, pointing at me. The man has a sense of humour.

That night, back at his home in Kalgoorlie, Joseph hosted a pool-side barbecue for his senior managers. He used the occasion to outline his future plans for Cawse, which included moving to a $1-billion second phase. This, he pointed out, was too big for him alone, and he would have to bring in other parties, possibly local, possibly multinational. Perhaps even the international mining giant Anglo American, with whom he had already been in contact. He allayed his managers' fears about his own commitment to Cawse, and assured them that he was there for the long haul and would seek to keep the current manage-ment style and structure in place. Meanwhile, he was busy tying up all the laterite deposits in the area.

Two months later, in November 1999, Joseph announced that he had indeed concluded a major deal with Anglo American and Anaconda. Under the deal, Anaconda would undertake a feasibility study for the $1 billion second phase, to be completed by 2001. Centaur and Anaconda would be 50:50 partners in the project up to the first 40,000 tonnes' annual production, with Anaconda's stake rising by 1 per cent for each additional 1000 tonnes produced until 50,000 tonnes, at which point the partnership would stabilise at 60:40. Joseph was delighted with the out-come: 'Centaur would not be able to achieve its goals without turning to a major partner like Anaconda to assist us,' he said.[7] There were good synergies for both parties. Anaconda had the financial muscle of Anglo American behind it at Murrin Murrin; while Centaur had the techno-logical edge at its Cawse plant, as well as a huge resource base.

For Joseph, the deal with Anaconda had a significant personal dimension. He had been involved with Anaconda boss Andrew Forrest for well over a decade, going back to the time when Forrest had worked as a broker involved in resource stocks before the 1987 stock market crash. 'We travelled together in Europe and raised money for Australian Gold Resources,' Joseph recalls.

> So I know him extremely well. I've had a very good relationship with him. What he's done in Anaconda is almost unprecedented. And the fact that he brought Anglo American as a major shareholder into Anaconda is just to be marvelled at. At the same time I was negotiating with Anglo American for Centaur. But they (Anaconda) had the mass resources, the economies of scale. Centaur has since built up its resource base through its strategic alliance with Heron, Julia Mines and Gilt Edge — so we've got almost the same mass. We've done a deal with Anaconda with Anglo as a major shareholder, so we're delighted . . .

The real upside for Joseph was, in fact, the access the deal gave him to Anglo American. 'Anglo wouldn't be talking to me if I didn't have the nickel,' he explains. 'It's introduced me to different people at Anglo, and you never know where it leads . . . My relationship with James Campbell, who's the head of Anglo Base Metals is very positive . . .' Joseph had had a bitter experience with Anglo in the past, through its De Beers/Stockdale subsidiary at Nabberu in the early 1990s. But he does not see that as a problem. On the contrary:

> Firstly, the Rebbe told me I should deal with De Beers if I make a big diamond discovery. And second of all you don't shoot yourself in the foot. I had a bad experience with them. You stand up and make sure you get compensation for what they did to you in the past. Some way I'll extract back what I lost through Anglo . . .

Joseph, quite simply, does not bear grudges. Or, more accurately, he does not allow past grudges to cloud his present judgement to his future detriment; he had demonstrated that in his dealings with J B Were, and was demonstrating it again in his dealings with Anglo.

As for the nickel project itself, Joseph wasn't quite sure where it would all lead:

> The Rebbe told me I'd find a whole lot of good things — not only gold and diamonds . . . I stumbled upon this. Who knows where it's going to lead me. And now with this laterite nickel, and the resources and the reserves that we have under our belt, there's a tremendous potential for having a

massive impact on ten to fifteen per cent of the world supply of an important base metal. Stainless steel, cobalt nickel. So it's very exciting, and I'll
keep my options open in regards to where this will lead me . . . You can
make a fortune in the good times with nickel. Whether laterites become a
new nickel boom for Australia, time will tell. Certainly it's very exciting.

In the meantime, Joseph points out, Cawse could turn out to be a
very good 'bridging project' for him — generating a potentially major
cash flow that would tide him over while the price of gold remained
low and its immediate future uncertain. And, for all Joseph's fundamental optimism about the long-term future of gold, it's immediate
future seemed very uncertain indeed.

◊ ◊ ◊

From the beginning of recorded history, gold has been the world's ultimate symbol of wealth. It has been sought and fought over more than
any other human possession. In ancient times, the Pharaohs had
buried it with them deep in their tombs, to assure their prosperity
and well-being in the afterworld. And golden vessels and jewellery
going back more than 5000 years have been unearthed at Ur in
Mesopotamia. An estimated 100,000 metric tonnes, or three billion
ounces, of gold have been mined since mining began more than 6000
years ago — half of it in the last four decades. Almost all of that gold is
still in circulation or is held in vaults. In more recent times, gold
became widely used as a currency of exchange, and by the beginning of
the twentieth century, most developed nations had adopted the so-
called 'gold standard' as the backing for their currencies. While this
has been largely abandoned since World War II, some 34,000 tonnes of
gold — or one third of all the gold ever produced — are still held by central banks around the world. In the mid-1990s, the United States alone
held over 8000 tonnes of gold in its vaults at Fort Knox, while the
International Monetary Fund (3200 tonnes) and western European
countries such as Germany (2960 tonnes), Switzerland (2590 tonnes),
France (2540 tonnes) and Italy (2000 tonnes) all held huge reserves.

But a strange kind of reverse alchemy has been taking place since
World War II. Gold, which from time immemorial has been a store of
value for both governments and individuals, appears to be losing its
mystique. Not, perhaps, for individuals — with some ninety per cent
of the 3400 tonnes of gold the world uses each year going to jewellery.
But a new generation of post-war central bankers has increasingly
challenged the age-old paradigm, forcing the world to come to terms

with the metamorphosis of gold into a commodity. And many central banks, especially in the West, now appear to see themselves as competitors rather than customers of the gold-mining industry, holding huge reserves of bullion that they can sell on the open market in competition with the traditional gold producers.

The Australian sell-off in the first half of 1997, as we have seen, precipitated a crisis in the gold industry, which propelled Joseph and Robert de Crespigny into their strategic alliance. Worse was to follow. Australia, with barely 250 tonnes before 1997, and less than 90 tonnes after, was a mere bit player when it came to holding gold. When it was reported a few months later, in October 1997, that one of the majors in the gold-reserves league, Switzerland, was considering dumping as much as half of the almost 2600 tonnes it held, gold markets around the world went into free-fall. In Australia, the Gold Index plunged by some sixty per cent and the local mining industry was decimated. The market value of Joseph's companies alone plummeted by more than $2 billion, down to $1.37 billion at the end of October from a high of $3.44 billion just a few months earlier. Quantum Resources had lost 81 per cent of its market value, Australian Gold Resources 74 per cent, Australia Wide Industries 73 per cent, Centaur 73 per cent, Mount Kersey 64 per cent, and Great Central 59 per cent. Joseph described the sell-off as 'mass panic' by smaller investors, but reaffirmed his own perennial faith in gold. 'I've no doubt that the gold sector is going to turn,' he said. 'At the end of the day, gold will endure the analysts and central banks, because it has always been a store of value. Paper currencies come and go.'[8] As one of Joseph's more historically minded mining colleagues, Sons of Gwalia chairman Peter Lalor, indicated — Australian miners might have a long wait before the cycle turned back in their favour. Australia, he pointed out, had been in the fifteenth year of its fourth gold-mining boom. The first three, beginning in the 1850s, the 1890s and the 1930s, had lasted an average of thirteen to fourteen years . . . [9]

The following year, 1998, was a tough one for the gold industry. Gold prices remained in the doldrums, and many smaller, less efficient producers around the world went to the wall. Joseph's optimism in the face of the industry doomsayers appeared to be vindicated, however, when, in the first few months of 1999, there were some encouraging signs of a rally in the price of gold. In fact, according to at least one respected American economist, the conditions were all set for a significant upturn in the gold market.[10] But, at precisely that moment, the Bank of England announced, at the beginning of May 1999, that it, too, would be selling off a large part of its gold reserves. Some 60 per cent, in fact. The result was predictable. Gold prices plummeted — and, once again, the gold industry around the world went into panic.

There were mutterings of some dark 'international conspiracy' at work. Some, particularly those on the far Right in US politics, saw gold's demise as a government plot to debase the precious metal to ensure the permanent dominance of paper currency. They argued that as currencies were issued by government, they could be influenced more by government policy than a 'real' substance, like gold. So it was a small jump from this to the proposition that there was 'a conspiracy in play to drive down the world gold price'.[11] Even more level-headed people were deeply suspicious of the Bank of England's motives. West Zurich Financial Services' David Hale, for example, pointed out that the world had been experiencing 'great asset inflation as a consequence of US monetary policy' at the time, and that there were genuine fears that this was starting to spread to gold. So people arrived at the conclusion that the Bank of England was colluding with the US monetary authorities 'to restrain inflationary psychology in the marketplace by depressing the gold price'.[12]

There was undoubtedly some truth behind these conspiracy theories, and it was clear that gold was no longer the central medium for exchange or the unchallenged repository of real value it had been for hundreds, if not thousands, of years. But its long-term future was by no means as bleak as some of the pessimists feared. An economic recovery in Asia, for example, which accounts for over half of the world's demand for gold (compared with twelve per cent for the United States), would certainly put some buoyancy back into gold prices. It was also pointed out that the enforced rationalisation of the gold industry, and the demise of many small miners, would help constrain gold supply and push up prices — while other central banks considering selling their gold reserves would be anxious to support the gold price, if only to secure the value of their own holdings. And it was not long before the central banks did, in fact, move to put an end to the gloom. At the end of September 1999, fifteen European central banks — which together held half of the world's total gold reserves — agreed not to sell any more of their gold for the next five years and committed to restrict sales already in the pipeline to no more than 400 tonnes a year during that period. The result of the move was dramatic. Gold prices surged, from lows of just over US$250, past US$300 for the first time in more than a year, before dropping back and appearing to stabilise at a new plateau of US$280 to US$300. A much needed degree of at least medium-term certainty and confidence, it seemed, had been restored to the industry.

◊ ◊ ◊

Joseph, as might have been expected, had remained largely optimistic throughout this period. While the slump in gold prices was being compared by some analysts with the Black Tuesday stock market crash exactly a decade earlier — 'The Crash of '97', the *Financial Review*'s Alan Deans dubbed the panic reaction to the Australian and Swiss moves in 1997[13] — Joseph was confident he would come through much better than he had then. 'I've been through this before, in 1987,' he remarked. 'But this time the companies have strong cash flows and we have a strategic alliance with Normandy . . .'[14] And his optimism was not misplaced, with both Great Central and Centaur proving to be surprisingly resilient, each reporting tidy net profits from their gold operations. He was also able to raise some $800 million for the two companies on US capital markets in the six months from November 1997 to April 1998. He was especially delighted that one of international financier George Soros's funds had bought a 5.4 per cent stake in Great Central. 'They've recognised our gold stock as an investment,' he said. 'It's an endorsement of their belief that the gold price has settled down.'[15]

Joseph also set about further consolidating his position in the Yandal belt. At the beginning of September 1999, he eventually acquired the Mount McClure mine just to the west of Bronzewing in a messy but ultimately successful takeover of Australian Resources, which had been placed in the hands of an administrator after the company collapsed in the midst of the takeover process. Great Central, which had already paid some $24 million for a substantial stake in AustRes before it went into receivership, managed to snap up Mount McClure from the receiver for just $8.5 million. This was a major coup, and for a total investment of just $32.5 million, Great Central had significantly broadened Bronzewing's resource base.

Joseph's optimism extended to his exploration activities in the Northern Territory as well, where two of his companies — Mount Kersey and Johnson's Well — hoped to find a gold province 'equal to the Witwatersrand in South Africa'. 'It's an area that our geologists and academics in our companies have focused on together with a South African geologist,' Joseph said. 'He has been studying areas for 10 years trying to find a similar model to the Witwatersrand which is South Africa's biggest goldfield. They have focussed on this area because they believe it's the number one area in the world similar to Witwatersrand.'[16]

Meanwhile, in March 1999, Joseph announced that one of the companies to be involved in the Northern Territory venture, Mount Kersey, was to be renamed Gutnick Resources. This sparked speculation that the company would be relaunched as his new public flagship now that Great Central had been privatised. Joseph conceded that putting his name to the company had been intended to prove a point: that he was in the mining industry to stay. As for the 'flagship' rumours, 'that's for other people to speculate', he said. But he revealed that the renamed company would be given 'much higher priority' and would be backed by a substantial exploration budget.[17] The company, Joseph said, had a vision of becoming 'the premier mining company' in the land. And its brochure, one commentator[18] observed, read like 'the most recent edition of the 10 Geological Wonders of the World'. Thus, Joseph's tenements in the Southern Laverton Tectonic Zone were 'transformed into replicas of the world's greatest geological structures, including Kalgoorlie's rich gold-veined Golden Mile', where Gutnick Resources would spend $4 million employing new drilling techniques that were better able to sample the bedrock beneath the heavy overburden. And, 200 kilometres away, $1.5 million was being spent trying to discover a massive 'Voisey's Bay-style' sulphide nickel–copper project in the Fraser Range (according to the brochure, Voisey's Bay was worth about US$13 billion). Not far north of Kalgoorlie, it found similarities between its Millennium base metals project and the world-class Kidd Creek base metals complex in Canada, valued at US$16 billion. And, finally, there was the optimistically named 'Rand Project' in the Northern Territory. Gutnick Resources' share price went from 50 cents to 70 cents in the three months to June, leaving it with a market capitalisation of about $43 million — gratifying to investors, but falling far short of the absurdly unrealistic market responses some of Joseph's offerings had provoked in headier times.

For all his optimism, the crisis in the industry was beginning to take its toll, even on Joseph. In March 1999, Centaur announced a $60.4 million first-half loss and the suspension of operations at its Ora Banda gold processing plant. Pressured by weak gold prices, Centaur bit the bullet, and put the plant on 'care and maintenance'. The loss was largely associated with a $55 million writedown on Centaur's gold operations plus a $11 million pre-tax loss due to a blowout in Centaur's already high operating cost of $438 an ounce.

More serious were the rumours that started circulating at about this time, that the phenomenally successful Joseph Gutnick–Ed Eshuys partnership was beginning to fall apart. The first signs that something was amiss came when Eshuys, Joseph's exploration chief since 1986, started offloading his shares in a number of Gutnick companies. While he remained a director of Great Central, he was said to have been distancing himself from the company ever since Joseph and Robert de Crespigny launched their joint takeover bid.

In April, the news came that Eshuys's board links with the Gutnick mining empire had been severed. In a short statement to the stock market, the Gutnick group said the 54-year-old award-winning geologist was no longer a director in any of Joseph's mining and exploration companies (he had, up to this point, held executive directorships in all of them), but would continue on 'a long-term consultancy arrangement . . . focussing on exploration and geological matters'. Eshuys himself refused to talk publicly about what had occurred, but Joseph initially denied there had been a parting of the ways. 'There's no split,' Joseph insisted. 'He's still being paid by the companies in the group. He's not working for anyone else.' He said it had been decided that Eshuys would be better able to serve the group without the distraction of executive and management responsibilities. 'Our relationship is still a good one,' he insisted.[19]

Joseph was fooling no one. It was clear an era had ended, not only for Joseph, but also for gold mining in Australia. Three years earlier, the *Financial Review*'s 'Chanticleer' columnist Ivor Ries had described Eshuys as 'one of the best mineral explorers this country has ever seen', while Joseph's bold approach to financing exploration — 'backing Eshuys's hunches with $10 million bets on single ore bodies' — made them 'clearly one of the most creative capital–intellect combinations at work in the share market'.[20] But the face of the mining industry had changed out of all recognition over the past two or three years. With gold prices at twenty-year lows, analysts believed there was no scope for the kind of swashbuckling but hugely expensive explorations that had been so spectacularly successful for them in the past. Especially with Joseph locked in with a super-conservative like de Crespigny, and his 'Woolworths' approach to gold mining. As the *Age*'s Barry FitzGerald put it, Eshuys 'no longer had a $50 million exploration budget to call his own' — and 'Eduard, the "pattern bomber" driller of the West, didn't like it . . .'[21]

Joseph concedes that Eshuys may have felt frustrated in this way — but it was by no means the most important reason for their parting. Great Central and his other companies were still heavily engaged in exploration: 'We're still drilling everywhere we want,' Joseph notes. 'We're doing less because the climate is for less. But one of the conditions of the shareholders agreement [with de Crespigny] is that there has to be aggressive exploration for three years'. Eshuys's wings had been clipped, Joseph points out, not so much when it came to exploration — but as manager and director of his companies:

> Ed's a great geologist, and should focus on geology and exploration, not on management . . . I think that over the years I got to rely too much on Ed on the day-to-day management, where I should have got more directly involved. He was de facto managing director, where I was more an executive chairman . . . Ed was too controlling. He didn't let some of the others do their thing . . . He inhibited me as well. We all felt a bit inhibited. We've now got a bit of space, to do our own thing. I'm much more hands on than I was. And I'm much more in the decision making.

Joseph might have been talking about Neil Balme or Cameron Schwab and the Melbourne Football Club. He himself makes the analogy: 'I feel a lot more involved in the day-to-day activities of the Melbourne Football Club,' he noted after Schwab had left the Demons — 'similar to in my business with Ed Eshuys going his way, we've had Cameron going his way and I think I'll get more involved in the club.' And, referring to Eshuys: 'We need a new coach, new areas, new ideas, different type of management style.' Mining is, of course, an infinitely more complex subject than Australian Rules football, and the stakes are infinitely higher. So Joseph had served a much longer 'apprenticeship' — almost thirteen years, in fact — before he felt confident enough to assert himself in this way. 'I've gained a lot working with Ed and with others,' he acknowledges. 'You can't put a dud past me too quickly. And I believe I've got my own flair in picking what a good gold deposit is.' But, he adds, as in football, 'I certainly rely on experts. And I've got a great team of people.'

While not denying Eshuys his due, Joseph suggests his role in the success of Great Central and his other companies has been overstated:

> I'm not taking away anything from Ed's credit. Ed is an outstanding, world-class geologist. But my success is not dependent on Ed Eshuys . . . Nothing is dependent on one man . . . There have been other geologists involved. Jim Wright. And we've got Dermot Ryan, Ian Hoberson, Alan Trench, Ken Hellsten, Darryn Head, Neil Phillips, Jonathan Law. Top people. Stephan Meyer . . . There is no question that Ed was a fundamental, a core driving force. But a lot of money was put his way. The question is if there would

have been another geologist who had the money that I gave would he have come up with the same discoveries? You can speculate from today until tomorrow.

In any case, Joseph argues, Eshuys has not necessarily been the infallible success story he is broadly perceived to have been — despite the huge sums of money Joseph had put at his disposal:

> I spent most money in my career in 1997 and 1998, under Ed Eshuys. And we didn't have two successful years. We spent a lot of money and didn't get the results that I would have liked. I spent a lot of money looking for diamonds under Ed's control. We didn't discover any.

Ultimately, Joseph insists, his success has not been due to Ed Eshuys or any other single geologist:

> It's a joint effort; geologists and God's blessings. And the Rebbe, not just Ed Eshuys. And that's what I'll prove in the future. So that's a very important point in Joseph Gutnick's story. I'm very grateful for what Ed Eshuys did, and for his involvement. But is it God's blessings and the Rebbe's blessings, or Ed Eshuys' skill and Joseph Gutnick's money that he just kept putting up for him, and my drive?

Joseph poses this as a hypothetical question; but there appears to be no doubt in his own mind as to the answer: 'I'm very grateful for what Ed contributed, and I wish him success. But the Gutnick show continues . . .'[22]

◊ ◊ ◊

As gold lost its glitter, rationalisation was forced on other parts of Joseph's mining empire as well. 'For as long as anyone can remember,' Ivor Ries wrote in June 1999, 'Joseph Gutnick's empire of eight listed mining and exploration companies has resembled something out of the monkey-puzzle game.' This involved, Ries explained, 'a tin can full of plastic monkeys with hook-shaped hands and feet: when you picked up one monkey, inevitably several others came along for the ride.' So it had been with Joseph's companies: 'Buy a share in one of his listed vehicles and — thanks to myriad cross-shareholdings — you end up having an interest in at least three or four companies.'[23]

This was the legacy of Joseph's bad old pre-1987 days as a market miner. And, as we have seen, he had tried to simplify and rationalise his impossibly Byzantine corporate structure in the mid-1990s to attract the big institutional investors who, for the first time, were showing a serious interest in some of his companies. But it remained an ugly, unwieldy affair, designed to perpetuate Joseph's own control and reward loyal long-term investors. With the wholesale rationalisation taking place throughout the industry, it was no longer sustainable. No more monkeys. So he bit the bullet and, at the beginning of June 1999, announced a plan to consolidate four of his independent mining companies — Centaur, Australian Gold Resources, Astro and Quantum — into one multifunctional exploration and mining company. Essentially, this was to entail a takeover by Centaur of the other three companies. It immediately spooked the large institutions like AMP and National Mutual, who dumped their holdings in Centaur and the other three companies, pushing the value of Joseph's empire to its lowest level in five years.

This might have been expected. It was the institutions, after all, that had earlier compelled him to rationalise his empire so that each of his companies would have a clearly defined focus, enabling them to invest in those that had proven assets and potential, and to avoid those engaged in more speculative ventures — such as Astro, and its obsessive search for the Rebbe's diamonds. Bringing them together might have made corporate structural sense — but, by once again co-mingling a variety of activities, some of them highly speculative, the proposed amalgamated company was much less attractive to conservative investors.

Analysts also queried the effect the merger would have on Centaur's shareholders — the very people Joseph had been so determined to protect in his earlier restructure. It was noted that their shares would be severely diluted as a result of the amalgamation, while Joseph, through his cross-holdings in all four companies, would almost double his own stake in the amalgamated company by some nineteen per cent. 'Sure, my ownership increases,' Joseph admitted. But he denied that this would be bad for the other shareholders. On the contrary. It would be in their best interests, he insisted. 'I will want to make the share price go up as much as anyone else. As my shareholding increases, my focus increases.' Analysts had criticised him for being too complex, he pointed out; 'this simplifies the structure and buys some quality assets at cheap prices'.[24]

In the end Joseph had to back down. KPMG Corporate Finance pulled the plug on the proposal at the beginning of September 1999, when it published a report finding that none of the three takeovers would be fair to Centaur and its shareholders. Joseph accepted the judgement philosophically, noting that KPMG had been 'very negative' on the value of Astro's, Quantum's and Australian Gold Resources' exploration portfolios. 'Time will tell if they were right,' he said,[25] hinting at his own much more positive evaluation of his companies' exploration prospects. Meanwhile, he signalled the possibility of pressing ahead with a scaled-down rationalisation, merging Centaur and AGR, with their gold/nickel focus, and Astro and Quantum, with their focus on the Rebbe's diamonds.

But it was Ries who, three months earlier, in June 1999, had put his finger on what was probably the main reason why many institutional shareholders of Centaur shares had been 'quietly fuming' about Joseph's takeover bid: it would seriously dilute their share in what was possibly the Gutnick group's most promising mining venture as it saw out the millennium — its nickel project at Cawse. 'Having suffered the near collapse of the company's share price — it was a fifth of its 1996 peak before the merger announcement — they now see their share of the upside in Cawse being diluted,' Ries observed:

> In round numbers, non-Gutnick shareholders end up owning 38 per cent less nickel production . . . In exchange for that they're being offered a share in the current assets of AGR, Astro and Quantum. The main assets of the three companies are nickel, cobalt, diamond and vanadium exploration leases, all of which are yet to be proved economic.

In essence, shareholders in Centaur were being asked to accept 'a large serving of exploration "blue sky" in exchange for a reduced share of Cawse'.[26]

With gold in the doldrums, Centaur's state-of-the-art nickel project at Cawse was by far the brightest spot on Joseph's immediate horizon at this time. It had largely been overshadowed in recent years by Joseph's dramatic and immensely successful performance as a gold explorer and his no less dramatic but rather less successful performance as a diamond explorer. But with commercial nickel and cobalt production due to come on stream in the last half of 1999, and a bright future predicted for nickel, Cawse was immensely attractive. Nickel was, in fact, the star performer in the base metals sector in 1999, and by the end of the year hit an eighteen-month high, virtually wiping out the impact of the Asian recession. And, analysts predicted, it was set for further gains in the year 2000. The revolution about to take place in laterite nickel processing was expected to boost the world's supply of nickel enormously — which would, of course, put downward pressure on nickel prices. But, with their much lower production costs, it would be the new high-tech producers like Cawse, rather than the far less efficient old-tech giants like WMC, that would reap the rewards. Or so it was hoped.

Officially opening Cawse in May 1999, with Western Australian Premier Richard Court present, Joseph spoke about his unabated 'passion to make major diamond, gold and base-metal discoveries'. He referred once again to the late Rebbe: 'The late Rabbi Schneerson's encouragement and blessing for exploration success continues to be a guiding light in all the above-mentioned projects.'[27] The Rebbe had said nothing specifically about nickel — but, Joseph explains, he had predicted he would find 'good things' in Australia's rich earth. And, as he began to face towards the new millennium, nickel was looking to be a *very* good thing.

Joseph 2000

'Look in the North, in a place that hasn't been explored yet, there are valleys and mountains of gold.'

The Lubavitcher Rebbe, circa 1991

FOR ALL HIS phenomenal success as a gold miner in the 1990s, Joseph doesn't believe he has even begun to achieve all the Rebbe had predicted — either in gold or in diamonds. True, Plutonic, Yandal and even Mount Pleasant were very significant finds — in the Australian context. 'But the Rebbe wasn't interested in just Australia,' Joseph points out. 'He was thinking in world terms. He was thinking in billions, not just millions.' Joseph relates how, even after the Rebbe was left without speech by his massive stroke in 1992, he had continued to encourage Joseph to keep up the search for the 'big one'. Just how big, Joseph wanted to know. 'I needed to know what I was meant to be aiming for,' he explains. He also needed to know whether the Rebbe was still lucid enough to be making his predictions with any degree of responsibility. After all, he was investing tens of millions of dollars every year in exploration. So he sought medical opinions from two of America's leading neurologists, who assured him that, when he wasn't in a state of deep exhaustion, the Rebbe was mentally alert and lucid enough to comprehend what he was being asked and to reply competently and responsibly. Joseph was satisfied. And the Rebbe's secretary would go in to the stricken Rebbe, at Joseph's behest, and ask: 'Three billion?' The Rebbe would gesture upwards with his hand — more. 'Four billion?' More. 'Five billion?' More. More . . .'The Rebbe's *brocha* [blessing] has to be not a Bronzewing or a Jundee,' Joseph insists:

There has to be something of world class, something that gets on the cover of *Time* magazine. Because otherwise the Rebbe wasted so much time and so much effort — for a Bronzewing? The way he talked: 'It's more than I

302

would ever imagine.' Remember, the Rebbe's ideas for wealth are greater than mine . . . Even before he had his stroke, he had said I would find gold and diamonds to rival South Africa.'

Hence Joseph's excitement when, towards the end of 1998, one of his leading geologists, Dr Neil Phillips, informed him that a South African colleague, Jonathan Law, had positively identified two huge basins in Australia that bore remarkable similarities to South Africa's fabulous Witwatersrand. The implications were staggering.

The Witwatersrand goldfields contain by far the world's largest accumulation of gold. They have produced over 1.5 billion ounces of the precious metal since they were discovered in 1886 — one third of all the gold ever mined. What is more, these two structures Phillips was talking about — the Ngalia and Amadeus basins — were situated not in Western Australia where Joseph had found all of his gold to date but in the Northern Territory. 'Look in the North, in a place that hasn't been explored yet, there are valleys and mountains of gold,' Joseph recalls the Rebbe saying. 'He told me a number of times about the North. Gold comes from the North. And all wealth comes from the North. The Rebbe mentioned a number of times about looking to the North . . . He also said it to Mottel [Mark] Feiglin. In the early '90s.'[1]

Neil Phillips had already been working for the Gutnick companies for some three years when he told Joseph about the Ngalia and Amadeus basins in Central Australia. A professor of Economic Geology who had been on the staff of the University of Western Australia, the University of Witwatersrand and James Cook University, Phillips was by this time an acknowledged world expert on the structure and formation of the Witwatersrand, having, some fifteen years earlier originated a theory on how this phenomenally rich gold deposit was formed. He went on to publish a series of seminal papers on the subject, including two with Jonathan Law,[2] who had been involved in Witwatersrand research and exploration since 1986 and was working as a senior geologist for one of the major South African gold-mining companies, Gencor. Between them, they revolutionised the theoretical basis of gold exploration in South Africa and elsewhere by challenging the conventional 'placer' or alluvial gold model for the formation of the Witwatersrand. Phillips explains:

Back in the past, people said, there were hills, and those hills had gold and quartz veins. Rain and rivers and weathering processes brought all that down and then deposited it in vast alluvial plains . . . They got covered up and much, much later we went back to mine those. Now that's the conventional ['placer'] model. We challenged that. 'Look,' we said. 'There just is no evidence up there for the amounts of gold you're talking about. You would need a Kalgoorlie — which is Australia's biggest gold deposit — every three or four kilometres for hundreds of kilometres. There's just no evidence of it, no sign that there was one there.'

And so they went looking for a better explanation, coming up with a new hydrothermal model which, Phillips insists, far better explains the phenomenal accumulation of gold in the Witwatersrand Basin:

We believe hot waters have come from deep in the earth's crust, dissolving gold and bringing that gold up into this area where it has been deposited. Now that model is very similar to how most people would agree that a Kalgoorlie, a Bendigo, a Ballarat deposit formed. So we're really taking existing ideas from somewhere else, big gold deposits, and saying maybe the Witwatersrand was formed in the same way.

There was considerable resistance to the idea at first. But by 1992 two of South Africa's leading gold mining companies, Anglo American and especially Gencor, came increasingly to accept the validity of the hydrothermal model for the Witwatersrand. Jonathan Law had been working for Gencor since 1990, during which time he was part of a major research project to evaluate the regional geological framework of the Witwatersrand Basin. This took over two years, further confirming and augmenting the validity of the hydrothermal model. The next step, Law relates, was to scour the world for similar geological formations. Law undertook the search in great secrecy over a period of about three years, between 1994 and 1997, looking at over 100 potential targets. He came up with a shortlist of ten basins that appeared to match the Witwatersrand — and the two most promising were the Ngalia and Amadeus basins.

Law's next move was to seek out a suitable exploration partner in Australia while keeping the precise identity of the Ngalia and Amadeus basins a closely guarded secret. 'We really needed someone we could respect in Australia to run it,' Law explains.

And we also felt that we needed someone with a knowledge of the Witwatersrand Basin to effectively apply these ideas. One way to ensure failure would really be to put a bunch of geologists who know nothing about the South African basin to do the exploration ... We needed a respected Australian partner, somebody who could deal with the Aboriginal issues in the area, and a group that was familiar with the Witwatersrand.

By this time Neil Phillips — whose knowledge of the Witwatersrand was second to none in Australia — was already working for the Gutnick companies, which, of course, had a remarkable exploration record and years of successful experience in dealing with Aboriginal land title issues in Western Australia. This would be a key element in any future exploration in Central Australia, where much of the target area was under Aboriginal jurisdiction. So Law began to speak, in confidence, to his old friend and mentor about the prospects of a joint venture in Central Australia between Gencor and the Gutnick companies. Not long afterwards, however, Gencor decided to get out of gold mining altogether. It was then that Law and Phillips decided, now that Gencor was out of the picture, that Phillips should approach Joseph with the proposition that the Gutnick companies might want to run with the Ngalia–Amadeus project on their own account.

Joseph, of course, jumped at the idea:

> Sometimes a project is too outlandish to even follow up. The whole theory that there could be another Witwatersrand — who else is out there saying they want a Witwatersrand apart from Joseph, because the Rebbe's *brochas* (blessings) have to be fulfilled? The first time I heard it I said, 'this is for me!' These fellows are saying there's a chance of Witwatersrand . . .

So Jonathan Law came out to Australia to head up, along with Neil Phillips, what came to be known as the Rand Project. It was, in a sense, a replay of Joseph's association with Mark Creasy in Western Australia a decade earlier. 'There are several reasons why there could be a Witwatersrand sitting in this part of Australia and not discovered,' Phillips explains. 'One is that if you're under very, very thin cover, five or ten metres of wind-blown sand, then the early prospectors would just walk across that and see nothing. You cannot do anything there unless you drill. And of course you can't drill unless you've got conviction and belief that you've got a good chance of something being there.' Creasy had said much the same about the Yandal belt in the late 1980s.

Now, as he had a decade before, Joseph had both the imagination and the faith to run with a revolutionary new idea that the more conservative companies had shied away from. What happened in the Yandal belt is now history: a tract of land rejected by generations of gold prospectors as unprospective is today one of Australia's most valuable gold provinces. That is nothing compared with what might be found in the Northern Territory if the Phillips–Law model proves even partially successful. 'You are comparing a cockroach with an elephant,' Joseph enthuses.

The sheer scope of the venture is mind-boggling. Joseph has taken out applications covering a staggering 68,000 square kilometres of Central Australia north and south of Alice Springs, extending across the Northern Territory from the Western Australian border for more than 600 kilometres, three-quarters of the way to the Queensland border. The area is so vast that Joseph had to make the applications in the name of two of his companies, Johnson's Well and Gutnick Resources, as the old Mount Kersey Mining was now known. About half the area was under pastoral leases, and the other half Aboriginal land. Exploration was going to be difficult, and would be subject to both complex negotiation with the local Aborigines and federal legislation. Joseph was confident, however, that both would be successful.

Meanwhile, Phillips and Law went about building up a geological database of the two basins using satellite photographs, aerial surveys, surface samples in the eastern pastoral-lease tenements, and the results of past seismic surveys and core-drillings associated with oil exploration in the area. By the end of 1999, after just a year in the field, the two geologists were prepared to say they were growing in confidence that they could be onto something very big.

First, there was the history of gold exploration in the area. There actually was an old gold-mining district in the region, just north-east of Alice Springs. It had not produced a lot of gold, but there was a reasonable resource there, estimated at about a million ounces. That mineralisation was more like the Kalgoorlie style of mineralisation, in that it was in shear zones. But it was on one of the big structures that extend right across the northern margin of the Amadeus Basin. 'In a sense, we're really looking at the structural extension of an existing site,' Law explains. Moreover, he continues, 'the very first discoveries in the Johannesburg area were exactly that kind of mineralisation. They didn't find the conglomerate mineralisation until ten or fifteen years later. The analogy is very similar . . .'

Even more encouraging, according to Law, has been the geology:

> There are two different ways [of assessing prospectivity]. One is the geological matching with the Witwatersrand. And . . . after the last year's work that we've been doing, we're very confident that that's a really good match. We put the ranking now at about 80 per cent. We think that the geology's more or less in the order of 80 per cent similar to South Africa. We haven't made it 100 per cent because no two basins are ever going to be exactly the same. But we believe that the geological match between the two basins is as good as any two basins are ever going to be.

The second aspect that we've looked at relates to the mineralisation, and whether the processes that are required for mineralisation have been taking place in that basin. Now when we initially started this work that ranking was very low because we basically knew nothing at all about the potential of the basin for gold. I think the ranking at the beginning of the year would have been about thirty per cent. Through the year, through geochemistry, looking at the rocks, looking at the metamorphic situation in the basins, we've been able to increase that ranking to the order of about seventy per cent. And again, we think seventy per cent from the reconnaissance geological perspective is probably as good as it's going to get. From here on out it really becomes exploration rather than ranking.

And that is where the Rand Project stood as the end of the second millennium approached. Joseph hoped to start drilling in the first half of the year 2000. He and his two senior geologists cautioned, however, that it would be nothing like the old Ed Eshuys-style 'pattern bombing' approach that had proven so successful in the Yandal belt and elsewhere. This was a whole new ball game, on a far grander scale and with far higher stakes. Paradoxically, perhaps, the exploration approach would be much more cautious, much more conservative. 'Every hole will be well thought out and targeted,' Joseph points out. 'It's based on a theory . . . This is "The Project". Much more scientific than in the past. Much more time. Much more, with the logical steps to be taken. Not missing out any steps.'

Realistically, Joseph's geologists believed they would need at least two or three exploration seasons before they would know for certain just what they were looking at. But with each passing month, the picture appeared to get brighter. The discovery of just one mine in the vast area they have under application, Phillips points out, would 'totally revolutionise the Australian gold industry'. It was an awesome prospect . . .

◊ ◊ ◊

Joseph had not, of course, forgotten the other leg of the Rebbe's prophecy as he moved into the 2000s: the diamonds. If anything, the possibility of finding a Witwatersrand in the Northern Territory might have encouraged him. 'This is something,' Joseph enthuses:

> The Witwatersrand! That's deserving of the Rebbe's blessings. That big discovery that the Rebbe said would come some day, that would be worth more than $10 billion — this is what you're talking about here. There has to be one like that in gold. And one like that in diamonds . . .

So the search continues. 'There won't be a rock I won't turn over looking for a diamond discovery,' Joseph says, insisting that he remains as determined as ever to vindicate the Rebbe. Even if it means searching further afield, in China, and now in India as well.

> We've done a deal in a very unexplored, exciting province in India. There's great potential for making a diamond discovery ... Stephan Meyer [Joseph's diamond exploration chief, who used to be the general manager exploration for CRA in Western Australia] thinks we should go out looking for different prospects in South Africa as well. Although Anglo told me to stick to India, China and Australia because in South Africa I won't find any new deposits. And so I'll look wherever I can ...

In Australia, while he is still looking in the Yilgarn and Kimberley in Western Australia, he is starting to look elsewhere as well. In late 1999 he acquired an extensive range of tenements in the Northern Territory, in Arnhemland, where he believes he might be successful.

But, although he would never concede this, one senses that much of the earlier urgency and enthusiasm may have gone out of Joseph's search for diamonds. Too many disappointments over the past decade appear to be taking their toll. He makes no secret of the fact that were it not for the Rebbe, he would long ago have given up the wild-goose chase after diamonds:

> I wouldn't be looking for diamonds today if the Rebbe hadn't said I'd find diamonds ... I'd be looking for nickel, I'd be looking for gold. Diamonds? Very high risk, very small chance of finding. It's a lot of risk capital money. And the reason that keeps me going, to be a diamond explorer, is no question the Rebbe ...

And, while he remains committed to finding the diamonds, Joseph concedes that he is not, in the present climate, throwing huge sums of money into the search:

> I'm not stupid. I'm not going to throw money through the door. If we get something encouraging I'll put big money into it. While we're still in this speculative situation, when things are tough, I'll cut down exploration. There'll be times when I spend a lot, and times when I spend a little bit ...

Joseph's father, Chaim, believes — with the wry, gentle wisdom so characteristic of him — that it is probably right and proper that his son should not have found the diamonds. Not yet anyway. For Joseph to have found the gems so soon after his brilliant success as a gold miner, he explains, 'would have been "too open" a miracle'.

And Heaven doesn't work that way. Heaven always works in such a way that leaves you a bit of doubt. You're never sure. If he would have found gold and the diamonds immediately, that means the Rebbe's prophecy came true — you can't have that.

Does that mean Joseph won't ever find them? 'No,' says Chaim. 'He may eventually find them — but the fact the Rebbe told him will wear off, be forgotten by the public . . .'

◊ ◊ ◊

Apart from the gold and diamonds, Joseph had several other irons in the fire as he moved into the 2000s. Centaur's nickel project at Cawse was one which, as we have seen, had huge potential. And some of his other companies were looking at vanadium and other base metals as well. He was also diversifying, into entirely new areas. Bayou — the old jock-strap company he had picked up before the 1987 crash and which he had used to promote the revolutionary LMMHD electricity-generation project in Israel in the late 1980s and early 1990s — has been recast as Baynet, with a brief to look into developments in the IT area. 'Baynet will be my vehicle that will be developing the new economy type opportunities,' Joseph says. 'It will be purely involved in IT related to the mining industry and medical research.' And, far more ambitiously, one of Joseph's core companies, Australia Wide Industries, has, since the beginning of 1999, been recast as Autogen — with a brief to ride what many economists believe will be one of the major growth waves in the new millennium: biotechnology.

Joseph's interest in biotechnology goes back several years, to the mid-1990s. His original involvement was purely philanthropic, and he gave considerable sums of money to medical research. But he was already aware of the huge commercial potential in this area, and in July 1996 Australia Wide Industries established a division to investigate the opportunities of investing in biotechnology research with the object of long-term commercialisation.

The initial focus was on research into the prevention of allergenic diseases and finding a cure for obesity and diabetes, and by 1998 Australia Wide had entered into an alliance with a major international pharmaceutical company, Merck-Lipha, with the aim of developing revolutionary new drugs for the treatment of obesity and Type-2 diabetes. A team of thirty-five scientists and technical researchers under Professor Greg Collier, one of Australia's leading authorities in the field, was assembled for the project, which is being carried out at Melbourne's Deakin University.

A second project, conducted concurrently by Professor Paul Zimmet, who is one of the world's leading authorities on metabolic diseases, was looking into the fundamental factors underlying these diseases and building up a major databank based on population groups throughout the Asia–Pacific region. A third project, conducted at Monash University in alliance with another major international company, Kyokuto of Japan, was developing an advanced new screening tool for the early diagnosis of Type 1 diabetes in children and young adults. A fourth project, based at the Prince of Wales Hospital in New South Wales, was looking into a possible cure for Type 1 diabetes by developing a new source of insulin-producing cells.

All of these projects were making encouraging progress, and by 1999 Australia Wide — which had undergone a number of radical transformations since Joseph had acquired it in 1982 — was formally renamed Autogen Ltd, with a brief to press ahead with rapid commercialisation. In particular, the identification by Professor Collier and his team at Deakin University of new genes associated with obesity and Type 2 diabetes — including the 'Beacon' gene, isolated as a result of pioneering studies on the Israeli sand rat, which has a metabolism remarkably similar to humans — has caused a stir in the industry, and Joseph is extremely optimistic that they are onto something of major significance:

> The scientists and the professors and the pharmaceutical companies are saying that I'm onto something very big . . . We've seen Lipitor — which is not a discovery of Autogen — which brings down the cholesterol count, which has sales of more than $4 billion. It's the fastest selling drug ever discovered. If you found a drug, which we're working on at the moment, which would alleviate the obesity problem — that has ramifications that are even greater than lowering someone's cholesterol. The fact is that all diseases, whether cardiac, or diabetes or other diseases, come from people being overweight . . . The potential of what we have reached now with the Deakin studies and also the human gene bank is just enormous . . . The base that we have and the technology that we have is just quite mind-boggling, where Autogen can go and lead . . . We talk about Witwatersrand. This is an area that could have as many, if not more ramifications than everything I'm doing in the resource sector . . .

So optimistic were they about the progress being made that Autogen's European strategic partner, Merck-Lipha, committed some $16 million to the Australian project at the end of 1999 (including a 10 per cent investment in Autogen) and made a further commitment to develop the Beacon gene into a drug, which they would market internationally, at a development cost of some $100 million. 'The fact that Merck-Lipha is showing the same excitement, that their drug is one of the most advanced drugs for diabetes, and they think that this one gene, Beacon, can possibly lead to a drug, and all the other new genes that we are finding,' Joseph enthuses, 'is quite staggering.'

The millennium countdown also marked a return by Joseph to the financial services sector — an area he had stayed clear of since the 1987 stock market crash. Valuations in the resources sector in 1999/2000 reflected historic lows, with many metal and mining companies trading below their book value. The resources industry was undergoing widespread consolidation, not only in Australia but all around the world, creating outstanding opportunities to invest in a sector with real assets at historic lows. It made more sense, in such a climate, to acquire existing, operating assets at bargain prices rather than invest in new exploration. And Joseph wanted to take advantage of this. But 'to raise funds by diluting equity in my existing companies would be ridiculous,' he points out. There had to be some other way to raise money that would enable him to take advantage of the situation. So, in late 1999, Joseph created a major new investment instrument, called the Capital Growth Resources Fund.

Registered in the Cayman Islands, the Capital Growth Resources Fund is quite unlike anything Joseph — or anyone else, for that matter — has done in the resources sector. Its goal is to raise approximately US$500 million worldwide and create a 'war chest' to take advantage of the opportunities that exist in the depressed global resources market. In stark contrast to Joseph's last foray into the financial services area before 1987, there would be no more mums and dads or little old ladies taking a punt with their life savings on a bunch of highly speculative stocks, as had happened with his pre-1987 ABC funds. The minimum investment is fixed at US$2 million, and Joseph is looking to large financial and other institutions around the world as his potential investors. The new fund enjoys the wholehearted support of the Chase Manhattan Bank, which has agreed to serve as its official adviser, and Anglo American, which is to take up a US$20 million placement and introduce the fund to other potential investors. With these two high-profile global players behind him, his own track record as one of Australia's most successful gold miners (this was internationally recognised in November 1999, when he was made a director of the World Gold Council), a professional team headed by Ian Currie (the highly rated chief financial officer of his group of companies)[3] and the vast infrastructure of expertise he has built up, Joseph believes he is ideally placed to emerge as a major investment player in the international resources industry:

> It's a very exciting phase in my involvement in the resource sector. Because if I raise US$500 million, we're allowed to lend 2:1, so we'd have a war chest of US$1.5 billion. And if we make some successful acquisitions, I'll go to the market to raise way more money. So there's no reason that in the resource sector we can't become a Soros-type fund ... I've watched the Tiger Fund and I've watched George Soros, what they've done with currency and what they've done in the industrial stockmarkets, and I thought there's no reason that a fund shouldn't be set up to take advantage of the opportunities that exist in the resource sector ... It will provide us with a tremendous amount of opportunities ...

Joseph's private holding company, Edensor Nominees, owns the fund and has access to twenty per cent of the profits, as part of an incentive scheme. Moreover, a certain percentage of the money in the fund can be invested in Joseph's own companies. 'For instance,' he points out, 'if we needed a partner in one of my projects here, and the advisory committee and independent experts say that it's not in any conflict and is fair and reasonable, then the fund could get involved.' But Joseph envisages the fund as far broader than simply a vehicle to raise money for his own companies. The aim is to build up a broad-based direct investment portfolio, an equities portfolio and a commodities portfolio right across the natural resources sector. 'It's a very big move for me,' he points out. I'm moving into a new field, a mixture of a hedge fund and an equity fund, to take advantage of the depressed resource sector worldwide, but with a focus on Australia.'

Like the Rand Project, the Capital Growth Resources Fund bears the mark of a new, more mature Joseph for the new millennium. His vision is, if anything, even more grandiose and ambitious than in the past. But he appears to have combined the innovative flair and imagination that had marked his earlier activities with a new-found caution and conservatism. It could be a potent combination.

◊ ◊ ◊

One area where Joseph, for all his sophistication, still continues to display what to the rational outsider might be a rather disconcerting naivete, is in his continued dependence on the Rebbe. It is difficult enough to come to grips with the way in which, when the Rebbe was still alive, Joseph appeared to have unquestioningly followed his judgement on complex business matters. It becomes even harder to comprehend how, six years after the Rebbe's death, Joseph still professes to be inspired and guided by him.

'I may not get the answers,' Joseph explains, 'I have to use a lot of my own brains now, based on the instructions I got in the past from the Rebbe.' But, he reveals, he still seeks the Rebbe's intercession from beyond the grave:

> Jewish tradition says if you pray by the graveside of a righteous person he can intercede on your behalf . . . Even the Rebbe, while he was alive used to visit the graveside of his father-in-law, the Previous Lubavitcher Rebbe, at least twice a month . . . If I were to write a note to the Rebbe and ask him for a blessing, he would write, besides the answer I would get: 'I will mention it on the graveside of my father-in-law.' And he trained us in that regard. In other words, we ask for a blessing and we hope that the spirit of this holy person will intercede on our behalf . . . [4]

Thus, Joseph notes, if you go on a Sunday or a Jewish religious holiday to New York and visit the Montefiore Cemetery in Queens, where the Rebbe is buried next to his revered father-in-law, thousands of people come and pray beside the Rebbe's grave:[5]

> Religious people, women, men and children. Not only religious Jews. You have people from all walks of life . . . even Solly Lew visited the grave site a few years ago. I don't think Solly would be ashamed to admit that he prayed by the graveside. Ronnie Perlman — who owns Revlon and is one of the wealthiest Jews in the US — he flies in in his helicopter and visits the grave. It's a landmark . . . When I arrive in New York, my first point, before I go to Manhattan, to whatever hotel I'm staying in, I drop in to the cemetery and I pray . . .

Living in Melbourne, Joseph is, of course, unable to make regular visits to the Rebbe's graveside in Queens, New York. But here, he explains, modern technology comes to the aid of ancient custom:

> I send faxes . . . I don't get answers — but I send faxes praying that I need this and this to happen. I send a fax to New York, which is ripped up and put on the Rebbe's graveside — thousands of people do that, from all walks of life . . . There's a full time person there. Twenty-four hours a day. Faxes coming in all the time . . . [6]

The observation made by Christopher Webb in the *Age* in July 1997 — that 'anyone who fails to understand the influence of the Rebbe on Gutnick fails to understand Gutnick' — remains as relevant as ever.

For all that, there is one question that still gnaws at me. I know perfectly well why I wanted to write Joseph's story. But just as

IT HAS BEEN barely nine months since that day last August when I first met Joseph and embarked upon this project. We were poles apart then, on just about everything imaginable: politics, Israel, religion — even football. And we are no closer today. Joseph still makes snide remarks about me and my 'lefties' in Israel, and I feel comfortable enough to take a dig at him and his 'Ayatollahs'. I'll still be taking immense delight when the Bulldogs thrash the living daylights out of his Demons — and there is no more likelihood that I will don a yarmulka and grow a beard than there is that he will become a kibbutznik. Yet, despite our very profound differences and my abiding antipathy for many of his views, I have found myself developing an intuitive liking, and genuine respect for Joseph as a person — quite apart from the fascination I have long had for him as a phenomenon.

For all that, there is one question that still gnaws at me. I know perfectly well why *I* wanted to write Joseph's story. But just why did *he* agree to cooperate with me? Was it vanity and egotism? — the irresistible lure of having a book written about him? I'm sure that that did play some part in his decision; Joseph does undoubtedly have a robust sense of ego and he thrives on publicity. But why a book by me? After all, I was perceived by him, and by most of his fellow right-wing and Orthodox Jews, as being hostile to much of what they stood for? And he would have only very little, if any, control over what went into the book; that had been made clear to him from the outset. If vanity were the prime motive, why hadn't he simply paid someone to write a book — a 'vanity biography' — over which he would have complete control. He wouldn't be the first to have done so, and he could certainly afford it.

I found it all quite puzzling. Until, I stumbled, quite by chance, on something in a collection of Biblical commentaries attributed to the Lubavitcher Rebbe.[1] In a commentary on the story of (the Biblical) Joseph's enslavement in Egypt, the Rebbe is said to have noted there were three ways Jews could deal with those hostile to them:

> The first is liberation through battle — one fights one's oppressor and vanquishes him. Yet although the enemy may be completely routed, such a victory is somewhat hollow, for in order to secure this liberation one had to lower oneself to the enemy's standards, up to and including the shedding of blood.

(Joseph might have let me go ahead and write a 'hostile' book — and then 'routed' me by suing me for all I was worth. A comparison of our respective bank accounts would show just how hollow a victory that would be!)

There is a superior form of victory and liberation — 'peace through strength'; i.e., the individual is so powerful that his enemy is afraid to engage him in battle. However, here as well, although actual bloodshed is avoided the victory is only temporary; the enemy still exists and if he becomes more powerful he may well engage in battle.

(Joseph might have sent me a solicitor's letter, daring me to go ahead with my book but warning that every word I wrote would be scrutinised by a team of the best defamation lawyers that money could buy. Gulp!)

The greatest form of peace and liberation from oppressors comes about when the oppressor himself is encountered and *transformed* into a steadfast friend. In this instance there is no need to worry about an eventual attack from the enemy, for the enemy has ceased to exist. He has become a friend.

Is *this* what Joseph had hoped to do? Effectively 'de-fang' me by befriending me, by taking me into the camp? And would Joseph's 'friendly co-option' have disqualified me as an 'objective' observer, and disarmed me as an effective critic? Or would it, perhaps, have made me a fairer and more balanced observer, by neutralising my perceived hostility?

While there can be little doubt that the kind of empathy such co-operation inevitably generates can be a great boon to writing a biography — it enables insights that are only possible through the willing suspension of judgement and the imaginative placing of oneself uncritically in the boots of one's subject — was there not a danger here, too? After all, even John Milton found himself accused of being 'too nice' to Satan in *Paradise Lost*!

I don't pretend to know the answers to these questions. But — as in all books about living people, where the author enjoys the co-operation of his or her subject, is privy to all sorts of first-hand inside information he/she would not otherwise have, and is to that degree in his/her subject's debt — they are questions that do need to be asked.

In the end, it is the reader who must judge in such cases to what extent 'objectivity' has or has not been compromised.

May 2000

Jewish terms

bar mitzvah   Every Jewish male, at the age of thirteen, becomes a '*bar mitzvah*' — literally a 'son of the commandments', meaning that he is now eligible for all religious privileges and duties.

Chabad   alternative name for the Lubavitcher (cf) movement, from the Hebrew acronym for *chochmah* (wisdom), *binah* (understanding) and '*da'at*' (knowledge)

Chabad House   centre of Lubavitcher activity, usually based around a synagogue

Chabadnik   member of Chabad; Lubavitcher (cf)

chutzpah   cheek, audacity

Diaspora   the 'dispersion', referring to Jews living outside Israel

Eretz Yisrael   the Biblical Land of Israel, promised by God to the ancient Hebrews as their birthright and claimed by their descendants, the Jews; refers to roughly the same area on the eastern lateral of the Mediterranean later known as Palestine

farbrengen   public rabbinical discussion, or 'teach-in'

Gemarah   part of the Talmud (cf)

gvir   wealthy benefactor

Hasid   (pl. *Hasidim*) literally, 'pious man' (also spelled *Chassid*). *Hasidism* is the joyous, mystic form of populist Judaism that emerged in the first half of the eighteenth century as a reaction to the dry, elitist, text-based Judaism of the time (adj. *Hasidic*)

Judea and **Samaria**   the Biblical names for the heartland of the Land of Israel, known since 1948 as the West Bank and under Israeli military control since the 1967 Six Day War

Litvak   the strict text-based 'Mitnagdic' tradition associated with the famous Vilna Gaon in Lithuania, which was vehemently opposed to the populist Hasidic movement from which the Lubavitcher movement emerged in the eighteenth century

Lubavitch   the small town in White Russia where the Lubavitcher movement originated in the eighteenth century (adj. *Lubavitcher*: member of the Lubavitcher movement)

mazel tov   the traditional Jewish toast (Yiddish), from the Hebrew *mazal tov*, or 'good luck'

mezuzzah   scroll containing the first words of the *Shma Yisrael*, the Jewish declaration of faith, enclosed in a small case attached to the doorframe of every observant Jewish home

mikveh   ritual bath

mitzvah   commandment, good deed (pl. *mitzvot*)

mohel   ritual circumciser

pikuach nefesh   the Jewish law venerating the sanctity of life

Reb   diminutive form of 'Rabbi'; colloquial honorific

Rebbe Hasidic (cf) rabbi and leader
Shabbat the Sabbath (Hebrew)
Shabbes the Sabbath (Yiddish)
shaliach emissary
shochet ritual slaughterer
shtetl Jewish village, or hamlet, in pre-Holocaust Eastern Europe (pl. *shtet-lach*)
smichah rabbinical certification
Talmud the vast body of Jewish Law and legend compiled between the first and fifth centuries
tefillin phylacteries; small leather boxes with thongs attached, containing parchment texts from the Torah (cf), bound around the forehead and arm during weekday morning prayers
Torah the Pentateuch (Five Books of Moses); by extension the whole body of Jewish religious literature; sometimes refers also to the scroll on which it is written
tsadik a perfectly righteous man
tsedakah charity, philanthropy
yarmulka (also yarmulke) skullcap
yeshivah religious seminary

Mining terms

alluvial relating to material transported and deposited by water
craton a relatively rigid and immobile region of the earth's crust
diamondiferous (diamantiferous) containing diamonds
greenstone rock sequences dominated by mafic rocks (rich in magnesium and iron) and ultramafic rocks (composed almost entirely of mafic materials)
kimberlite a form of rock low in silica and high in magnesium in which diamonds are formed
laterite/lateritic red residual deposits formed at the earth's surface in formerly humid, tropical regions
mineralisation process by which minerals are introduced and concentrated within a host rock, and the product of this process
open pit type of mine were ore is excavated from the surface
RC (reverse circulation) percussion drilling method by which non-contaminated samples are returned through the drill rods
resource a body of mineralisation to which conceptual tonnage and grade figures are assigned, but for which exploration data are inadequate to calculate geological reserves
sulphide mineral in which one or more metals are in combination with sulphur
tenement area of land held or applied for by a company or individual to explore for, or mine minerals

Abbreviations

Age	The *Age*
AFR	The *Australian Financial Review*
AJN	The *Australian Jewish News*
BRW	*Business Review Weekly*
Good Weekend	'Good Weekend' supplement in the *Age* and *Sydney Morning Herald*
HS	The *Herald Sun*
SMH	The *Sydney Morning Herald*

Prologue: Yossel and Me

1 *Shtetl* — Jewish village, or hamlet, in pre-Holocaust Eastern Europe (pl. *shtetlach*). The *shtetl* best known to most Jews, and many non-Jews, is almost certainly Anatevka in the popular musical *Fiddler on the Roof*. In reality, however, *shtetl* life was somewhat grimmer than as portrayed in this romantic blockbuster; it was one of grinding poverty, whereby Jews struggled for centuries to survive in a hostile Gentile environment. But it was certainly character-building. Of necessity, Jews in the *shtetl* were highly dependent on each other, and this led to a strong ethos of mutual support and philanthropy, as well as to the evolution of a wide range of communal organisations and structures. Both that ethos and many of those communal structures are recognisable, in modified form, in contemporary Jewish Australia. So, too, is the fundamentally inward-looking mindset that characterised life in the *shtetl* — although this is beginning to break down as Jewish Australians grow to feel more comfortable and at home in the broader Australian community.

2 Although it is used more widely in contemporary colloquial language — by both Jews and, increasingly, non-Jews — the word *kosher*, from the Hebrew *kasher* (fit), applies literally to food that is 'fit to eat' according to Jewish law. For strictly observant Jews, 'keeping kosher' means rigorously following a complex set of rules governing the kind of food that can be eaten (no pork or shellfish, for instance), how it is slaughtered, and how it is prepared and served (no mixing of meat and dairy). Non-observant Jews disregard most of these rules most of the time, although some might still have a residual cultural aversion to certain gross violations, such as eating pork.

3 Distinguished by their distinctive black attire and beards (men), and wigs or headkerchiefs (women), the Ultra-Orthodox (or *Haredi*) Jews are the most strictly pious and religiously observant of all Jews. The two main Ultra-Orthodox communities in Australia are the Adass Israel and the Lubavitchers. Both have their own schools, synagogues and spiritual leaders, although the Lubavitchers — unlike their Adass co-religionists, who have little to do with the general Jewish community — seek actively to proselytise, with some considerable success, among secular or 'lapsed' Jews, in the belief that this will hasten the coming of the Messiah. Joseph Gutnick is a leading member of the Lubavitcher community.

Chapter 1: In the Beginning . . .

1 Except where otherwise indicated, all quotes attributed to Rabbi Chaim Gutnick in this chapter are from an extensive interview I conducted with him in August 1999.

2 There are generally believed to be about 14 million Jews in the world today, the vast bulk of whom live in North America (about 6 million), Israel (about 5 million), and the former Soviet Union (about 2 million). The remainder are spread throughout the so-called Diaspora, with an estimated 100,000 in Australia. The official figure for Australia, according to the 1996 Census, is somewhat smaller — 79,805, about 0.4 per cent of the population. But because the Census question on religion is not compulsory and for ideological or historic reasons many Jews decline to answer it, many demographers have adjusted the figure upwards. Most Australian Jews live in Melbourne (35,383) and Sydney (31,450), with a sizeable Jewish community in Perth (4,487 — boosted by recent migrants from South Africa) and smaller communities in the other capitals as well as some coastal areas like the Gosford region of New South Wales or the Gold Coast of Queensland. The Jewish presence in Australia goes back to the beginning of white settlement (there were at least twelve known Jews on the First Fleet). But while there are a few fifth- and even sixth-generation Australian Jews, the vast majority are either post-World War II European migrants or the children of these migrants. In fact, Australia, per capita, has the highest proportion of Holocaust survivors outside Israel. More recently there has been significant migration of Jews to Australia from the former Soviet Union, South Africa and Israel.

3 Anti-semitism, or Jew-hatred, has a long history in Western civilisation, and is rooted in Christian demonology that for centuries stigmatised Jews as 'Christ-killers'. This resulted in tens of thousands of Jews being slaughtered over the centuries in religiously sanctioned blood libels, ritual murders and pogroms. It wasn't until the accession of Pope John XXIII (1958–63) that the Catholic Church finally convened Vatican II and exonerated the Jews of the charge of deicide. However, other, non-theological, strains of anti-semitism persist, including that based in various conspiracy theories of Jewish world domination of the kind described in the late nineteenth century Russian forgery *The Protocols of the Elders of Zion.*

One of the most infamous anti-semitic documents ever written, the *Protocols* purport to be the 'record' of a secret meeting of Jewish leaders conspiring to take over the world. It was first circulated by the Russian secret police in the late 1800s, and has been a standard text for anti-semites and Jew-hating conspiracy theorists throughout the world ever since. Adolf Hitler had recourse to it in formulating his own anti-semitic ideas, and it was used to drum up Jew-hatred in Germany by persuading millions of people that the Jews were a deadly menace to civilisation and had to be exterminated. Hence the Holocaust. Various Arab propagandists have used, and continue to use, the forgery in their war against Israel. The work is still in print, translated into many languages, and widely distributed — including by anti-semitic and racist fringe groups in Australia.

4 Yiddish, a 'hybrid' of Biblical Hebrew and Medieval German, was the universal language of millions of Jews in Central and Eastern Europe before World War II, and the repository of a vast and rich Jewish secular culture.

Most Yiddish speakers perished in the Holocaust, and when Israel turned its back on the despised 'Diaspora tongue' in favour of Hebrew — the 'original' Jewish language, the language of the Bible — the latter replaced Yiddish as the Jewish vernacular, at least in the Jewish state. Yiddish is still spoken, but mainly by the vanishing generation of Holocaust survivors and by Ultra-Orthodox Jews, both in Israel and in the Diaspora. Most Jewish Australians know a little Yiddish, even if only the few words remembered from Yiddish-speaking parents or grandparents. Those who went to a Jewish day school know some Hebrew, with varying degrees of proficiency. But for the overwhelming majority English is the mother tongue and, for many, the only effective language.

5 AJN 9/12/38. Cited by P Medding in *From Assimilation to Group Survival: A Political and Sociological Study on an Australian Jewish Community*, (Melbourne: F W Cheshire, 1968) p. 160.

6 According to Jewish law, animals for consumption have to be slaughtered with a single, swift cut to the throat which causes minimum distress and almost instantaneous death to the animal. Meat from animals not slaughtered in this manner, by a specially trained *shochet* (ritual slaughterer), is not considered kosher and cannot be eaten by observant Jews.

7 The story of Rabbi Mordechai Ze'ev Gutnick is told (in Hebrew) by Rabbi Motty Liberow, in the 10 December and 17 December 1998 issues of the official Lubavitcher publication, *Kfar Chabad*.

8 Edward Hoffman, *Despite All Odds: The Story of Lubavitch* (New York: Simon and Schuster, 1991) p. 17.

9 Samuel Heilman, *Defenders of the Faith: Inside Ultra-Orthodox Jewry* (New York: Schocken Books, 1992) pp. 21–2.

10 Heilman, pp. 22–3.

11 Hoffman, p. 18.

12 Thus, Rabbi Schneur Zalman (known as the '*Alter Rebbe*' — the Old Rebbe) was succeeded by his son, Rabbi Dov Baer (1812), who in turn was succeeded by his son-in-law Rabbi Menachem Mendel (1827), who was succeeded by his son, Rabbi Shmuel (1866), who was succeeded by his son Rabbi Sholom Dov Baer (1882).

13 Chaim relates that the Rebbe selected his father for the job in London over one Menachem Mendel Schneerson. 'The Rebbe must have had something else in mind for him,' Chaim says modestly of the man destined to marry the Rebbe's daughter and eventually succeed him as the Seventh and, it seems for the moment, last Lubavitcher Rebbe.

14 Circumcision (*Brit Milah*) is the oldest ritual in Judaism. According to the Bible, Abraham, at the age of ninety-nine, was instructed by God to have himself circumcised along with his thirteen-year-old son Ishmael (Genesis 17:9–14 and 24–25). Later (Genesis 21:4) Abraham was commanded to circumcise Isaac when he was eight days old — the age at which all Jewish males are traditionally circumcised by a ritual circumciser (*mohel*). Nowhere in the Bible is a rationale given for the rite, but throughout much of history circumcision has been the physical mark that has distinguished Jewish males from their non-Jewish neighbours (in more recent times, of course, medical fashion in some Western countries, including Australia, has seen circumcision become common in the general male population, for supposed health and hygiene reasons). Circumcision, while accepted

unquestioningly by the overwhelming majority of Jews, has come under scrutiny at different times in Jewish history. In the nineteenth century some leading figures in Reform Judaism — including Rabbi Abraham Geiger who referred to it as a 'barbaric bloody rite' — wished to see circumcision abolished. In more recent times Jewish groups and individuals in the United States and Great Britain have publicly questioned the practice. But there has been no serious challenge to the rite, in either Orthodox or Reform Judaism. This is true of Australia, too, where circumcision is universally practised — although some individual Jews are known to have refused to have their infant sons mutilated.

15 Although all contemporary Jews claim to be the descendants of the ancient Hebrews — or, more precisely, the ancient Tribes of Judah and Benjamin — they are deeply divided, some would say almost to the point of schism, between Orthodox and Progressive (sometimes also called Liberal or Reform) Jews. The major difference between the two is that Orthodox Jews, in theory, at least, hold the Bible and the entire body of Jewish Law (known as *Halachah*) to be God-given and hence immutable, while Progressive Jews take a less fundamentalist and more pragmatic approach to *Halachah*, which they are prepared to reinterpret and amend to suit changing circumstances. Thus, for instance, women have a much more equal role in Progressive Judaism, participate fully in Progressive synagogue ('Temple') services, and can even serve as rabbis. In Orthodox synagogues, by contrast, a strict gender 'apartheid' pertains, symbolised by the partition (or *mechitzah*) behind which women are confined and from where they can observe but not take an active part in the service. Progressive Judaism is also seen as much more accepting of non-Jewish converts, and it is the 'door' through which most non-Jews tend to enter the Jewish faith.

Most affiliated Australian Jews, nominally at least, would define themselves as 'Orthodox' or 'Traditional'; that is, they belong to Orthodox synagogues — even if few go to synagogue more than two or three times a year, on the so-called High Holy Days. Most are not religiously observant, beyond ascribing to the standard Jewish 'Rites of Passage' rituals — circumcision, bar mitzvahs, weddings and funerals. The more observant observe the Jewish dietary laws, refrain from desecrating the Sabbath, and attend synagogue more or less regularly.

16 *Good Weekend* 12/12/98.

17 Hilary Rubinstein, *The Jews in Australia: A Thematic History* (vol. 1), (Melbourne: William Heinemann, 1991) p. 264.

18 More than 33,000 Jews died in this atrocity just outside the Ukrainian city of Babi Yar, carried out by the infamous Nazi *Einsatzgruppen* which accompanied the German invasion of the Soviet Union in 1941 with an express brief to round up and slaughter every Russian Jew they could find, often with the enthusiastic help of virulently anti-semitic local Ukrainian collaborators. Although by no means the only such atrocity, Babi Yar is the best known and was commemorated in a famous poem written in 1961 by the Russian poet Yevgeny Yevtushenko, which was later set to music by Dmitri Shostakovich.

19 Respondents were asked in this survey: 'Who do you think are the three most important Jews in Melbourne? Why?' Rabbi Chaim Gutnick was the

fourth most frequently mentioned, and his 'liaison via TV *Epilogue*' was given as the reason for his importance. He rated just behind the prominent QC Maurice Ashkenazy ('born here, can approach all English people'), the charismatic Progressive Rabbi Dr H Sanger ('mixes with Jews and English'), and St Kilda Synagogue's Rabbi Jacob Danglow ('mixes with both, a head for Jewish people we wouldn't be ashamed of — he can talk intelligently with them and they won't look down on him'.) Rabbi Gutnick was placed ahead of such prominent Jews as Judge Trevor Rapke and Professor (later Sir) Zelman Cowen — later to become Australia's second Jewish Governor-General, and was singled out by respondents to the questionnaire as being 'active, makes Jewish people known and liked; a symbol.' — Medding, p. 178.

20 The Jewish National Fund (JNF), along with the United Israel Appeal (UIA) are two of the Australian Jewish community's largest and most effective philanthropic organisations, raising millions of dollars from the community each year for Israel. While there is considerable scepticism about the value of this kind of so-called 'chequebook Zionism' (especially among Israelis), giving money to the JNF and the UIA does enable many Jewish Australians to express their commitment to Israel in a practical way, while at the same time tapping into the age-old Jewish tradition of *tsedakah*, or giving to charity.

21 AJN 12/7/91.

22 HS 31/8/96.

Chapter 2: The Sage of New York

1 Hoffman, p. 26.

2 *loc. cit.*

3 The *Australian Magazine* 12/7/92.

4 The atmospherics of typical Lubavitcher *farbrengens* is well described by Hoffman, pp. 31–6. See also Simon Jacobson's introduction to his book *Towards a Meaningful Life: The Wisdom of the Rebbe* (New York: William Morrow, 1995) pp. xi–xiii, for a concise account of the Rebbe's discursive 'style' and 'technique' at a *farbrengen*.

5 David Landau, *Piety & Power: The World of Jewish Fundamentalism* (New York: Hill & Wang) p. 67.

6 Landau, p. 25.

7 Jacobson, p. xiv.

8 The Rebbe produced many millions of words of wisdom, almost entirely in Yiddish and Hebrew, during his long lifetime, and most of these have been transcribed, collected and compiled in hundreds of bound volumes. The most concise and accessible source in English of the Rebbe's teachings is Simon Jacobson's *Towards a Meaningful Life*. Rabbi Jacobson — who had prepared the Rebbe's talks for publication over a period of some fourteen years and is the editor-in-chief of Vaad Hanachos Hatmimim, a foundation dedicated to perpetuating the Rebbe's teachings — describes his book as a simplified, introductory overview of the Rebbe and his message as seen through the lens of the author's own 'scholastic experience and understanding of the Rebbe'. Accordingly, he makes no claim that what he has written are verbatim representations of the Rebbe's teachings. While acknowledging that no publication can 'possibly capture the authenticity

of his teachings in their original form' (p. xvii), Rabbi Jacobson has striven to produce what he calls in his introduction 'a genuine representation of the Rebbe's wisdom, unfiltered, without any extraneous interpretation or commentary' (p. xix). It is on this understanding that I have quoted the following passages from Rabbi Jacobson's book as being true and accurate representations of the Rebbe's ideas.

9 *Talmud*, Megillah 6b.

10 It is forbidden, by religious Jewish custom, to spell out God's name (Yahweh, or Jehovah). However, many Ultra-Orthodox Jews, and all Lubavitchers, extend the prohibition to the more generic 'God' as well, which is thus rendered 'G-d' in its ineffable form.

11 The modern state of Israel was established in May 1948 on the basis of a Partition Plan approved by the United Nations General Assembly in November 1947. Palestine, then under a British Mandate (Britain had captured it from the Ottoman Turks in 1918 and had pledged to facilitate the creation of a Jewish 'homeland' there), was divided by the plan into a Jewish and an Arab state. Australia was one of the countries that voted for partition, and was one of the first countries to recognise the new Jewish state. The Australian Foreign Minister at the time, Dr H V Evatt, was a staunch supporter of Jewish statehood. While the Jewish state came into being, and even expanded its boundaries in the course of a war launched against it by the surrounding Arab countries, the planned Palestinian state never eventuated. The bulk of the territory allocated to that state (the West Bank) was annexed by Jordan, and, in the 1967 Six Day War, was captured by Israel which proceeded to administer it as an 'occupied territory' pending a final peace agreement with the Palestinians.

12 Unless otherwise indicated, the Rebbe's statements relating to Israel are quoted from a special compilation published in the official Lubavitcher magazine *Kfar Chabad* (30/4/98) to mark the fiftieth anniversary of the State of Israel (in Hebrew).

13 Quoted by Edward Hoffman in his book *Despite All Odds*, p. 43.

14 There is, of course, a fundamental debate raging in Israel over whether or not giving back land would, in fact, entail a greater risk to life than hanging on to it. Both military experts and rabbinical authorities are deeply divided on this issue (see Chapters 6 and 7).

Chapter 3: The Young Tyro

1 After the 1987 stock market crash Harry Cooper became less and less involved with Joseph. 'I was going through tough times,' Joseph recalls. 'Probably he was fighting for his own survival . . . Also, I wasn't exactly Mr Success Story after the '87 crash, so [Cooper] went his way with Solly [Lew]'. Not, however, before Cooper had introduced Joseph to the chief of the State Bank of Victoria's ill-fated merchant-banking subsidiary Tricontinental, Ian Johns, with whom Cooper had a strong relationship. That introduction sowed the seeds of what was to be one of the most harrowing and controversial episodes in Joseph's business career — the negotiation of a series of loans which Joseph claims were grossly mismanaged by the State Bank and ended up needlessly costing the Victorian taxpayer tens of millions of dollars (see Chapter 5).

2 Apart from this sole venture in the early 1980s, Joseph has been surprisingly uninterested in mineral exploration in Israel. He has since been approached by individuals claiming to have found oil in northern Israel, 'in the Ground of Joseph', hoping the Biblical connection with his own name would fire his interest. To no avail. 'Oil exploration is just too risky,' Joseph explains. 'I'd love to become involved, if there were gold or minerals, the field I'm in; I'd spend some money there . . . But the Land of Israel has different kinds of rocks. There are rocks when you go to Hebron, en route to Hebron . . . every rock is filled with sacrifice and love and blood and tears. . . . That's the spiritually important land. The physical land, where there are gold and diamonds, where we can help the spiritual land, is here in Australia.'

3 Henry Herzog was not from a Lubavitcher family but, like Harry Cooper, later became closely involved in and identified with the Lubavitcher community. His daughter married a Lubavitcher, Levi Mochkin, a young American-born stockbroker who, until a falling out in the late 1990s, was Joseph's main point man in the stock market. It was Henry's brother Izzy (who owns the swish luxury car dealership on the ground floor of Joseph's present corporate headquarters in South Melbourne) who initially got Joseph involved in the fight to save the Melbourne Football Club in August 1996 when he introduced him to one of the men leading the fight, former Demons champion Brian Dixon (see Chapter 14). Henry's involvement with Joseph was nowhere near as extensive or as significant as Harry Cooper's had been. But he did retain a small stake in Kingsway, and was a director of the company until he, too, parted ways with Joseph in the late 1980s.

4 Joseph takes some delight in telling the story of how Larry got his comeuppance after he died in 1989:

> There was this fellow at Larry's funeral from the *Chevra Kadisha* [Jewish burial society] in Israel who had a long beard, unkempt, a long coat. I don't know how he got there. And there, of course, were all the dignitaries from the secular community, and when they put the coffin into the grave, there was no one to take the spade and cover the coffin. I couldn't do it — I'm a *Cohen* [a member of the Jewish priestly caste, forbidden to come into contact with the dead] — and that guy happened to be there. He was the one who shovelled soil over Larry's coffin. Here was this man all his life complaining about this type of Jew, and for whatever reason he turns up at his funeral and poured the earth over his coffin. It's so eerie — because it would be the last type of person who Larry would have wanted to bury him. He was also giving out little bottles of the Rebbe's *mashkeh* [vodka]. I was embarrassed myself — giving out the Rebbe's vodka at the funeral!

5 *Australian* 22/8/90.
6 AFR 28/8/85.
7 Emmanuel Althaus's family was one of the five original Lubavitcher families sent to Shepparton in country Victoria after World War II. He was 'a very loyal, dedicated lieutenant,' Joseph says, and 'gave good service for many, many years' on the boards of several Gutnick companies before departing in 1996 to manage his own mining company, Golden Triangle Resources. The parting was amicable, and he and Joseph remain on good

terms. He was replaced by Dr David Tyrwhitt, a high-profile figure in the Australian mining community.

8 'CBD', SMH 25/8/87.

9 SMH 30/9/88.

10 AFR 24/3/87.

11 *Australian Business* 15/4/87.

12 *Australian Business* 10/8/88.

13 This, along with Trevor Sykes's feature 'Little Joe's Comeback', also in *Australian Business* the following year (10/8/88), are the most comprehensive and insightful contemporary accounts of Joseph's activities in the 1980s and provide an invaluable record of the period.

14 *Australian Business* 10/8/88.

15 Martin Summons, *Australian Business* 8/3/89.

16 *Australian Business* 15/4/87.

17 5/8/87.

18 Mendel New first made *Business Review Weekly*'s 'Rich 200' list — with a personal fortune estimated to be $45 million — in 1994. BRW noted at the time that, while he ran a textile wholesaling business in his own name, 'the bulk of his wealth' came from his holdings in two of Joseph's companies, Great Central and Centaur. His fortune peaked in 1997, when BRW assessed it at $105 million, noting: 'New built a substantial textile and clothing business, through which he provided a start for his son-in-law, and he remains a large shareholder in the Gutnick stable of mining companies.'

19 *Australian Business* 10/8/88.

20 BRW 14/8/87.

21 *Australian Business* 5/8/87.

22 Both quotes SMH 9/5/87.

23 Reflecting on the episode more than a decade later, in 1999, Joseph hadn't the slightest doubt that he had done the right thing, for, once again he believed, the Rebbe had shown himself to have more foresight about the ways of the world even than a man as supposedly worldly-wise as Larry Adler:

> Now, when you look back, where's Larry and FAI? It's not listed any longer . . . If I had been on his board, resources wouldn't have survived. I would never have been able to do what I did with my exploration. They would never have given me the funds. Larry died. Rodney took over. They went from a capitalisation of $2 billion to $80 million, before it was sold. It was a total reversal. FAI was on top of the world. Who would have said in 1988, that I'd be still around with companies and big discoveries, and FAI would be off the map? So that was only the great vision of the Rebbe. That's why everything he says will come true. It may take a little longer than we like, but . . .

24 All quotes Skeel, *Australian Business* 15/4/87.

25 AFR 30/3/87.

Chapter 4: Crash

1 AFR 18/10/97.

2 *Australian Business* 10/8/88.

3 *Australian Business* 28/10/87.

4 *loc. cit.*

5 *loc. cit.*

6 Sykes, *Australian Business* 10/8/88.

7 4/11/89.

8 22/4/93.

9 SMH 4/11/89.

10 Looking back at the 'Class of '87' a decade later, *Business Review Weekly*'s Narelle Hooper noted (26/5/97) that in 1987, the galloping equities market had catapulted a record 44 new members on to the BRW 'Rich 200' list. By 1988, 46 had dropped off, of which 6 had been gaoled and, at least 8 were bankrupted (and some, both) and almost 30 of whose companies had collapsed or whose assets had been sold up by the banks, or who had been financially diminished. In addition to Christopher Skase and Abe Goldberg, half a dozen found residences overseas more to their liking.

11 SMH 4/11/89.

12 *Australian Business* 10/8/88.

Chapter 5: The Comeback Kid

1 AFR 17/12/87.

2 *Australian Business* 10/8/88.

3 Ben Hills, SMH 4/11/89.

4 Professor Herman Branover is a trained scientist from the Soviet Union who had been drawn to the Lubavitcher movement while still in Moscow. He had been a prominent dissident and was among the wave of Jews who left the Soviet Union for Israel in the early 1970s. An impish, charismatic man with extreme right-wing political views, Branover had one great dream: to harness the scientific potential being brought to Israel by the flood of highly trained Soviet–Jewish scientists and technicians, and turn the Jewish state into a technological superpower.

5 See Hoffman, p. 150.

6 Hoffman, p. 152.

7 *Australian Business* 3/8/88.

8 *Australian Business* 10/8/88.

9 *Australian Business* 25/3/88.

10 *Australian Business* 10/8/88.

11 AFR 29/11/88.

12 Hugo Armstrong, *Tricontinental: The Rise and Fall of a Merchant Bank* (Carlton: Melbourne University Press, 1995) — edited excerpt relating to Tricontinental's deal with Centaur in HS 20/9/96.

13 *loc. cit.*

14 Cited by Armstrong.

15 *Age* 15/7/89.

16 SMH 4/11/89.

17 SMH 4/11/89.

18 Hoffman, p. 46.

19 Hoffman, p. 42.

20 *Australian Business* 8/3/89.

21 Adam Shand, in the *Australian* 22/8/90.

22 *Australian* 22/8/90.

23 *Australian* 22/8/90.

24 Armstrong.
25 24/8/94.
26 HS 20/10/94.
27 HS 23/12/95.
28 HS 28/9/96.
29 AFR 4/11/91.

Chapter 6: The Rebbe's Man in Israel
1 Landau, p. xx.
2 Landau, pp. 330–31.
3 From a Lubavitcher perspective, another possible analogy might be that the Rebbe saw Joseph as 'Aharon' (Aaron) to his 'Moshe' (Moses). The Rebbe, in one of his commentaries, discussed the relationship between the two Biblical figures:

> Our Sages relate that Aharon would sometimes stretch the truth in order to bring about peace between people who were at loggerheads. The Torah condones such behaviour when it is the only possible way to make peace; as our Sages say, 'One may modify a statement in the interest of peace.' The very essence of Moshe, however, was the personification of truth. It was therefore impossible for him to bring about peace between people if it would necessitate him telling an untruth. Although such conduct is permitted in the Torah, it went against the grain of Moshe's essence ... Since both these manners of conduct are in accordance with the Torah, it is to be understood that each possesses a quality lacking in the other. The merit in Moshe's conduct was that he didn't deviate in the slightest from the truth. The merit of Aharon's conduct was his ability to affect even so lowly an individual who could be reached only by stretching the truth ...'

(*The Chassidic Dimension: Interpretations of the Weekly Torah Readings and the Festivals, based on the talks of the Lubavitcher Rebbe Rabbi Menachem M Schneerson*, compiled by Rabbi Sholom B Wineberg (New York: Kehot Publication Society, 1990) p. 272.)
4 *Kfar Chabad*, 14/1/99.
5 SMH 14/6/94.
6 The thirteenth and last of the Principles of Faith listed by Maimonides, the twelfth- century codifier of Jewish law, states: 'I believe with perfect faith in the Coming of the Messiah, and even though he tarry, nevertheless I will await him every day.' David Landau, in his book *Piety & Power* (p. 79), notes that 'many a believing Jew has gone to the stake, or to the gas-chamber, with that declaration on his lips'.
7 Landau, p. 79.
8 AJN 10/2/95.
9 Resurrection of the dead is another of Maimonides' Thirteen Principles of Faith: 'I believe with complete faith that there will be a resurrection of the dead when the Creator wills it.'
10 Paul Heinrichs, *Sunday Age* 18/5/96.
11 HS 14/6/94.
12 AJN 8/7/94.
13 AJN 10/2/96.

14 AJN 14/6/96.

15 Cited by Abraham Rabinovich, *Australian* 12/5/99.

16 It is sometimes difficult to comprehend how so much importance can be attached to seemingly so little. But religious Jews like Joseph are well versed in a tradition of exegesis and *Midrash* that regularly builds great edifices of interpretation and commentary on the smallest of clues in the Holy Texts. One has only to think how the complex rules of *kashrut* governing the strict separation of milk and meat in Orthodox Jewish households — with all its physical infrastructure of separate crockery, cutlery, pots, pans, sinks, refrigerators, dishwashers and even stoves — derive ultimately from a single brief injunction that occurs in three separate places in the Bible: 'You shall not seethe a kid in its mother's milk' (Exodus 23:19, 34:26; Deuteronomy 14:21).

17 *Australian* 18/2/97.

18 AJN 14/6/96.

19 AJN 20/9/96.

20 SMH 23/1/97.

21 *Australian* 18/2/97.

22 *Age* 22/2/97.

23 *Australian* 12/5/99.

24 AJN 22/1/99.

25 SMH 15/5/99.

26 The *Yediot Achronot* campaign, and Joseph's and Netanyahu's responses, were reported in AJN, 2/4/99.

27 *Australian* 12/5/99.

28 AJN 11/12/98.

29 *Kfar Chabad* 14/1/99.

30 *Jerusalem Post* 22/7/98.

31 Joseph did place 'two or three advertisements in the Israeli press urging Israelis to vote for a right-wing government'. This was cited by the Israeli State Comptroller in a report, published in February 2000, criticising widespread intervention by Diaspora Jews in the 1999 Israeli election — overwhelmingly in support of Labour's Ehud Barak. Joseph was unfazed by the report and denied any wrongdoing: 'I believe in the democratic right of an individual to put an ad in a newspaper.' (AJN 18/2/00.)

32 AJN 21/5/99.

33 *Kfar Chabad*, 14/1/99.

Chapter 7: A Reluctant Radical

1 AJN 14/2/97.

2 Kurt Zentner, AJN 28/2/97.

3 Shmuel Gurewicz, AJN 28/2/97.

4 AJN, 21/2/97.

5 *Good Weekend* 12/12/98.

6 In the event, I saved Joseph the trouble — and the money — by quitting the paper in April 1999, over a controversial cartoon I had published comparing the 'ethnic cleansing' of Kosovo's Albanians with the exodus of 700,000 refugees from Palestine when Israel was created fifty years earlier. Three months later, Joseph was quite happy to talk to me for this book — which must say something about his sense of irony, if not about his tolerance.

7 See Ellingsen *loc. cit.* and Abraham Rabinovich, *Australian* 12/5/99.

8 HS 1/4/97.

9 *Australian* 18/2/97.

10 *loc. cit.*

11 *Good Weekend* 12/12/98.

12 'The Rebbe and the Arabs', AJN 17/5/96.

13 Cited by Abraham Rabinovich, *Australian* 18/2/97.

14 *Age* 6/12/97; 26/11/97.

15 AJN 28/11/97.

16 *Age* 6/12/97.

17 *Age* 26/9/98.

18 Betty Sutton of Surrey Hills, Vic. 28/11/97; Paul Madigan of Brunswick, Vic. 1/12/97; Jonathan Scutt of Broadmeadows, Vic. 16/1/99.

Chapter 8: Diamond Joe

1 SMH 18/4/91.

2 18/4/91.

3 18/4/91.

4 HS 16/4/93, citing a 10-minute video presentation used by Joseph to promote Great Central's diamond hunt at Nabberu in early 1993. Joseph made the same point, even more graphically, to Peter Ellingsen in December 1998, when Ellingsen accompanied him on a visit to one of his gold mines in Western Australia:

> Beside Joe Gutnick on the hard rim of the open cut is his 'rock hopper', geologist Ed Eshuys, who tells him that the rock containing the gold is more than five billion years old. But the Rebbe . . . said the earth was 5,759 years old. Gutnick, who scored 100 for commercial studies at school, smiles. 'At the end of the day,' he shrugs, 'the Rebbe is right. It is 5,759.'

(*Good Weekend*, 12/12/98.)

5 *loc. cit.*

6 AFR 15/11/91.

7 Joseph's father, the generally tolerant and broad-minded Rabbi Chaim Gutnick, found this so offensive that he complained to the newspaper, which apologised for any hurt but denied there had been anti-semitic intent (see Chapter 13).

8 Article, cartoon and comments: SMH 18/2/92.

9 AFR 2/4/93.

10 By 1994 Levi Mochkin was arguably the richest broker in Australia, and the youngest person on BRW's 'Rich 200' list with a fortune estimated at $40 million. According to BRW, the bulk of his wealth was in Joseph's companies: Great Central, in which he was the fifth-largest shareholder, Centaur and Johnson's Well. By 1996, his fortune had doubled, on the back of another lucrative investment in a Gutnick company, Mount Kersey, whose shares had increased ten-fold following the Silver Swan nickel discovery in Western Australia. Mochkin had invested almost $2.8 million in the company. That was the peak, however, and by 1998 his fortune had declined along with the plunge in gold, and he had dropped out of the BRW rankings. By 1999 he had fallen out with Joseph as well. That, however,

was in the future. For the moment, Mochkin was busy selling Joseph to the New York investment community.

11 AFR 23/3/93.
12 SMH 23/3/93.
13 *Age* 3/4/93.
14 HS 5/4/93.
15 *Age* 6/4/93.
16 HS 6/4/93.
17 SMH 8/4/93.
18 HS 7/4/93.
19 *Australian* 19/4/93.
20 BRW 27/1/97.
21 HS 23/9/93.
22 AFR 21/4/93.
23 AFR 19/4/93.
24 12/4/93.
25 SMH 15/4/93.
26 AFR 16/4/93.
27 AFR 10/1/94.
28 HS 12/4/93.
29 HS 17/4/93.
30 Joseph's American roadshow and the reactions to it are described in some detail in AFR 2/4/93 and BRW 9/4/93.
31 Cited by Abraham Rabinovich, *Australian* 12/5/99.
32 *Bulletin* 6/4/93.
33 HS 15/4/93.
34 HS 16/4/93.
35 SMH 19/4/93.
36 HS 16/4/93.
37 *Sunday Age* 26/5/93.
38 AFR 26/5/93.
39 Reported in HS 25/5/93.
40 AFR 28/7/93.
41 SMH 3/8/93.
42 16/8/93.
43 20/8/93.
44 AFR 30/9/93.
45 HS 17/12/93.
46 AFR 19/10/94.
47 SMH 2/6/94.
48 HS 14/9/96.
49 SMH 16/9/96.
50 Bruce Hextall, in SMH 18/9/96.
51 HS 24/10/96.
52 *Age* 20/11/96.
53 BRW 27/1/97.
54 HS 30/8/96.
55 David Walker, director of resources at the broker ABN AMRO Australia Hoare Govett, quoted by Mark Davis in BRW 27/1/97.
56 AFR 19/9/96.

57 HS 23/5/98.

58 AFR 20/7/98.

59 *Australian* 22/4/93.

60 *Age* 29/12/96.

61 Asked about how he got along with his high-profile new mate, Joseph said he was aware Hawke had 'strong views' about the rights of the Palestinians — but added: 'I might not necessarily agree with him on some issues, but we have agreed to disagree.' (*Age* 9/11/96)

Chapter 9 Sister Act

1 SMH 12/3/97.

2 HS 21/2/97.

3 SMH 6/12/97.

4 *Age* 20/4/97.

5 *Age* 20/4/97.

6 HS 21/2/97.

7 SMH 6/12/97.

8 HS 15/10/97.

9 AFR 15/10/97.

10 AFR 20/12/97.

11 SMH 6/12/97.

12 SMH 6/12/97.

13 HS 16/7/98.

14 SMH 22/8/98.

15 HS 29/8/98.

16 SMH 6/12/97. Pnina was even more specific in a February 2000 interview with the AJN: 'What's kept me going, firstly, is the faith and belief that I'm going to be successful because of the Rebbe's blessings to my family. I just believe that what the Rebbe says happens eventually. God may be a bit slow, but he gets there.' (AJN 18/2/00.)

17 SMH 6/12/97.

18 AFR 21/3/97.

19 SMH 16/7/97.

20 HS 8/3/99.

Chapter 10: Going for Gold

1 Mark Smith, AFR 11/5/94.

2 AFR 28/6/94.

3 SMH 29/1/94.

4 AFR 11/5/94; 13/5/94.

5 BRW 22/1/93.

6 *Bulletin* 6/4/93.

7 31/12/92.

8 *Bulletin* 6/4/93.

9 Not everyone in AMP approved the flirtation with Great Central, though, and it was challenged at AMP's annual general meeting the following May, when perennial dissident Jack Tilburn voiced concern about taking a punt on 'Joe Gutnick bringing home the bacon' — a none-too-kosher cliché which prompted an ironic comment on the quality of Tilburn's 'research' from the editor of the *Australian Financial Review*'s 'Rear Window' (AFR 11/5/95).

10 BRW 27/1/97.
11 AFR 25/10/94.
12 AFR 27/1/95.
13 *Age* 4/1/95.
14 Both quotes: BRW 12/8/96.
15 SMH 11/7/95.
16 AFR 15/3/95.
17 Both quotes: SMH 17/7/95.
18 AFR 17/7/96.
19 David Walker, director of resources at the broker ABN AMRO Australia Hoare Govett, quoted in BRW 27/1/97.
20 BRW 27/1/97.
21 HS 26/10/96.
22 AFR 6/11/96.
23 HS 9/1/97.
24 HS 21/12/96.
25 The Australian Jewish community is, by any standard, a wealthy one. Many Jews have made huge fortunes in Australia, as emerges each year in the annual *Business Review Weekly*'s 'Rich 200' list, which invariably contains a grossly disproportionate number of Jewish names. This does not mean that all Jews are significantly better off than their non-Jewish fellow Australians. A surprising number are even quite poor: the 1996 Census, for instance, showed that 22.9 per cent of Jews, many of them older people and students — had an annual gross income of $8268 or less per annum. The majority, however, would probably fall into the middle-class, middle-income demographic.

Chapter 11: If I Were a Rich Man . . .
1 *Australian Business* 25/9/91.
2 8/10/97.
3 *The Jerusalem Report* May 1996.
4 *Age* 12/12/98.
5 SMH 6/2/96.
6 Joseph Gutnick was not the only Orthodox Jewish businessman whose ownership of a corporate jet drew the attention of the media. The Reichmann brothers in Canada — who, according to the *Economist*, once owned the world's largest portfolio of office property before they ran into difficulties, including London's gigantic Canary Wharf project — also owned a jet, which the *Economist* referred to as the 'only suggestion of tycoonery' about the Ultra-Orthodox Jewish businessmen–philanthropists. As in Joseph's case, the magazine noted that the jet was made necessary by their frequent business trips from their base in Toronto to Canary Wharf in London. Before the collapse of their company, Olympia & York, in 1992, caused by overextending themselves at Canary Wharf, Paul, Albert and Ralph Reichmann were unquestionably the most prominent Ultra-Orthodox Jewish philanthropists in the world. Many Ultra-Orthodox religious institutions in Israel and around the world were the beneficiaries of the Reichmanns' famous largesse, and suffered considerable hardship when the brothers' fortunes went into decline. Like Joseph, even at the height of their wealth, they lived relatively unopulent lives in Toronto,

where the family had arrived as refugees from Vienna-via-Tangier in the early 1950s. Although not Lubavitchers, and much less flamboyant and more publicity shy than Joseph is, they, too, wore their beards and yarmulkas with pride and felt perfectly comfortable leading their strictly Orthodox Jewish lifestyle while fully engaging in broader Canadian society — which, very much like Australia's, has become increasingly open to multicultural diversity since World War II. (See Landau, pp. 269ff.)

7 HS 8/11/96.

8 7/12/96.

9 HS 11/12/97.

10 Jana Wendt, *60 Minutes*, CBS, September 1999.

11 *Good Weekend* 12/12/98.

12 *Mishpachah* 23/9/99.

13 p. 168.

14 BRW 9/4/93.

15 *Australian* 18/2/97.

16 *Halachah*, or Jewish law, requires that every Jew allocate a tithe — ten per cent — of their income for charity, stipulating twenty per cent as a 'sensible ceiling'. David Landau notes in his *Piety & Power* (p. 268) that, because a rich man's standing in the Ultra-Orthodox community is determined by his philanthropy rather than his wealth, the social pressure to give more than one can sensibly afford is 'sometimes a contributory factor in the over-extension and eventual decline or even collapse of personal fortunes'.

17 Like the Amish in Pennsylvania, so wedded is the Adass community to the past, and so zealously do members of the community seek to preserve their way of life, that the outgoing principal of the Adass school in Melbourne is reputed to have replied, when asked what he thought his greatest achievement had been in the forty years he had headed the school: 'The fact that I am leaving it exactly as I found it.'

18 The Orthodox religious establishment does not recognise Progressive Judaism as 'authentic', nor does it recognise the authority of Progressive rabbis or the legitimacy of their rulings. Hence, only marriages, conversions, etc. that are performed by an Orthodox rabbi are considered legitimate by the Orthodox establishment.

19 2/6/97.

20 Both quotes: BRW 2/6/97.

Chapter 12: The Rabbi

1 The festival of Chanukah celebrates the recapture of the Temple in Jerusalem from the Syrian Greeks by the Maccabees in the year 165 BC. Legend has it that there was only one day's supply of sacred oil left for the lamp in the Temple, and this miraculously burned for eight days until a new supply of oil was prepared. The miracle of the oil has become a symbol of the Maccabee revolt, which, in turn, is a powerful symbol of Jewish freedom and resistance to oppression. The central ceremony marking the so-called 'Festival of Lights' is the lighting, over eight consecutive days, of the eight-branched menorah, or *Chanukiya*.

2 See Hoffman, pp. 129ff.

3 Chanukah has, in fact, become increasingly familiar to Australians in recent years. Thus, it was not surprising to hear the chaplain at

Melbourne's Wesley College — a private school run by the Uniting Church which traditionally has had a sizeable number of Jewish students — wish students at the end of one school year 'a merry Christmas and a happy Chanukah'. Unfortunately, displaying a little theological confusion, she added: 'In the name of the Father, the Son and the Holy Ghost!'

4 Promoting the ethical values of Judaism to the wider world has been a fundamental tenet of the Lubavitcher movement, and the Rebbe is said to have instructed his emissaries around the world to bring the 'seven Noahide Laws' to the attention of world statesmen and political leaders 'as a cardinal foundation for ethical behaviour'. (Landau, p. 70.) According to *Halachah*, or Jewish law, Gentiles, or 'descendants of Noah', are required to observe seven commandments (as against the 613 binding on Jews). These are the Biblical injunctions against idolatry, blasphemy, murder, robbery, incest, and tearing flesh from a living animal; and the duty to set up courts of law.

5 *Defenders of the Faith: Inside Ultra-Orthodox Jewry*, p. 41.

6 *Sunday Age* 26/9/97.

7 p. 175.

8 p. 284.

9 AJN 24/9/99.

10 *Sunday Age* 6/7/97.

11 HS 28/12/96.

12 HS 14/12/96.

Chapter 13: The Oldest Hatred

1 SMH 18/1/97.

2 HS 28/9/96.

3 HS 21/5/98.

4 Both quotes: *Age* 19/5/98.

5 HS 20/5/98.

6 *Australian* 23/5/98.

7 Ironically, the first time I ever heard the 'bacon-and-eggs' analogy was at a Jewish function in Melbourne in the early 1990s. Visiting Israeli journalist Hirsh Goodman amused his large Jewish audience by using the analogy to describe the difference between Jews in the Diaspora, who merely contributed to Israel's well-being from afar, and Jews in Israel, who were totally committed to the Jewish state and were prepared to lay down their lives for its survival.

8 *Age* 19/8/98.

9 In the same issue (21/8/98), the *Age* published an article of mine, 'Gutnick v. J B Were: Why all the Fuss?' in which I questioned the paper's handling of the affair. 'Was this the stuff of several front-page stories in the *Age*,' I wrote, and did it justify a public apology by J B Were to 'the leaders of the Jewish community'? Did what the *Age* had reported of the incident up to that point 'really qualify as serious racist or anti-semitic conduct?' Or did it simply reflect 'little more than a kind of mindless, tasteless, but ultimately innocuous garden-variety bigotry on the part of two of the firm's employees that we were all susceptible to and guilty of succumbing to at one time or another'? In the final analysis, I wrote, all the publicity about what appeared to be, at worst, 'a tasteless but rather trivial incident had the

potential to unnecessarily alienate many people from the idea of multiculturalism, if it were perceived that multiculturalism meant one had
constantly to walk on eggs when referring to someone of a different cultural or ethnic background, for fear of causing offence'. Perhaps even more
seriously, I felt that any ordinary person reading the *Age* up to that point
would consider this a relatively trivial matter and believe such sensation-
alist treatment of it could serve to divert attention from and trivialise the
real issues of racism facing Australia. 'With the challenge thrown down by
Pauline Hanson and her One Nation Party,' I wrote, 'we can ill afford such
distractions.' (*Age* 21/8/98)

10 HS 20/8/98.

11 Joseph also took me to task in that article:

> Mr Bernstein clearly implies that my concerns were overstated and that
> the *Age* was wrong to deal with the issue in the manner which it has . . .
> It is clear Mr Bernstein did not take the time to properly research his
> 'opinion'. If he had, he would then, like any good journalist, have had
> regard to the 'source' material — in this case, transcripts tendered to the
> Magistrate's Court in committal proceedings. These transcripts contain
> numerous anti-Semitic statements of the grossest and most repugnant
> kind . . .

It was difficult to argue with Joseph's last statement once the transcripts
were made public, and a public explanation from me was in order. This
appeared in the *Age* two days later, on 26 August:

> My article 'Gutnick v. J B Were' (*Age* 21/8) was, I believe, fair and rea-
> sonable comment on all that had been published on the affair up to that
> point. Like any other reader of the *Age*, I had no reason to assume that
> the transcript referred to contained anything more offensive than the
> material that had been reported. Had I been aware of some of the fur-
> ther comments that Mr Gutnick and the *Age* have now published, I
> would have written that article quite differently.

(*Age* 26/8/98)

12 *Age* 26/8/98.

13 HS 26/8/98.

14 AFR 22/5/99.

15 Quoted by Leo D'Angelo Fisher in 'Merchants of Venom', *Bulletin* 22/9/98.

16 *loc. cit.*

17 In a telling footnote to Gutnick v. Were, a resource paper for final-year
high-school students preparing for the Victoria Certificate of Education,
published in the *Age* in June 1999, listed the incident among the major
milestones in the history of Australian race relations over the past 200
years (*Age* Education Section 23/6/99). Along with such seminal events as
New South Wales's Governor Philip King ordering Aborigines to be driven
out of Parramatta, Prospect and Georges River on 1 May 1801; the
Premiers' Conference of 4 March 1896, which agreed that all colonies
should amend anti-Chinese legislation to restrict immigration of all
coloured races; Immigration Minister Arthur Calwell's announcement on
28 January 1948 that all coloured people who found refuge in Australia
during World War II must leave the country; the successful 1967

Referendum to end constitutional discrimination against Aborigines; the 3 June 1992 High Court of Australia Mabo ruling, which put an end to the notion of *terra nullius* and for the first time legally recognised the principle of Aboriginal ownership of Australia prior to white settlement — one finds the following entry:

> August 1998
> The head of Melbourne stockbroking firm, J.B. Were, apologises to mining magnate Joe Gutnick for 'offensive remarks made about him and the wider Jewish community'.

Chapter 14: Demon Joe

1 Since Mr Michaelis's time, there have been several Jewish club presidents: Dr Jacob Jona at Melbourne in the 1930s; Dr David Berman at North Melbourne (1924 and 1935–37); G Morris Jacobs at Geelong (1929–39), Reuben Sackville at St Kilda (1947–56); Ern Joseph at Fitzroy (1966–70); and David Smorgon at Footscray (Western Bulldogs) in the 1990s. In addition, there was the flamboyant Dr Geoffrey Edelsten, who owned the Sydney Swans franchise in the late 1980s, and Gold Coast hotelier Reuben Pelerman who owned the Brisbane Bears for a while in the early 1990s (both as part of the eventually successful drive to establish Australian Rules football in the tradition of Rugby League strongholds of New South Wales and Queensland, respectively).

There have even been a handful of successful Jewish players over the years, including Ian Synman who played 154 games for St Kilda between 1958 and 1969 (including the club's only winning premiership game in 1966, which happened to fall on Yom Kippur, the holiest day in the Jewish calendar!); Keith Baskin, who played 75 games for South Melbourne between 1964 and 1974; Mordy Bromberg, who played for St Kilda between 1978 and 1982; and Henry Ritterman, who played 23 games for Melbourne between 1971 and 1973. Other Jewish players who have had a briefer flirtation with football at the top level have included Michael Zemski, who played 8 games for Hawthorn in 1973 and 1974; Trevor Korn, who played 3 games for Melbourne in 1981; Rick Marks, who played 1 game for Richmond in 1983; and Julian Kirzner, who played 4 games for Essendon and North Melbourne between 1994 and 1997 (see Ashley Browne, 'People of the boot,' AJN 24/9/99).

2 *Age* 21/9/96.

3 AJN 30/8/96.

4 Quoted by James Button, *Age* 31/8/96.

5 *Age* 31/8/96.

6 *Age* 31/8/96.

7 All quotes: *Sunday Age* 15/9/96.

8 *Age* 31/8/96.

9 Quoted by Paul Heinrichs, *Age* 27/8/96.

10 HS 27/8/96.

11 *loc. cit.*

12 *Age* 27/8/96.

13 HS 27/8/96. Columnist Les Carlyon lampooned Joseph's press conference in the *Age* about ten days later, setting the scene in 'the shower room at

Punt Road Oval'. Instead of Joseph, it is the Palestinian leader Yasser Arafat — a 'pallid man wearing a tea-towel' — who sits at a trestle table flanked by associates who carry assault rifles disguised as mobile phones. He is holding a press conference to announce his takeover of the embattled Richmond Football Club. Presumably taking his cue from Joseph's red-and-blue Demons yarmulka, the 'tea towel' has been 'newly dyed black and yellow' — the Richmond Football Club colours. Asked why he and his Palestine Liberation Organisation want to save Richmond, Arafat replies, with Joseph-like fervour: 'I've always been passionate about Richmond. Heck, Lou Dyer . . . the whole culture of the club . . . gets in your bones, it does.' And when did he become a Richmond member?: 'Tomorrow'. Asked if all this might just possibly 'have anything to do with Joseph Gutnick taking over Melbourne', the yellow-and-black *kefiyyeh*ed Arafat replies: 'Well, of course. You can't pull a rabbi out of the hat and pretend the Middle East peace process hasn't been compromised.' And so on (*Age* 5/9/96). It was clever, but quite cruel: Arafat, in Joseph's eyes, was evil incarnate. Joseph, however, had long been fair game in his dramatic business career for those wielding a sharp pencil. This was about par for the course.

14 AJN 30/8/96.

15 *Age* 27/8/96.

16 AJN 30/8/96.

17 *Age* 8/9/96.

18 HS 28/8/96.

19 BRW 30/9/96.

20 HS 28/8/96.

21 One can only speculate about what the Rebbe might have thought of his protégé's involvement in Australian Rules Football. He had repeatedly stressed the need for a Jew to live openly and proudly in the Gentile world, and rejected the argument, put forward by those Jews who preferred to remain 'invisible', that Jews courted anti-semitism by making themselves too 'obvious'. On the contrary, he argued, anti-semitism *increases* when Jews seek to assimilate and abandon their heritage, for such behaviour breeds suspicion rather than admiration. He totally rejected the 'old, long discredited assimilationist approach' — 'Be a Jew at home but a person [*sic*] outside' — noting that it 'did not take long to become apparent that one who is ashamed of his Jewishness in the street soon becomes weak in his Jewishness at home'. And anyone who clung to the belief that Jews should 'keep quiet and not be too blatant about their Jewishness', he declared, was 'seriously out of touch with reality' given what had befallen Jews who had followed this path in Europe and elsewhere in this century (Hoffman, p. 142).

It is highly unlikely that the Rebbe, when he uttered these words, would have had in mind one of his protégés one day donning a red-and-blue yarmulka and defying the world of Aussie Rules to accept him, on his own terms, as president of the country's oldest and most establishment football club. But one imagines he might have been smiling gently on high and nodding his head in approval when Joseph Gutnick burst onto the Australian football scene on that memorable day in August 1996, in a blaze of unprecedented publicity, and set about saving the Melbourne Demons from oblivion. Here was one Jew who refused to 'keep quiet and not be too blatant about his Jewishness'.

22 HS 27/8/96.
23 *Age* 28/8/96.
24 HS 31/8/96.
25 *Age* 28/8/96.
26 *Sunday Age* 1/9/96.
27 *Sunday Age* 1/9/96.
28 HS 27/8/96.
29 HS 28/8/96.
30 HS 30/8/96.
31 *Age* 28/8/96.
32 Both quotes: HS 27/8/96.
33 HS 27/8/96.
34 Helen Carton from Watsonia, quoted in HS 27/8/96.
35 HS 30/8/96.
36 *Age* 3/9/96.
37 Both quotes: HS 3/9/96.
38 *Age* 3/9/96.
39 *Age* 3/9/96.
40 HS 3/9/96.
41 HS 8/9/96.
42 HS 12/9/96.
43 All quotes in this paragraph and the next are from reports in the *Age* and HS 13/9/96.
44 *Age* 16/9/96.
45 *loc. cit.*
46 The merger meeting at the Dallas Brooks Hall was covered by a battery of reporters from both Melbourne dailies, and the event received blanket coverage in the sports pages of the next day's papers. The following account is based on several reports published in the *Age* and HS the following day (17/9/96).
47 HS 17/9/96.
48 *loc. cit.*
49 HS 18/9/96.
50 HS 19/9/96.
51 *Age* 19/9/96.
52 HS 19/9/96.
53 AJN 30/8/96.
54 *Age* 21/9/96.
55 *Age* 2/6/97.
56 AJN 30/9/96.
57 *loc. cit.*

Chapter 15: Mister President
1 *Age* 19/9/96.
2 *Age* 4/10/96.
3 HS 1/11/96.
4 Caroline Wilson, *Age* 14/8/99; see also Ian Cockerill, 'The Schwab dynasty', *Sunday Age* 12/4/98.

5 HS 30/11/96.
6 *Sunday Age* 15/12/96.
7 *Age* 5/9/98.
8 *Sunday Age* 24/11/96.
9 *loc. cit.*
10 *Age* 2/5/97.
11 HS 30/3/97.
12 *Age* 2/5/97.
13 Transcript in HS 5/5/97.
14 *Age* 5/5/97.
15 HS 5/5/97.
16 HS 5/5/97.
17 *Age* 5/5/97.
18 HS 5/5/97.
19 *Age* 6/5/97.
20 HS 7/5/97.
21 *Sunday Age* 11/5/97.
22 *Age* 7/5/97.
23 HS 26/5/97.
24 *Age* 30/5/97.
25 HS 31/5/97.
26 *Sunday Age* 1/6/97.
27 HS 31/5/97.
28 HS 1/6/97.
29 *Sunday Age* 1/6/97.
30 HS 30/5/97.
31 *Age* 2/6/97.
32 *Age* 2/6/97.
33 *loc. cit.*
34 Caroline Wilson, *Age* 14/8/99.
35 *Age* 4/6/97.
36 HS 4/6/97.
37 *Age* 3/6/97.
38 HS 11/6/97.
39 *Age* 8/7/97.
40 *Sunday Age* 29/6/97.
41 *Age* 29/7/97.
42 *Sunday Age* 31/8/97.
43 HS 12/9/97.
44 *Sunday Age* 16/11/97.
45 *Sunday Age* 16/11/97.
46 *Sunday Age* 12/10/97.
47 HS 8/10/97.
48 *Age* 3/12/97.
49 *Age* 20/4/98.
50 *Age* 20/4/97.
51 HS 5/5/98.
52 HS 16/5/98.
53 HS 18/5/98.
54 *Age* 18/5/98.

55 It is a bit of a myth that most club presidents do, in fact, have a strong football background. Of the sixteen club presidents surveyed by HS's Damian
Barrett in April 1999, it emerged that while a few did once have serious
football ambitions, not one had played so much as a single game at the
highest level. Carlton's John Elliott had a trial with Hawthorn but was
deemed 'too slow', and Hawthorn's Ian Dicker trained twice with South
Adelaide before opting for tennis instead. A few even played AFL football
at the junior level — Collingwood's Eddie McGuire for North Melbourne
Under-19s and Essendon's Graeme McMahon for Essendon Under-19s.
The best credentialled was probably Adelaide's Bob Hammond, who was 'a
prominent SANF identity with North Adelaide and Norwood and coached
Sydney for part of 1984'. Others reached reasonable heights at the amateur
level, including Fremantle's Ross McLean and Sydney's Richard Colless,
who played in the WA amateur league, and Richmond's Leon Daphne who
played more than 200 games for Surrey Hills. For the rest, their football
experience didn't go much past secondary-school level — and even then,
the Western Bulldogs' David Smorgon conceded he had to do 'second year
Matric' to get a game for Brighton Grammar, where St Kilda's Andrew
Plympton also played, as a self-confessed 'dreadful wingman — most
people thought I was the third umpire running the wing'. West Coast's
Michael Smith described his football experience as 'Nil, but I did captain–coach two games, which we lost by 15 goals, for a hotel I was working
for at the time' (HS 25/4/99). So Joseph, with his kick-to-kick background
at Yeshivah College, wasn't as far out of his depth in the company of his
fellow presidents as was often assumed.
56 HS 16/8/98.
57 HS 26/8/98.
58 HS 1/9/98.
59 *Age* 8/9/98.
60 *Age* 8/9/98.
61 HS 14/9/98.
62 HS 18/9/98.
63 *loc. cit.*

Chapter 16: The 'Outsider'

1 *Age* 2/3/99. Joseph put out the following formal statement on 1 March
1999, explaining his action:

> The Melbourne Football Club has today formally requested the
> Australian Football League (AFL) conduct a full inquiry in relation to
> past breaches of the AFL's salary cap by the Melbourne Football Club.
> As a result of the AFL's recent investigations into salary cap breaches
> by another AFL club, I deemed it appropriate to confirm that the
> Melbourne Football Club had complied fully with the AFL's salary cap.
> Unfortunately, certain past breaches have been identified. We believe
> those breeaches occurred around 1994. Whilst it was personally dis-
> tressing for me to learn of these breaches, I determined that it was nec-
> essary and appropriate to forthwith disclose the breaches to the AFL
> and to request that the AFL undertake a full investigation of the iden-
> tified breaches and the club's compliance with the salary cap. The

Melbourne Football Club has provided all relevant information to the AFL and will continue to provide the AFL with its full co-operation. The AFL was not aware of the breaches prior to my informing Mr Wayne Jackson chief executive of the AFL of their existence. The board of the Melbourne Football Club believes it has a fundamental duty to its members, supporters, players and employees, and to the game itself, to ensure that the club conducts itself with complete honesty and public openness. It is for this reason that the AFL and the public have been informed of the breaches. The Melbourne Football Club has a great future and we will not allow the disclosure of these past breaches or the AFL's investigations to affect our on-field performances. I urge all our members and supporters to stand by their great football club whilst these errors of the past are addressed and cleaned up.

(Reproduced in HS 2/3/99.)

2 HS 5/3/99.
3 HS 3/3/99.
4 *Age* 13/8/99.
5 HS 2/3/99.
6 *Age* 2/3/99.
7 *Age* 3/3/99.
8 HS 5/3/99.
9 *Age* 17/3/99.
10 *Age* 20/3/99.
11 HS 23/3/99.
12 *Age* 22/3/99.
13 HS 28/3/99.
14 *Age* 12/3/98.
15 *Age* 20/3/99.
16 HS 24/3/99.
17 HS 8/5/99.
18 *Age* 23/3/99.
19 HS 28/6/99.
20 *Age* 7/8/99.
21 All quotes: *Age* — 9/8/99, 7/8/99, 9/8/99 respectively.
22 *Age* 9/8/99.
23 *Age* 10/8/99.
24 Andrew Williams, Richmond, *Age* 12/8/99.
25 HS 27/8/99.
26 *loc. cit.*
27 *Age* 27/8/99.
28 HS 27/8/99.
29 *Age* 1/9/99.
30 HS 6/8/99.
31 *Age* 7/8/99.
32 *Age* 10/8/99.
33 *Age* 14/8/99.
34 HS 18/8/99.
35 HS 23/3/99.
36 *Age* 10/8/99.
37 *Age* 10/8/99.

38 HS 18/8/99.
39 SMH 19/6/99.
40 *Bulletin* 24/8/99.
41 *Sunday Age* 8/8/99.
42 BRW 27/1/97.
43 *Bulletin* 15/10/96.

Chapter 17: The Odd Couple
1 Quoted by Trevor Sykes, AFR 15/5/99.
2 *Good Weekend* 12/12/98.
3 Rod Myer, *Age* 16/1/99.
4 'The relationship that's good as gold,' in AFR 15–16 May 1999.
5 SMH 7/3/97.
6 SMH 25/3/97.
7 AFR 1/5/97.
8 AFR 2/5/97.
9 AFR 2/5/97.
10 AFR 26/6/97.
11 *Age* 5/7/97.
12 *Age* 12/7/97.
13 *Age* and AFR 10/7/97.
14 12/7/97.
15 'Chanticleer', AFR 16/7/97.
16 *loc. cit.*
17 Trevor Sykes, AFR 15/5/99.
18 AFR 1/11/97.
19 AFR 27/8/97.
20 *Age* 22/8/97.
21 AFR 22/8/97.
22 AFR 8/9/97.
23 SMH 29/11/97.
24 AFR 8/9/97.
25 AFR 22/8/97.
26 *Age* 22/8/97.
27 HS 23/8/97.
28 BRW 29/6/98.
29 AFR 31/7/98.
30 HS 28/11/98.
31 AFR 17/6/99.
32 *Age* 17/6/99.
33 HS 22/6/99.
34 *Age* 25/6/99.
35 AFR 11/12/99.
36 *Age* 11/12/99.
37 AFR and *Age* 11/12/99.
38 AFR 15/5/99.

Chapter 18: All that Glitters . . .
1 AFR 24/11/95.
2 HS 23/12/95.

3 *West Australian* 24/11/95.

4 HS 6/5/96.

5 Joseph's former stockbroker, Levi Mochkin, told the Victorian Supreme Court in November 1999 that he himself had invested almost $2.8 million in Mount Kersey — 'mainly, he claimed, because he, like many of the Jewish investors he dealt with as a broker both in Melbourne and in New York, took the Rebbe's blessings to Joseph seriously.' He told the court — which was hearing the long-running J B Were insider-trading trial that had exposed the anti-semitic comments about Joseph in August 1998 (see Chapter 13) — that the Rebbe had said on many occasions the Gutnick companies would make major discoveries, and that when he heard that Mining Project Investors had made a major nickel discovery at Silver Swan, adjacent to ground held by Mount Kersey, he had decided to take a punt. Asked whether many fellow Orthodox Jews had likewise invested in Mount Kersey because they believed Joseph had been blessed by the Rebbe and would find nickel there, he replied that while a 'lot of people from my community dealt with me', his clients were not solely from the Jewish community. (*Age* 5/11/99)

6 AFR 30/8/96.

7 *Age* 19/11/99.

8 *Age* 28/10/97.

9 *Age* 1/11/97.

10 David Hale of West Zurich Financial Services, quoted in the *Age* 8/7/99.

11 AFR 31/5/99.

12 *Age* 8/7/99.

13 *Age* 8/7/99.

14 AFR 29/10/97.

15 *Age* 9/5/98.

16 HS 3/5/99. See next chapter.

17 HS 6/5/99.

18 Kate Askew, SMH 26/6/99.

19 HS 27/4/99.

20 AFR 6/11/96.

21 *Age* 27/4/99.

22 The Rebbe was aware, Joseph points out, that Eshuys would not be with him forever. He recalls the 1991 encounter between Eshuys and the Rebbe in New York (see Chapter 8): 'The Rebbe told Ed at that famous meeting in New York: "You should have success when you work for other people also." So the Rebbe knew that there would come a day — I didn't believe it would ever happen — that Ed would work for someone else . . . But now it's happened. If someone had told you five years ago that Joseph Gutnick and Ed Eshuys were going to split, you'd say they were mad . . . But the Rebbe saw . . .'

23 AFR 12/6/99.

24 AFR 12/6/99.

25 *Age* 9/9/99.

26 AFR 12/6/99.

27 SMH 17/5/99.

Chapter 19: Joseph 2000

1 This was about the time Joseph had started to look at the Yandal belt, which is about 400 kilometres north of the Lady Bountiful–Mount

Pleasant area. Perhaps that was what the Rebbe had had in mind? 'No, No, No, No. He said it should be North. North. North. It's got to be prominently North,' Joseph insists, reading from what he believes was the Rebbe's source for the pronouncement. 'Gold comes from the North.'

2 'The role of fluids in the origin of the evolution of the Witwatersrand Basin', *South African Journal of Geology,* vol. 93 (1990) and 'Hydrothermal Origin for Witwatersrand Gold', *SEG Newsletter,* No. 1, October 1997.

3 A former South African, Ian Currie had been the Chief Financial Officer of the Gutnick group of companies since the mid-1990s. 'He's extremely intelligent, with good business acumen,' Joseph says of Currie. 'He's very dedicated, works long hours. He's very passionate about the work he's doing and has a wide network of contacts. He's also got the confidence of the bankers. So he's an integral part of the team with regards to the new millennium.'

4 Rabbi Yehudah Krinsky, one of the most powerful figures in the Lubavitcher movement since the Rebbe's death and the father-in-law of Joseph's eldest daughter Rivka, explains: 'The righteous are greater in death than in life, say our sages. Commentaries explain that while freed from their physical limitations, they are able to be more selfless, more unlimited, in their blessings for us left behind.' (AJN 26/11/99)

5 Joseph has had a major role in facilitating this practice by purchasing three large houses adjacent to the Rebbe's grave for the use of visitors to the grave.

6 The sheer naivete of all this calls to mind a peculiar building I once saw in Hong Kong. This was a large block of luxury apartments, prominently situated on the slope of one of the mountains overlooking the harbour, with a huge gap in the middle. There was no obvious architectural or aesthetic reason for this strange feature, which must have cost the developer many millions of dollars in lost income from the sale of the seven or eight 'missing' apartments. But the building had been built smack in the middle of the path used, according to local legend, by a sacred dragon as it made its way down the hillside to drink from the waters of the harbour. And the developer was not about to incur the dragon's wrath by impeding his passage — whatever the cost in lost revenue. To the rationally minded outsider, it is hard to fathom how otherwise hard-headed, high-powered businessmen can defer to the drinking habits of imaginary dragons or appeal to the intercessionary powers of dead rabbis before making major business decisions. But the fact is they can, and they do — to a degree that is quite awesome.

Epilogue

1 *The Chassidic Dimension* pp. 44–5.